ROBERT BIERSTEDT
Department of Sociology
New York University
ADVISORY EDITOR TO DODD, MEAD & COMPANY

Family in Society

Family in Society

Floyd Mansfield Martinson

Gustavus Adolphus College

DODD, MEAD & COMPANY

New York   1971

Preface

The experiences of human life are almost limitless. To write meaningfully about the complicated world of human experience one must find ways of bringing order into the data, ways of focusing on and highlighting certain experiences. This is the purpose of a perspective. Viewing the American family in sociological perspective, then, this book is an attempt to describe and analyze the American family within the context, first, of its involvement with society and, second, of its involvement in the lives of individuals.

Thus, in the following chapters the family is viewed not as an isolated phenomenon but as a unit significant and essential to society. The family is a social system that is responsive to the cultural and social milieu in which it operates. By limiting the scope of the analysis of the family to one society—American society—we avoid the oversimplification that might result from a comparative analysis of the family in a large number of societies.

The comparative method utilized in intersocietal or cross-societal description and analysis of family structure and function tends by its eclecticism toward the danger of superficiality in family-to-family comparisons. In the process of such comparison the unit of comparison, in this case the family, is "freed" from the social and cultural milieu in which it is formed and in which it operates. Comparative analysis of this sort is markedly useful in assessing the breadth of human ingenuity in handling the sex-marriage-family functions, but it does little to aid the student in understanding the role of the family within society. Hence there are some advantages in intrasocietal comparisons—comparison of the goals of the society with the goals of the family; comparison of the structure and functions of the family with that of other subsystems in the society (the polity, the economy, the school, the church—along with consideration of the interplay between the family and the other social systems); and comparison of the contemporary family *in situ* with earlier forms of the family *in situ* during precedent periods of history. As Ruth Benedict points out in *Patterns of Culture* (1934), aspects of family living are not special items of human behavior with their own generic drives and motivations which have deter-

v

mined their past history and will determine their future, but are the occasions "which any society may seize upon to express its important cultural intentions." From this point of view the significant sociological unit to utilize in understanding aspects of family life is not the family *per se* but rather the society in which family functions are performed. The study of the family or any other social system requires attention to the unique social forces that influence, determine, and perhaps dominate adaptive social systems, such as the family.

Contemporary students of the family thus have taken a cue from earlier researchers who studied the family from the institutional point of view and who analyzed the "famliy in community." It should be noted, though, that American family sociology, in contrast to European family sociology, still appears to be disproportionately oriented toward treatment of the family as a closed system, not a social system *in situ*.

We must avoid taking a monolithic view of American society, however. American society has often been pictured as an extreme example of lack of integration. Its "huge complexity" and rapid changes from generation to generation make inevitable a lack of harmony between its elements that may not occur in simpler societies. As we have said, though, by limiting the scope of our analysis to one society we may avoid some of the danger of oversimplifying a complex society. As Oscar Lewis experienced, based on intensive studies in Mexico, "the more homogeneous (and I might add superficial) the picture we get of a single society, the more contrasting will it appear in comparison with other societies. On the other hand, the more we know about the range of behavior within any society, the more readily can we perceive the cross-cultural similarities as well as the basic human similarities." To paraphrase Benedict, one society understood as a coherent organization of behavior is more enlightening than many touched upon only at their high points.

For many students of the family it may be relatively more valuable to understand the family in the society in which they will live and work than to be familiar with data about other societies, especially if knowledge of other societies is gained at the expense of thorough analysis of their own society.

There is also some question as to the value of emphasizing such universal aspects of the family system as the nuclear family. We are tempted to say that to study the family in any society is to study a universal phenomenon; but to assume that all societies are alike in that they have a recognizable nuclear family system consisting of husband and wife, parents and children, and existing more or less as an autonomous or private social system, disengaged in part from the other social entities, may be to cloud rather than clarify the nature of existent primary groups. Certain essential functions will of course persist. However, we cannot speak with certitude regarding structural family systems resembling our own nuclear family.

While today the small group stands in the focus of sociological research, most of this research has been done in the United States and by Americans. Studies from other societies (India and Turkey, for instance) do not necessarily corroborate the American results. This may be due to different experimental conditions, but it is not improbable that the small group does not play the same role in these societies, and that consistency of results in American studies are the result of strong conformist tendencies in American society.

There is another reason for restricting the present study to the American society. The American family has existed for over three hundred years of recorded history in a society whose basic polity has been characterized more by evolution than by revolution. In other words, to study the American family sociologically is to study the family in and of one of the oldest continuous sociopolitical systems possessed of a recorded history. To understand the American family it is necessary to see it not only in horizontal (contemporary) perspective but also in vertical (historical) perspective. The contemporary American family is an emergent out of the past and bears the marks of the past.

This is a sociology, not a history of the American family. We do not trace the development of the family in each epoch of the history of this country. Only selected epochs in the development of the family and society are considered. The American family has gone through various periods in time that can be viewed as "natural experiments." Since the family sociologist is handicapped in his research by the limited opportunity which he has to conduct experiments, he must, therefore, take advantage of the varied "experiments" which nature and society provide. He can do this either by focusing his attention on the past and contemporary family experiences in a society with a long history or by focusing on family experiences of a variety of societies.

An advantage of studying the family experiences in America is that America has had a variety of "natural experiments." Our technique is to "take soundings" at significant epochs or at times of "disturbing or prodding" events that have affected the family. In this way American experience, historical and contemporary, provides partial answers to a number of questions (or "hypotheses") about the family. What happens to the family under a totalitarian, legalistic oligarchy? Puritan New England, and especially the Massachusetts Bay Colony, provides one answer. What happens to the family if personal freedom and democracy are exalted as core values of the society? The period beginning with the birth of American independence is instructive here. What happens if every vestige of personal freedom is removed and persons are treated as chattels? Slavery and its aftermath in America addresses these questions. What happens to the family in a society characterized by rapid change from a rural-agricultural to an urban-industrial economic system? The experiences of migrant and immigrant families in America around the turn of the century are pertinent. A last "natural experiment" is the experience of the family in a society characterized by bigness in most social systems and by national community —the contemporary American scene. This receives major emphasis in the present study.

But this is only one-half of the sociological perspective employed herein. The perspective employed deals not only with interchanges and transactions between the family and society (macrosociology), but also with the internal workings of the family (microsociology), the individual in the family, organization and activity within the family, and relationships between family members. Here the emphasis is on the relationship of the individual to the family and the other socio-sexual systems (dating, mate selection, and marriage), procreation and socialization in the family, and the adjustments involved as the individual leaves his natal family (family of orientation) and establishes his own heterosexual unit (family of procreation).

A final section of the book deals with crises situations in marriage and the family and with resolution of these crises either in restoration or dissolutionment of the respective social systems.

It should be pointed out that family and society receive major emphasis when the family in earlier epochs of American society is considered, while a more balanced emphasis on "macro" and "micro" aspects of family life characterize the contemporary chapters. This split in emphasis occurs out of necessity. In the first case we are dependent on the record kept by historians and others, not by sociologists. In the latter case, we have available the vast resources of contemporary sociological and other social scientific research to draw upon.

Appropriate sociological concepts for the two perspectives are introduced in the text at points when they seem to the author to be most appropriate to the discussion. Teachers wishing to introduce all of the concepts at the beginning of the course will find them conveniently listed in the index.

For the teacher wishing to compare American family experience with that of other societies there are a number of books written from a comparative or cross-cultural perspective that can be utilized as supplementary texts. They include the following: Victor A. Christopherson, *Readings in Comparative Marriage and the Family* (New York: Selected Academic Readings, A Division of Associated Educational Services, Incorporated, 1967); William J. Good, *Readings on the Family and Society* (Englewood Cliffs, N.J.: Prentice-Hall, 1964); H. Kent Geiger, *Comparative Perspectives on Marriage and the Family* (Boston: Little, Brown, 1968); M. F. Nimkoff, *Comparative Family Systems* (Boston: Houghton Mifflin, 1965); William N. Stephens, *The Family in Cross-Cultural Perspectives* (New York: Holt, Rinehart, and Winston, 1963).

FLOYD MANSFIELD MARTINSON

Contents

TABLES

FIGURES

PART I

Introduction

CHAPTER 1

Family in Society:
An Overview

THE FAMILY UNIT containing father, mother, and child is referred to as the *nuclear* family. In many societies, the nuclear family is part of a larger unit of kinsmen living together.[1] But even when larger groups of kinsmen live together, time and space is commonly reserved for at least minimal interaction of the nuclear unit.

The network of which the nuclear family is a part varies from society to society. It may include a group of relatives who live together with the nuclear family and are subordinate to the same authority, as in the case of the traditional Chinese family, in which a patriarch, his wife, his unmarried daughters, his sons, his son's wives, their children, and their children's children for as many generations as possible live together as a cohesive unit. This is called an *extended* family. It may include a number of families who habitually camp together, as the bands of the American Cheyenne Indians. It may involve a group of agricultural families living in a concentrated cluster of homes at the center of or in close proximity to the source of livelihood—cultivated lands, pastures, and forests. The latter is a more common type of settlement in Europe than in the United States. It is referred to as an agricultural village, *dorf* (German), or *mir* (Russian).

In Middle West America, where the land was plotted in rectangular sections with each family living on a farm, the local social network included a number of farm families on adjoining farms who associated informally with one another. This type of settlement has been referred to as a neighborhood, or, if it is a larger grouping clustering around a village as a trade center, it is referred to as a community.

[1] The word "family" is derived from the Latin *familia,* a term which in classical Rome applied to the entire group living in the house—husband, wife, small and grown-up children, and servants.

FAMILY AND KIN

As a part of a kinship system, a system composed of blood relatives, their spouses, and their offspring, the nuclear family has contacts with persons and groups beyond the limits of the local community. In societies where the larger kinship system is regarded as a major and significant unit of association, many functions on behalf of the nuclear family and its members are carried on outside the local community. These functions are supervised by an official of the larger kinship group. Life-crises observances—as birth, marriage, death—are frequently carried on by this larger kinship group. While the choice of a marriage partner in our society involves the two persons immediately concerned in the choice, in some societies choice is totally out of the hands of the prospective marriage partners and is regulated by representatives of the larger kinship group. A most common task of the kinship group is the regulation of the selection of marriage partners. For example, Nahas reporting as recently as 1956 indicates that most marriages in Iraq are arranged by parents or by elders rather than by the marriage partners themselves.[2]

THE FAMILY AND NONKINSHIP ASSOCIATIONS

Kin groups play a relatively smaller role for nuclear families in modern industrialized societies than they do in some primitive societies, but nonkinship systems—social, political, economic, educational, and religious—involve the family and its members in many social patterns. In American society with its vast communications network and rapid, convenient transportation, a family might be said to be in touch with the whole society.

THE FAMILY AND SOCIAL ORDER

Sexual expression is never free from social control. Some prohibitions, such as the prohibition of sex relations between blood relatives, are universally in force. There are prescriptions as well as proscriptions, for sexual cohabitation is necessary to the perpetuation of the race. Offspring are born, and these must be nurtured and tended. Families deal with basic human needs—sexual, economic, reproductive, educational, disciplinary. Without provision for meeting these needs human society would cease, and human life would cease as well. With few exceptions—"so curious and contrived that they emphasize the ubiquitousness of the institution of the family"— all human societies structure a nurturant relationship between adults and dependent children.[3]

[2] M. K. Nahas, "The Married Life in Iraq," *Studies of the Family,* ed. Nels Anderson, (Tübingen: J. C. B. Mohr [Paul Siebeck], 1956), p. 194.
[3] Margaret Mead, "The Contemporary American Family as an Anthropologist Sees It," *American Journal of Sociology,* LIII (May, 1948), 453.

THE FAMILY AND SOCIAL INTEGRATION

In small, isolated primitive societies, the kinship system in itself can meet most of the basic individual and social needs. In such societies there may be little economic, political, or religious activity outside of families. But in complex societies differentiated structures emerge to meet basic and acquired needs. Market, government, and school take their places alongside the family in meeting the needs of individuals and groups.

Changes in society necessitate changes in its various systems. When a nation declares war, for example, the family, the economy, the school—in fact all systems of society—are affected. It is logical to assume that changes in the whole will affect changes in the parts more than changes in the parts will affect the whole. Family, in American society, is not a dominant system, hence it is apt to be more affected by rather than affecting. The family operates within a social milieu which helps to bring the family into being, to support it, to shape it, and often even to destroy it.

THE FAMILY AND CULTURE

No people are without a past—a history, survivals,[4] and traditions. Certain activities come to be regarded as right and proper, and certain ways of carrying them out become standardized solutions to collective problems. These accepted activities and procedures become normative for the society. One is applauded when he follows the norm and punished when he does not; in other words, sanctions are applied. Thus man interprets all of his environment in ideological terms. He gives his environment meaning in terms of the why, the what, and how of life. Availability of a thing is not enough; whether or not one will utilize it and how he will utilize it depend on the meaning attached to it.

Family life is dependent on the culture of the society of which the family is a part. In American society a particular family system, the monogamous nuclear family, came to be recognized as a crucial element. No system in American society has been more circumscribed by normative patterns than has the family.[5]

THE FAMILY AND RAPID SOCIAL CHANGE

One question that has concerned social scientists, especially American sociologists, is what happens to the family—this small, adaptive, vulnerable part of the total social structure—in complex societies characterized by

[4] "Survival" is here used in the technical, anthropological sense to refer to the continuance of some aspect of social behavior—a custom, a ritual—after the circumstances in which it originated or which gave it meaning no longer exist.

[5] Morris Zelditch, Jr., "Values Institutionalized in the Family," *The Antioch Review*, Winter, 1957–58, pp. 455–468; John Sirjamaki, "Culture Configurations in the American Family," *American Journal of Sociology*, LIII (May, 1948), 464–470.

rapid social change. More specifically, what has happened to the American family during the rapid emergence of America as a complex society? This question cannot be answered as satisfactorily as we might like with available evidence, but it can be answered in part, and the question and its answers are crucial to an understanding of the American family.

Disintegration

There are students of the family who say that the Western family, and particularly the American family, has shown signs of disintegration that are actual and absolute. Sorokin develops the theme that the family has become more and more unstable until it has reached the point of disintegration.[6] He predicts that the family as a sacred union of husband and wife, or parents and children, will continue to disintegrate until the differences between socially-sanctioned marriages and illicit sex-relationships disappear. He sees the functions of the family decreasing until the family will become "a mere incidental cohabitation of male and female," while the home becomes "a mere overnight parking place mainly for sex relationships."[7]

Loss of Function

Other sociologists speak of loss of function when explaining what happened to the American family.[8] The loss-of-function sociologists point out that the family at one time performed many functions on behalf of its members, on behalf of the community, and on behalf of society, and that it has gradually lost these functions. Historically, the family was both an important productive unit (making soap and clothing and processing food) and an important protective unit (against wild animals and savages). Not only has the family lost these and other functions; it has not taken on any significant new ones. Hence the family's relative importance in society has declined, say these sociologists.

Adaptability

Still other sociologists recognize that social change has taken place but view change as having had a favorable effect on the family. Burgess sees the emergence of a type of family characterized by adaptability—a family that can adapt not only to changing conditions but also to divergent personalities with diversity of cultural backgrounds.[9] Adaptability, Burgess asserts, makes for stability in the long run. Not a stability brought about by external pres-

---

[6] Pitirim A. Sorokin, *The Crises of Our Age* (New York: Dutton, 1941).

[7] Pitirim A. Sorokin, *Social and Cultural Dynamics* (New York: American Book, 1937), IV.

[8] W. F. Ogburn, *Recent Social Trends* (New York: McGraw-Hill, 1933), pp. 661–708.

[9] Ernest W. Burgess, "The Family in a Changing Society," *American Journal of Sociology*, LIII (May, 1948), 417–422.

sures—public opinion, norms, law—but a stability brought about by the "strength of the interpersonal relations of its members, as manifested in affection, rapport, common interests and flexibility." But flexibility of personality is not in itself sufficient to insure family adaptability to a changing society, according to Burgess. Family members must be culturally and educationally oriented to the necessity of making adjustments. Adaptability is more than favorable attitudes toward adjustment; it requires knowledge and skills of adaptation. Education and counseling based upon social science research are seen as the best means of preparing family members for the adaptations necessary to good adjustment in a changing society. Along with disintegration and loss of function, the adaptability point of view can be supported with empirical evidence and it does illuminate a part of the situation.[10]

The "Colleague" Family

Blood and Wolfe in a survey of empirical data conclude that the American family has not for many decades been highly integrated and authoritarian in structure. They conclude that the patriarchal family—a family ordered under a strong, authoritarian father figure—was already weakened by 1912 and "died a sudden death in World War I."[11] They find the family today to be like a corporation that "makes its decisions in staff conferences but executes them through technical experts," with husband and wife having clearly differentiated roles.

Miller and Swanson call this type of family the "colleague" family because it resembles co-workers rather than companions—interdependent, but each with distinct and mutually recognized competencies.[12] To label the contemporary pattern as "colleagueish" may be to describe only one emergent family type, however; the American family in its variety escapes any easy monolithic category.

Improvement

Other sociologists see the American family not as disintegrating but as improving. More of the population is marrying; marriages—when death rate and divorce rate are considered together—are lasting longer; more people are remarrying; divorce-rate increase has been checked, at least for the present; more and more couples are establishing homes of their own and

[10] Robert C. Angell, *The Family Encounters the Depression* (New York: Scribners, 1936); Ernest W. Burgess and Paul Wallin, *Engagement and Marriage* (Philadelphia: J. B. Lippincott, 1953).

[11] Robert O. Blood, Jr., and Donald M. Wolfe, *Husbands and Wives: The Dynamics of Married Living* (Glencoe, Ill.: Free Press, 1960), p. 27.

[12] Daniel R. Miller and Guy E. Swanson, *The Changing American Parent* (New York: Wiley, 1958), pp. 196 ff.

are having children.[13] America is seen as a family-affirming society, and the American people by their actions as family-affirming people.

Differentiation

In answering the question "what has happened to the nuclear family in our rapidly changing society?" perhaps it would be more accurate to use less evaluative terms than "disintegrating" or "improving" and to use instead terms more in keeping with a sociological tradition. Differentiation (the transfer of family functions to other more specialized social systems) is a characteristic of societies that are increasing in complexity. As we have already pointed out, there are so-called primitive societies in which the kinship system does carry out many functions, and influences the carrying out of many more. But in highly complex urban and industrialized societies, more functions are transferred to other social structures, such as the market, government, school, and church. These systems are not extensions of the kinship system but are innovations in the society with specialized structures for specialized activities. Education at mother's knee comes to be displaced by new educational structures—the elementary school, the secondary school, the vocational school, the university, and in-service training in industry. To say that the family has thereby lost the educational function may be to prejudice the data with an interpretation that fails to do justice to the fact that there are many functions which the family simply cannot perform effectively. America may have developed a new type of nuclear family, "one in which the family is more specialized than before, but not in any general sense less important, because the society is dependent *more* exclusively on it for the performance of *certain* of its vital functions."[14]

The "Civilization-Adequate" Family

It is instructive in a review of theories of family change to review the early over against the later of one of the sociological "prophets of doom," Carle C. Zimmerman. In his *Family and Civilization* (1947), Zimmerman quoted with approval Sorokin's gloomy predictions about the family. Zimmerman concluded that, "There is little left now within the family or the moral code to hold this family together. . . . The United States as well as the other countries of Western Christendom, will reach the final phases of a great family crisis between now and the last of this century."[15] Theoretically, the family could stay as it was, decay further, or show a "resurgence of Victorian morality." But to Zimmerman it was already so completely

---

[13] Talcott Parsons and R. F. Bales, *Family Socialization and Interaction Process* (Glencoe, Ill.: Free Press, 1955); Paul H. Landis, *Making the Most of Marriage* (New York: Appleton-Century-Crofts, 1955).

[14] Parsons and Bales, *op. cit.*, pp. 9–10.

[15] Carle C. Zimmerman, *Family and Civilization* (New York: Harper, 1947), pp. 798–799.

atomized that it produced no stable social body in which to solidify. Yet he assumed that Americans had the intelligence and the educational and propaganda agencies necessary to bring about a reinstatement of the family if the "learned classes" understood the basic meaning of the family to society.

Two years later, in 1949, Zimmerman published an extension of the same argument. But Kinsey's data on the sexual behavior of American males had been published by then, and Zimmerman saw a hopeful and optimistic sign in the "puritanical" behavior of the intellectual classes. Zimmerman wrote, "This is the first time in Western history when we have had a family crisis in which the intellectuals have not been to a much greater extent than the other classes the leaders in the new freedom from restraint."[16]

Later Zimmerman noted that the family system had begun "some changes of its own" toward a stronger socially-creative family unit. Zimmerman saw this "ethical good," or "civilization-adequate" family as isolating itself and surrounding itself with a buffer of other families of similar ethical views. "In essence, 'good families' now surround themselves with similar families and the world of the child seems 'good.' "[17] Hence in the span of his observation of American family life, Zimmerman after predicting a great crisis observes a hopeful trend: the "good" families slowed the tide of family disintegration if not in fact turned that tide.

What has happened to the family in America with its history of rapid change? Is it disintegrating (Sorokin)? If disintegrating, has the disintegration been slowed or perhaps even brought to a halt (Zimmerman)? Has the family lost most of its important functions (Ogburn)? Should the changes in the American family be viewed as social differentiation rather than as loss of function (Parsons and Bales)? Has the family adapted to rapid social change (Burgess; Blood and Wolfe)? Is the condition of the family improving (Parsons and Bales; Landis)? The reader may wish to withhold judgment about the effects of change until the family's place in American society has been described and analyzed in subsequent chapters.

SUMMARY

A variety of networks of human relationships are structured to meet human needs; the family is one of these networks. Besides the family, there are governmental, economic, educational, social, and religious structures. A society operates through the various differentiated structures in meeting the needs of people. The more complex the society the greater the variety of specialized social structures. It is important that these specialized social

[16] Carle C. Zimmerman, *The Family of Tomorrow* (New York: Harper, 1949), p. 282.

[17] Carle C. Zimmerman, "The Family," *Contemporary Sociology*, ed. Joseph S. Roucek (New York: Philosophical Library, 1958), pp. 92, 93, 95.

structures be integrated with each other and with the society as a whole. Families are bound together with other social structures into larger groupings—bands, neighborhoods, villages, communities, kinship groups. The family performs a vital part of the functions necessary to individual and group life.

The family is affected by the nature and the rate of social change in society. Some behavioral scientists see the family as disintegrating as a result of the direction and rapidity of social change. Others see it as achieving a new vitality and stability.

BIBLIOGRAPHY

Joan Aldous and Reuben Hill. *International Bibliography of Research in Marriage and the Family, 1900–1964.* Minneapolis: University of Minnesota, 1967.

Robert C. Angell. *The Family Encounters the Depression.* New York: Scribners, 1936.

Norman W. Bell and Ezra F. Vogel. *A Modern Introduction to the Family.* Glencoe, Ill.: Free Press, 1960.

Robert O. Blood, Jr., and Donald M. Wolfe. *Husbands and Wives: The Dynamics of Married Living.* Glencoe, Ill.: Free Press, 1960.

Gunnar Boalt. *Family and Marriage.* New York: McKay, 1965.

Elizabeth Bott. "A Study of Ordinary Families," *Studies of the Family,* ed. Nels Anderson. Tübingen: J. C. B. Mohr [Paul Siebeck], 1956. Pp. 29–68.

Ernest W. Burgess. "The Family in a Changing Society," *American Journal of Sociology,* LIII (May, 1948), 417–422.

Ernest W. Burgess and Paul Wallin. *Engagement and Marriage.* Philadelphia: J. B. Lippincott, 1953.

Harold T. Christensen. "Development of the Family Field of Study," *Handbook of Marriage and the Family,* ed. Harold T. Christensen. Chicago: Rand McNally, 1964. Pp. 3–32.

Joseph F. Folsom. *The Family and Democratic Society.* New York: Wiley, 1934.

Börje Hanssen. "Dimensions of Primary Group Structure in Sweden," *Studies of the Family,* ed. Nels Anderson. Tübingen: J. C. B. Mohr [Paul Siebeck], 1956. Pp. 115–156.

Börje Hanssen. "Group Relations of Peasants and Farmers," *Studies of the Family,* ed. Nels Anderson, Vol. III, Göttingen: Vandenhoeck and Ruprecht, 1958. Pp. 57–92.

Daniel R. Miller and Guy E. Swanson. *The Changing American Parent.* New York: Wiley, 1958.

George Peter Murdock. *Social Structure.* New York: Macmillan, 1949.

W. F. Ogburn. *Recent Social Trends.* New York: McGraw-Hill, 1933.

Talcott Parsons. *The Social System.* Glencoe, Ill.: Free Press, 1951.

Talcott Parsons and Robert F. Bales. *Family, Socialization and Interaction Process.* Glencoe, Ill.: Free Press, 1955.

Margaret Park Redfield. "The American Family: Consensus and Freedom," *American Journal of Sociology,* LII (November, 1946), 175–183.

John Sirjamaki. "Culture Configurations in the American Family," *American Journal of Sociology*, LIII (May, 1948), 464–470.

Clark E. Vincent. "Familia Spongia: The Adaptive Function," *Journal of Marriage and the Family*, XXVIII (February, 1966), 22–36.

Morris Zelditch, Jr. "Cross-Cultural Analysis of Family Structure," *Handbook of Marriage and the Family*, ed. Harold T. Christensen. Chicago: Rand McNally, 1964. Pp. 462–500.

Carle C. Zimmerman. *Family and Civilization*. New York: Harper, 1947.

Carle C. Zimmerman and Lucius F. Cervantes. *Successful American Families*. New York: Pageant, 1960.

PART II

Family in Society: The Historical Perspective

WHAT HAS HAPPENED to the family during the period of rapid emergence of America as a complex society? One obvious and important piece of evidence is that it has survived. Not only has it survived emigration from Europe, Africa, and Asia, it has also survived Puritan colonialism, the American Revolution, slavery, the Civil War, industrialization, urbanization, the great depression of the 1930's, and numerous wars. Its survival has not been without modification in form and function, but the important point is that the family has survived at all.

In the interactions of human life, even in a society composed historically of a plurality of disparate elements, a society with a common culture emerges. America is such a society; though the elements which make it up have been varied, a common culture has developed during America's long history as a social system. America's three and a half centuries may be a short time in the life span of a civilization, but it is a long span of time under one continuous political system. In these three and a half centuries a culture has developed which contains patterns sufficiently diversified and yet sufficiently integrated to enable the American people to fulfill the basic requirements of personal and group life. The test of the unity of the society was met during the Civil War when the centralized government of the country prevailed. Developments of the 1950's and 1960's, in attempting to extend recognition and opportunities to American minorities, have brought some aspects of the common culture into serious question and have provided the national government with one of its greatest challenges.

Historically speaking, the patterns of family life in America are numerous and varied. There are rural and urban families; Jewish, Catholic, and Protestant families; immigrant and native-born families; Negro and white families; and other patterns *ad infinitum*. No one would question that there are both cultural and functional differences in these families. However, to the extent that the family is a dependent part of society and adaptive more than dominant, it follows that trends toward uniformity of cultural patterns in the nation as a whole are reflected in uniformity in the family system.

13

Uniquely American cultural configurations become part of family life even in the families of recent immigrants, particularly as the breadwinner and the children become involved in community life. New patterns of behavior bring conflict between parents and children in the immigrant home, but a bend toward American culture is likely to emerge.

The American family as it emerges has gone through a variety of "natural" experiments—experiments which nature and society provide. By taking soundings at significant epochs—times of disturbing and prodding events in history—we can provide partial answers to a number of questions about the family in a dynamic society.

The several chapters that follow deal with family life in a few selected critical periods in American history. In each chapter we attempt to answer certain questions within the limits of the data available. What was the nature of the society during the critical epoch? What ideological principles, activities, and procedures became normative for society and for the family? What part did the family play in society? What was the internal nature of the family? What was the relationship between the family and the individual? As well as giving the reader an understanding and appreciation of the family in American society at certain critical periods in its history, it is the aim of these chapters to show what the impact of these periods has been on the development of the contemporary American family. The four periods chosen are (1) the colonial period, which left a heritage of religious and moralistic values in personal and family life; (2) the revolutionary period, which fostered the development of a libertarian and democratic tradition; (3) the period of slavery, which placed a significant minority of the American population in bondage and continues to influence the character of American life at the present time; and (4) the period of emergence of America as an industrialized urban nation, which established the family as an adaptive (rather than a dominant) system in American economic and political life. In point of time there is overlap between the periods. This is especially true of the period of slavery, but the impact of slavery on the family is so unique that it must be treated as a separate unit.

CHAPTER 2

Puritanism and the Family

OF THE SOCIAL EXPERIMENTS that have been tried in America, Puritanism was one of the most significant. It has been referred to as "the fullest amalgam of religion, economics, and politics within a single mold that Americans ever achieved."[1] Never before and never since has the family operated under a stricter polity nor under more stringent attempts to apply that polity to family life. It should be noted, however, that although Puritanism was a dominant way of life, it was not the only one that existed during the colonial period. Puritanism and minority ways of life coexisted within the society at the same time, and there were also regional differences in family types during the period.

The large group of Puritans who landed at Salem in Massachusetts Bay was controlled by capable members of the British middle class, men of trade and commerce who came from the urban centers of Great Britain. Among them also were squires, yeomen, and not a few who had attended British universities. Tocqueville observes that these men possessed, in proportion to their numbers, a greater mass of intelligence than was to be found in any European nation.[2]

From its start in 1630 the Massachusetts Bay settlement, unlike many of the colonies, was a family settlement. The Puritans and their descendants became the primary leaders of the emerging American society during the colonial period—and the colonial period occupies nearly half of the entire course of American history from the founding of the first colony in 1607 to the present time. Thus these early settlers "established Puritanism—for better or worse—as one of the continuous factors in American life and thought."[3]

[1] Max Lerner, *America as a Civilization* (New York: Simon and Schuster, 1957), p. 719.

[2] Alexis de Tocqueville, *Democracy in America* (New York: Knopf, 1951; first published in France in 1835), p. 31.

[3] Perry Miller, ed., *The American Puritans: Their Prose and Poetry* (Garden City, N.Y.: Doubleday, Anchor, 1956), p. ix.

THE PURITAN VALUE SYSTEM

The concept of a covenant was the master idea of Puritanism.[4] It was believed that God agreed on a way of life with a group of men and that they were in turn committed, as a political system, to a specifically enunciated political program carrying out the dictates of the covenant with God. The Massachusetts Bay colonists believed they had made such a covenant. No activity was seen as falling outside its holy purposes. So concerned were they with the rules of morality that Puritan theologians set about defining and cataloging them—frugality, industry, liberality, and parsimony. None of these virtues were new; what was new about them was their double orientation—towards God, who exacted obedience from his elect; and toward the world, in which obedience was to become manifest by a man's devotion to his calling or occupation.[5]

The Puritan's calling provided him with seemingly contradictory norms. He was to be diligent in his "worldly businesses," while at the same time being "dead" to the world. Puritanism emphasized the duty of work in this world, at worldly tasks. Through working the Puritan escaped the temptation to which the idle were susceptible. The Puritan's work was never done, for it was labor itself, not any of its products, that God commanded.

FAMILY ADAPTATION TO THE ENVIRONMENT

New England did not lend itself readily to the establishment of large family estates. The land was rocky and the terrain uneven. In addition, the short summers were not conducive to extensive agriculture. Land was distributed to persons in small plots, with each person holding title to his land. This meant that the majority of family heads were free entrepreneurs. This enhanced the father's role in the eyes of other family members.

Such outside labor as was used by the farm family was usually obtained in the neighborhood and was seasonal. On special occasions—such as barn raisings, house raisings, or the building of a public facility such as a school or meeting house—all able-bodied members of the community might turn out and help. The demanding nature of the settlement is evident in the use made of children as laborers. Many of these were neglected or needy children. "Friendless boyes and girles" twelve years old and older were in demand.[6]

---

[4] Perry Miller, *The New England Mind: From Colony to Province* (Cambridge: Harvard University, 1953).

[5] Karl H. Hertz, "Max Weber and American Puritanism," *Journal for the Scientific Study of Religion,* I (Spring, 1962), 189–197.

[6] Arthur W. Calhoun, *A Social History of the American Family* (New York: Barnes and Noble, 1945; first published in 1917), p. 285.

In the seventeenth century the term "servant" was applied to anyone who worked for another in whatever capacity, whether in agriculture, commerce, or industry, as well as in the work of the household. The servant was family-free in terms of his own commitments; but his life as a servant, whether voluntary or involuntary, was not a pleasant one. The servant was required to do whatever the master expected of him and not to do anything without the master's consent. However, a good Puritan did not treat his servant harshly, if there were other means available to him. His religion did not permit it, and most of the servants were only temporarily in servitude, eventually becoming the equals of their masters as free persons in the community.

INTERCHANGES BETWEEN THE FAMILY AND THE GOVERNMENTAL SYSTEM

Puritan society was a totalitarian society run by a theologically-inclined oligarchy devoid of democratic inclinations as we think of them today. Puritans exercised rights of sovereignty in naming magistrates, enacting laws, and making police regulations, as "if their allegiance was only to God."[7]

Characteristic of the legislation of the period is the code of laws promulgated by Connecticut in 1650. The laws were borrowed almost directly from the text of the Old Testament. Sorcery, adultery, fornication, rape, and blasphemy were to be punished with death; disobedience of a son to his parents could also meet with the same penalty. The legislators in their concern with orderly conduct and good morals in the community constantly invaded the domain of conscience.

The Puritan value system provided a major role for the family; indeed, the Puritan believed that God in creating systems of control began with the family. The chief problem of the state was to see that family heads did their duty. The assumption upon which Puritan leaders acted was that the state was made up of families rather than persons. A commonwealth results from "many familyes subjecting themselves to rulers and laws."[8]

Taking care to bring everyone under the authority of a family ruler, the state did its utmost to support such rulers in the proper exercise of their authority. The strict punishments prescribed for disobedient children were

---

[7] De Tocqueville, op. cit., p. 37; Stanley Elkins and Eric McKitrick, "A Meaning for Turner's Frontier," Political Science Quarterly, LXIX (September, 1954), 321–353, and (December, 1954), 565–602.

[8] Thomas Hutchinson, ed., A Collection of Original Papers Relative to the History of the Colony of Massachusetts-Bay (Boston, 1769), p. 67; as reported in Edmund S. Morgan, The Puritan Family: Essays on Religion and Domestic Relations in Seventeenth Century New England (Boston, Mass.: Trustees of the Public Library, 1944), p. 84.

extended to include servants. Protection was given family governors from outsiders who might undermine their power. For example, a tavern-keeper or anyone else who entertained children or servants without the consent of their parents or masters was punished.

Since colonial officers (selectmen) relied heavily upon the family, they took care to see that family rulers were worthy of their responsibilities. Men who did not deserve to have charge over a family could be prevented by the courts from setting up households. The selectmen themselves regularly inspected families to see that parents fulfilled their educational and regulatory duties. Parents found negligent might have their children taken from them and placed with someone more worthy. When Robert Stockpiles, a family man of Dorchester, was presented before the court for negligence in his calling and not submitting to authority, he was ordered to "put forth" his children.

The system of state supervision of the family might appear as an odious interference with liberty. It doubtless was odious to the unregenerate against whom it was directed, but a good Puritan father looked upon it as an indispensable support to his authority. Rather than interfering with his private rights it provided him with the power to maintain them. There was no reason for conflict between the state and the governor of a well-ordered family; the avowed purpose of both was the same.

As settlements grew, it became more and more difficult for the selectmen and constables to supervise the government of all the families, and in later years a group of officers for the specific purpose of inspecting and reenforcing family government was established. In interchanges between the governmental system and the family system, government was clearly dominant. The family was a significant, though adaptive social system.

FAMILY-CHURCH INTERCHANGES

The church was established as a tax-supported system working in cooperation with the governmental system of the colony. It was an authoritarian system claiming a monopoly on religious truth. Religious freedom was denied. The church possessed both requisites of civil control—influence and power; the minister as the official representative of the church often came to be a leader in the community.

The congregation made heavy demands on the family and supposedly had high regard for it. The parent-child relationship was a crucial one, religiously speaking. Membership in a believing family came close to being regarded as a prerequisite to membership in the congregation.

Ministers did their best to make it difficult for the unregenerate servant to enter a godly family; they advised the heads of families not to hire ungodly servants lest their children be corrupted by contagion, and they condemned marriages of church members with the unregenerate. Thus, while the unregenerate were admonished to get into godly families, the heads of godly families were admonished to keep such influences out of their families!

The congregation could censure and admonish all families, but it could employ the threat of excommunication only in dealing with its members. The records indicate that these weapons were freely used to reform family disorders. Congregations, as well as the state, adopted the practice of home inspections. The First Church of Boston voted unanimously "that the elders should go from house to house to visit the families and see how they are instructed in the grounds of religion."

Despite close cooperation between the autonomous local congregations and the state, ecclesiastical and civil functions were distinctly separated. The civil government had authority to punish the wrongdoer, but it could never excommunicate a person. The functions of the "tithing man," the colonial visitor of homes, were beyond the jurisdiction of the churches. He was appointed by the parish, not by the congregation, and he had no official role in the enforcement of church discipline.

In interchanges involving the religious system and the family system, it was again the family system that played the adaptive role.

FAMILY AND COMMUNITY

Each agricultural village had facilities near the center for a village green, a meetinghouse, a schoolhouse, a burial ground, the minister's house, pillories, stocks, a signpost. That is, there were facilities for community services: economic, governmental, educational, religious. Plots of land large enough to provide for a house, a barn, other outbuildings, a kitchen garden, and a somewhat larger garden in back were available to each family. Outside this cluster of public buildings, homes, and outbuildings stretched the tillable land, meadows, pastures, and woodland. In new settlements strips of land were distributed among the settlers by lots with each receiving some of the best and some of the poorer land. Communal pasture lands were under the supervision of herdsmen hired by the villagers.

The tithing man not only visited families, he also kept a close check on single persons entering the village. The concepts of a closed community and an open family are helpful in appreciating the nature of the Puritan family in the New England village, in that the tithing man had free access to the family while at the same time keeping the community closed to "undesirable" persons.[9] The town of Dorchester, for instance, passed an ordinance requiring that "the tithing men in their several precincts should

[9] C. D. Saal, "Causes of the Delay in Western European Family Research and Some Notes of the Investigation of the Dutch Rural Family," *Studies of the Family*, ed. Nels Anderson (Tübingen: J. C. B. Mohr [Paul Siebeck], 1956), pp. 228–245.

inspect all inmates that do come into each of their precincts, either single persons or families, and to give speedy information thereof unto the selectmen from time to time or to some of them that order may be taken about them."[10]

Despite precautions, Puritan villages were not as pure in terms of population composition as the true believers would have liked. They had not imagined that the immigration from England would bring such "a hoard of average, lusty Elizabethan Englishmen." In the total population of the Bay colony there were perhaps more unregenerate than regenerate. The regenerate controlled the positions of power in the community and in the congregation, however.

Community influences on the family were not as wholesome as the regenerate would have liked. Drinking to the point of intoxication became a problem, and ministers in New England thundered at the practice from the pulpit. The colonists were known to consume liquors on all important occasions—"baptisms, weddings, funerals, barn raisings, church raisings, house raisings, ship launchings, ordinations, perambulations, or 'beating the bounds,' and meetings of commissions and committees, and in taverns, clubs, and private houses."[11] Taverns, which also doubled as inns, were to be found in all the colonies, in towns, on the traveled roads, and at the ferry landings. Laws against intoxication were enacted at an early date.

INSIDE THE PURITAN HOME

There were houses of almost every description. In the country districts small houses of one story were common; they were made of roughhewn or sawn flat boards, had few windows and no panes of glass, were unpainted and weatherstained. Another common type was the frame house, a story and a half high in front and one story high in the rear, with a single pitched roof that sloped from the front of the house to the rear. There were four rooms and a hall on the first floor, with a kitchen in back, and three or four rooms on the second floor. The Puritans were not given to luxury; this is reflected in their houses. The ordinary farmhouse "was hardly so well built, so spacious, or so warm as that of a well-to-do contemporary of Charlemagne."[12]

There was great diversity in the household effects of colonial homes. Chairs, bureaus, tables, bedsteads, buffets, cupboards were in general use.

[10] Calhoun, *op. cit.* (see above, fn. 6), p. 74.

[11] Charles M. Andrews, *Colonial Folkways: A Chronicle of American Life in the Reign of the Georges* (New Haven: Yale University Press, 1919), pp. 104–105.

[12] Henry Adams, *The United States in 1800* (Ithaca, N.Y.: Cornell University Press, Great Seal Books, 1955; consisting of the first six chapters of Volume I of Adams' *History of the United States of America During the First Administration of Thomas Jefferson,* published in 1889), p. 12.

Some people had silverplate, mahogany, fine china, and copper utensils; others owned china, delftware, and furniture of plainwood with perhaps a few silver spoons, a porringer, and an occasional mahogany chair and table; still others, and these by far the largest number, used only pewter, earthenware, and wooden dishes with the simpler essentials—spinning wheel, flatirons, pots and kettles, lamps and candlesticks—but no luxuries.

An interesting phenomenon in the New England community was the large number of half-finished houses. Apparently a man would build the first section of a house for occupancy by his family, and, when his son married, the remainder of the house would be finished for his use. Family dwellings had to be fairly large since households commonly contained members who were not of the immediate family. In the household of a prosperous Massachusetts merchant might be found unattached relatives, boys apprenticed to him, both male and female indentured servants, and wage employees who worked for him, ate at his table, and lived under his roof.

FAMILY TASKS

Economic Tasks

The equipment of the average New England country household included not only the household furnishings but also shoemaker's tools and shoe leather, surgeon's tools and apothecary stuff, salves and ointments, branding irons, pestle and mortar, lamps, guns and perhaps a sword, harness and fittings, occasionally a still or a cider press, and outfits for carpentering and blacksmithing.

Tasks performed within the home reflected the family's economic relationships with external systems. The internal activity of a home was governed in part by the requirements of the interchanges with other systems in the community and in part by the kind and amount of goods obtained in these interchanges. In the case of the Puritan family there was very little economic interchange. The family was a major and virtually independent production unit. Nine-tenths consisted of farmers who performed most tasks for themselves. All family members worked, labor dividing along sex lines with men employed in the fields and women carrying on the housework and caring for the children.

Religious Tasks

Ideally, every morning and every evening in a godly Puritan home the father led his household in prayer, in scriptural reading, and song. At mealtime thanks were offered to the Lord. Sabbath-day services commonly lasted two hours or more, but devotions in the home were reasonably brief. The proper Puritan kept work and worship in balance; by and large weekdays were for work.

Besides the daily rituals, once a week children and others in the home were to be catechized in the grounds and principles of religion, or at least to be taught some short orthodox catechism. This religious instruction was not a mere formality; parents were expected to try to make religion understandable, meaningful, and significant in the lives of their children.

The father was obligated to seek the salvation of the souls under his charge, servants as well as children. Cotton Mather wrote in his diary on April 21, 1700: "This day, my Servant, was offered unto the Communion of my Church. But in the Account that she gave to the Church of her Conversion, she Declared her living in my Family to have been the Means of it, and that she should forever bless God for bringing her under my Roof. Others of my Servants formerly (almost all that ever lived with me) have joined unto my church when they have lived with mee; and blessed God for their Living in my poor sinful Family."

Woman's Work

Woman's place was in the home. It was her duty to "keep at home, educating all her children, keeping and improving what is got by the industry of the man." She was to see that nothing was wasted or prodigally spent; that all had what was suitable in due season. Bearing and caring for children, processing food and fiber, and managing a large household left little time or energy for her to contemplate her place in society. Nevertheless, the number of women that performed the numerous tasks unaided by servants while bearing and rearing many children was probably not much greater than it is today.[13] The number of children who did not survive infancy was great and adult unmarried women, unpaid servants, or other kindred living with the family assisted with the household tasks.

LEADERSHIP AND AUTHORITY IN THE FAMILY

There can be no question of the situational factors that led to authoritarianism, but this is not adequate to explain the authoritarianism of the New England Puritan family. The law prescribed the death penalty for disobedience of children to parents, following the precepts of Mosaic law; the father was the representative of the oligarchy in the home. "The sway of the housefather, though in the main just, became in theory despotic."[14] But so far as is known, the death penalty was never imposed for the crime of disobeying parents.

Women had a role subordinate to that of men. Married women could not hold property of their own. Legally, the wife's personality was largely ex-

---

[13] Calhoun, *op. cit.* (see above, fn. 6), p. 98.
[14] George E. Howard, *A History of Matrimonial Institutions* (Chicago: University of Chicago Press, 1904), II, 152.

tinguished, for her personal property became her husband's and he was responsible for her behavior. In Puritan theology the souls of men and women were equal but few would advocate social equality. Modesty, meekness, compassion, and piety were regarded as "solid feminine virtues." A good wife was expected to submit to her husband's authority, meet his needs, and cater to his whims. When a wife of the first governor, John Winthrop (who married four times), lost her mind, her Puritan women friends attributed the calamity to "her desertion of her domestic duties and meddling in a man's sphere."[15] In similar vein, Governor Winthrop believed that the young wife of the Governor of Connecticut had gone insane by giving herself wholly to reading and writing. Had she "not gone out of her way and calling to meddle in such things as are proper for men, whose minds are stronger, etc., she had kept her wits and might have improved them usefully and honorably in the place God had set her."

The husband's authority was strictly circumscribed, however. Lawfully, he could not strike his wife, nor could he command her to do anything contrary to what were regarded as the laws of God. She held a place of honor in the home; she was parent to the children and mistress to the servants. In relation to these members of the household she stood in a position of authority equal to that of her husband. The case of Daniel Ela and his wife Elizabeth is a case in point. When Daniel told his wife Elizabeth that "shee was none of his wife, shee was but his Servantt," the incident was reported to the authorities; and in spite of Elizabeth's protest that she held no charges against her husband, the county court levied a fine against Daniel.

FAMILY INTEGRATION AND SOLIDARITY

A great deal of the integration of the Puritan family was perpetrated by external conditions rather than internal activity. The integration of the family was also advanced by strictures on communal pleasures that were considered to be morally dangerous.

That the demands of a primitive agriculture and the severity of Puritan religion and moral standards caused strained relationships in the family is to be expected. We have indications of the tense situation that developed as the Puritan father attempted to carry out the requirements of parenthood, especially the requirements that he be responsible for the souls of his children. Both Cotton Mather and Judge Samuel Sewall report problems in this regard. An entry in Cotton Mather's diary indicates the dedication and intensity he felt as he attempted to carry out his religious function as a Puritan father, indicating also the unreasonableness of the task and the release from tension that the situation produced through the shedding of tears.

[15] Calhoun, *op. cit.* (see above, fn. 6), p. 90.

Cotton Mather writes in his diary on a Lord's Day as follows:

I took my little daughter, Katy, inty my Study; and there I told my Child that I am to dy shortly, and shee must, when I am Dead, Remember every Thing, that I said unto her.

I sett before her, the sinful and woeful Condition of Her *Nature,* and I charged her, *to pray in secret places,* every Day, without ceasing, that God for the Sake of Jesus Christ would give her a *New Heart,* and *pardon* Her Sins, and make her a Servant of His. . . .

At length, with many Tears, both on my Part, and hers, I told my Child, that God had from Heaven assured mee, and the good Angels had satisfied mee, that shee shall be brought Home unto the Lord Jesus Christ, and bee one of His forever. . . . But I therewithal told her, that if she did not now, in her Childhood seek the Lord, and give herself up unto Him, some dreadful Afflictions must befall her, that so her Father's Faith may come at its accomplishments.

I therefore made the child kneel down by mee; and I poured out my Cries unto the Lord and Hee would lay His hands upon her, and bless her and save her and make her a Temple of His glory. It will bee so; it will bee so![16]

THE PURITAN FAMILY AND THE PERSON

There is some value in making a distinction between *individual* and *person* in that "individual" is a generic term applicable to biological organisms, human and animal, while "person" is a specific term applied only to human beings. If this distinction is accepted, it can be argued that the human infant at birth is more correctly designated as "individual" than as "person," thus reserving the term "person" for human beings who have been shaped by the socialization process. ("Socialization" is a term that denotes the process by which a human being learns to adjust to the way of life, or life style, in a society by acquiring patterns of behavior of which his associates, particularly his adult associates, approve. This process normally begins in the family. It continues in the school and in association with playmates and other children and adults.)

Children were "providential accidents," but they were prized both for religious and practical reasons. While there were many births, there were also many deaths. The infant mortality rate was high even in advantaged families. Only two of Cotton Mather's fifteen children survived him and only three of Judge Sewall's fourteen children outlived their father.[17]

In spite of the high infant mortality rate, the colonial family proved to be remarkably adequate in adding to the population. Families with ten children were fairly common, and families with twenty or more children were not unusual. Most of the large families were the offspring of at least two mothers, however.

[16] As quoted in Morgan, *op. cit.* (see above, fn. 8), p. 81.
[17] Calhoun, *op. cit.* (see above, fn. 6), pp. 105–106.

The demands of Puritan theology and the demands of the environment complemented each other; for the theology saw idleness as a source of sin for children as well as for adults, and the demands of nature called for long hours of labor by the children. Harsh as the pattern of piety, rigid discipline, and hard work might appear, it did match the times. In the world that children could expect to enter as adults, labor was in demand and capital was scarce. Thus, it was somehow consistent with prevailing conditions when the will of the headstrong child was broken. All children were taught that it was wrong to find fault with their meals, their apparel, or their lot in life.[18]

Children, it was believed, were born evil; since the stain of original sin defiled the soul of the newborn, he was promptly taken to the church on the Sabbath to be baptized. The fear of Hell was greater than the fear of pneumonia or other children's diseases that might be aggravated by so early exposure.[19] The Puritans also believed that children were born without knowledge. They assumed, however, that much of the effect of both evil and ignorance could be overcome by training and education. If parents performed their duty, the child could be led away from the evil to which he was naturally prone. Evil nature could be curbed and disciplined into right behavior only if training started early. The pious parent had to fill his children's minds with knowledge and he had to make them apply knowledge to right action.

The basic personality of the child was not formed as a result of intensive contacts between parent and child alone. Puritan farm children living in the New England village had extensive contacts with many people within the larger household and outside of it. The personality of the Puritan child was influenced by his kin, by others of the household, and by neighbors in the village.

Beyond the usual teaching of skills, the Puritan family was responsible for teaching the child a calling. According to law, every father had to see that his child was instructed "in some other trade profitable for themselves, and the Commonwealth if they will not or cannot train them up in learning to fit them for higher imployments."[20] Puritan children often lived outside the parental home. A boy chose his calling between the ages of ten and fourteen, and if it was to be a trade the training was gained through an apprenticeship of seven years to some master of that trade.

Children left the parental home not only to live with the masters to whom they were apprenticed; they frequently went to live with a schoolmaster. Judge Sewall's granddaughter attended boarding-school in Boston at the age of nine. Children also made long stays in the homes of friends, and not

[18] George R. Clay, "Children of the Young Republic," *American Heritage,* XI (April, 1960), 46–53.

[19] Calhoun, *op. cit.,* pp. 107–108.

[20] Max Farrand, ed., *The Laws and Liberties of Massachusetts,* (Cambridge, Mass.: Harvard University Press, 1929; reprinted from the 1648 edition), p. 11.

always voluntarily. There was a precedent in England for the practice of placing children outside the home, one justified on the grounds that children learned better manners when they were brought up in another home. The Puritans continued the practice. They felt that God gave them through birth to their natural parents and as Reverend Deodat Lawson put it, children belonging to God rather than to man were in reality "put out" by God for purposes of training and education when they were placed in the parental home. Hence, by extension, children were "put out" whether they were in the parental home, in the home of kinfolk, or in another home. Rather than putting disobedient children to death, as the law allowed, the selectmen or the court placed them until they came of age with families who would more strictly supervise their upbringing.

THE FAMILY-FREE ADULT

It was "common practice in diverse places for young men irregularly and disorderly to watch all advantages for their evil purposes, to insinuate into the affections of young maidens by coming to them in places and seasons unknown to their parents for such ends, whereby such evil hath grown amongst us to the dishonour of God and damage of parties," according to a Massachusetts law of 1749.[21] We learn from a Massachusetts statute that there was "a loose and sinful custom of going or riding from town to town . . . ofttimes men and women together, upon pretence of going to lectures, but it appears . . . merely to drink and revel in ordinaries and taverns, which is in itself scandalous, and it is to be feared a notable means to debauch our youth and hazard the chastity of those that are drawn forth thereunto."[22] Later Jonathan Edwards told of young men in Northampton who had become "addicted to night-walking and frequenting the taverns, and leud practices," and how they would "get together in conventions of both sexes for mirth, and jollity, which they called frolics; and they would spend the greater part of the night in them."[23]

Sunday night "dating" apparently grew out of the way in which the Sabbath was celebrated. It was customary in New England to celebrate the Sabbath from sundown on Saturday through sundown on Sunday, and this gave rise to the practice of celebrating the close of the religious services by company-keeping on Sunday evenings. The various families of the church would call on each other, and apparently the young people went so far as to keep company apart from the rest of their respective family.[24] In some

---

[21] As reported in Howard, *op. cit.* (see above, fn. 14), II, 165.
[22] From Whitmore, *Colonial Laws of Massachusetts,* as quoted in *Ibid.,* II, p. 154.
[23] From Adams, *Some Phases of Sexual Immorality,* as quoted in *Ibid.,* II, p. 198.
[24] Herbert Wallace Schneider, *The Puritan Mind* (Ann Arbor: University of Michigan Press, 1958; first copyrighted in 1930 by Henry Holt and Company, Inc.), pp. 102–103.

parts of Connecticut it was reported that courtship was carried on in the living room in the presence of the family; while an early English traveler said of Boston that on the south there was a small but pleasant common, where the gallants, a little before sunset, walked with their maidens till the nine o'clock bell rang.

A custom in New England as well as in New York and other Middle Colonies was that of bundling, which involved the couple courting while in bed, with the mutual understanding that innocent endearments should not be exceeded. The couple courted in bed apparently for considerations of convenience and privacy. There is some evidence that the custom was practiced particularly among the less privileged classes "whose limited means compelled them to economize strictly to their expenditure of firewood and candle light."[25] Precautions were taken against undue physical stimulation or involvement—they were fully clothed; in some instances the girl was expected to don additional clothing when bundling; and beds were sometimes equipped with a center partition separating the bed partners.

Bundling was regarded as a gross licentious practice by the Puritans, but how common the practice was and how commonly it led to sexual involvement is not known. Burnaby, a visitor to Massachusetts Bay Colony, told of such a custom (under the title of "tarrying") which he observed took place between the permission to "pay court" and the banns. Another observer attributed different motives to young men and young women; women bundled with chaste purpose, but "in time the men had their way."[26]

It is possible that those who introduced bundling were influenced by the Dutch custom of "queesting," for there does not seem to be evidence of bundling in Old England. In Ireland, Scotland, Wales, and Germany there were comparable customs.

Puritan proscriptions on sexual behavior were difficult if not impossible to enforce. Sexual irregularities both before and after marriage were common. Lord Dartmough, secretary for the Colonies, referred to the commonness of illegitimate offspring among the young people of New England as a thing of accepted notoriety. There were a number of contributing factors. Settlers had brought from England a fund of coarse sensuality, perhaps only veneered with asceticism.[27] It was difficult to keep adults in subjection in a pioneering area where the cooperation and the labor of each person was so sorely needed. Even young ladies enjoyed a relatively large amount of liberty. The need for laborers brought "undesirables" into the communities. Lastly, the form of sexual indulgence that developed may have reflected the

[25] Howard, *op. cit.* (see above, fn. 14), pp. 181–185.
[26] As reported in Sidney Ditzion, *Marriage, Morals and Sex in America: A History of Ideas* (New York: Bookman Associates, 1953), p. 213.
[27] Arthur Wallace Calhoun, "The Early American Family," *The Annals of the American Academy of Political and Social Science,* CLX (March, 1932), 11.

stern morality that did not allow for a class of prostitutes. If fornication was common, apparently prostitution was exceedingly rare in the colonial period.

All of the above were contributing factors no doubt, but observers have generally agreed that there were norms built into the very structure of Puritan society that contributed to the problem. First, the New England Puritans had preserved an ancient English usage—that of the precontract or betrothal—and in some instances gave it a legal status. This ceremonial betrothal preceding marriage often took place before a witness, and after the ceremony the terms "husband" and "wife" could be used. An understandable confusion regarding the privileges and obligations of the new status existed. Indeed, a greater leniency toward the betrothed was reflected in the law. For fornication between the betrothed the punishment was usually one half, or less than one half, what it would have been if the couple had not been betrothed. It is possible that bundling involving Puritans had its chief significance as an adjunct of precontract.

Sex Laws

The Puritans tried to do everything in their power to prevent sexual behavior outside of the marriage bonds. Private morals were brought under the purview of the magistrate. It was ordered that all single persons who merely for their pleasure took journeys, especially in mixed company, "shall be reputed and accounted riotous and unsober persons, and of ill behavior . . . and shall be committed to prison for ten days, or pay a fine of forty shillings for each offense."

There was also the "seven months rule," aimed at couples who had committed fornication after precontract but before marriage, who had, however, married before the birth of their child. This rule called for the couple to humble themselves before the congregation by making confession of the fact that they had had sexual intercourse prior to marriage. Added to the humiliation of public confession in church was the fact that subsequently these cases usually came before the county court for trial and the infliction of a penalty.

The fear for the welfare of their offspring no doubt drove many couples to confess. By the "seven months rule," children born in less than seven months after marriage were refused baptism and were thereby put in period of eternal damnation, unless the parents made public confession before the congregation.

Casual and illicit behavior involving unmarried young people led to laws governing mate selection. Massachusetts law specified that "whatsoever person from hence forth shall endeavour, directly or indirectly, to draw away the affection of any Mayd in this jurisdiction, under pretense of marriage, before he hath obtained liberty and allowance from her parents or Governors or in absence of such of the nearest magistrate, he shall forfeit for the first offense five pounds, for the second toward the partie ten pounds, and be bound to forbeare any further attempt and proceedings in that unlawful design, without or against the allowance aforesayd. And for the third offense upon information of complaint by such parents or Governors or any Magistrate, giving bond to prosecute the partie, he shall be committed in prison . . . untill the Court of Assistants shall see cause to release him." In other words, an indeterminate sentence for the third offense! The courts were not without employment under this statute. The Puritans believed that God was concerned with mate selection and that the power to dispose of a son or daughter in wedlock was a gift of heaven.

Mate Selection

Where love is highly controlled by society, as it was among the Puritans, it does not enter prominently into mate selection. This generalization seems to apply to the New England Puritans, for Puritan love differed radically from the romantic conception. Romantic love would have seemed idolatrous and blasphemous to the orthodox Puritan. The love which they embraced more closely resembled that characteristic of the rationalistic model, wherein the affections are subservient to the will under the guidance of reason. It was held that where passion and affection ruled, there man was deprived of sense and understanding.

It was expected that there would be a personal element in mate selection, however. Parents could not merely contract for a spouse for their offspring. A young man was expected to seek and obtain the consent of a prospective bride, although the parents frequently determined or helped to determine what young lady he should seek to win. There was even greater control over the activities of a daughter, and parents commonly determined what young man should be given a chance to court their daughter. The usual factors governing consent to court were the character and personality of the young man, his religion, and his ability to provide for a wife and family.

The diary of Judge Sewall provides a case study in parental involvement in courtship and mate selection. It is reported that Judge Sewall superintended the whole procedure of lovemaking for his daughters with never-flagging zeal; on the other hand, as one of Judge Sewall's letters to his daughter Betty shows, he was anything but a ruthless autocrat overriding the sensitivities of his daughter.

> Mr. Hearst waits upon you once more to see if you can bid him welcome. It ought to be seriously considered, that your drawing back from him after all that has passed between you, will be to your Prejudice; and will tend to discourage persons of worth from making their Court to you. . . . I do not see but the Match is well liked by judicious persons, and such as are your Cordial Friends, and mine also.

Yet not withstanding, if you find in yourself an imovable incurable Aversion from him, and canot love, and honour and obey him, I shall say no more, nor give you any further trouble in this matter.

According to the record, Betty Sewall married Mr. Hearst the following year.

The Puritan father exercised his authority in the negotiations over financial arrangements accompanying marriage. The boy's parents might withhold their approval if a girl's dowry was not large enough. The "higgling of dowries" was one of the most "singular practices" of New England life.[28]

Young people had recourse from family decisions in regard to mate selection. First of all, parents could not insist that a child marry someone whom he disliked—the reason being that the child would then not be able to love his mate, which was a duty of a Puritan spouse. Sternness in matters regarding courtship must not be confused with injustice. The court allowed appeal to be made if the parent or guardian withheld his consent through any sinister or covetous desire.

Bachelors and Spinsters

The adult who remained unmarried was no less under the surveillance of the selectmen and their representatives, the tithing man, than were families. Spinsters were looked upon with disapproval, and an "ancient maid" of twenty-five or thirty years of age might be disparagingly referred to as a "thornback." Single, unattached men were viewed with suspicion if not with contempt. The law made no distinction between men and women in ordering that they live in licensed families so that a family governor might "observe the course, carriage, and behavior, of every such single person."[29]

Outside of domestic service, marriage and parenthood was the major, if not the only, career open to a young woman. Wives and mothers were in short supply; marriages were formed early and widows were wooed almost at the bier of the departed. Apparently colonial society admitted women into the world of work outside the home but more out of necessity than out of conviction. Outside and inside the home men were predominant, in spite of the fact that women were found serving as proprietors of taverns, shops, grocery stores, hardwares, and in the professions of teaching, nursing, and writing. Though women engaged in all of these activities, the total number of women wage earners in New England (outside of domestic service) was small.

Bachelors and "thornbacks" were not the only family-free adults who caused the tithing man anxiety. He also kept a watch on married persons who were living apart from their spouses. It was conceivable that one's

---

[28] Howard, *op. cit.* (see above, fn. 14), pp. 126–134.
[29] From *New Haven Colonial Records,* II, as quoted in Howard, *op. cit.,* p. 153.

spouse might be living in the old country and that courtship might then take place between such a married person and some single person in the colony. Living apart from one's spouse was frowned upon even if a person was circumspect in his behavior and even if there were grounds for living apart. The case of Abraham Hagborne shows the extremes to which the courts would go. Hagborne had come to the colony forty-two years before; he lived with his wife for fourteen years until she left for England. He then sent for her to return to America and provided for her transportation; yet when she did not comply the court "was pleased to require him to depart the Countrie and repayre unto his wife."

MARRIAGE

Marriage Law and Custom

Old England had no clear-cut marriage norms to offer the Puritans at the time they left to establish homes in a new land. English marriage law was in an anomalous and chaotic state. The Protestant Reformation had brought no real change in the canonical conception of the form of wedlock. On the one hand was the church (with state support), trying to enforce ecclesiastical rights and to secure publicity by requiring banns, parental consent, and registration. On the other hand was common-law marriage, entered by private agreement without any of the ecclesiastical or legal safeguards.

The continuity of English marriage law and custom in the New England colonies is striking. But so are the innovations.[30] There was a strong reaction in favor of temporal power in matters regarded in England as pertaining to the spiritual jurisdiction. In no respect was the change more remarkable than in the administration of matrimonial law and in the conception of the marriage contract. The Puritans regarded marriage not as a sacrament but as a civil contract in which the intervention of a priest was unnecessary and out of place.

Governor Winthrop, in commenting upon an important marriage that was to be solemnized at Boston in 1647, expressed the prevailing sentiment. "We were not willing to bring in the English custom of ministers performing the solemnity of marriage, which sermons at such times might induce, but if any ministers were present and would bestow a word of exhortation, etc., it was permitted." Generally, early colonial law required that all marriages should be celebrated before a justice of the peace or other magistrate. This emphasis on civil marriage helps to explain why the marriage ceremony commonly took place at home instead of in the church.

So intent were the Puritans in emphasizing the secular character of marriage that in the statutes the words "holy" or "sacred" as applied to

[30] Howard, op. cit., pp. 125–134, 143, 151, 200–203.

marriage seldom, if ever, appeared. "Honorable" or some similar epithet was usually the strongest term employed. There does not seem to have been any direct legislation regarding matrimony for many years. A positive legal sanction may well have been deemed superfluous while public opinion was united.

The demands as well as the opportunities afforded by pioneer life contributed to marriages being universal, early, and repeated. Andrews reports that a Miss Sarah Hext married John Rutledge when she was fourteen years of age and that she was the mother of seven children before she was twenty-five; that Ursula Byrd married Robert Beverley, had a son, and died before she was seventeen; Sarah Breck was only sixteen or seventeen when she married Jonathan Edwards, as was Hannah Gardiner when she married Doctor McSparran.

Sentiment in Marriage

The record left in diaries, correspondence, and books attests to the fact that Puritan married life was not without its pleasant side. Such expressions as "my dearest Life," "my only beloved spouse," "my chief love" were not uncommon in letters exchanged by spouses. Nevertheless, the highest love was reserved for God himself; no human object of interest, even one's spouse, could take his place. To prize one's spouse too highly was idolatry, in that it ultimately endangered one's love of God. Governor Winthrop saw fit to qualify his expression of love for his wife in the words, "My only beloved spouse, my most sweet friend, and faithful companion of my pilgrimage, the happye and hopeful supplye (next Christ Jesus) of my greatest losses."

Tension and the Dissolution of Marriage

The course of love—even Puritan love—did not always run smoothly. The colonists were a litigious people; and members of even some of the best families did not hesitate to bring their matrimonial difficulties into court. Sometimes a jilted lover sued his fickle sweetheart; in other cases a forlorn maiden sought satisfaction from her unfaithful betrothed spouse. The Puritans believed that human depravity so deprived man of control of his affections that it was not easy for him to properly love proper objects. Court records reflect broken promises, cruelty, adultery, desertion, and divorce.

Since the Puritans had rejected the sanctions of the sacramental theory of marriage and had established marriage as a civil right, marriage could be dissolved by the civil authorities; and many petitions for divorce were entertained by the courts. Puritan thought on divorce has been referred to as the most liberal of the times. Dissolution of the bond of matrimony was granted for such causes as breach of the marriage vows, cruelty, or desertion. However, as long as a couple were lawfully married, the church required that they live together despite disagreements between them.

Originally, death was the penalty prescribed for adultery and at least two persons were condemned and executed for it in Massachusetts. Generally, though, the courts shrank from pronouncing sentence according to the limit of the law and satisfied themselves with lesser punishments, such as imprisonment, banishment, or whipping. Eventually the scarlet letter was substituted for the death penalty—a capital *A* "of two inches long and proportionate bigness, cut out of cloth of a contrary color to their clothes, and sewed upon their upper garments, on the outside of their arm, or on their back, in open view." But the magistrates seemed to hesitate to prescribe the letter, too, thus giving the accused benefit of a more lenient interpretation of the law. In some cases the juries declined to convict for the offense charged, though the evidence seemed clearly enough to sustain a verdict.

The law with regard to incest was similar to that for adultery; persons guilty of incest were forced to wear an initial letter as in the case of adulterers. In Massachusetts, for instance, exactly the same penalty in the same words was imposed for the punishment of incest as for adultery, except that in the case of incest the capital letter *I* was to be worn.

While the adulterer might evade punishment by the civil authorities, he could be fairly certain of summary excommunication if the church found out about it. The rule against adultery apparently furnished the basis of more ecclesiastical prosecutions than any other provision in the Decalogue.

THE FAILURE OF PURITANISM

Puritanism and Personality

What was the effect of the Puritan family upon its individual members? This is somewhat difficult to determine because of lack of empirical evidence. Hatch and Hatch have made an ingenious attempt to test the effect of Puritanism using historical and contemporary data available for one family over a number of generations. They attempt to show by reference to the persons in this highly integrated Puritan family how consistent abandonment by the person of his own desires and ascetic controls from outside leads to disturbances in the integration of the person, in his relationship with others, and in his relationship to work.[31]

Members of this family never forgave themselves for falling short in any respect; they regarded love or passion as dangerous. The men of the family thought that their wives and children had their reward in being related to a successful man. The lack of strong affection between husband and wife

[31] David L. Hatch and Mary G. Hatch, "An Unhappy Family: Some Observations on the Relationship between the Calvinistic Ethic and Interpersonal Relations over Four Generations," *Marriage and Family Living*, XXIV (August, 1962), 213–223.

seemed to be compensated for by both parents centering their affection on the children.

This case does not prove but it does illustrate the thesis that personality difficulties were inherent in the Puritan system. Members of the family were schooled from childhood to live for future rewards; there was little regard for the uniqueness of the person. There was an indefinite deferment of feeling. "When they come to the end, few of the family have ever done anything they wanted to do. They have conscientiously done what they did not want to, and they have very little to show for their trouble except their secret rage."[32]

Rigidity of Puritanism

Almost from the beginnings in America signs of the eventual failure of the Puritan experiment were evident. The system was a rigid system not prepared for the modifications that a new situation demanded. Out of this system came much of the intolerance that left a stain on the pages of early New England history. The Salem witchcraft outbreak, for instance, was a logical outcome of the long policy of repression that hanged nonbelievers and destroyed independent thought in its attempt to imprison man "in a strait jacket of Puritan righteousness."[33]

Puritanism held so uncompromisingly to its principles that it alienated the adherents it needed. It found itself engaged in an impossible task; growing democracy and liberalism in a virgin, well-endowed land could not be stifled.

Some reasons for the failure of the Puritan experiment were closely related to a dedication to the family as the basic social and religious system. The Puritan strategy was to depend on the family as the basic system responsible for providing covenanted citizens for the state. When it became apparent that their children did not convert easily, they intensified the campaign; they wrote, they preached, they prayed, they threatened. It became clear that religious commitment was not hereditary!

THE LEGACY OF PURITANISM

Today, the major designs of the Puritan social system are nothing more than museum pieces capable of titillating the minds of the historically curious. What, if any, was the legacy of New England Puritanism to American society in general and to the American family in particular? In a nation made up of successive waves of immigrants, there is some advantage in having been an early arrival in the land. There is always the possi-

---

[32] *Ibid.*, p. 223.

[33] Vernon Louis Parrington, *Main Currents in American Thought* (New York: Harcourt, Brace & Co., 1930), I, 131.

bility that the culture of the early arrivals will become established and will gain prestige, and that the culture of the later arrivals will be expected to modify in the direction of the established culture. This is in part the story of the American experience. Aspects of Puritan life that remained were a spirit of religion and a rigid moralistic pattern of personal life.[34] Puritanism also "protected" early American society from some of the more democratic social aspects of the Renaissance and the Protestant Reformation. Furthermore, Puritanism drew sharp lines around the family and in a sense strengthened it, as opposed to the reform influences in Europe that tended to unsettle it. Theoretically, both the Renaissance and the Reformation exalted personality at the expense of the social systems, including the family. These reform movements called for a self-reliant man always conscious of his rights, not always conscious of his duties. Since the first wave of reform to strike the American shore was Puritan, for better or worse some of the impact of the more personalistic tendencies of the reform movements in Europe were modified or at least postponed.

Another of the lasting effects of Puritanism is to be found in the penal codes of the United States and in many of the states. These made a negative impression on some European visitors, Gustave de Beaumont, for instance, and have been an exasperation to American social reformers.[35] Beaumont, visiting America in 1831–32 wrote, "This austerity appears not only in daily habits but in laws as well. . . . Puritanism, dominant in New England, influences nearly all the states of the Union: thus, the penal code punishes with imprisonment any intimacy between unmarried men and women.[36]

---

[34] On the basis of an extended analysis Williams distinguished activity and work, achievement and success, and moral orientation as among the fifteen major value-belief clusterings that are salient in American culture. See Robin M. Williams, Jr., *American Society,* 2nd ed. (New York: Knopf, 1961), pp. 372–470. It would be impossible to demonstrate empirically whether or not or to what extent colonial Puritanism was a source of these values in contemporary American culture.

[35] See "Sex Offenses," a special issue of *Law and Contemporary Problems,* XXV (Spring, 1960).

[36] Gustave de Beaumont, *Marie or Slavery in the United States* (Stanford, Calif.: Stanford University Press, 1958; first published in France in 1835). Beaumont was quite right in his generalization, for traditional American sex law makes potential criminals of much of the adolescent and adult population. The statutes proscribe every sexual act involving a male and a female, except for coitus within marriage. Prohibited is aberrant and potentially dangerous behavior such as forcible rape, forcible sodomy, and the sexual abuse of children, as well as heavy petting, mutual masturbation, and premarital coitus. Those who would reform these sex statutes are of the conviction that Puritan sex law introduced a confusion into American thought between what is private and what is public interest, between what is immoral and what is illegal, and between what is crime and what is sin. It is widely held that Puritanism erred in giving to the state and the law a role as guardian of private morality that should be left to the individual and the family.

SUMMARY

Since the colonial period occupied nearly one half of the course of American history from the founding of the first colony to the present, aspects of Puritan thought became one of the continuing factors in American culture. The Puritans covenanted with God in forming a society; indeed, many of the rules and statutes of the social order were taken verbatim from the Old Testament. Their society was at first a totalitarian one run by a theologically-inclined oligarchy.

The Puritan social system provided a major role for the family, for it was believed that God in creating systems of control began with the family. Both state and church put heavy demands on governance in the family. The state expected the family head to maintain order and discipline; the church expected him to assist in the religious conversion of his children and to supervise their religious education and devotional life. Observers from both state and church invaded the privacy of the home to check on the performance of family functions. The man deemed unfit to superintend his children could have them "put out" under worthy governance. Children also left the home at an early age as apprentices or to receive a formal education.

The Puritans believed in free choice of mates, but youthful indiscretion led to various kinds of parental control and legal statutes. Punishment for illicit sexual behavior was severe. Marriage was a civil rather than a religious contract. Expressions of affection were not unknown to Puritan marriage, but to prize one's spouse was idolatry; the highest love was reserved for God. Marriage could be dissolved by civil action, and many petitions for divorce are on record.

Puritanism was religious rather than humanistic; personal needs and desires were not indulged. The individual lived to serve here and to enjoy his reward in the hereafter.

Puritanism failed as a social system. A spirit of religion; a rigid, moralistic pattern of personal life; and some puritanical federal and state laws continued as survivals after the death of Puritanism as a social system.

BIBLIOGRAPHY

Henry Adams. *The United States in 1800.* Ithaca, N.Y.: Cornell University Press, Great Seal Books, 1955, consisting of the first six chapters of Volume I of Adams' *History of the United States of America During the First Administration of Thomas Jefferson;* first published in 1889.

Charles M. Andrews. *Colonial Folkways: A Chronicle of American Life in the Reign of the Georges.* New Haven: Yale University Press, 1919.

Panos D. Bardis. "Family Forms and Variations Historically Considered,"

Handbook of Marriage and the Family, ed. Harold T. Christensen. Chicago: Rand McNally, 1964. Pp. 403–461.

Gustave de Beaumont. *Marie or Slavery in the United States.* Stanford, Calif.: Stanford University Press, 1958; first published in France in 1835.

Arthur W. Calhoun. "The Early American Family," *The Annals of the American Academy of Political and Social Science,* CLX (March, 1932), 7–12.

Arthur W. Calhoun. *A Social History of the American Family.* New York: Barnes and Noble, 1945; first published in 1917–19.

George R. Clay. "Children of the Young Republic," *American Heritage,* XI (April, 1960), 46–53.

Sidney Ditzion. *Marriage, Morals and Sex in America: A History of Ideas.* New York: Bookman Associates, 1953.

Stanley Elkins and Eric McKitrick. "A Meaning for Turner's Frontier," *Political Science Quarterly,* LXIX (September, 1954), 321–353; and LXIX (December, 1954), 565–602.

David L. Hatch and Mary G. Hatch. "An Unhappy Family: Some Observations on the Relationship between the Calvinistic Ethic and Interpersonal Relations over Four Generations," *Marriage and Family Living,* XXIV (August, 1962), 213–223.

Karl H. Hertz. "Max Weber and American Puritanism," *Journal for the Scientific Study of Religion,* I (Spring, 1962), 189–197.

George E. Howard. *A History of Matrimonial Institutions,* Vol. II. Chicago: University of Chicago Press, 1904.

Florence R. Kluckhohn. "Family Diagnosis: Variations in the Basic Values of Family Systems," *Social Casework,* XXXIX (February–March, 1958), 63–72.

Manford H. Kuhn. "American Families Today: Development and Differentiation of Types," in Howard Becker and Reuben Hill, *Family, Marriage, and Parenthood* (2nd ed.). Boston: Heath, 1948. Pp. 131–168.

Herman R. Lantz, Raymond Schmitt, Margaret Britton, and Eloise C. Snyder. "Pre-Industrial Patterns in the Colonial Family in America: A Content Analysis of Colonial Magazines," *American Sociological Review,* XXXIII (June, 1968), 413–426.

Don Martindale. *American Society.* Princeton, N.J.: Van Nostrand, 1960.

Nathan Miller. "The European Heritage of the American Family," *The Annals of the American Academy of Political and Social Science,* CLX (March, 1932), 1–6.

Perry Miller (ed.). *The American Puritans: Their Prose and Poetry.* Garden City, N.Y.: Doubleday, Anchor, 1956.

Perry Miller. *The New England Mind: From Colony to Province.* Cambridge: Harvard University Press, 1953.

Edmund S. Morgan. *The Puritan Family: Essays on Religion and Domestic Relations in Seventeenth Century New England.* Boston, Massachusetts: Trustees of the Public Library, 1944.

Emil Oberholzer, Jr. *Delinquent Saints: Disciplinary Action in the Early Congregational Churches of Massachusetts.* New York: Columbia University Press, 1956.

Henry Bamford Parkes. *The American Experience: An Interpretation of the History and Civilization of the American People.* New York: Knopf, 1947.

Vernon Louis Parrington. *Main Currents in American Thought*. New York: Harcourt, Brace and Co., 1930.

Herbert Wallace Schneider. *The Puritan Mind*. New York: Holt, 1930.

John Sirjamaki. "Cultural Configurations in the American Family," *American Journal of Sociology*, LIII (May, 1948), 464–470.

Alexis de Tocqueville. *Democracy in America*. New York: Knopf, 1951; first published in France in 1835.

Frederick Jackson Turner. *The Frontier in American History*. New York: Holt, 1920.

Robin M. Williams, Jr. *American Society* (2nd ed.). New York: Knopf, 1960.

CHAPTER 3

The Family and a New Nation

FOR THE FAMILY, the period of national emergence was in some ways threatening because some of the ideological tendencies of the times were to lead to family experimentation the likes of which America had never seen before and has not seen since. The period is one of emergence from regional to national perspective; from dependence on England to political independence; from conservative, highly articulated rules to liberal, vague, abstract principles of freedom and democracy. What bridges the gap? How do we get from a Puritan theocratic model of society to an ideology stressing personal dignity, freedom, and democracy?

This is not the place to trace the intricate themes that make up America's social and intellectual history; but unless some of the major themes are briefly sketched, Puritan culture and the Puritan family become meaningless even as catalysts for the unique American cultural and family systems that emerged. Not that the colonies had been totally Puritan in culture and polity nor totally without models of freedom and democracy, but Massachusetts Bay and its "satellite" colonies provided a massive Puritan influence beyond their numbers and beyond their region.

THE NEW PHILOSOPHY: A FAITH IN MAN

In 1758 Jonathan Edwards died and his death signaled Puritanism's loss of validity. Samuel Johnson, Edwards' intellectual successor, disillusioned with the Puritan philosophy, substituted human happiness for the glory of God as the chief end of man. This change in philosophy helped to pave the way for the humanitarian revolt against Puritanism.[1] As Puritanism crumbled, free thinkers, liberals, Whigs, "new lights," and "independent reflectors" flourished. To exalt vindictive justice at a time when the liberals were preaching a benevolent God was unpopular doctrine.

Self-reliance found expression in the beliefs of Jonathan Mayhew and

---

[1] Kenneth S. Latourette, *A History of Christianity* (New York: Harper, 1953); Herbert W. Schneider, *The Puritan Mind* (New York: Holt, 1930).

Charles Chauncey. Mayhew declared that true religion was comprised of a love of liberty and country, and the hatred of all tyranny and oppression. Chauncey saw the whole human race as made for happiness. Such ideas expressed the spirit of a revolutionary generation. Mayhew, Chauncey, and others like them were educated men of English descent fighting for their rights as Americans. Through the writings and lectures of liberal thinkers the prosperous, confident, commercial Yankees were able to disregard or at least to rationalize the Puritan pretense of their utter dependence on God and transform their theology into a Declaration of Independence.

It was left to Benjamin Franklin to separate the Puritan ethic from its theological sanctions and to attempt to preserve the ethic without the theology. Franklin held that the old-fashioned Puritan virtues of frugality, industry, and the rest were necessary if one wanted to succeed, but he made no attempt to prescribe what the end of life should be. He merely established the personal discipline that was necessary to success. Edwards and Franklin represent opposite poles of Puritan thought. Edwards attempted to induce New Englanders to lead a godly life; Franklin succeeded in teaching Americans to lead a sober but not necessarily a godly life.

Unitarianism also supported the nascent humanitarian trend.[2] It regarded authority as the prop of the weak, dogma as the body of a faith that is dead. The Unitarian was a seeker, open-minded and free. He did not regard himself as the sole custodian of truth as had the Puritan.

The new philosophy received additional support from Emerson and the transcendentalists. To a Unitarian human nature was excellent; the transcendentalist saw it as divine. The transcendentalists were romantics; authority, dogma, and creed were swept away by faith in an indwelling divinity, with intuitive sanctions. They saw nature as sinless and man as a sinless being; they elevated him to a dizzy eminence.[3]

Perfectionism was an even more extreme and permissive philosophy of the day. If its logic were followed, perfectionism would have made short shrift of political parties, of loyalty to government, of the political state itself.

The new philosophy can perhaps be summed up best in the thought of Thomas Jefferson, among the leading politically influential philosophers of the age. Assumptions of Jefferson include the following: man is basically good; he can be counted on to act rationally; the masses of men, if given freedom of choice, will choose the wise and good. Jefferson's was a faith in personality and not a faith in social systems. The latter were to serve man to the end that his human capabilities might be fully developed.

[2] Vernon Louis Parrington, *Main Currents in American Thought* (New York: Harcourt, Brace & Co., 1930), II, 379–383.

[3] Randall Stewart, *American Literature and Christian Doctrine* (Baton Rouge: Louisiana State University, 1958), pp. 43–52.

INTERCHANGES BETWEEN FAMILY, POLITY, AND THE ECONOMY

In 1782, when Great Britain conceded the independence of America, probably as many as a third of the whole American population had Loyalist (British imperialistic) inclinations and involvements. The Loyalists included many of the aristocratic families in New England, New York, and Pennsylvania.[4] Because of their loyalty to Great Britain their property was confiscated, and they were deprived of political and legal rights. An estimated eighty thousand Loyalists went into exile during the war. Shiploads of families whose heads included some of the most cultivated persons in America were driven from their homes to seek refuge in "Hell, Hull, or Halifax." State legislatures, in an attempt to democratize the ownership of property, divided Loyalists' estates into small farms and either sold them or distributed them to soldiers in the form of bounties. The prospect of an elite dynasty of aristocratic families gaining positions of political and economic power for the family system was markedly curtailed with the defeat and emigration of the Loyalists.

Other wealthy families of the Atlantic seaboard and the South, though not Loyalists, were also out of sympathy with democratic principles. These monied classes believed that their rights would be endangered by any democratic system of government based on outright majority rule. They hoped to work out a framework of government appropriate to the families of farmers and planters, especially those interested primarily in agriculture and not in land speculation. The theory of the equality of all persons could not be reconciled easily to the European aristocratic practices of entail (settling property inalienably on a person and his descendants) and primogeniture (giving an explicit right of inheritance to the firstborn). In English law, it was the eldest son's right to receive all the real estate possessed by his father to the exclusion of all women and younger male descendants, except for what aid he might extend to them.

The holders of large estates did not prevail; Virginia, in 1776, was the first state to abolish entail, and before the end of the eighteenth century primogeniture had been abolished generally. In America, land was too abundant to require that estates remain intact for economic reasons, and emerging democratic principles frowned on making land an "ensign of nobility." Entail and primogeniture never had popular support in America; but their demise, legally, along with the defeat of the Loyalists, dealt a serious blow to the prospect of the family becoming a dominant social system in American society.

---

[4] Henry Bamford Parkes, *The American Experience: An Interpretation of the History and Civilization of the American People* (New York: Vintage Books, 1959), p. 92.

An important factor contributing to the division of American families into isolated nuclear units with small holdings was the law governing the alienation of land in areas beyond the original colonies. The rectangular survey was adopted as a way of dividing the virgin land in the West. This provided for the division of land into townships consisting of thirty-six sections of one square mile each. The sections were divided into farms of 160 acres each. This system provided an almost infallible method of describing property; but the gridiron pattern contributed to a dispersion of land with modest holdings for each family.

Not that the influence of economically powerful family dynasties was lost entirely, however. Besides families of wealth who had supported the Revolution rather than the Loyalist cause and hence had been spared from both financial ruin and exile, there was a new group of speculators and merchants who grew rich on the war effort. Inflation and general disorder created an atmosphere in which shrewd and unscrupulous entrepreneurs could profiteer off speculation in land, currency, and government contracts. Fortunes were made and a *nouveau riche* emerged to replace partially the Loyalist aristocracy, an aristocracy less cultured and less public-spirited, however.[5]

THE FAMILY SYSTEM AND EXPERIMENTAL COMMUNITY SYSTEMS

In the period of unrest and torment that ushered in the birth of the new nation, when all major social systems were being subjected to critical reappraisal, it is to be expected that the family would also undergo reappraisal. There were, both in Europe and in America, groups who were looking for a social and intellectual climate wherein they could experiment with community and family systems.[6] Before enthusiasm for family reform subsided about the middle of the nineteenth century, most of the logically possible types of marriage reforms had been aired and a number had been tried out in practice. Among them were the Shakers' concept of celibacy; the Mormons' practice of polygamy and celestial marriage; the Oneida Community's practice of male continence; and Robert Dale Owen's emphasis on birth control.[7]

What were the major issues of community and family systems that were

[5] Henry Bamford Parkes, *The American Experience: An Interpretation of the History and Civilization of the American People* (New York: Alfred A. Knopf, 1959), p. 105.

[6] Nathan Miller, "The European Heritage of the American Family," *The Annals of the American Academy of Political and Social Science,* CLX (March, 1932), 1–6; Parrington, *op. cit.,* pp. 317–382.

[7] Sidney Ditzion, *Marriage, Morals and Sex in America: A History of Ideas* (New York: Bookman Associates, 1953), p. 68.

being debated, researched, and experimented upon? The major issue was the question of equal rights. The egalitarians thought equal rights would solidify the family; the upholders of benevolent authoritarianism thought that an organization without a leader would disintegrate.

Some crucial questions were being raised. Up to what point could a person be permitted to exercise his freedom? Who was to be responsible for setting the standards of propriety and morality? Does the person himself decide whether monogamy or polygamy is the best marriage system? Should marriage as a system be retained or abolished?

Two among many examples of experimental family and community systems of the times were New Harmony, established by Robert Owen, and the Oneida Community, established by John Humphrey Noyes.

New Harmony

Robert Owen asserted that the architects of the American Revolution had intended the family reforms that he would detail; their hesitancy had been due only to the fact that they did not want to endanger their immediate objectives. Owen told his hearers that man, up to that hour, had been a slave in all parts of the world to "a trinity of the most monstrous evils that could be combined to inflict mental and physical evil upon his whole race." He was referring to private property, "absurd and irrational systems of religion," and marriage "founded on individual property combined with some of these irrational systems of religion."[8]

Owen saw as destructive of human happiness the very social systems which other social leaders considered essential to civilization. In 1827, he published his proposals for improving the social system. His principles of marriage were designed to overcome the difficulties of the prevailing system. The couple desiring to be married were to give notice of their intentions in writing to a community committee. They were to repeat their notice three months later with the signatures of two witnesses affixed. The secretary of the committee was to call a community meeting on the following day, at which the parties would declare themselves husband and wife. If the marriage did not turn out to their satisfaction, they could utilize the same procedure to undo it, for they were responsible only to each other.

Owen was of the opinion that no law could successfully stimulate love or extinguish hatred. "Love," said Owen, "withers under constraint; its very essence is liberty: it is compatible neither with obedience, jealousy, nor fear; it is there most pure, perfect and unlimited, where its votaries live in confidence, equality, and unreserve."

Robert Dale Owen, who carried on the work of his father, Robert Owen, was a thinker, serious researcher, and writer in his own right. In a world

[8] *Ibid.,* p. 79.

bent on progress Robert Dale Owen viewed constancy of any kind, including marriage, as no virtue. He did not regard man as perfect but as a pliable creature who learned from experience; he needed freedom to correct his errors. Some persons would find their happiness in a permanent marriage while others would find happiness in change. Under a free system there would be more real and less affected constancy.

Part of Robert Dale Owen's ammunition for his attack on prevailing monogamous marriage came from a report of the New York Magdalen Society, an apparently reliable source. It was asserted in the report of the Society (c. 1830) that there were 20,000 women engaged in prostitution in New York City. Owen, allowing for possible error in the figures, pointed out that even if there were only 10,000 prostitutes in all, with three visits daily per prostitute, this would mean 10,000,000 contacts annually. Owen used the report as evidence supporting his call for sex education and the need for marriage and divorce reform.

Owen's *Moral Physiology, or A Brief and Plain Treatise on the Population Question,* was ahead of its time in recommending population adjustment through birth control. Owen questioned the emphasis the Christian church had put on propagation as the first if not the sole purpose of sex in marriage and emphasized personal and mutual happiness as the goal of marriage. This was not a new idea even in 1831, but no one had attempted to couple it with specific, albeit inadequate, instruction in birth control. Though the little treatise was condemned, as were others of Owen's writings, 1,500 copies were sold within five months. One female correspondent assured Owen that nine-tenths of his women readers would approve of the book though they would not dare to admit it openly.

But this first, largest, and best-known of the utopian communities begun by Robert Owen on a 20,000-acre tract at Harmony, Indiana, was doomed to failure almost from the start. Owen did not give necessary attention to the detail of organization nor did he screen the applicants for admission to the community. Due to wide publicity and the general invitation extended by Owen to one and all to come, the community became a mixed collection of nonconformists without the necessary unifying convictions of a carefully structured social system.[9]

The Oneida Community

In certain respects the Oneida Community was the most radical and at the same time the most successful of the experimental communities. After an earlier attempt at Putney, Vermont, the group settled at Oneida, New York, and continued until what had been called one of the greatest pressure campaigns that has been waged against any religious group in history forced

[9] Charles A. Madison, *Critics and Crusaders: A Century of American Protest* (New York: Holt, 1947), pp. 87–88.

them to modify their pattern of life. The undisputed leader of the Oneida Community was John Humphrey Noyes.[10] To Noyes the chief obstacles to a community system based on love were private ownership of property and the exclusiveness characteristic of the sexual relationships as experienced in paired marital relationships. Noyes proposed to abolish both.

Ten years prior to the establishment of Oneida Community, Noyes had proposed marriage to Harriet Holton, daughter of a prominent Vermont family. That he was prepared to practice what he advocated is apparent from his letter of proposal. He wrote as follows: "I desire and expect my yoke-fellow will love all who love God, whether man or woman . . . as freely as if she stood in no particular connection with me." Miss Holton accepted his proposal.

Noyes rejected promiscuity; he proposed instead what he called "complex marriage." He saw Oneida Community as a family system, as separate and distinct from promiscuous society as ordinary households were distinct from promiscuity. The community of property and the community of love were to be coterminous, with all the wealth of the community pledged to the maintenance, protection, and education of all its citizens. Man should not embrace one woman exclusively any more than he should hold property privately.

The regulations for complex marriage permitted any man and woman regardless of previous marital commitment to apply to a central committee for the right to cohabit. They would declare their affection for each other and then a committee would decide on the validity of their application. If the application was approved, the couple could retire to their quarters and begin their life together.

Noyes' plan also called for a strict control of births until the facilities in the community were adequate for the care of children. The method employed in controlling conception was male continence, but male continence of a special kind. Noyes believed that sexual intercourse should be permitted but that the male should exercise ejaculatory control. This method of conception control, known as *coitus reservatus,* involves sexual intercourse without ejaculation. Self-control was to be developed through training. Until young men had mastered ejaculation control, they were expected to limit their experience to sexual relations with older women. Despite the skepticism of knowledgeable persons, the system of male continence apparently worked. The community appears to have had remarkable success in postponing child bearing. Noyes extolled the practice, asserting that its use had not only spared them unwanted pregnancies but had increased satisfaction both for himself and for his wife.

Eventually the community was ready for the birth of children and at this point selective breeding—stirpiculture—was introduced. At first a stirpicul-

10 Pierrepont Noyes, *My Father's House* (New York: Farrar and Rinehart, 1937).

ture committee and later the cabinet of the community decided who was qualified to reproduce and in what combination the members should mate. This was as close as Noyes came to his goal of scientific propagation. Within a ten-year period, approximately a hundred men and women were selected to be parents and these matings reportedly produced between fifty and sixty children. Noyes was one of those selected to propagate; a number of the children claimed him as father.

We must reiterate that New Harmony and Oneida are only two of the many family-community experiments that were proposed or attempted during the time that America began its experiment in individualism, equality, and democracy. No succeeding period in American history has witnessed more revolutionary, experimental attitudes toward the family.

INSIDE THE FAMILY

Family life for most Americans continued to be considerably more conservative and traditional than was life in the experimental communities.

De Tocqueville observed that there was no country in the world where the tie of marriage was more respected and conjugal happiness more highly or more worthily appreciated than in America. He saw the breadwinner as coming home to a family characterized by order and peace. Other European observers were struck more with the appearance of coldness and formality in the American home, with the head of the house showing little more familiarity with his wife and children than with his neighbors.[11]

Family Integration and Solidarity

Perceptive observers searched beyond the apparent lack of closeness in the family to the total setting of the times. Expanding economic opportunities and the exaggerated emphasis on individualism and independence turned the eyes of family members outward from the family; men were too busy to know their little ones, to enjoy much of their wives' company, or to lavish family members with affection. The claim that husbands neglected their wives was one of the most common criticisms of American marriage as viewed by Europeans traveling in America. Family ties appeared to be looser than they were in Europe because of the mobility of the American. Americans appeared to have little affection for the place of their birth; young members left the place of their birth with seeming indifference, and parents did not make undue sacrifices to keep their children around them.

[11] See Arthur W. Calhoun, *A Social History of the American Family* (New York: Barnes and Noble, 1945), p. 131; and Frank E. Furstenberg, Jr., "Industrialization and the American Family: A Look Backward," *American Sociological Review*, XXXI (June, 1966), 326–337.

Family Leadership

Despite the growth of democratic ideas in political and social thought, law and much of public opinion continued to support the authoritarian family. The husband-father was still the only person recognized by law, and all rights over the property and person of wife and child were lodged in him. This concentration of authority in the hands of a single individual supported the traditional belief that with its statutory support the nuclear family should continue as a strong and coherent unit, for the pattern remained without fundamental changes for at least half of the nineteenth century in the midst of profound changes in other social systems.

Few changes were made during and following the Revolutionary period in the section of English common law governing the relations of husbands and wives, though the situation varied somewhat from state to state. As a general rule, the husband had entire right to the person of his wife and might use "gentle means" to constrain her liberty. Yet most European observers remarked that American women were treated with extraordinary deference and respect, though some saw the respect as superficial and deceptive.

Under English common law during this period the husband had the sole right to the remedies for legal wrongs committed against the person of his wife. He could maintain suits for injuries to her person; she could not sue on her own behalf. She could not execute a deed or valid conveyance, without the concurrence of her husband. At marriage the woman lost entire personal control over her property, and such property as money, goods, animals and moveables of all descriptions was vested immediately and absolutely in her husband. On his death, this property—being regarded as entirely his— went to his representative. He entered by marriage also into possession of his wife's real estate, had the power to manage it, and, finally, had entire use and profit of it.[12] It is understandable that some European observers saw woman's position as ambiguous. Her lower status was at odds with democratic ideology.

Experiments like those led by Robert Owen and John Humphrey Noyes attracted a minority of the populace; more were agreeing that men should be "the patriarchal sovereigns," and women the "queens of their household;" the "sanctuary of domestic life" was to the women "the place of safety as well as the 'post of honor.' "[13]

[12] Edward Mansfield, *The Legal Rights, Liabilities and Duties of American Women* (Salem: John P. Jewet and Company, 1845); as reported in Willystine Goodsell, "The American Family in the Nineteenth Century," *The Annals of the American Academy of Political and Social Science*, CLX (March, 1932), 15–16.

[13] *Woman in America* (New York: Harper, 1858), pp. 45 and 60; as reported in Goodsell, *ibid.*, p. 16.

De Tocqueville, as well as a number of other European travelers, was impressed by the great loss of freedom women suffered when they married[14] and by the resulting difference in independence between single and married women. Married women were "irrecoverably lost in the bonds of matrimony." Tocqueville saw the young girl as making her father's home "an abode of freedom and pleasure" while the wife lived in the home of her husband "as if it were a cloister," with a constant sacrifice of her pleasures to her duties, which was seldom demanded of her in Europe. The reason for withdrawal of married women from social life appears to have been their demanding domestic obligations.[15]

THE FAMILY AND THE INDIVIDUAL

The birth rate continued to be high as it had been during the colonial period. The limited birth control literature was supplemented by the appearance of Dr. Charles Knowlton's tract, *The Fruits of Philosophy, or, The Private Companion of Young Married People* (1832). Also, Noyes's success with *coitus reservatus* at Oneida gave that method of control some notoriety. What contraceptive information was available circulated largely by word of mouth.[16] Francis Wright, a Scotswoman lecturing and writing in this country in the early 1800's, asserted that people needed to be educated to a realization that they should bring into the world only as many children as they could comfortably feed, clothe, and educate.

On the other hand, there were those who urged early marriages and an increased population. Benjamin Franklin for one had strongly approved of early marriage and his ideas were in print. His optimism concerning early marriage and high birth rates derived from the unusual opportunities presented by the new world, where in his time there seemed to exist a limitless expanse of arable land.

"Men of feeling and men of religion" reacted violently to the suggestions of population control—"ungodly, inhuman, wicked bundle of ideas." It was thought that neither providence nor natural law indicated that such matters should be left to legal enactment and moral law; all should marry (and preferably marry early) and beget children.

Socialization

The observations of foreign visitors gave insights into socialization practices. A Mrs. Duncan was impressed by the precociousness of American children. She observed that the "little creatures feed themselves very neatly"; they were "trusted with cups of glass and china, which they grasp firmly,

[14] Alexis de Tocqueville, *Democracy in America* (New York: Knopf, 1951), p. 201.
[15] Furstenberg, *op. cit.*, pp. 326–337.
[16] Alvah W. Sulloway, *Birth Control and Catholic Doctrine* (Boston: Beacon Press, 1959), pp. 5–7.

carry about the room carefully, and deposit, unbroken, at an age, when, in our country mama or nurse would be rushing about after them to save the vessels from destruction."[17]

Some observers were less favorably impressed. Wrote one, "As soon as he can sit at table [the American child] chooses his own food, and as soon as he can speak argues with his parents on the propriety or impropriety of their directions." A German visitor in the 1820's saw girls "in convulsive anger at their parents" and boys "in quarrel with old people, pick up stones and threaten to fling them at the old man that wanted to punish them." Parents were seen as too anxious to make money to give their children the attention they needed. Permissive child-rearing patterns apparently were widespread at this time, attesting to the lack of general salience of some of the child-care pattterns introduced earlier as a part of Puritan culture. European visitors noted a distinctly American attitude toward children: a curious combination of parental overindulgence coupled with neglect that encouraged both confidence and willfulness in children.

Three points of view characterized the "child guidance" literature of the first half of the nineteenth century. The first was a continuation of the Puritan view which saw the infant as born in sin and needing to be redeemed at all costs, even at the cost of breaking his will. A second view aimed at hardening the child for a difficult life. For instance, cold baths such as the Indians were thought to take were recommended. A third view placed emphasis on leading, not driving; persuading, not commanding the child. In this view corporal punishment was seen as too severe a discipline for the tender child.

THE FAMILY-FREE ADULT

The first ten amendments of the Constitution established a charter of freedom for the citizen. In it his beliefs, thoughts, and feelings were protected; he was given the right to be let alone. A robust individualism grew as a consequence of these democratic and humanistic ideas. It is difficult to measure the full effect of these ideas—the effect of the theory of the indefinite perfectability of man, for instance. Men living in a democratic society soon discovered that they were not confined or fixed by their present state or fortune, but that they could alter it through effort. If opportunities are theoretically limitless, individuals are drawn into excessive activity.

An account of the effect of restless activism and puritanical morality on two American artists is instructive. Greenough, a young American sculptor, went to Rome in 1825. The thing which particularly delighted him about Italian society was the tone and tempo of Roman life. The impression it

[17] As quoted in George R. Clay, "Children of the Young Republic," *American Heritage,* XI (April, 1960), 49.

made upon him was that leisure was not necessarily evil, but that it might even be a duty. In America none of his friends seemed to possess his impulse to inactivity; in fact, anyone who did not work at his trade from morning till night six days a week was looked upon as an idler or a parasite. In Rome, he found a community of artists who believed in the virtue of irregular hours. Story, another American artist in Rome, wrote, "As the time draws near I hate more to leave Rome. . . . How shall I ever again endure the restraint and bondage of Boston?"[18]

Americans accepted a principle of personal mobility rather than a principle of status. According to the principle of status a minor position may be worthy, while the principle of mobility regards such a station as the penalty for and the proof of personal failure. Status as a fixed, differential social position was in disrepute.[19] Individual mobility destroyed values inherent in traditional class society—namely, the importance of the relationship between the person, and his family and community in establishing the person's status. The achievement of equality for women proved to be a long and hard battle, but women as well as men were affected by the economic opportunities and the other liberties insured in the mobile, democratic society.

A number of European visitors commented on the seeming urgency for children to become independent of their families. Writers frequently characterized American children as self-confident, independent, poised, and mature. Michael Chevalier presents a case history of the emergence of girls as independent persons in his essay, "The Factory Girls of Lowell."[20] Chevalier visited Lowell, Massachusetts, and wrote his impression of this new industrial town. One of the things that impressed him was the number of young women working away from home—and the orderliness of their life and their behavior also. They were young women from seventeen to twenty-four years of age, the daughters of farmers from the New England states. They were in Lowell far from their families and on their own. After a few years in factories, they would quit and get married.

Chevalier could not conceive of such a situation existing in his homeland, France. He observed that the training given American girls drew round each "a line over which it is difficult to step"; they commanded and expected respect. These girls though far from home, were under the safeguard of a public faith that presupposed an extreme reserve of manners. Life might have a somewhat somber hue under this system, but when Chevalier reflected on what would have happened to the daughter of the poor so far

[18] Margaret Farrand Thorp, "Literary Sculptors in the Cafe Greco," *American Quarterly*, XII (Summer, 1960), 174.

[19] David M. Potter, *People of Plenty: Economic Abundance and the American Character* (Chicago: University of Chicago, 1954), p. 105.

[20] Michael Chevalier, *Society, Manner, and Politics in the United States,* ed. John William Ward (Garden City, N.Y.: Doubleday Anchor Books, 1961; first published in France in 1834).

from home under the system prevailing in France, he felt that Anglo-American prudery had its merits.

Of three French visitors who observed life in America in the 1830's—Chevalier, Tocqueville, and Beaumont—all were convinced that the education of women for life in a democratic and equalitarian society had to be different from the education of women in traditional aristocratic societies. They recognized this need and at the same time regretted it. Religion plus reason became the basis of education of the American girl. There was no choice: to protect woman from the dangers in democratic social systems surrounded by men, her will and her reason had to be developed.

What were the regrettable results of such education? According to Gustave de Beaumont, women brought up in this way had "well-informed minds but little imagination, and more reason than sensibility." They lacked "two qualities which are so charming in youth; candor and naivete." They needed knowledge to be chaste, yet they knew too much to be called innocent. Their thoughts were serious and their character had a certain masculinity. For instance, Beaumont recalled a girl of twelve years of age discussing which of all types of government was the best. Beaumont summed it up: "This coolness of the senses, the supremacy of the mind, this masculine behavior among women, may find favor with one's intellect; but they hardly satisfy the heart."[21]

Dating and Mate Selection

Beaumont observed that unchaperoned dating was common in America in the early 1800's. Couples went about together unaccompanied. Girls also entertained boyfriends in their homes, being permitted to converse in the drawing room without any other adults present. Girls even invited boys not previously met by the parents.

Marriages were not alliances of families but unions of persons—unions brought about by their own free choice. Already in the eighteenth century the opinion that unhappiness in marriage could be due to parental interference was extant.[22] Even young people who had reached the common-law age of fourteen for boys and twelve for girls sometimes married without first receiving the consent of parents.[23] Theoretically, parental consent was required, but writers of the time agree that generally speaking it was not taken seriously.

If courting and mate selection involved more reason than affection, the woman was not alone to blame. American men, according to one stereotype, had neither the time nor the temperament for tender sentiments or

---

[21] Gustave de Beaumont, *Marie or Slavery in the United States* (Stanford, Calif.: Stanford University Press, 1958; first published in France in 1835), pp. 16–17.

[22] Ditzion, *op. cit.* (see above, fn. 6), p. 32.

[23] Goodsell, *op. cit.* (see above, fn. 11), p. 19.

gallantry. The American was said to be gallant, if at all, only once in his life and that when he wished to marry. He conducted a business affair rather than a love affair. He had neither the leisure for love nor the desire to make himself loved. He was neither preoccupied with pleasing women nor skillful in winning them.[24]

It could be said on the American's behalf, however, that what he lacked of a Frenchman's doting and gallantry he made up for with a respect for women. So things were equal: everyone was engaged in business and American girls had their business, too—that of finding the right husband. Unlike the French coquette, the American girl when she flirted was less desirous of pleasing than of marrying. Her flirtation was more a calculation than a passion. Young women often came under the criticism of being cold. Women trained to conform to a chilly society did not have hearts "made for the burning passions of the wilderness." Since, therefore, men were businesslike and women rational, it was said that there was more esteem than enthusiasm in their relationships.

Compared with some of the European countries, America had high standards concerning premarital sexual behavior. This could be assumed in a society that emphasized morality and reason over romance in dating and courtship. Most books, novels not excepted, supposed women to be chaste; and no one related "affairs of gallantry."

The principle of equality is not without significance in explaining the reason for the strict moral standards. Since women were coming to be regarded as equals, a woman's honor was protected: rape, for instance, was a capital offense. The seducer of a young girl commonly became her husband regardless of whether a marriage between the two was well advised. Whoever seduced a girl contracted the obligation, by that very act, of marrying her. This was quite different from aristocratic societies in other countries with their permanent class distinctions. If a young man of an aristocratic class seduced a girl of a lower class, it might not cause a scandal, and he would certainly not be expected to marry her.

The brevity of courtship also militated against a high rate of premarital intimacy. American couples did not dally; they married early. "Society thereby gains moral married men in place of licentious bachelors," according to Gustave de Beaumont. When two people thought they were suited for each other, they promised to marry each other. Betrothal was a private affair resolved without public ceremony and without binding forces beyond the good faith of the contracting parties; the precontract of Puritan days was not longer generally employed. The promise of betrothal was soon ratified by marriage.

---

[24] Beaumont, *op. cit.,* p. 20; Furstenberg, *op. cit.* (see above, fn. 10), pp. 326–337.

MARRIAGE

With the demise of Puritanism as a social system, the laws requiring civil marriage were set aside even in New England. The prejudice against ecclesiastical rights subsided and laws were enacted allowing the ministers of all denominations to perform the marriage ceremony.[25]

The attitude toward marriage was optimistic, and European visitors observed that American women were dutiful wives. Magazine articles glorified marriage, regarding it as the essence of virtue and well-being, and as something that was to be encouraged.

Swift's "Letter to a Very Young Lady on Her Marriage" was included in both the 1750 and 1793 editions of Benjamin Franklin's *Reflections on Courtships and Marriage*. In it Swift cautioned women to be as modest and reserved in marriage as they were as virgins. They were advised to be completely undemonstrative toward husbands in public, there being enough private hours in which to ape the behavior of a French romance! Whether the behavior of a French romance ever characterized their moments of intimacy is doubtful; their training had hardly prepared them for it. "I am aware," wrote Tocqueville, "that an education of this kind is not without danger; I am sensible that it tends to invigorate the judgment at the expense of the imagination and to make cold and virtuous women instead of affectionate wives and agreeable companions to man."[26] Some European observers, on the other hand, characterized American women as affectionate wives. There was no doubt variation in norms and behavior from region to region and between social classes. While Lantz, Snyder, Britton, and Schmitt report from a content analysis of colonial magazines, "the romantic love complex . . . may have been a common pattern among large sections of the upper status groups,"[27] the evidence is too scattered and inadequate to make firm generalizations about dating and courtship practices of the period.

In most of the states divorce was permitted and the laws specified causes for which divorce would be granted. Both men and women sought relief from intolerable marriages by legal action.[28]

Attempts began as early as the 1800's to free the person and the property of the married woman from absolute control of her husband, to open opportunities for higher education, and to secure for her other fuller political rights. Connecticut led the way in 1809 by granting to married women a

[25] George E. Howard, *A History of Matrimonial Institutions* (Chicago: University of Chicago Press, 1904), II.

[26] Tocqueville, *op. cit.* (see above, fn. 13), p. 200.

[27] Herman R. Lantz, Eloise C. Snyder, Margaret Britton, and Raymond Schmitt, "Pre-Industrial Patterns in the Colonial Family in America: A Content Analysis of Colonial Magazines," *American Sociological Review*, XXXIII (June, 1968), 420.

[28] Goodsell, *op. cit.* (see above, fn. 11), pp. 19–20.

limited right to make disposal by will of such of their property as their husbands could not legally claim. Prior to the Civil War, at least seven states had followed the lead of Connecticut; and six others had enacted laws according to married women the right to own and manage property by gift or request.[29] General reforms for the emancipation of women had to wait until the decades after the Civil War. Thus ideas of equality, freedom, democracy, and respect for personality—values salient in American culture today[30]—vied with other traditional and emergent forces in the physical and social milieu of a developing nation.

SUMMARY

American society during the latter part of the eighteenth century and first half of the nineteenth century—the period of growing individualism and of the emergence of America as a nation—was in a state of flux and rapid change. The contrast with the ready-made social system that the Puritans had hoped to put into effect is striking. The period under consideration here was a period of growth—from local to national; from political dependence to independence as a nation; from conservative, articulated rules to liberal, vague, abstract principles as marked by Unitarianism, transcendentalism, perfectionism, and the political and social ideals of Jefferson and others supporting personal freedom and democracy. It was a period when high idealism clashed with traditional conservative social systems.

The period was marked by the ruthless destruction or removal of many of the aristocratic families of culture, education, and property (the Loyalists). The *nouveaux riches* who supplanted them were destined not to become a repetition of the landed aristocracy of Europe since the abolition of entail and primogeniture contributed greatly to removing the possibility of developing a socially powerful family system.

The birth of freedom and democracy invited family experimentation in practice as well as in principle—New Harmony and the Oneida Community, among others. The laws governing equality of men and women were slow in responding to the growing demands for change. Yet, this was a time when women as well as men were asserting their freedom from the family of orientation and moving out into the world to make their own way; the aesthetic niceties of male-female relations in courtship, love, and marriage were largely set aside. Young people were prepared for self-disciplined individual accomplishment in the world of farming, business, industry, and the professions; and they had neither the preparation or the taste for the leisure that love requires.

---

29 *Ibid.*, p. 21.

30 Robin M. Williams, Jr., "Individual and Group Values," *The Annals of the American Academy of Political and Social Science,* I (May, 1967), p. 33.

BIBLIOGRAPHY

Henry Adams. *The United States in 1800.* Ithaca, N.Y.: Cornell University Press, Great Seal Books, 1955, consisting of the first six chapters of Volume I of Adams' *History of the United States of America During the First Administration of Thomas Jefferson;* first published in 1889.

Gustave de Beaumont. *Marie or Slavery in the United States.* Stanford, Calif.: Stanford University Press, 1958; first published in France in 1835.

Arthur S. Calhoun. *A Social History of the American Family,* Vol. II. New York: Barnes and Noble, 1945; first published in 1918.

Maren Lockwood Carden. *Oneida: Utopian Community to Modern Corporation.* Baltimore: Johns Hopkins, 1969.

Michael Chevalier. *Society, Manner, and Politics in the United States,* ed. John Williams Ward. Garden City, N.Y.: Doubleday, Anchor, 1961; first published in France in 1834.

George R. Clay. "Children of the Young Republic," *American Heritage,* XI (April, 1960), 46–53.

Norman Cousins. *'In God We Trust': The Religious Beliefs and Ideas of the American Founding Fathers.* New York: Harper, 1958.

Sidney Ditzion. *Marriage, Morals and Sex in America: A History of Ideas.* New York: Bookman Associates, 1953.

Frank E. Furstenberg, Jr. "Industrialization and the American Family: A Look Backward," *American Sociological Review,* XXXI (June, 1966), 326–337.

Nathan Miller. "The European Heritage and the American Family," *The Annals of the American Academy of Political and Social Science,* CLX (March, 1932), 1–6.

Vernon Louis Parrington. *Main Currents in American Thought,* Vol. II. New York: Harcourt, Brace & Co., 1930.

David M. Potter. *People of Plenty: Economic Abundance and the American Character.* Chicago: University of Chicago, 1954.

Herbert Wallace Schneider. *The Puritan Mind.* Ann Arbor: Ann Arbor Paperbacks, University of Michigan, 1958; first published in 1930.

Lindsay Swift. *Brook Farm: Its Members, Scholars, and Visitors.* New York: Corinth Books, 1961; first published in 1900.

Alexis de Tocqueville. *Democracy in America.* New York: Knopf, 1951; first published in France in 1835.

Robin M. Williams, Jr. "Individual and Group Values," *The Annals of the American Academy of Political and Social Science,* I (May, 1967), 20–37.

CHAPTER 4

Slavery and the Black Family

ALONG WITH IDEAS of equality and freedom, contra-values of racism and group superiority are also salient in American culture today. A life style contributing to such values was slavery. No "natural experiment" so thoroughly destroyed the family as an organized, functioning social system as did slavery. The migration of the majority of blacks that settled in America was a forced migration. Cultural patterns from the mother country, patterns that would have helped to keep the family intact, were destroyed. There was little opportunity in the United States for a slave to meet one of his own people on the plantation where he resided. Memory of the homeland was effaced, and the slave system gave the slaves little freedom to develop a social system of their own.

What happens to the family system if cultural systems supporting it are destroyed and the persons who adhere to them are scattered and placed in bondage in a foreign, hostile society?[1] What we are dealing with is not just any case of bondage but a particular one at a particular time in history, namely the experience of Afro-American slaves in the United States beginning in 1619 and continuing, officially, until the Emancipation Proclamation.

THE VALUE SYSTEM SUPPORTING SLAVERY

The motive for enslavement was economic: it was not at the outset designed to destroy a people and their culture. It was designed rather to facilitate the adaptation of a landowning class to a situation presenting an abundance of land and a market coupled with a severe shortage of labor. Both the plantation economy and the church supported an inceptive aristocracy.[2]

[1] For a detailed discussion of the black family in America see E. Franklin Frazier, *The Negro Family in the United States* (Chicago: University of Chicago, 1939), and Jessie Bernhard, *Marriage and Family Among Negroes* (Englewood Cliffs, N.J.: Prentice-Hall, 1966).

[2] Clement Eaton, *The Growth of Southern Civilization, 1790–1860* (New York: Harper, 1961); Rupert D. Vance, "Regional Family Patterns: The Southern Family," *American Journal of Sociology,* LIII (May, 1948), 426–429; Paul Jacob Reiss, *The Extended Kinship System in the American Urban Middle Class* (Cambridge: Harvard University, 1960); Charles M. Andrews, *Colonial Folkways: A Chronicle of American Life in the Reign of the Georges* (New Haven: Yale University, 1919); and

For a number of decades it would have been difficult to predict whether equalitarian idealism or economic realism would mark the value system of southern life. Gradually equalitarian idealism lost out to a pragmatic policy based on a frank recognition of the slave system as essential to the economy.

The emerging economic system was in need of some clarifying logic that would resolve the conflict between the reality of the situation calling for cheap labor and the rising spirit of democracy. Caught between the forces of democracy and a slave economy, southern thought found the most rational compromise in the Greek ideal of inequality of status. Southern intellectuals claimed that every civilization rested on labor exploitation of some kind and that the patriarchal ties between planter and slave were more humane than the impersonal wage system by which employer and employee were related in industry. Slavery, an institution which the North supposedly abhorred, came to be the very foundation of social order in the South.

THE PLANTATION COMMUNITY

Natural conditions determined the site of each plantation—an adequate water supply, rich soil, well-drained fields, timber for fuel and for buildings. As a result most of the planters and their families lived in almost complete isolation from other families. The plantation was a largely self-sufficient and independent biracial community. Millers, blacksmiths, carpenters, tanners, shoemakers, seamstresses, and laundresses as well as farmhands were part of the work force on a plantation.[3]

Plantations were often planned with some eye for beauty and symmetry, with the house of the master (by no means always a mansion) situated in pleasant surroundings of live oak and pine trees and gardens of shrubs and flowers. At a distance were the kitchen garden, the smokehouse for processing meat, the laundry, the bakery, the machine shops, and finally the barns and the quarters for slaves. Fine mansions on the plantation were relatively rare. The presence of a mansion in town often meant that the planter was an absentee owner; he placed his land in the hands of overseers who managed it and supervised the slave laborers.

BLACK ADAPTATION TO A SLAVE LABOR SYSTEM

Some blacks brought to America in the earliest years came as indentured servants; they were not slaves and were entitled to earn their freedom.[4] The first shipload of slaves arrived in 1619. By the end of the seventeenth cen-

Vernon Louis Parrington, *Main Currents in American Thought* (New York: Harcourt, Brace, 1930), II.

[3] W. D. Weatherford, *The Negro from Africa to America* (New York: George H. Doran, 1924).

[4] Abbott Emerson Smith, *Colonists in Bondage: White Servitude and Convict Labor in America, 1607–1776* (Chapel Hill: University of North Carolina, 1947), pp. 3–4.

tury there were only about five thousand slaves in the South. When traffic in convict white labor from Europe came to an end, the slave trade flourished. There were already some 400,000 slaves in America by the time of the American Revolution. As soon as they were landed in this country, slaves were divided and shipped in small numbers, frequently no more than one or two, to a plantation. It was easier to deal with slaves if they were separated from their kinsmen. Furthermore, because of the obvious labor advantage, slave traders aimed particularly to transport young men.

The slave belonged to a man's estate, not to his person. Thus the slave was not a sign of ostentation but an economic asset—an "animate tool," a part of the agricultural machinery.[5] The completely subservient positions of the slaves invited cruelty and there were slaveowners who took advantage of it. On the other hand, since a prime male slave cost $1,800 or more, he was too valuable an economic asset to mistreat or to maim. Health records indicate that the physical abuse of slaves was not common; except for the havoc raised by epidemics of cholera, the planters did not suffer unduly from loss of labor due to illness of their slaves.

In the long-range planning of a planter, a high birth rate and a low maternal and infant mortality rate were viewed economically as assets. Thomas Jefferson, as one example, was concerned over the lack of understanding of the relative importance of the breeding and child-care functions by his overseer. He wrote to an overseer in 1819 as follows: "The loss of 5 little ones in 4 years induces me to fear that the overseers do not permit the women to devote as much time as is necessary to the care of their children; that they view their labor as the first object and the raising of their child but as secondary. I consider the labor of a breeding woman as no object, and that a child raised every two years is of more profit than the crop of the best laboring man."[6]

During the 1930's social scientists at Fisk University and Southern University in Louisiana collected testimony from ex-slaves as to their treatment. Some retained nostalgic memories of kind masters, good food, and simple pleasures, while others remembered frequent whippings, poor food, overwork, miscegenation, cruel overseers, and the fear of being separated from their families by the slave trade.

Strict controls were imposed on the activities of slaves as a result of slave revolts. Slaves could not leave their plantation without a written pass and there was a curfew time when they had to be in their houses at night; nine o'clock was a common time for curfew.[7]

---

[5] Gustave de Beaumont, *Marie or Slavery in the United States* (Stanford, Calif.: Stanford University Press, 1958; first published in France in 1835), p. 199, and E. Franklin Frazier, *The Negro Family in the United States* (Chicago: University of Chicago, 1939), pp. 359–360.

[6] *Thomas Jefferson's Farm Book*, pp. 42–43, as reported in Eaton, op. cit., p. 63.

[7] Eaton, *op. cit.* (see above, fn. 2), p. 77; Henry Adams, *The United States in 1800* (Cornell University, Great Seal Books, 1955, consisting of the first six chapters of

The slave owed to his master and to all members of the master's family "respect without bounds" and absolute obedience. He was to execute all orders received from any one of the master's family. A saving grace of the code of absolute obedience was that though comprehensive and severe it was often only laxly enforced.

The attitude toward the educating of black children varied. In New England the education of the children began almost with the beginning of their enslavement and was stepped up after the Revolution. In the South, on the other hand, education of blacks was a crime. In Alabama a fine of not less than $250 and not more than $500 could be imposed on anyone convicted of teaching a slave or a freed slave to spell, read, or write. The fine for encouraging literacy was $200 more than the maximum fine for torturing a slave. Despite the concern to keep the slave ignorant and in subjection, some remarkable black personalities did emerge despite the slave system. Planters often apprenticed capable young slaves to skilled artisans to learn trades; others became skilled in plantation concerns and were consulted by their masters concerning plantation policy.[8]

Blacks as House Servants

The style of life of a planter's family was as varied as the types of dwellings they lived in and as varied as the value of the plantation operation would permit. The southern antebellum way of life has come to be synonymous in the popular mind with life in luxurious mansions, however. In such a mansion, a visitor would find that a household slave would come to his room to build a fire, to polish his boots, and to brush his clothes. Because of an abundance of cheap labor and overseers to supervise the work, the master and members of the master's family were free to accompany the guest in any activity they chose to pursue and on any day of the week.

The romantic life in a Charleston or Natchez mansion must be balanced, though, against the more common isolated and lonely life of the modest plantation operation. The letters of Sarah Williams, a New York girl who married a doctor and turpentine planter in North Carolina, tell of that life. The mistress of the plantation often worked harder and had more activity to supervise than did her counterpart in the North. She sewed clothes for the slaves, she doctored them, she supervised the gardening, and she took care of the chickens.

Volume I of Adams' *History of the United States of America During the First Administration of Thomas Jefferson;* first published in 1889), p. 108. The present author found while conducting interviews in a southern town in 1958 that the local police were enforcing a nine o'clock curfew, the time when blacks and whites were supposedly each to be in their own section of town.

[8] Jared Sparks, ed., *Letters and Recollections of George Washington* (New York, 1906), as reported by Eaton, *op. cit.* (see above, fn. 2), p. 85.

Catherine Ann Edmondston reports such a strenuous round of activities on a cotton plantation.[9] The mistress cultivated her flower garden, made blackberry wine and brandied peaches, prepared hams for smoking, vaccinated the numerous slave children, and taught them the catechism. An operation using slave labor often lacked organization; and according to Sarah Williams, households were not run with much efficiency. Household slaves would "wash, bake, or iron, just as the fit takes."[10]

Little attention was given to the personal privacy of growing slave children. One traveler, Elkaneh Watson, was shocked to find on one of his trips in Virginia that young slaves of both sexes, from twelve to fifteen years old, ran about the house and even tended table in the master's house "as naked as they came into the world." What surprised him even more was the fact that several young women at the table with him did not seem disturbed by the presence of these naked adolescent servants. Observed Watson, "I find custom will reconcile us to almost everything."[11]

The Black "Mammy"

Birth rates among the white population were high; genealogical records indicate families of ten to fifteen children as not uncommon in white families in the South. Caring for children was eased for white mothers because of the presence of household slaves. A "mammy" might begin her responsibility before the birth of the child as she attended her mistress during pregnancy. She took the infant under her care as soon as it was born. She might even serve as wet nurse; in any event she was expected to give the master's children continued and devoted service and to show them partiality even over her own offspring. The mammy was an important part of every household with children, and if her charge was a girl she might serve the girl without interruption until she was grown. Oftentimes a warm and lasting attachment was formed between a mammy and the white children she nurtured.

SLAVE LIFE

Housing

Slave houses varied greatly in size and quality. It is reasonable to assume that the planter would regard adequate shelter and adequate rest as important to the health and endurance of his labor supply, but the evidence does not always support the contention. The houses varied all the way from

[9] *Diary of Catherine Ann Edmondston,* May 2, 18, 1861; May 8, 1862 (North Carolina State Department of Archives and History), as reported in Eaton, *op. cit.* (see above, fn. 2), p. 188.

[10] Eaton, *op. cit.* (see above, fn. 2), p. 187.

[11] Quoted in E. S. Turner, *What the Butler Saw: Two Hundred and Fifty Years of the Servant Problem* (New York: St. Martin, 1962), p. 189.

twelve-foot-square log cabins without windows, with chimneys of sticks and mud, and with no trees, porches, or shade of any kind, to the brick cottages built by Henry Clay for his slaves. Not uncommonly slave houses were one-room cabins providing little or no privacy.

The household furnishings in the slave cabin were modest. Furnishings might include rough wooden beds with slats or corded rope for springs, a pallet or two on the floor, homemade chairs, a table, perhaps a chest, and wooden pegs on the walls for hanging clothing. Utensils might include a large pot, an oven, a skillet, a coffee pot, a few crude dishes, a wooden pail, and a gourd dipper.

On large plantations the majority of males worked in the fields and were housed separately from the women and children. Adult males, adult females, and children living together was a more common pattern among the house servant and artisan classes.

Clothing

The clothing allotment of field slaves, like their lodgings, represented minimum standards. The slave owner who reported that he gave his slaves "four full suits of clothes with two pairs of shoes, every year, and to my women and girls a cabin dress and two handkerchiefs extra" was perhaps the exception rather than the rule. Young children wore only a shirt, while men might be issued two cotton shirts and two pairs of cotton pants in summer and woolen pants, a jacket, a hat, a pair of rough brogans, and blanket every second or third year. Women were given cloth to make dresses and a kerchief or sunbonnet. Besides doling out rations to the slaves, some planters expected or at least allowed them to supplement their meager possessions by gardening or hunting.

Task Performance—Bearing and Rearing Children

Women slaves employed at field labor generally were expected to accomplish only three-fourths of the task of an able-bodied field hand because of their child-bearing function. They returned to the field within a month after delivery, but they were allowed to leave the job in the field as many as four times a day for the purpose of nursing the babies.

On the best-managed plantations, slave children were well cared for. They were supervised by one or more responsible older slave women who had successfully reared children of their own. Women who served as nursery attendants were not required to work in the fields. One planter with pride over his good fortune in the rearing of slave children described the procedures in practice on his plantation as follows:

> A large house is provided as a nursery for the children, where all are taken at daylight, and placed under the charge of a careful and experienced woman, whose sole occupation is to attend to them, and see that they are properly fed

and attended to, and above all things to keep them as dry and cleanly as possible, under the circumstances. The suckling women come in to nurse their children four times during the day; and it is the duty of the nurse to see that they do not perform this duty until they have become properly cool after walking from the field. In consequence of these regulations, I have never lost a child from being burnt to death, or, indeed, by accidents of any description; and although I have had more than thirty born within the last five years, yet I have not lost a single one from teething, or the ordinary summer complaints so prevalent amongst the children in the climate.[12]

Not all planters were so fortunate; it was said of one planter that despite good treatment only sixteen babies were born on his plantation in a period of twelve years and only seven lived. Nevertheless, it is not unlikely that slave women might have viewed the experience of pregnancy and childbirth with favor since the resulting offspring were a reason for preferential treatment.

Children did not regularly work in the fields until they were twelve years old, and then a master might assign duties commensurate with their strength and ability. One rule was that a twelve-year-old was expected to do one-fourth of the work done by an able-bodied male hand.

THE STATUS OF SLAVE MARRIAGES

When a master ordered his slaves to "get married," what he meant was that he wanted them to copulate.[13] On the other hand, some planters tried to discourage or prevent illicit sexual activity of slaves. Male slaves were known to have been castrated for attempted rape of female slaves; in later times only slaves convicted of attempted rape of white women were so treated.[14] More than one planter was frustrated in his attempt to control sexual behavior among these demoralized people thrown together without regard to personal feelings. Among "Christianized" slaves excommunication from church was threatened for those having illegitimate children.

A prevailing opinion is expressed in the words of a North Carolina judge in 1858: "The relation between slaves is essentially different from that of man and wife joined in wedlock . . . for with slaves it may be dissolved at the pleasure of either party, or by the sale of one or both, depending on the caprice or necessity of the owners."[15] In the State v. Samuel

[12] As quoted in Weatherford, op. cit. (see above, fn. 3), p. 153.

[13] Andrew Jackson, Narrative and Writings of Andrew Jackson of Kentucky (Syracuse, New York, 1847), p. 8.

[14] Eugene D. Genovese, "The Medical and Insurance Costs of Slaveholding in the Cotton Belt," The Journal of Negro History, XLV (July, 1960), 141–155; Arthur S. Calhoun, A Social History of the American Family, I (New York: Barnes and Noble, 1945; first published in 1917), 328.

[15] Quoted in Helen T. Catterall, Judicial Cases Concerning American Slavery and the Negro (Washington, D.C.: Carnegie Institution, 1926), II, 221.

(North Carolina), in 1836, the state of marriage for slaves was defined as "only that concubinage . . . with which alone, perhaps, their condition is compatible."

De facto slave marriages were a reality. Some marriages were encouraged out of the master's humanity, sometimes because religious conviction would not permit him to stand by and see his slaves living in a state of nature. An Andover clergyman suggested a formula for slave marriage in which each would promise to perform the part of a spouse as "far as shall be consistent with the relation" of his status as a slave and to remain faithful to each other only "so long as God in his Providence, shall continue your and her abode in such place (or places) as that you can conveniently come together."[16]

Perhaps in more cases than not stable slave marriages were an expression of the humanity of the blacks themselves. Since they were not necessarily legally bound, the attitudes of slave husbands and wives toward their relationships depended on their affections or the extent to which they assimilated the sex and family norms of an African or American culture. House servants were often treated quite differently from field hands and sometimes elaborate weddings and feasts marked their unions.

SLAVE FAMILY INTEGRATION AND SOLIDARITY

The slave family developed in part as a natural organization based on familiarity and feelings of affection and sympathy that sometimes resulted from close association of persons in the same cabin, living under the same conditions of servitude. And close association there had to be, for life within the cabins was generally characterized by overcrowding and lack of privacy, and slaves were often closely confined to their cabins when not in the fields. A slave cabin might house persons "of all ages, sexes, and sizes."[17]

A Mississippi planter spelled out the orders for his plantation as follows: "It shall be the duty of the driver, at such hours of the night as the overseer may designate, to blow his horn, and to go around and see that every negro is at his proper place, and to report to the overseer any that may be absent; and it shall be the duty of the overseer, at some hour between that time and daybreak, to patrol the quarters himself, and see that every negro is where he should be."[18]

It is likely that nascent slave families first centered around the natural organization based on the physical and emotional ties between the mother and her offspring. The husband-father played a less important role; his

16 As reported by Arthur W. Calhoun, "The Early American Family," *The Annals of the American Academy of Political and Social Science,* CLX (March, 1932), 11.
17 Charles Ball, *Slavery in the United States* (Lewistown, Pa., 1836), p. 107.
18 Weatherford, *op. cit.* (see above, fn. 3), p. 150.

fortunes depended on his relations to master and overseer and the prospects of being sold or retained by his owner. As already pointed out, the law did not require that relationships between slave husbands and wives be honored when they were being sold. Slave mothers and their young children were often treated as a unit, but only two states—Louisiana and Arkansas, and the latter only after 1852—prohibited the sale of children under ten years of age apart from their mothers.

Humane masters went to great lengths to respect the sanctity of slave families. Owners sometimes stipulated in their wills that slaves should be sold only in family groups, and some endeavored to unite families with members living on different plantations by offering to buy or sell family members. On the other hand, there were tragic scenes of inhuman treatment as family members were separated despite their pleas to the contrary. Any restriction on the power to separate slave from slave was reflected in the marketplace. No planter was eager to buy a slave who had any rights, such as conjugal rights, safeguarded by law.[19]

INTERRACIAL INTERCHANGES AS A THREAT TO FAMILY INTEGRATION AND SOLIDARITY

Sexual liaisons between blacks and whites were a constant threat to the solidarity of both black and white families during slavery. Interracial intimacy between the sexes was not from the first confined to white males and black females. Afro-Americans also came to America as indentured servants, and colonial records indicate instances of illegitimate children of black men and indentured white women. Relations between black males and white servant females were sometimes encouraged by white masters who desired thereby to increase the number of their bound servants. In South Carolina a grand jury in 1743 took note of the "too uncommon practice of criminal conversation with Negro and other slave wenches as an enormity and evil of general ill-consequence."[20]

Traffic in mulatto women especially for purposes of prostitution became a regular part of the slave trade in southern cities. Slave women usually sold for as much as one-fourth less than did men, but "fancy girls" sometimes sold for $2,500 or more. Where an interracial relationship was a private affair, involving a black or mulatto woman and only one patron, it resembled and merged into the quasi-legitimate system of concubinage that flourished in New Orleans and some other southern cities. Persons of all classes of whites in the South, from the industrial and planter classes down to the landless poor whites, were involved in personal relations with slave

---

[19] Stanley M. Elkins, *Slavery: A Problem in American Institutional and Intellectual Life* (Chicago: University of Chicago, 1959), pp. 53–54.
[20] Andrews, *op. cit.* (see above, fn. 2), p. 203.

women; but concubinage was the privilege of only the economically well-off.

There were advantages to be gained by slave women surrendering to white men for sexual purposes. It could mean freedom from field work, better food, and fine clothing. There was also the prospect that her mulatto offspring would enjoy certain privileges and perhaps in time receive their freedom, but this could not be taken for granted. Besides those masters who developed a deep and lasting attachment for their Negro mistresses and mulatto children, there were others who would tire of and abandon their mistresses and even sell their own mulatto children to other masters. Being mulatto could be a mark of social status, however; and mulattos of aristocratic ancestry were known to look with disdain on poor white people.

Even if a master honored his liaison with a slave woman, it did not follow that his white wife or his white relatives would be tolerant. The legal wife might attempt to have the slave woman and her mulatto children sold; and if she did not accomplish this during the lifetime of her husband, she was almost certain to get revenge when he died. Resentment was expected particularly if the master showed any affection for his concubine or her offspring. Not only was the colored woman a rival for the affections of the husband; she might also be a competitor for a share of his property. White families sometimes went so far as to seek court action declaring the errant male mentally disabled.

Black male-white female sexual liaisons became illegal under any circumstances when slavery became an established system. It might be a trespass for a white man to rape a slave woman; it was a capital offense for a black man to rape a white woman. Even for a male slave to look at a white woman could be interpreted as lustful.

The household servants and the mulatto offspring of slave-master relations became the main channels through which the subservient blacks were exposed to white culture. Mulatto children who received preferential treatment in the form of separate and preferred care, training, and even education, assimilated not only the grosser aspects of the slave-owner culture but also some of its niceties. Entire communities of persons of mixed blood practicing the white man's culture developed in some parts of the country. It was especially here that a new family system became established among the black population prior to the Civil War.

SLAVE FAMILY LEADERSHIP

Under slavery the male did not control his person or his tools. He worked away from home for someone else and earned no income. Thus he lacked the prerequisites for being effective as the head of a household. The father's authority over his wife and children was subject at all times to his master's will; legally he had no authority over his children since he was a chattel not a person and was possessed rather than possessing. His offspring belonged to the master in the same way as an increase of the livestock belonged to the master.

The slave mother of small children, on the other hand, was more free to regulate her own activity and to assert herself. The desire on the part of the owner for good care of the offspring was an economic reason for treating mother and child as a unit. It was also economically important that children derive their status from their mother rather than from their father. Had the child's status been defined according to the father's condition, the interpretation of the status of mulatto children would have had economic consequences. It would have meant that a category of free mulattos would have been created with a relationship to their father that society did not want to recognize. This problem was resolved by jurists through the universal adoption of the principle that "the father of a slave is unknown to our law." This freed the white father of legal responsibility for his mulatto offspring, but it also had implications for the role of a black father in relation to his offspring. A slave husband had no legal rights to his marital bed and could not sustain an action against any other man who would violate his "rights." In the opinion of Daniel Dulany, Esq., attorney general of Maryland, "A slave has never maintained an action against a violator of his bed. A slave is not admonished for incontinence, or punished for fornication or adultery; never prosecuted for bigamy. . . ."[21]

AFTER SLAVERY

The South's social system based on inequality crumbled under the impact of the Civil War and the Emancipation Proclamation, having never become a clear-cut system of superordination and subordination. The slave was both animate and human, and the economic methods appropriate to most dealings with chattel property did not entirely prevail. Slavery was "a curious blend of force and concession, of arbitrary disposal by the master and self-direction by the slave, of tyranny and benevolence, of antipathy and affection."[22] The lives of the master class intertwined with those of the slaves—least with the field hands, most with the household servants and concubines. As a consequence of the system of slavery there began "that long, long piteous problem of interracial morality so entirely incapable of solution under the chattel regime, and so lingering in its consequences to later generations."[23]

[21] William Goodell, *The American Slave Trade in Theory and Practice* (New York: American and Foreign Anti-Slavery Society, 1853), pp. 106–107; as quoted in Elkins, *op. cit.*, p. 55.

[22] Ulrich B. Phillips, *Life and Labor in the Old South* (Boston, 1929), p. 217.

[23] Calhoun, *op. cit.* (see above, fn. 16), p. 8.

Emancipation resulted in social disorder and personal demoralization among the slaves. Many left the plantation immediately upon being emancipated, for the right to move was a crucial test of freedom. "After the coming of freedom," wrote Booker T. Washington, "there were two points upon which practically all the people on our place were agreed, and I find that this was generally true throughout the south: that they must change their names, and that they must leave the plantation for at least a few days or weeks in order that they might really feel sure that they were free."[24] Negroes flocked to army camps by the thousands, creating both problems of discipline and health; others were drawn to the towns and cities; still others drifted about aimlessly.[25] For the second time in his brief history in America, the black individual and the black family were stripped of a supporting moral system; the first time by enslavement, and the second time by emancipation.

Emancipation was abrupt; and chattel status did not provide circumstances wherein life patterns appropriate to a state of freedom could be developed. Subsequent to the end of the Civil War, a national plan of reconstruction and rehabilitation for the South was developed, but Congress was not prepared to accept the program. With emancipation, blacks were enfranchised and, with them voting for the first time, new governments were elected. Illiterate emancipated slaves found that suddenly a measure of political power was theirs. But without adequate protection of their rights by the federal government, it was only a matter of time until a hostile southern white population invented Jim Crowism as an alternative to slavery.

Black Family Stability after Emancipation

The vast majority of blacks eventually settled down to a way of life which was in many ways more a modification of than an exception to the plantation system. The sudden emancipation of field hands called of course for a modification in the operation of the plantation. Attempts were made to organize the free blacks into work squads under the supervision of an overseer, but the desire of the blacks to be out from under the supervision of an overseer and to farm for themselves rendered the system ineffective. In accommodation, the row of slave cabins disappeared and tenant houses were scattered over the plantation. It was with the end of slavery that the cabin in the cotton made its appearance. Typically, the plantation was broken up into twenty-acre sharecropping units with a sharecropper's cabin on each tract. A system developed wherein the tenant looked to his white landlord for advances in food and clothing until the crop was harvested. When the crop was harvested and the bills were paid, the tenant was likely to "sign up" for another year. If the price were poor or the landlord unscrupulous, the

24 Booker T. Washington, *Up From Slavery* (New York: 1902), p. 23.
25 Frazier, *op. cit.* (see above, fn. 5), p. 78.

former slave might find himself still in debt at the end of the year. If this situation continued, he became a new type of indentured servant beholden to his landlord until he could work his way out of debt. Life for the uneducated black sharecropper moved in an orbit formed by an economic system beyond his control or understanding.

Thousands of emancipated slaves deserted the plantation for ever. Some cut themselves loose from both family and friends and wandered from place to place in search of work and adventure. Sawmills, turpentine camps, and roads were common work sites for these unskilled laborers. Women who left the plantations alone had their best chance for work as domestics in nearby towns.

The lumber and turpentine camps were often sites of free and spontaneous matings as persons so recently released from external restraint attempted to find their way in a new, strange, and supposedly free world. Couples, with or without benefit of clergy, lived together. The marital associations formed were often marked by impulsive behavior, quarreling, and fighting as mates attempted to adapt to each other as persons, not as chattels.

Families that had developed some stability under slavery frequently made the transition to freedom without major disturbance to family life. In fact, the hardships of adapting to a new social order became a test of the strength of family ties. Where the family of husband, wife, and children had already been firmly established, the husband assumed the responsibility for family support under freedom.

The black father's authority in family relations after emancipation was facilitated in instances when economic subordination of women occurred. It was chiefly through the acquisition of property that his interest in his family was established on a permanent basis. Even before emancipation, some free black fathers acquired a proprietary interest in their families by buying wife and children and in so doing brought family members under their own authority. Such families formed a part of the nearly half-million blacks who were free before the Civil War. It was among the free blacks that the first black nuclear families in America were formally established.

There were also some outstanding black persons living under slavery who succeeded in establishing permanent homes for their families, and in getting education for themselves and for their children. The emergence of these families from the mass of the slave population created small nuclei of stable families. Along with the free blacks, they represented the highest development of black family life up to the time of the twentieth century.

MATRICENTRIC BLACK FAMILIES

Generally speaking, the principle of subordination of women to male authority had not been transmitted to the black wife and mother either by the slave system or by economic necessity. In many cases emancipation only confirmed her feeling of sufficiency apart from a man who was an authority figure. For her to maintain her family after emancipation, apart from the paternalism of the plantation, was difficult. Most of these mother-centered families attempted to subsist on the sharecrop system. Mothers with young children were generally not able to farm a plot of more than six to eight acres, and their advances of corn meal and bacon from the landowner were correspondingly small. They maintained small vegetable gardens as they had under slavery. The restricted diet left many suffering from pellagra. Women who were able to pay for a piece of land of their own were better off; but the system of credit and the relations with the white (and still "master") race continued to make for a precarious life for the matricentric family.

Sometimes the matricentric household was made up of several women and their children, with a grandmother as the focal point of family authority. Farming on a larger plot with greater resulting cash and subsistence produce was then possible.

Because of the transitory nature of man-woman relationships, the grandmother continued to play a peculiarly significant role in the black family after emancipation. Wise, experienced older women who had cared for children and helped maintain order and emotional stability on slave row had authority. These older women also cared for orphaned and abandoned children. It was often these women who kept the generations together.

THE BLACK FAMILY IN THE CITY

Contemporary black American family life bears the marks of a culture shattered by slavery, emancipation, and mobility. By 1910, four hundred thousand blacks had left the South and were living almost exclusively in northern industrialized cities. During and following World War I, more than a half-million blacks migrated to four northern metropolitan areas.[26] The pattern has continued.

The black worker class that developed in industrial cities gradually formed its own family systems. For some, isolation was broken down and the black industrial worker's ideals and patterns of life began to approximate those of industrial workers in general. In housing and neighbor settings, blacks were set apart from other industrial workers, however, as prejudice and limited resources forced them to concentrate their homes in overcrowded and in other ways undesirable residential areas.

[26] Frazier, *op. cit.* (see above, fn. 5), pp. 210 ff.

FIGURE 4.1. NONWHITE POPULATION IN CENTRAL CITIES

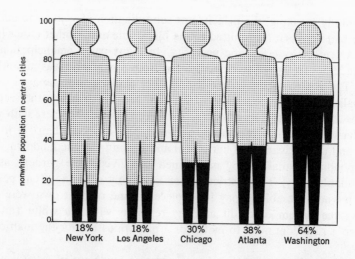

Between 1950 and 1960, 21 central cities lost population while the suburbs around them grew. As middle-class white families moved out, their places in most of the central cities were taken by nonwhite and lower income families.

SOURCE: Wilbur J. Cohen, "Social Planning and Urban Development," *Health, Education, and Welfare Indicators,* October, 1966, p. 18.

EXTERNALLY ADAPTIVE AND ACCULTURATED BLACK FAMILIES

Queen and Habenstein delineate two general types of family structure descriptive of black families in America today—the adaptive urban matri-centric family and the acculturated middle majority family.[27]

The adaptive urban matricentric black family is an outgrowth of male-female relationships developed during slavery and its aftermath, marked by mobility and economic insecurity. It is a family form commonly found in the blighted inner city, in the heart of the black ghetto; hence it is isolated from some of the major elements of the majority culture, and is marked by economic insecurity and constant threats from the disorganizing and demoralizing elements present in the inner city. Bernard refers to this family type as "externally adapted" in counterdistinction to what an internally adapted family would be like.[28] For example, the female family head may hold attitudes traditional to American culture toward sexual behavior and illegiti-

[27] Stuart A. Queen and Robert W. Habenstein, *The Family in Various Cultures,* 3rd ed. (Philadelphia: Lippincott, 1967), pp. 313–339. See also Jessie Bernard, *Marriage and Family Among Negroes* (Englewood Cliffs, N.J.: Prentice-Hall, 1966), especially the "externally adapted" and the "acculturated" family types, pp. 32 ff.

[28] *Ibid.,* p. 33.

macy, while at the same time permitting and practicing behavior that is externally adaptive, though immoral in her own eyes.

The father in the adaptive family, especially among those in the lowest-income brackets, is absent from the home occasionally or permanently, depending largely on his relationship with the mother of the children. As another example of the externally adaptive nature of this way of life, at least some of the men attached to the adaptive matricentric family reportedly enter marriage with the same ideals as men oriented to the dominant cultural patterns. They feel that they are making lifetime commitments when they marry and hope to carry through on them. The responsibilities of parenthood coupled with limited resources are factors in their withdrawal, as the role of father becomes too difficult and expensive for their personal and economic resources. With the adult males absent or itinerant, one or more married daughters and their mother commonly live together and share the responsibility for support of the household and care of the children.

FIGURE 4.2. CHARACTERISTICS OF POOR FAMILIES COMPARED WITH ALL FAMILIES

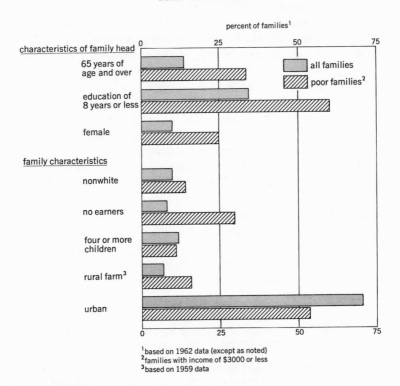

[1] based on 1962 data (except as noted)
[2] families with income of $3000 or less
[3] based on 1959 data

SOURCE: U.S. Department of Health, Education, and Welfare, *Health, Education, and Welfare Trends,* 1964 Annual Supplement, p. xvi.

Acculturated black families are referred to as such because they have taken on family life patterns present in the culture of the white majority. Acculturated black families are not necessarily characteristic of any one social class in that there are acculturated families in the lower as well as in the middle and upper classes. What does divide acculturated and adaptive families is "a great social and psychological chasm." The acculturated family's leadership coalition accepts the monogamous marital pattern and the ideal of permanent marriage.

Already in the nineteenth century family stability and conventional behavior were cherished values of certain elements within the black population. World War I marked a time of decline in the status of family stability and conventional morality as the primary criteria of social status—as income, education, and occupation came more and more to differentiate black families.

The acculturated idea includes the concept of the nuclear family group of husband, wife, and children living in their own home and managing their own affairs. Both economic and social factors commonly hamper the acculturated black family in its search for a single family dwelling or an apartment in a desirable residential setting.

Developments since the middle of the twentieth century indicate that the "travail of civilization" for the black American is not at an end. "There is a considerable body of evidence to suggest the conclusion that Negro social structure, in particular the Negro family, battered and harassed by discrimination, injustice and uprooting, is in the deepest trouble, while many young Negroes are moving ahead to unprecedented levels of achievement, many more are falling further and further behind."[29] Between 1960 and 1963, median nonwhite family income in relation to the income of white families decreased from 55 percent to 53 percent of white income.

Over the past generation, the proportion of nonwhite women twenty to forty-four years of age separated from their husbands increased from an estimated 15 percent in 1940 to about 25 percent in 1964. During this same period the proportion of white women separated from their husbands has remained constant at about 5 percent.[30] If the rise in nonwhite marital instability is in part due to the disruptions attendant on migration to urban areas, then the separation rates and family instability in the nonwhite population will probably remain high as that population becomes increasingly urbanized.

[29] *The Negro Family: A Case for National Action* (Washington, D.C.: Office of Policy Planning and Research, United States Department of Labor, March, 1965), p. 4.

[30] United States Bureau of the Census, "Marital Status and Family Status, March, 1964 and 1963," *Current Population Reports,* Series P-20, No. 135, April 28, 1965, p. 2.

The majority of black families are bi-parental and stable, and this fact is often overlooked. Staples, a family sociologist with personal identity and participation in the black community, states the case as follows based on his own research and a review of the literature on the black family:

> "Our central theme is that the Negro family has magnificently withstood the assaults on its integrity by the forces of poverty, racial discrimination and degradation and involuntary servitude throughout the last three hundred years; that the majority of Negro families, which are stable, adequately prepare their children to be good citizens; and that any deviation of the Negro family from the American norm may be attributed to the peculiar circumstances and conditions of life under which Negro Americans are forced to live."[31] . . . . In summation, research on the Negro family demonstrates that it has undergone certain changes in adapting to the circumstances in which it found itself. Yet it has survived as an important social unit to fortify its members against the vicissitudes of American racialism.[32]

SUMMARY

There is little evidence that African culture had any marked influence on the development of black family culture in America. The memories of social life among African forebearers that may have stirred the imagination of the older generation failed to take root. A family folklore based on a history of African tradition gave no real support in the struggle for status in American society.

Other subdued peoples have continued their traditional way of life within the intimate circle of their kinsmen. But American slavery destroyed the kinship system as it destroyed bonds of sympathy and affection between men and women of the same household. In order to survive they had to acquire a new language, adopt habits consistent with forced agricultural labor, and attempt to imitate the social systems of the "master" race. Their slave children knew only the plantation system of inferior status and developed modes of behavior appropriate to that system.

Emancipation, while it brought a measure of freedom, also destroyed certain patterns of life and relationships that had developed under slavery. Jim Crowism established new and different barriers to interracial associations. Life in the urban ghetto added burdens to a culture and a family life shattered by slavery and its aftermath. Reflecting these burdens, what the black family will be in the future is in large part contingent upon changes that might come about in the social condition of black people.

---

[31] Robert E. Staples, *The Lower Income Negro Family in Saint Paul* (St. Paul, Minn.: St. Paul Urban League, 1967), p. 7.

[32] Robert E. Staples, "Research on the Negro Family: A Source for Family Practitioners," *The Family Coordinator*, 18 (July, 1969), 208.

BIBLIOGRAPHY

Frederic Bancroft. *Slave Trading in the Old South.* Baltimore: Furst, 1931.

Gustave de Beaumont. *Marie or Slavery in the United States.* Stanford, Calif.: Stanford University, 1958; first published in France in 1835.

Jesse Bernard. *Marriage and Family Among Negroes.* Englewood Cliffs, N.J.: Prentice-Hall, 1966.

Andrew Billingsley. *Black Families in White America.* Englewood Cliffs, N.J.: Prentice-Hall, 1968.

Arthur W. Calhoun. *A Social History of the American Family,* Vol. II. New York: Barnes and Noble, 1918; 1945.

St. Clair Drake and Horace Cayton. *Black Metropolis.* New York: Harcourt, Brace, 1945.

Clement Eaton. *The Growth of Southern Civilization, 1790–1860.* New York: Harper, 1961.

Stanley M. Elkins. *Slavery: A Problem in American Institutional and Intellectual Life.* Chicago: University of Chicago, 1959.

E. Franklin Frazier. *The Negro Family in the United States.* Chicago: University of Chicago, 1939.

Ludwig L. Geismar and Ursula C. Gerhart. "Social Class, Ethnicity, and Family Functioning: Exploring Some Issues Raised by the Moynihan Report," *Journal of Marriage and the Family,* XXX (August, 1968), 480–487.

George E. Howard. *A History of Matrimonial Institutions,* Vol. II. Chicago: University of Chicago, 1904.

Camille Jeffers. *Living Poor.* Ann Arbor, Mich.: Ann Arbor Publishers, 1967.

Elliot Liebow. *Tally's Corner.* Boston: Little, Brown, 1967.

Robert E. Park. "The Conflict and Fusion of Cultures with Special Reference to the Negro," *Journal of Negro History,* IV (April, 1919), 111–133.

Vernon Louis Parrington. *Main Currents in American Thought,* Vol. II. New York: Harcourt, Brace, 1930.

Stuart A. Queen and Robert W. Habenstein. *The Family in Various Cultures* (4th ed.). Philadelphia: Lippincott, 1967.

David A. Schulz. *Coming Up Black.* Englewood Cliffs, N.J.: Prentice-Hall, 1969.

Francis Butler Simkins. *The South: Old and New.* New York: Knopf, 1947.

Abbot Emerson Smith. *Colonists in Bondage: White Servitude and Convict Labor in America, 1607–1776.* Chapel Hill: University of North Carolina, 1947.

Charles S. Sydnor. *Slavery in Mississippi.* New York: Appleton-Century-Crofts, 1933.

Daniel Thursz. *Where Are They Now?* Washington, D.C.: Health and Welfare Council of the National Capitol Area, 1966.

George Brown Tindall. *South Carolina Negroes: 1877–1900.* Baton Rouge: Louisiana State University, 1952.

Rupert D. Vance. "Regional Family Patterns: The Southern Family," *American Journal of Sociology,* LIII (May, 1948), 426–429.

W. D. Weatherford. *The Negro from Africa to America.* New York: Doran, 1924.

Paton Yoder. "Private Hospitality in the South, 1775–1850," *The Mississippi Valley Historical Review,* XLVII (December, 1960), 419–433.

The Negro Family: A Case for National Action. (The Moynihan Report.) Office of Policy Planning and Research, U.S. Department of Labor, March, 1965.

CHAPTER 5

The Immigrant Family and the City

THE DYNAMIC SETTING for family life that we now consider—the period of emergence of America as an industrialized urban nation—eventually led to a relatively high standard of living for a majority of families but also contributed to the economic and cultural poverty of many families. During the time of America's emergence as an industrialized nation, family life for the great masses of industrial laborers was often sorely tested. Technological advance and the resulting urban concentration and congestion of population were two of the most significant factors in American history bringing about an imbalance between the family and other social systems—an imbalance that resulted in a subordinate or adaptive role for the family, especially in its interchanges and transactions with the economic system. Technological advance and urban growth contributed significantly to the fluidity and facility for change characteristic of American life, change that was sometimes disadvantageous to the family. The history of modern America has been called a story of the impact of industrialism on every phase of human life;[1] not least was the impact felt on the family.

In 1815, Hezekiah Niles, editor of *Niles' Weekly Register,* a newspaper of early nineteenth-century America, remarked that the distinguishing feature of the American character was the almost universal ambition to get ahead. But this personal ambition to get ahead required facilitating social circumstances. The American economy up to 1815 was relatively static. America had not yet entered what has been called the "take-off" period of economic growth. After 1825 (the date of the completion of the Erie Canal), the boom in transportation and the incredibly rapid expansion of the economy gave substance and impetus to the American ambition. Between 1820 and 1930, America increased forty-fold the supply of energy which it could command per capita through exploiting new sources of power.

The industrial revolution of the nineteenth and twentieth century is the major economic force responsible for the modern American family. The factory, which had become too large to be housed in the home or staffed by any one single family, became the unit of production instead of the home.

[1] Samuel P. Hays, *The Response to Industrialism, 1885–1914* (Chicago: University of Chicago, 1957), p. 1.

Early industrial sites were influenced by the availability of water. Later, the coal areas became the place of concentration of heavy industry—iron and coal mining, smelting, machine production, etc. Thus, heavy industry and population came to be concentrated north of the Ohio River and east of the Mississippi. Pittsburgh, for instance, was situated in the middle of extensive coal fields.

The development of sources of power was not a sufficient cause of the development of industry; labor had also to be marshalled and disciplined to perform simple, precise, and repeatable operations before the American assembly line could attain its remarkably high rate of production of a uniform product. The new "industrialization" worker appeared to many as "a different specimen from the peasant and the artisan who have made up the bulk of the population in civilized lands since the dawn of history."[2]

With the promise or the hope of work in industry, individuals and families migrated from the farms and small towns of America. Industry was the new frontier; the last important tracts of free land for settlement were gone. Moreover, agriculture was being rapidly mechanized, dispensing with the need for thousands of agricultural laborers. At the beginning of the Civil War, only about 16 percent of American people lived in cities; while by 1900 over 30 percent were urbanites, including thousands of blacks who left the South and migrated to northern metropolitan areas.

But not all the laborers in industry came from American farms, plantations, and small towns. With the closing of the free-land frontier, the possibility of the immigrant from Europe establishing himself on the land was slight; the new frontier for him had to be the urban-industrial cities. The immigration of Europeans during the period of industrial growth was the largest such movement in all history. It was so heavy that it radically altered the nationality composition of America; by 1920 only about 40 percent were of Anglo-Saxon descent. During the decade from 1900 to 1910 alone, over eight million immigrants arrived. In 1914, the peak year, nearly three-fourths of the total immigrants came from southern and eastern Europe, and less than 15 percent from northern and western Europe. A reaction against the heavy wave of new immigration gradually developed until the immigration acts of 1921, designed to end the numerical imbalance between northern European immigrants and southern and eastern European immigrants, were passed.

Over against the few who became captains of industry, the vast majority of those attracted into industry were wage or salaried workers. The newcomers, particularly the foreign-born whites and the blacks, encountered difficult conditions of life and work. Wages for unskilled laborers were pitifully low, and almost none came equipped to carry out skills peculiar to

[2] A. J. Muste, "The Tug of Industry," *The Survey,* LIX (December 1, 1927), 281.

the emergent industries. Unskilled newcomers found employment in construction, railway maintenance, coal mining, and urban public works.

Many of the jobs in industry were dangerous jobs without proper safeguards. Industrial accidents in the United States in the 1920's annually caused about twenty-five thousand deaths. Many additional workers suffered permanent disabilities, and there were millions of temporary disabilities of a few days' duration. Humanitarian voices spoke out against what was regarded as flagrant disregard for the safety and security of the worker and his family. With a mixture of fact and feeling characteristic of the times, Muste wrote, "In a good many instances management might have provided safeguards or given instructions that would have prevented trouble, but failed to do so because it may be cheaper for a particular employer or industry, in the short run at least, to cut off a worker's arm, throw him on the scrap heap, and hire another man, than to prevent the accident."[3]

Work in industry could also be uncertain, and the wages offered, misleading. The total yearly income was adequate only if work was reasonably steady. In the bituminous fields of Illinois, Ohio, Indiana, or Pennsylvania, for instance, it was said that a worker was lucky if he had two hundred days of work a year; the same could be true in the building trades, railroads, and other industries. Many family heads found it difficult if not impossible to maintain a consistently adequate level of living. Of 122 housewives who gave information regarding readjustment occasioned by unemployment in Middletown, eighty-three reported unemployment during the preceding fifty-seven months. Many made changes in their routine habits of living to meet the emergency; forty-seven cut on purchases of clothing; forty-three cut on food; twenty-seven worked for pay either at home or away from home; fourteen of sixty carrying some form of insurance got behind on payments; six moved to cheaper housing; five of twenty having a telephone had it taken out; four of thirty-five with children in high school took a child out of school. These changes did not usually come singly; families that felt the need to retrench did so in several areas.[4]

Even where work was steady and wages were increasing (textile workers received perhaps twice as much in the pay envelope in 1925 as they did in 1890) workers were often discontented, feeling that wage increases were not commensurate with increases in productivity. Muste voiced the sentiment of many American industrial workers and their wives when he observed that "American workers, as a whole, do not yet have the food, clothing, housing, leisure, the access to culture and education opportunities that cannot on any reasonable grounds be denied to human beings. This

---

[3] *Ibid.*, p. 284.
[4] Robert S. Lynd and Helen Merrell Lynd, *Middletown: A Study in Modern American Culture* (New York: Harcourt, 1929), p. 62.

drive for a higher standard of living ought to have the unqualified support of those interested in the integrity of American family life."[5]

VALUES SUPPORTING INDUSTRIAL EMERGENCE

The industrial supremacy achieved by America was partly due to material factors—that is, natural resources—but material factors alone would not have produced such a result if Americans had not supported a view of life compatible with technological advancement and industrial growth.

Dominance of Nature

From their Puritan-Calvinistic and pioneering past, Americans had acquired a bent toward the dominating of nature. Self-control and thrift coupled with the conquest of nature had come to characterize their way of life; contemplation and enjoyment for its own sake were eschewed. It was all right to contemplate if one's contemplation resulted in some outcome that had practical, utilitarian value. Mastery-over-nature was of the first order. Nature in all its forms, including human nature, was to be overcome and put to some useful purpose. "Rivers everywhere are spanned with bridges; mountains have roads put through and around them; new lakes are built, sometimes in the heart of a desert; old lakes get partially filled in when additional land is needed for building sites, roads, or airports; the belief in man-made medical care for the control of illness and the lengthening of life is strong to an extreme; and all are told early in life that 'the Lord helps those who help themselves.' "[6]

Preference for Mobility

The American preference for mobility and versatility rather than for the development of specialized professional skills was in harmony with the techniques of mass production developed in American industry. On the assembly line, which emphasized simple, repeatable operations, a worker could acquire the sufficient degree of skill for a particular job in a short time; no lengthy apprenticeship or other training that would bind him to a particular occupation for life was required. The black, for instance, as he moved about the country, sloughed off the traditional attitudes and beliefs that had provided a philosophy of life in the world of the folk in exchange for a philosophy supportive of the urban-industrial revolution.[7]

[5] Muste, op. cit., p. 283.

[6] Florence R. Kluckhohn, "Family Diagnosis: Variations in the Basic Values of Family Systems," Social Casework, XXXIX (February–March, 1958), 67.

[7] E. Franklin Frazier, The Negro Family in the United States, rev. and abridged ed. (New York: Dryden Press, 1948; first published in 1939), pp. 210–225.

Future Orientation

Americans looked toward a future that was expected to be bigger and better than the present. Techniques and procedures were not considered good just because they were traditional and dominant; Americans were seldom content with the present. This view resulted in a high value being placed on change, providing change did not threaten the so-called American way of life.[8] Pragmatism was in the American tradition. When "doctrine got in the way of practicality, the doctrine lost out."[9] Already in 1834, Chevalier saw the American people as "a people which, above all things, strives to save time, and which is so much given to haste and dispatch that its most suitable emblem would be a locomotive engine or a steamboat. . . . The work on the railroad from Boston to Providence was going on à l'americaine, that is to say, rapidly."[10]

As an ideology capitalism holds that maximum efficiency is achieved when business and industry are under the ownership and control of free men who operate them for private profit. Both labor and management supported the capitalistic ideology.

Social Darwinism

Economic views popular at the time of urban-industrial emergence treated the notion that personal and family misery caused by economic change was inconsequential compared with its benefits. One of the most extreme views has been labeled social Darwinism, the notion that success comes to those who are able to survive the rigors of struggle, and the poor are poor simply because they are less fit. Classical economies denied that a conflict existed between private and public interest. According to this view, private competition among individuals would automatically produce the greatest social good. The rise of social Darwinism in the United States coincided with the accumulation of vast amounts of wealth by early captains of industry. John D. Rockefeller explained this philosophy to his Sunday School class by explaining that "The growth of a large business is merely survival of the fittest."[11] Herbert Spencer, known as the father of social Darwinism, and a man with tremendous popularity in the United States during the period of industrial emergence said that prosperity comes about through the competitive struggle of individuals. The struggle is natural and therefore good, whereas social action tends to limit the struggle and is artificial and there-

[8] Kluckhohn, op. cit., p. 67.
[9] William H. Whyte, The Organization Man (New York: Simon and Schuster, 1956), p. 24.
[10] Michael Chevalier, Society, Manner and Politics in the United States, ed. John William Ward (Garden City, N.Y.: Doubleday and Company, Anchor Books, 1961; first published in France in 1834), p. 74.
[11] As quoted in Richard Hofstadter, Social Darwinism in American Thought (Philadelphia: University of Pennsylvania Press, 1945), p. 45.

fore bad. Social interference "should not be so paternal as to check the self-extinction of the morally ill-constituted" and "social interference should not so limit the struggle for existence as to nullify the selective process."[12]

The aim of the drafters of the Constitution was to give the government powers to carry out basic activities designed to facilitate the conduct of business—regulate trade, coin money, legislate protective tariffs, establish credit, and redeem securities. According to the political ideology supporting capitalism, *laissez-faire*—or the least government interference in economic affairs—was regarded as producing the greatest economic efficiency. Not that ideology and practice are always the same, for the government from the beginning gave active support to business and industry. America's rapid economic growth was made possible by social capital, that is, by governmental investment. Rather than capitalism supported by a political philosophy of *laissez-faire,* the American economy even in its early stages was a mixed economy with the government playing a major role. Government support to business and industry was substantial; government support to families was minimal. Families needing special governmental support were regarded as families that had failed.

THE URBAN COMMUNITY AND FAMILY

Though the economy of the city had a more important effect upon the destiny of man in the city than did the family, life in the city did not form into an integrated community around this industrial economy.[13] In fact, business interests often initiated some of the major disharmonies in urban life. While economic events are a major influence in patterning the life of a city, they do not bring a stability and consistency to the city.

Two key reference points in the city are the factory and the slum. In the interchange and transactions over sites, the family lost out to the factory. All other aspects of urban life tended to be subordinated to the factory. Chemical, cotton, iron, and other industries usually obtained the sites most favorable for their operations near the waterfront, where large quantities of water needed for the productive processes were available. The general result was that other major buildings were forced back from the scenic spots on the waterfront. Not only did industry command the best sites; it also transformed those sites through pollution of land, water, air, and the added noise of industry into blighted areas unpleasant and unhealthful for human activity and human occupancy. The total environment was apt to present a mixture of unsightly slag dumps, soot and grit in the atmosphere, danger-

---

[12] As quoted in E. A. Ross, *Social Control* (New York: American Book Company, 1901), pp. 423, 425.

[13] Don Martindale, *American Society* (Princeton, N.J.: Van Nostrand, 1960), p. 195.

ous chemicals and waste in the water, and unpleasant foul odors every-where.[14] The surrounding area was developed less with an eye to beauty than with an eye to simplicity of settlement and a profitable return to the owners of the land mass involved. The first step in preparing an area for urban sites was to destroy most of the natural features, and hence the natural beauty. Hills were leveled, swamps were filled, the course of streams and rivers were changed or efficiently contained within concrete retaining walls. After the troublesome natural features were modified as much as it was economically feasible to modify them, the area was plotted in rectangular blocks of identical size separated by streets and sidewalks of standard width. Facilities for bringing in water, light, and gas, and for disposing of waste in the residential areas were a late development of the period of urban-industrial emergence. It was with the necessity of a large labor supply and the accessory services required by a large population that the industrial movement came to be associated with urban living.

All available space was used for housing, and tenement houses five or more stories high and running ninety feet back from the street were built to house the influx of population. Each floor was divided into numerous rooms, some without direct light or air. Whole families would live in one or two ill-equipped and unpleasant rooms, sometimes in cold-water flats with no plumbing facilities except for a common basin in the hall. A growing number of hotels, lodging houses, and boarding-houses provided housing for single and other unattached persons, but there was little public effort to control or improve them before the 1890's. Some of the reasons for public concern with housing between 1890 and 1915 were the tendency of male immigrants from southern and eastern Europe to live first by themselves as unattached roomers or boarders for several years before they brought their women over; the new openings for women in industry and commerce, and the fact that women in large numbers had to live away from home to take these jobs; the white-slaving of immigrant women; the occasional fires that broke out in old rooming houses and the publicity they received.[15]

Cramped living conditions were reflected in small industrial cities as well. In Middletown in the 1880's the usual size of the lot on which a house was built was sixty-two and a half feet fronting on the street with a depth of one hundred and twenty-five feet; the standard lot in 1924 had a frontage of only forty feet. Whereas the city block of 1890 usually contained eight lots, the same blocks in 1924 contained ten, twelve, and even fourteen lots. A common practice in 1924 was to divide a lot and build an additional house on the back half of the lot fronting on the side street. Houses were crowded closer to the front paving-line, and the flowers and shrubbery

[14] Lewis Mumford, *The Culture of Cities* (New York: Harcourt, 1938), p. 143 ff.
[15] Arnold M. Rose, "Interest in the Living Arrangements of the Urban Unattached," *American Journal of Sociology*, LIII (May, 1948), 483–493.

gave way as the lawn shrank to allow a driveway to the garage. In many working class families, smaller yards and closer neighbors reduced the backyard to an overflow storage place since the newer houses lacked attics, storerooms, or barns.[16]

Nels Anderson discussed the situation dramatically and graphically when he said:

> The city home has been so stripped and depleted and backed to the wall that in sections like Manhattan it bids fair to lose out entirely. Family life, too, seems to be going by the board. Soaring of land values and pyramiding of rents pinch the city dweller into ever narrowing quarters where for the advantage of location he sacrifices one after another of the comforts of home. The press for space takes away the front yard and then the back yard. It takes away pets and plants and penalizes him for having children, so he gives up the nursery. The parlor and sitting room are narrowed and combined. He is forced to exchange the four poster for an in-a-door bed, the kitchen becomes a kitchenette and the dining room a dinette, while the pantry has all but vanished. The home declines as family headquarters, a place for eating, sleeping and passing leisure. It becomes a mere address, a place where members of the family leave things they do not care to carry around with them. Unless he submits to the clipping process he must submit to what is more uncompromising, the increasing cost of retaining these ancient comforts.[17]

The immigrant from southern and eastern Europe found the American city a singularly strange place. On the other hand, the mass of newcomers maintained customs that were strange to the American native. They spoke peculiar languages, dressed differently, had revolting personal habits, and practiced the Catholic religion; they had not mastered the subtleties of respect due American values, symbols, and heroes, nor did they seem to care about them. Moreover, they were involved—though not necessarily by choice—with the most vulgar and unpleasant features of industrial society. They worked at menial tasks and lived in the least desirable section of the city, where the most distasteful dives and bawdy houses were located. Immigrants from Europe (as well as migrants from the farmlands and towns of America) came mostly from established neighborhoods and communities. Most of their home communities were reasonably closely integrated by tradition and personal ties. The move to American industrial cities ushered in a decline of the community and neighborhood as integrated units and a decline of their influence upon individuals and families, except in those cases where strong ethnic communities temporarily held off some of the effect of the impersonal city. In the pages to follow we will concentrate our attention on the community and family life of two of the immigrant groups —the Italian-American and the Polish-American. The patterns described

---

[16] Lynd and Lynd, *op. cit.* (see above, fn. 4), pp. 94–95.
[17] Nels Anderson, "Bedroom Towns," *The Survey*, LIX (October 15, 1927), p. 92.

could be repeated *ad infinitum,* with some variations for the great variety of racial and ethnic groups that formed the population mosaic of the American city.

Ethnic Communities—Italian[18]

Ethnic communities tried in various ways to meet the challenge of the city; for Italian-Americans social organizations were formed on the basis of the part of Italy from which people had come. Village and provincial groups from both the North and South of Italy organized mutual benefit societies for their social life and for mutual aid in case of sickness or death. The number of these societies was legion, and even their names were often not known outside of their own membership. A few of the more prosperous societies had their own clubrooms. It was only the experience of being in a foreign land which made many of the immigrants feel themselves to be Italians at all rather than citizens of a particular town or province.

Time brought change in these Italian communities. In some cases the community's structure was broken, partly through loss of members through migration to outlying parts of the city, partly through the impact of American institutions, partly through urban development, and partly because the old provincial alignment ceased to be relevant as newly developed interests cut across old lines.

The provincial societies made no appeal to the younger generation raised in America. In contrast to the ethnic organizations of some other groups in America whose educational and cultural programs have attracted and held at least part of the younger generation within the bonds of ethnic consciousness, the provincial emphasis of these organizations tended to represent to the young Italian-American the worst aspect of his heritage and to be associated with the "backwardness" of his parents.

Ethnic Communities—Polish[19]

If a Polish immigrant found work that paid well and promised to be permanent in a locality where there was no Polish settlement as yet, he would try to attract his friends and relatives from other Polish-American communities. Usually a small group of Polish workmen could be formed. Their first attempt—partly for economic, partly for social reasons—would be to organize a Polish boardinghouse. Often some one of them with some money and a wife would assume the initiative, rent a large apartment, and

[18] This discussion of the Italian community follows the analysis of Caroline F. Ware, "The Breakdown of Ethnic Solidarity: The Case of the Italian in Greenwich Village," *Greenwich Village, 1920–1930* (New York: Houghton Mifflin, 1935), pp. 152–202.

[19] This section on the Polish community follows the analysis of W. I. Thomas and Florian Znaniecki, *The Polish Peasant in Europe and America,* II (New York: Dover Publications, 1958; an unabridged and unaltered republication of the 2nd ed.).

take the others as roomers or boarders. Frequently, the initiative came from a group rather than an individual, with all the workers pooling their money, renting and furnishing an apartment, and inducing one of their number with a wife or fiancée to be in charge. In this case the workers bought the food while the wife cooked and cleaned house and received one or two dollars a week for her services with the tacit understanding that she and her children could live on the boarders' surplus food.

With the growth of a new community came progress in unity and cohesion, especially in the form of a "society." The first purpose for which such a society was usually established was the same as it was for the Italians and other immigrant groups—namely, mutual help in emergencies (sickness, death, and, more seldom, lack of work). Any Pole who accepted the help of American social agencies was considered disgraced personally as a pauper and was considered also as disgracing the whole Polish community.

The society founded in a new community was much more than a mutual insurance system. Not only did it bring the scattered members together periodically, thus actively encouraging social intercourse, but it became the social organ of the community—the source of group initiative and the instrument for the realization of plans initiated.

When a parish was organized, the mutual help association ceased to be the central and only representative agency in the Polish community. Leadership passed into the hands of the priest. But the association did not surrender entirely any of its social functions; it simply shared the initiative in communal matters and in the representation of the community. The priest, far from limiting the activities of local associations, favored their development and utilized them consistently as instruments for all purposes connected with the progress of the parish. The community had only a small stock of traditions left from Poland and it could not efficiently enforce even these unless the individual chose to participate actively in common life.

No community center established by American social agencies would expect to even approximately fulfill the social function of a Polish parish. The American social agency was a system imposed from the outside, instead of being freely developed by the initiative and cooperation of the people themselves and this, in addition to its ethnically unfamiliar character, was enough to prevent it from exercising any deep social influences. Its managers usually knew little or nothing of the traditions, attitudes, and native language of the people with whom they had to deal, and therefore could not become genuine social leaders under any conditions. Whatever common activities it tried to develop were almost exclusively leisure-time activities. The parish as an instrument for the unification and organization of the Polish-American community was thus quite unrivaled.

The Polish-American parish was then much more than a religious association for common worship under the leadership of a priest. The unique power of the parish in Polish-American life, much greater than in even the most conservative peasant communities in Poland, could not be explained by the predominance of religious interests. The parish was the old primary community reorganized and concentrated. In its institutional organization, it performed the functions which in Poland were fulfilled by both the parish and the commune. In spite of the great vitality which the parish had as social system, the authority of the church as religious system was much weakened, perhaps for the very reason that the existence of the Polish-American church depended on the free will of the members.

Interchanges Between Family and Community

For native Americans or immigrants who were not a part of any ethnic community, the move to the city resulted not in an integrated community or neighborhood, but in a more or less accidental grouping of sleeping quarters. Eliot[20] described an incident typical of this type of settlement pattern. "I walked out of my front door one morning and saw an undertaker's car in front of a house almost directly across the street. I suddenly realized that I didn't even know the name of the family who lived in that house, and that now it was too late to inquire. Neighborliness—the natural human impulse to be kind to one's neighbor in his time of trouble—had ceased to bear any direct relation to the fact of physical nearness. That could not have happened to my father or mother. It could not have happened fifty years ago."

In settled, integrated communities, there are important interchanges between family and community. Family life is in many respects conditioned by the community; the family also has an important part in creating and changing the community. The sense of responsibility which comes with the consciousness of belonging to a community gives meaning and value to family life. The family opens up to such a community; if it wants to protect itself, it closes to an impersonal and disorganized community.

The Lynds observed the lack of interchange in the pattern of family friends in Middletown. Their observations and the comments of some of the individuals interviewed reveal an impersonal character to life in the city. One in eight of the business class and one in three of the working class had either no friends at all in Middletown or no intimate friends.

The following answers are characteristic of the forty of the 118 workers' wives who had no friends or no intimate friends:

It doesn't pay to be too friendly.
I never chum with anyone; it's dangerous.
I have no best friends. In town you never know who is your friend.

20 Frederick M. Eliot, "The New Neighbors," *The Survey*, LIX (December 1, 1927), 304.

Even your best friend will do you dirt. I never run around with people. I let everyone alone.

I haven't any friends in the city. I see plenty of people at church and clubs, but I treat them all alike.

Our neighbors used to be good friends and we had lots of good times together, but in the last seven or eight years that is all gone. People don't pay much attention to each other any more.

I don't even know the names of the people next door and we have lived here a year.[21]

THE SETTLEMENT HOUSE AND THE IMMIGRANT FAMILY

In settlement houses American middle-and upper-class individuals sought to learn firsthand of immigrant life, to encourage the newcomers to express their own culture, and to try to persuade Americans to appreciate the unique contributions that foreign peoples could make to their community. College students and others of troubled humanitarian conscience, often anxious to give expression to humanitarian values, associated themselves with the settlement-house movement. Some settlement houses became centers from which the positive qualities of immigrant life were interpreted to the wider community; and the most famous of them, Jane Addams' Hull House in Chicago, became a cultural and inspirational center for the whole humanitarian movement.

William F. Whyte, an American sociologist viewing settlement-house activity from the perspective of the Italian immigrant, was not impressed with its accomplishments on behalf of individuals or families. The workers whose actions defined the role of the settlement house were middle-class people of non-Italian stock. The boards of directors also were composed of upper-middle class and upper-class people of northern European background. The only Italians connected with the settlement houses had subordinate jobs, teaching special classes or doing clerical or janitorial work. Not one of the social workers could speak Italian, although some had spent as much as twenty years in the district; not until 1940 was a non-Italian proficient in the language hired. The workers had no systematic knowledge of the social backgrounds of the people in their homeland, nor had they made much of an effort to get to know the local social organization in the Italian-American community which they served. The social workers did not think in terms of interchange between the settlement house, representing American society, and the Italian-American community. They thought in terms of a one-way adaptation: the Italian-American community was expected to adapt itself to the standards of the settlement house. Some people made the adaptation; most people did not. None of the first-generation men

[21] Lynd and Lynd, *op. cit.* (see above, fn. 4), pp. 272–273.

met in the settlement; the settlement houses got a cross section of the population among the small boys and girls, but as the children grew older, the selection became less diversified.[22]

The results of the movement were not spectacular; the extent to which settlement houses served to moderate the cleavage between native American and foreign-born is open to question.

After World War I, the drive to socialize ("Americanize") the immigrant took the form of bringing every possible pressure to bear upon aliens to become American citizens. Never before in history had a nation incorporated such a vast number of aliens into its corporate body without undergoing any essential change itself.[23]

THE POLITICAL MACHINE AND THE IMMIGRANT FAMILY

No one was responsible, officially, for meeting the new arrival in the city and helping him to become established and sustained. Industry was interested in him as a worker, but, in many cases, the only group that paid attention to him as a person and paid attention to his family was the political machine. The political boss through the ward heeler stood ready to help the immigrant find a job and to provide welfare services if he was not already committed to receive them from a mutual aid society operated by his ethnic community. The machine would provide an allotment of coal to a family in need, help arrange for a funeral if the family lacked funds and a close tie with the church, intercede with the authorities in case of a petty arrest, and protect one of the immigrant's social centers, the saloon. And on top of it all, the immigrant family might receive a basket of food at Christmas. All the political boss asked in return was the newcomer's vote in subsequent elections.

Social reformers interested in social justice scorned the machine as an instrument of corruption and partisan patronage, but to the newcomer, selling his vote for the benefits and protection he received was not an unreasonable interchange. "In a society that rejected the immigrant's right fully to belong, the boss remained one of the few sources of power in the community which the foreign-born could reach, and the political machine provided one of the few opportunities for him to rise to a position of influence and prestige."[24]

---

[22] William F. Whyte, *Street Corner Society: The Social Structure of an Italian Slum* (Chicago: University of Chicago, 1943), pp. 98–99.

[23] Henry Bamford Parkes, *The American Experience: An Interpretation of the History and Civilization of the American People* (New York: Vintage Books, 1959; first published in 1947), p. 256.

[24] Hays, *op. cit.* (see above, fn. 1), p. 99.

THE TRADE UNION MOVEMENT AND THE FAMILY

A major step in the adjustment of the urban-industrial worker's family came when the workers organized themselves across nationality lines. The emphasis on specialization in mass-production industry had stripped artisans of their roles of manager and salesman and reduced them to the sole task of selling their labor to others. For several decades they attempted to reverse the trend through programs aimed at destroying the wage system or at helping themselves to escape from it. Gradually they became reconciled to the values emergent in the American urban-industrial system and concentrated on working out their destiny within it. The early national trade unions were job-and-wage-oriented and concentrated on creating economic power to advance the condition of workers within the wage system. The labor movement, which came fully into its own following the economic depression of the 1930's, was a major factor in providing material resources, stability of work, and so-called fringe benefits essential to the functioning of the working man's family.

INSIDE THE URBAN FAMILY

The Italian-American Family[25]

At the time of the great population movement from Italy to America beginning at the end of the nineteenth century, the southern Italian peasant family came from a folk society with a culture that was highly integrated. The intimate interchanges between the various parts of a folk society make it difficult to isolate—even for the sake of study—any one part, such as the family. There was intimate interplay of the peasant family with religious practices, the planting and gathering of food, the celebration of feasts and holidays, the education of the children, the treatment of the sick, the protection of the person, and all other aspects of small-village folk life.

The family was the center of Italian culture. In one way this made Italian culture easier to transplant than cultures which depend upon complex and differentiated social systems. Embedded in the intimacy of family relations, fundamental Italian attitudes were almost beyond the reach of many influences that affected external interchanges with the urban community. Whatever tended to place the Italian tradition in disrepute or to draw the members of the group away from it, struck directly at the Italian family. "Any agencies which sought to amalgamate this group with the American community thus had the choice of accepting its Italianness and

[25] In this section we are particularly indebted to Paul J. Campisi, "Ethnic Family Patterns: The Italian Family in the United States," *American Journal of Sociology*, LIII (May, 1948), 443–449; and Ware, *op. cit.* (see above, fn. 18).

dealing with it in family groups or of attempting to deal with a group of individuals who were not only traditionless but socially disorganized as well."[26]

Campisi delineates three stages in the process of adjustment of the Italian family in America: (1) the initial-contact stage, (2) the conflict stage, and (3) the accommodation stage.

In the first decade of Italians living in America—the initial-contact stage —the structure of the old-world family was still fairly well intact, but interchanges within and outside the family were beginning to modify the old-world peasant pattern. Producing this incipient distortion were the following: the very act of physical separation from the parental family and village culture; the necessity to work and operate with a somewhat strange and foreign body of household tools, equipment, gadgets, furniture, cooking utensils, and other physical objects, in addition to making an adjustment to a different physical environment and tenement living arrangements; the birth of children and the increasing contact with American medical practices regarding child care; the attendance of Italian children in American parochial and public schools; and the increasing pressure by American legal, educational, political, and economic systems for the Americanization of the foreigner.

In the conflict stage, the first-generation family experienced its most profound changes and finally broke with old-world foundations. Interchanges were characterized by conflict between two ways of life—the one American and the other Italian—and a generation gap between parents and children. This phase began roughly during the second decade of living in America— specifically, when the children unhesitatingly expressed their acquired American expectations and attempted to transmit them in the family situation and when the parents in turn attempted to reinforce the pattern of the old-world family. It was the parents who had the most to lose, for their complete acceptance of the American way of living meant the denial of the old-world ideals.

Of all the elements in the traditional pattern, none was in more fundamental conflict with the new environment than the tradition of the patriarchal family. It was under fire from practically every American institution which the family came in contact with, for, with the exception of the family welfare agencies, American social systems had been designed to deal with people as individuals rather than people in family groups. Democracy, community participation, public school education—all rested on individualistic assumptions. Recreational agencies such as settlement houses dealt with their members in individual terms, and Protestant churches stressed the

26 Ware, *op. cit.* (see above, fn. 18), p. 173.

ultimate separateness of the individual. Activities of all types were character-istically planned for and carried on by the several age groups rather than by young and old acting together. In interchanges in the community in which this Italian population thus found itself—except for old-world traditions they attempted to perpetuate—there existed little or nothing to reinforce and many things to undermine the unity of the family group.

American pressures penetrated below the family's external unity and gave its internal structure a severe wrench. The breakdown of Italian cul-ture was traceable in the changing position of Italian women and girls; for whatever operated to individualize the women and the children upset their subordination to the group as a whole, and to the man who was the head of the family. As this occurred, the most fundamental of all traditional Italian relationships was destroyed.

Health agencies and recreation and church groups joined in taking the married women out of the home, building up a taste for club activities, and developing the attitudes and sense of importance of clubwomen.

The development of clubs was opposed by husbands in the more con-servative homes. One husband told a worker from the center at which the club met, when the worker called to find out why his wife had not been attending, "I won't have her go because they learn her things there."[27] This attitude was not so prevalent, however, as to keep the enrollment of the clubs from rising rapidly.

Club activity significantly altered the relation of the women to their families and their homes, primarily by giving them the idea of living for themselves rather than exclusively for the family group of which they were a part. But at the same time that the American urban community gave Italian women a life outside of their families, it removed the traditional basis for their prestige. In a patriarchal family, childbearing was a woman's principal source of distinction, for the economic usefulness of children in an agricultural society, reinforced by the teaching of the church, made a large family proverbially a blessing, while pressure toward family limitation was very strong in the American urban community.

In an effort to determine where the pattern of old-world life was crum-bling the fastest and where it was holding most firmly, interviews were held with 144 residents in one Italian-American community. Family-related items and percentage differences for those over and under 35 years of age are shown in the accompanying table.[28]

The accommodation stage began with the realization by parents and children that the continuation of hostility, misunderstanding, and contra-ventive behavior could result only in deterioration of the family. The am-bivalent attitude of the children toward the parents—of great affection on

[27] *Ibid.*, p. 177.
[28] Adapted from Ware, *op. cit.* (see above, fn. 18), p. 133.

the one hand, and hostility on the other—tended to be replaced by a more tolerant disposition. This stage began when the offspring reached adulthood and married and established households of their own, for by this time the control of the parents was greatly lessened.

TABLE 5.1. DIRECTION OF THE DISTORTION OF THE ITALIAN CULTURE PATTERN: PROPORTION WHOSE ANSWERS DEPARTED FROM THE TRADITIONAL PATTERN

Family	Under 35 years of age Percentage	Over 35 years of age Percentage	Difference
Does not believe that:			
Marriages should be arranged by parents	70	99	29
Large families are a blessing	48	86	38
Girls should not associate with men unless engaged	45	83	38
Husband's authority should be supreme	34	64	30
A child should sacrifice his personal ambition to welfare of family group	31	54	23
Divorce is never permissible	12	61	49
Children owe absolute obedience to parents	2	15	13

Among the many factors which operated to bring about a new stability in the Italian-American family were the realization on the part of the parents that life in America was to be permanent; the adult age of the offspring; the almost complete dependence of the parents on the offspring, including use of the children as informants, interpreters, guides, and translators of the American world; recognition on the part of the parents that social and economic success could come to the offspring only as they became more and more like other Americans; the conscious and unconscious acculturation of the parents themselves with a consequent minimizing of many potential conflicts. The success of the first-generation family in instilling in the offspring respect and affection for the parents, and the gradual understanding by the children that successful interaction with the American world was possible by accepting marginal roles and that complete denial of the old-world family was unnecessary were also factors.

The second-generation household tended to pattern itself after the contemporary urban American family. Intermarriage, the advanced age of the parents, the loosening of ties with the Italian neighborhood, and the development of intimate relationships with non-Italians made the transition of the second-generation family easier.

The Polish-American Family[29]

Polish peasants had been socialized to the life of a permanent agricultural community, settled for many hundreds of years in the same locality and changing so slowly that each generation adapted itself to the change with very little effort or abstract reflection. They were not accustomed to expected unfamiliar happenings in the corners of life; and if such happenings occurred they relied upon the group, which not only gave assistance when necessary, but helped them recover the feeling that life in general was normal in spite of the unexpected disturbances. The peasant drew his social stimulations, prohibitions, and suggestions from direct contact with his milieu; and the steadiness and efficiency of his life-organization depended on the continuity of interchanges with his own group. He was a member of a politically and culturally passive class and did not interact directly with any of the larger impersonal social systems that existed in his homeland.

Each extended family took care to enforce the traditional rules of behavior upon its own married members and at the same time was ready to defend these members against any break of the rules committed by another party. If the extended family overstepped the principles for which it was meant to stand or was unable to influence its nuclear families, the community increased its rights of control over both the nuclear family and the extended family. In the United States, the extended family was no longer a real social unit with common interests, for usually only a few members had emigrated and these were often scattered.

The social control to which a nuclear family in the old country was subjected by the extended family and the community bore upon the nuclear family as a unit and had the interests of the unit in view. The role of the social milieu was not to stop between husband and wife and arbitrate between their personal claims as those of separate individuals, but to uphold their union when threatened by the action of either. The misbehaving individual was made to feel that he had sinned against the sacredness of marriage, not that he was wrong in his contest with another individual. Therefore, the control of the old social milieu increased the institutional significance of the conjugal bond. On the contrary, the interference of the American legal institution meant an arbitration between husband and wife, who were treated—officially and unofficially—as contesting parties, as individuals between whose claims a just balance should be established.

Interchange between the Polish-American family and social systems responsible for law and order made appeals to solidarity difficult if not meaningless because the social worker or the judge was not a member of the Polish community and had no direct, vital interest in the family. Moreover, the action of the American systems differed in nature from that of a Polish

---

[29] This section follows the analysis in Thomas and Znaniecki, *op. cit.* (see above, fn. 19).

community by being sporadic and putting the matter on a rational basis, whereas the old-world social milieu acted continuously and by emotional interdependence rather than by reasoning.

Task Performance

During the past two or three thousand years in Europe, the family had reached a high point as a functioning social system. The functions of the family declined very rapidly after the development of the factory, aided by innumerable other mechanical inventions. In the agricultural era which preceded the industrial age, six major functions were performed largely by the family—affectional, economic, recreational, protective, religious, and educational. The family lost functions particularly in the city, and it was only with difficulty that it maintained equilibrium in its hostile environment. Spinning, weaving, sewing, and production of soap, laundering, and even the preparation of food left the aegis of the family in whole or in part— changing the nature of the employment of men and women, and particularly taking away from women their ancient employment. The loss of economic functions was most noticeable in the large city among apartment-house dwellers; it was less developed among families in the smaller towns and in the country.[30]

Woman acquired a new role in a new division of labor, however. With her husband away from home, held to a rigid time schedule, it fell to her, first of all, to use the family's income to take care of the family's needs. While the husband changed from a producer to an earner, the wife changed from a processor to a consumer in a society where consumption was an increasingly important economic function. It was the advent of the money economy, in which the income was the index of achievement and the housewife was the only worker who did not get paid.[31]

Interchanges between the family and the economic system were increasingly contractual, established through the major breadwinner and other members of the family. The family was not self-sufficient, but it was expected to be self-supporting. For persons moving from a peasant-agricultural to an urban-industrial way of life, the change from a productive to consumption unit was abrupt. The family could not possibly retain the old type of division of labor and authority structure in the face of such drastic changes.

Family Leadership

With the change of economic function of the family and the loss in authority as a natural outcome of the loss of economically-productive activity, the period of industrial emergence was a period of confusion and

---

[30] W. F. Ogburn, "Our Social Heritage," *The Survey*, LIX (December 1, 1927), 278.

[31] David M. Foster, "American Women and the American Character," *Stetson University Bulletin*, LXII (January, 1962).

disorganization within the family as members found difficulty in defining their new roles as individuals and family members in the urban setting. The husband might continue to expect his wife and children to be docile, if not devoted, members of his work force, while they might aspire to careers and to social, civic, or recreational activities outside the home. Activities previously not available at all could now be engaged in by family members apart from the presence of the husband and father. It was only natural and inevitable that the patriarchal control of the husband-father over his wife and children should suffer in this process.[32]

Integration and Solidarity

How were the new adjustments to be made? Not by clinging to the old beliefs and customs, for the old conditions of agriculture and home industry could not be brought back into society as it was now. The family had to work out new adjustments as a unit held together less by economic and social bonds. What would bind the new urban family together as a replacement for the old interests and restraints? It did not seem probable that the family could recover the functions it had lost. But even if the family did not produce thread, cloth, soap, and food, it could still produce affection and happiness. However, making personal affection the central binding force within the family was to be debated by social scientists and family-life educators for decades to come.

THE FAMILY AND THE PERSON

Birth Rate

Interchanges of the family with the industrialized city were accompanied by a reduction in birth rate and in size of family households. In 1790, the average number of persons per family household in the United States was 5.7; in 1920, the first year in which the United States Census showed America to be more urban than rural in residence of population, the average had dropped to 4.3.

The burden of carrying out the changing attitudes toward family limitation were not always equally shared by husband and wife. This was true certainly of the Italian-American community. Evidence from doctors and others consistently agreed that the men of the older generation would take no precautions. In fact, women could expect no support from their husbands, their tradition, or their church in their desire to limit family size.

Socialization

In Polish peasant life, the children began at an early age to participate in all the activities of the parents—economic, recreational, social, religious

[32] Ernest W. Burgess, "The Family in a Changing Society," *American Journal of Sociology*, LII (May, 1948), 417–422.

—and thus unreflectively absorbed and imitated the parents' way of life. The parents introduced the children into the traditions and the present life of the community and thus prepared them to supplement whatever deficiencies there might have been in their early education from the principles and examples offered by the community.

All this was radically changed in America. The children no longer took part in the activities of their parents. They went to school or ran the streets while the parents worked, or played in their own separate milieu. There was still some community of interests and occupation left between the girl and her mother, but the boy had very little in common with his father. Education by imitation was no longer possible. And even if the boy did have an opportunity to participate in his father's activities, he did not gain much by it, for these activities had little social meaning—unless, of course, the father was one of the active builders of the Polish-American community. Furthermore, the family was no longer the medium through which the child was introduced into the social life of his wider milieu. On the contrary, not only were his contacts in the community for the most part direct and independent of the selective control of his elders, but he was often called to mediate between his parents and American institutions whose real meaning he may not have understood any better than they, but with which he had a superficial acquaintance.

The position of a girl in an immigrant family differed from that of a boy in that the claims which the family put upon her were greater. But the difference between her own education and the traditions of her parents produced estrangement too; and in view of the traditional supremacy claimed by the older generation, there was little chance of her gaining personal freedom.

Perhaps the girl would settle down without revolt to this ordered life, however dull; but the apparent possibilities of an entirely different life, full of excitement, were continually displayed before her eyes in the city. Quite apart from the idea of democracy—which though it may not mean much to her politically, taught her to think that the only social differences between people were differences of wealth—she might well feel through exposure that some small part of a glamorous life actually was within her reach.

In Polish-American communities attempts were made to control the socialization of the children by organizing parish schools. There were many parishes—five in Chicago alone—whose schools were attended by more than 2,000 children. The teachers were mainly nuns of the various teaching orders. Polish and English were both employed as teaching languages, the proportion varying in different schools. Some large and wealthy parishes went further and established high schools. One—the parish of St. Stanislaw Kostka in Chicago—even founded a college.

Immigrant children who attended the American public school found there a great stress on a high standard of living. In the words of one young

Italian man, "They made us feel at school as if we were being actually un-patriotic—almost traitors—if we did not achieve a high standard of living." Where earnings were low, a high standard of living was incompatible with a large family, and the younger people could not long accept the traditional "rich in flesh" attitude.

Some of the immigrants and most of the children were ambitious to be-come Americanized and socialized into the American way of life as rapidly as possible. The children quickly learned the American language and Amer-ican standards as they saw them where they lived, and second- and third-generation children of immigrants became almost indistinguishable from earlier Anglo-Saxon immigrants. The particular process of socialization, in which millions of immigrants' children repudiated the traditions of their ancestors and assumed for themselves "the memories of the Mayflower and the Declaration of Independence," was largely the work of the public schools. The welding of different groups into a national unity, and not the maintenance of intellectual standards, was the primary social function of the American educational system.

In some parts of the city the socialization process produced high rates of delinquency. These areas of greatest concentration of delinquency were in the low-rent, congested rooming-house areas of the city. Gang life, prosti-tution, vice, and organized, illicit liquor and dope traffic operated in the same locale, presenting a distorted view of American life to the newly arrived immigrant.

Child Labor

Learning to work in the factory was a part of the socialization process for many children and youths. Many children worked long hours in the factories under unfavorable working conditions. This, along with black servitude, is regarded as one of the worst chapters in the history of America.

The child's presence in the industrial labor force did not signal his eman-cipation from the family. Children, when they grew up, were expected to preserve family solidarity at least to the extent of turning over to the family most of their earnings, so that whatever expenses the family incurred to support them until working age were treated as an investment of the family funds from which a return was expected.[33]

Child labor legislation was nonexistent or administratively weak and poorly enforced in this country until after the Civil War. In 1832 as many as two-fifths of all persons employed in New England factories were between seven and sixteen years of age. Hours of labor were never less than ten, sel-dom less than twelve, often fourteen or fifteen or more.[34] The number of

[33] Thomas and Znaniecki, *op. cit.* (see above, fn. 19), p. 1516.
[34] Raymond G. Fuller, *Encyclopedia of Social Science,* ed. Edwin K. Seligman, III (New York: Macmillan, 1930), 414.

children ten to fifteen years of age engaged in gainful occupations as determined by the U.S. Bureau of the Census for the years 1880, 1900, and 1910 were as follows:

1880	1,118,356	16.8%
1900	1,750,178	18.2%
1910	1,990,225	18.4%[35]

A study of the health of children attending continuation school in New York City in 1924 showed that of the 412 boys and girls examined only eighteen were without some serious deficiency or impairment.[36] In mills in the South, boys of fifteen and nineteen had a death rate twice as high as those not employed in the cotton mills, and girls of the same age had rates that were even higher. From two to three times as many children as adults in proportion to the number employed were killed or injured in industry.[37]

Local child welfare campaigns eventually produced juvenile courts, recreational facilities, and compulsory school laws. Legislation to limit child labor provoked special controversy, but laws were enacted in almost every state outside the South prior to 1912. In the South, the main opposition came from the textile industry, which employed many children. Not until the 1930's was a national child labor law enacted.

FAMILY-FREE ADULT

Industrialization and urbanization were effective in providing opportunities quite early for older children and for women to secure a life relatively free from family ties. The way was now open for spinsters, widows, and orphaned children to know financial independence. As has already been pointed out, the change weakened the patriarchal family; in addition it paved the way for the emancipation of women and relieved men from the ancient burden of caring for unmarried female dependents. By the close of the nineteenth century, public opinion had changed from the belief that unattached women must be supported by their male relatives—fathers, brothers, or uncles—and had accepted the view that it was respectable if not obligatory for dependent women to support themselves.[38]

When industry was transferred from the family to the factory, both women and children followed the work to the factory. The movement of

[35] Raymond G. Fuller, *Child Labor and the Constitution* (New York: Thomas Y. Crowell, 1923), p. 2.

[36] New York Department of Labor, *The Health of the Working Child*, Special Bulletin No. 134 (Albany, 1924), p. 66.

[37] Fuller, *Child Labor and the Constitution, op. cit.*, pp. 102, 105.

[38] Willystine Goodsell, "The American Family in the Nineteenth Century," *The Annals of the American Academy of Political and Social Science*, CLX (March, 1932), 14.

women outside the homes soon came to include women of the middle classes who sometimes worked in factories, but who also became sales persons, typists, teachers, and nurses.

Legislative commissions collected facts, the most extensive being the voluminous report on the conditions of child and women wage earners which Congress authorized in 1907. These data showed low wages, long hours, and poor working conditions; the close relationship suggested between the low wages paid to women and prostitution particularly excited the public.

Dating and Mate Selection Among Italian-Americans

Traditionally among Italian peasants any interaction between the sexes after adolescence was assumed to be solely with a view to marriage.[39] Outside social activities were not favored and work contacts were restricted to a minimum. All relations between the sexes were to be under the supervision of parents or relatives, and no man should enter a girl's home unless serious in his intention to seek her hand in marriage or unless he had been accepted as her suitor. Physical contact was regarded as defiling and was taboo. Intimate acquaintance began with marriage or, perhaps, with betrothal.

The girl was treated pretty much as she would have been in a rural and small-town situation where marriage was a matter of families rather than of individuals, where the houses containing marriageable men were known, and the problem of each family was to negotiate a relationship as favorable as possible to the social and economic standing of the family. In the American city, the parents could not know who all the eligible young men were. Since each marriage meant a new household rather than the carrying on of an inherited farm, marriage came to be more an individual and less a family matter. It was difficult for the parents to find suitable husbands for their daughters, and, embued with a spirit of freedom, daughters more and more opposed the traditional mate-selection process. Furthermore, the prohibitions against girls going out, especially in the company of men, lasted beyond the time when parents could reasonably be expected to find a husband for their daughter. In the words of one girl, "Our parents think you can just sit home and wait for a man to come asking for your hand—like a small town in Italy. They don't realize that here a girl has got to get out and do something about it."[40]

Efforts were made to prevent contacts between men and girls, thereby making it most difficult for a girl to find a man. At the same time, she was expected to find a man, since her parents were not in a position to do so for her. She was expected to find a suitable mate, but she was not free to date potential eligibles in the process. In congested housing areas, one could

[39] The following draws again on the development by Ware, *op. cit.* (see above, fn. 18), pp. 180 ff.

[40] *Ibid.*, p. 182.

hardly help meeting people, however. The first step—allowing the daughter to go down and sit on the stoop in front of the house—did not offer much opening, but being allowed to go out for an evening stroll with another girl did. Nearly everybody had a ready fund of stories of ways in which they had defied their parents, and the tales of how girls got their husbands were well stocked with episodes involving deception. Neither their cultural heritage nor their parents were prepared to show them how relations between young men and young women could be enhanced through the "new" principles of love and romance. The children had dropped the idea that marriage involved a union of families and that love was a secondary consideration; but love and the idealization of the person had no place in a peasant tradition of almost total subordination of the individual to the group. The city was the setting *par excellence* for personal contacts, but the immigrants who settled the cities represented familistic, not individualistic, ways of life. This situation was a major source of parent-child conflict and family disorganization.

Home played a much smaller part in the activities of the son than of the daughter of immigrant parents. Whyte found, as a participant observer in a slum district of an eastern city inhabited almost exclusively by Italian immigrant families, that except when he ate, slept, or was sick, the boy was rarely at home, and his friends always went to his corner first when they wanted to find him.[41] Even the corner boy's name indicated the dominant importance of the gang in his activities. It was possible to associate with a group of men for months and never discover the family names of more than a few of them. Most were known by nicknames attached to them by the group. The corner boy could be found on his corner almost every night of the week.

The corner boy knew that if he visited a girl in her home it would be assumed by her parents (and by everyone else) that he intended to marry her. Consequently, until he was sure of his own intention, the corner boy remained outside of the house. He even hesitated to make a date with a girl, for if he did take her out alone it was assumed that he was her "steady." When he centered his attention upon one girl, he arranged to meet her on the street corner. Good girls were not expected to "hang" on the corner, but the men considered it perfectly respectable to keep appointments on the corner.

The sex life of the corner boy began when he was very young. One of them wrote:

> In Cornerville children ten years of age know most all the swear words and they have a good idea of what the word 'lay' means. Swearing and describing sex relations by older people and by the boys that hang on the corner are overheard by little children and their actions are noticed and remembered.

[41] This section follows the analysis in Whyte, *Street Corner Society: The Social Structure of an Italian Slum, op. cit.* (see above, fn. 22).

Many of the children when they are playing in the streets, doorways, and cellars actually go through the motions which pertain to the word 'lay.' I have seen them going through these motions even children under ten years of age.

Most all the boys that I know and all my friends carry safes (condoms). Most boys start carrying safes when they are of high school age.

Safes are purchased from necktie salesmen as cheap as a dozen for fifty cents. Some boys buy them and then make a profit by selling them to the boys at school. You can get them in some of the stores around here.[42]

The sex play of young boys was relatively unregulated. The code of sex behavior crystallized only as the corner boys reached maturity.

The corner boy code strongly prohibited intercourse with a virgin. Thus the most desirable of women was also the most inaccessible. A good girl could submit to a limited amount of kisses and caresses without compromising her reputation.

Relations between corner boys and women cannot be described in uniform terms since there were variations in behavior, depending upon the category in which the woman was placed and the man's qualifications for access to women of various categories. The local classifications of women which were explicit or implicit in corner boy attitudes and behavior can be represented in the three categories shown in the following tabulation. The most highly valued type of woman was placed at the top of each category.

Sex Experience	Physical Attractiveness	Social-and-Ethnic Group Position
1. "Good girls"	Beautiful	1. Superior groups
2. "Lays"	to	2. Italian nonslum
a. One-man girls	ugly	3. Italian slum[43]
b. Promiscuous		
c. Prostitutes		

An additional factor making for change in boy-girl behavior, other than those brought about by the urban milieu, was the rapid means of transportation—the streetcar and, especially, the automobile. The change in sex behavior of young people in the years when the automobile came into vogue caused great concern on the part of parents and other guardians of traditional moral standards. Cars could carry young people to secluded lovers' lanes or to anonymity in hotels or tourists' cabins. As Frederick Lewis Allen wrote, "One of the cornerstones of American morality had been the difficulty of finding a suitable place of misconduct; now the cornerstone was crumbling."[44] The automobile was a veritable living room on wheels. In their review of the records of the juvenile court in Middletown, the Lynds reported that over half of the girls charged with sex crimes in 1924 had

[42] *Ibid.,* p. 25.
[43] *Ibid.*
[44] Frederick Lewis Allen, *The Big Change* (New York, Harper, 1952), p. 123.

committed the offense in an automobile.[45] In a sample of forty-one females who had experienced premarital sexual intercourse, Kinsey and associates found that only 18 percent of those born before 1900 had had such experiences in an automobile, 38 percent of those born between 1900 and 1909, and 44 percent of those born between 1910 and 1919.[46]

MARRIAGE AND DIVORCE

As the influence of the extended family declined, individual members were no longer as concerned with the interests of the group as a whole when they contemplated marriage, but were increasingly concerned with their own individual benefit or loss, liking or disliking. The break of the conjugal relation brought little if any harm to the social prestige or economic security of the relatives, so there was less that prevented the parents, cousins, or even friends from stirring up trouble in the marriage group if they desired. Motives were easily found and if either of a young couple was amenable to such influences, the break was often produced. Close relatives were particularly dangerous in the early period of married life; interference became less effective later as husband and wife were estranged from their respective families—a natural result of the American conditions—so that even such imperfect community of economic and progeny interests as might be established between the married pair in the heterogenous American city was sufficient to counterbalance external interference if there were no other special factors leading to a break.

An entirely new element was introduced into the conjugal life of the immigrant by the interference of the state, which from his standpoint included not only court and police action but also the activities of private or half-private American institutions, because he could seldom distinguish a purely social institution from one maintained by the state, particularly as the former did or could, or at least was thought to be able to, make use of courts and police. After a careful study of many hundreds of cases, Thomas and Znaniecki were of the opinion that in not a single instance did official interference strengthen the conjugal bond. In a great majority of cases, the immediate additional strain put on the marriage bond by actual or threatened state interference was apparent.

The parish was the core institution in attempting to maintain group characteristics among the southern and eastern European immigrants.[47] The prohibition on marriage outside the group was maintained by most groups

---

[45] Lynd and Lynd, *op. cit.* (see above, fn. 4), p. 258.

[46] A. C. Kinsey, W. B. Pomeroy, C. E. Martin, and P. G. Gebhard, *Sexual Behavior in the Human Female* (Philadelphia: Saunders, 1953), p. 336.

[47] Thomas and Znaniecki, *op. cit.* (see above, fn. 19), p. 1523; John L. Thomas, *The American Catholic Family* (Englewood Cliffs, N.J.: Prentice-Hall, 1956), p. 149 ff.

attached to these parishes. This prohibition was reinforced by the Catholic church's attitude toward interfaith marriage.

American churches joined the national parishes of the Roman Catholic church in its attempt to sustain ingroup marriages, intrafaith marriages, and stable marriage in general during the critical period of the new immigration and rapid urbanization. Tendencies on the part of the church to put restrictions on the entrance to matrimony were also in part due to the rise of the divorce question and the resultant investigations of marriage. The churches had all along had their doctrines of divorce, but these assumed new importance with the increase in divorce. The Protestant churches' efforts to cope with the problem consisted largely of official warnings and of exhortations to the clergy to preach against it and to refuse to celebrate marriages not consonant with customs and beliefs prevalent in the church. At the General Council of the Evangelical Lutheran Church in 1899, the president deplored the frivolity with which marriage, divorce, and remarriage were treated; he also deplored the contradictory laws of various states. He advised a petition to Congress in behalf of uniform marriage and divorce laws for the whole country.

SUMMARY: RETROSPECT AND PROSPECT

As Michael Chevalier said in 1834, "No people can count itself in the first rank of nations if it is not advanced in the course of industrialization."[48] No supply of free land, however great, would, by itself, have raised the American standard of living very far. The base for American abundance was supplied by the bounty of nature, but abundance has also been socially created by an advanced technology and industrial organization.

The United States has so improved the technology of food production alone that, while in 1820 over 70 percent of the working population were needed in agriculture in order to feed the rest, in 1960 the less than 8 percent of the working population engaged in agriculture feed themselves and the remaining 92 percent of the population as well. If the proportions of 1820 still prevailed, almost forty-eight million of the labor force would be required in agriculture, rather than the fewer than five million presently so engaged. When technology enabled 8 percent of the labor force to produce food for the entire population and more, it freed the rest of the labor force to engage in business and industry, creating other goods and services which add to a high standard of living. The wealth in goods and services is awesome, reaching a level that a few decades ago would have been regarded as impossible.

In 1910, there were about eight million more people in the rural than in the urban areas of the United States, but by 1920 urban population out-

48 Chevalier, *op. cit.* (see above, fn. 10), p. 14.

numbered the rural population by over three million. Today, almost two-thirds of the population live in or near large metropolitan complexes. Furthermore, the third of the population remaining in rural areas are less isolated than they were. Thus the number living in towns has almost tripled in the past fifty years, but the number on farms is declining rapidly.

FIGURE 5.1. PEOPLE ARE LEAVING THE FARMS

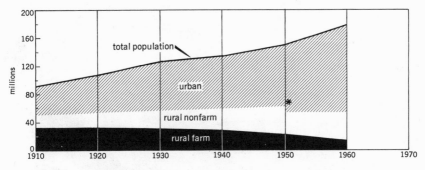

*difference due to new urban and rural definition adopted for use in 1950 census

SOURCE: U.S. Bureau of the Census, *U.S. Census of Population: 1960, Number of Inhabitants, U.S. Summary.*

Americans have always been a mobile people, but today they are moving faster and farther than ever before. Mobility varies by state and by region. In Pennsylvania at the time of the last census (1960), twelve percent of the residents had been born in some other state. State and regional variation in mobility is shown in Figure 5.2.

While the economic system was producing great wealth, it was also producing great inequalities in family income during the period of urban-industrial emergence, including some colossal private fortunes. By the time of the stock-market crash in 1929, over 600,000 families were receiving incomes of ten thousand or more dollars a year. The total income of the sixteen million poorest families, on the other hand, including most of the immigrant families, was substantially smaller than was the total income of the six hundred thousand richest families. At this time, 15 percent of the working population belonged to the business and professional classes, 69 percent were wage earners in industry and other enterprises, and the remaining 16 percent were farmers.

How a family fared in the burgeoning urban-industrial cities was markedly influenced by how the family and particularly the major breadwinner fared in the economic system. In this chapter we have stressed the plight

FIGURE 5.2.   TWENTY-SIX PERCENT OF THE PEOPLE NO LONGER LIVE
IN THE STATE WHERE THEY WERE BORN

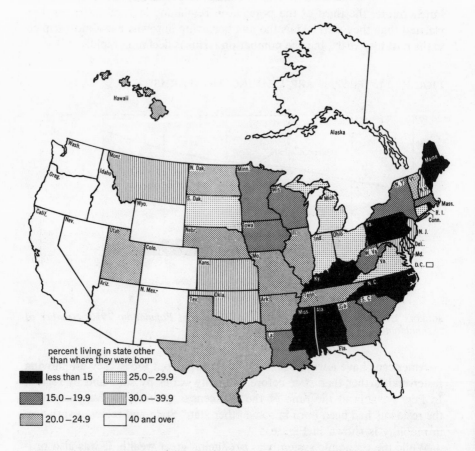

percent living in state other
than where they were born

■ less than 15		▦ 25.0−29.9	
▨ 15.0−19.9		▥ 30.0−39.9	
░ 20.0−24.9		☐ 40 and over	

SOURCE: U.S. Bureau of the Census, *U.S. Census of Population: 1960, State of Birth.*

of the newly arrived families, especially those coming from foreign lands.
Are conditions any different in the center of the city today? Robert S. Allen
notes that the various cities have developed impressive facades—parkways,
boulevards, civic centers, schools, etc.—but that beneath the surface there
are the same slums, vice, disease, graft, and disregard of public health that
were present when the muckrakers made their exposés. It is abundantly
clear that the central cities still contain much of the blight accumulated
beginning with the industrial revolution.

America has been in the process of building cities almost from the time
of its establishment as a nation, and at the present time wherever there is
growth of population, it seems to take place in the city. The hope in early

urbanization was that the movement to the city would result in comfort, opportunity, and glamour; but in some ways the city became the acme of discomfort—congested, dirty, noisy, dark, and gloomy—as every unplanned American city created its slum area. The total population of the five largest cities grew from 7.6 million in 1900 to 17.3 million in 1960. One out of every ten United States citizens lives in these five cities. Today, the greatest part of population growth continues to be in the metropolitan agglomerations.

New York City is a case in point; the enormity of its problem can be suggested by the loss of a middle-class white population of some 750,000 in a seven-year period and the attendant gain of some 650,000 low-income black and Puerto Rican populations in the central city. This shift of population has led to the expansion of the slums and to overcrowding in such housing as could be obtained by the new residents. Though almost 600,000 people are housed in public housing erected largely since World War I, and in spite of the accelerated growth of private housing with or without government subsidy, there are still an estimated 6,000 or 8,000 acres of slums in existence in the city. In addition, city planners point to the "gray ring" of vulnerable housing which surrounds the slums. These houses, built as private residences, are now over fifty years old and unlikely to withstand the rigors of the population "pile up."[49]

Thousands of families are being displaced by site-clearance programs in urban renewal projects in the large cities; the Urban League of Chicago reported that in the period from 1948–56 alone, approximately 86,000 persons were displaced by various urban-renewal projects. When news comes that an area of a city is going to be rebuilt, those who can do so start moving, creating loss of morale in the neighborhood. This means that marginal groups in New York City most frequently Puerto Ricans, move into the vacated houses; the area around one settlement house became forty-five percent Puerto Rican "almost overnight."[50]

The shift in population composition further demoralizes the neighborhood and makes it almost incapable of collective action. The new residents of the area are without roots in the institutional life of the area. They know that they will have to move out, and the landlords are reluctant to improve property that will soon be taken from them.

When the eviction notices are posted, panic tends to result. The slum landlords prepare for this day by cutting up apartments adjacent to the area to be evacuated and preparing them for rent increases. The bulldozer approach to urban renewal has come under attack as being callous to human values and stifling to the creativity of the human spirit. People without

49 Dan W. Dodson, "Family and Agency Equity in Urban Renewal," *Journal of Educational Sociology*, XXXIV (December, 1960), 182.
50 *Ibid.*, p. 200.

power fight impersonal and financially powerful organizations in order to preserve for themselves some modicum of continuity in living.

The suburbs of the larger cities have their own problems, but they also create problems for the central city. The movement of people to the suburbs has brought a new crisis to America's big cities. Older settlements are hemmed in by rapidly growing suburbs, and the city is forced to maintain essential services at increasing costs for its population while many affluent citizens work in the city but live and pay taxes in a suburb. The suburbs, on the other hand, contain a high socio-economic status group which maintains a more stable family structure.

What a President's commission said in 1960 in regard to living conditions could as appropriately have been said in 1900, namely that slum conditions must be remedied, that the process of decay in the larger cities must be reversed, and that the necessity for low-income and minority groups to concentrate there must be relieved. The President's commission went on to say that solutions should be sought for haphazard suburban growth and that an equitable sharing of the cost of public services between central cities and suburbs should be provided. In many parts of the country, said the commission, the goal should be a regional pattern providing for a number of urban centers, each with its own industries, its own educational, cultural and recreational institutions, and a "balanced" population of various income levels and backgrounds. They also pointed to the needs of a growing population for parks and recreation, needs which must be met.[51]

In the following sections of the book we turn from the historical toward the contemporary American family. As we have tried to show, however, the American family, while engaging in interchanges with persons and with other systems in contemporary society, is not unmarked by its history. In Part II we have pointed out what some of the historical influences have been on the family as it survived and as it adapted to (1) restrictive, oligarchic, moralistic Puritanism, (2) the birth of a nation espousing a heady ideology of freedom and democracy, (3) the humility of chattel status and racism which affected the culture and socio-sexual systems of the black minority and the white majority in American society, and (4) the urban-industrial city with its wealth, glamour, and slums.

BIBLIOGRAPHY

Robert S. Allen. *Our Fair City*. New York: Vanguard, 1947.

Nels Anderson. "Bedroom Towns," *The Survey,* LIX (October 15, 1927), 93–94.

Bernard Berelson, *et al.* (eds.). *Family Planning and Population Programs.* Chicago: University of Chicago, 1966.

[51] President's Commission on National Goals, *Goals for Americans* (Englewood Cliffs, N.J.: Prentice-Hall, 1960), p. 13.

Ernest W. Burgess. "The Family in a Changing Society," *American Journal of Sociology*, LIII (May, 1948), 417–422.
Arthur W. Calhoun. *A Social History of the American Family, III: From 1865 to 1919.* New York: Barnes and Noble, 1919; 1945.
Paul J. Campisi. "Ethnic Family Patterns: The Italian Family in the United States," *American Journal of Sociology*, LIII (May, 1948), 443–449.
Michael Chevalier. *Society, Manners, and Politics in the United States*, ed. John William Ward. Garden City, N.Y.: Doubleday, 1961; first published in France in 1934.
Frank B. Copley. *Frederick Winslow Taylor.* New York: Harper's, 1923.
Dan W. Dodson. "Family and Agency Equity in Urban Renewal," *Journal of Educational Sociology*, XXXIV (December, 1960), 182–189.
Solomon Good. " 'Boom Babies' Come of Age: The American Family at the Cross Roads," *Population Bulletin*, XXII (August, 1966), 61–79.
H. Theodore Groat and Arthur G. Neal. "Social Psychological Correlates of Urban Fertility," *American Sociological Review*, XXXII (December, 1967), 945–959.
Philip M. Hauser and Leo F. Schnore (eds.). *The Study of Urbanization.* New York: Wiley, 1965.
Samuel P. Hays. *The Response to Industrialism, 1885–1914.* Chicago: University of Chicago, 1957.
Edward P. Hutchinson. *Immigrants and Their Children, 1850–1950.* New York: Wiley, 1956.
Paul Lerman. "Individual Values, Peer Values, and Sub-Cultural Delinquency," *American Sociological Review*, XXXIII (April, 1968), 219–235.
Robert S. Lynd and Helen Merrell Lynd. *Middletown: A Study in Modern American Culture.* New York: Harcourt, 1929.
Floyd M. Martinson. "Personal Adjustment and Rural-Urban Migration," *Rural Sociology*, XX (June, 1955), 102–110.
Lewis Mumford. *The Culture of Cities.* New York: Harcourt, 1938.
A. J. Muste. "The Tug of Industry," *The Survey*, LIX (December 1, 1927), 281–285, 343–344.
Henry Bamford Parkes. *The American Experience: An Interpretation of the History and Civilization of the American People.* New York: Knopf, 1947.
David M. Potter. *People of Plenty: Economic Abundance and the American Character.* Chicago: University of Chicago, 1954.
Mark Perlman (ed.). *Human Resources in the Urban Economy.* Baltimore: Johns Hopkins, 1963.
Arnold M. Rose. "Interest in the Living Arrangements of the Urban Unattached," *American Journal of Sociology*, LII (May, 1948), 483–493.
Leo F. Schnore. *The Urban Scene: Human Ecology and Demography.* New York: Free Press, 1965.
Karl E. Taeuber and Alma F. Taeuber. *Negroes in Cities.* Chicago: Aldine, 1965.
John L. Thomas. *The American Catholic Family.* Englewood Cliffs, N.J.: Prentice-Hall, 1956.
W. I. Thomas and Florian Znaniecki. *The Polish Peasant in Europe and America.* New York: Dover, 1958.
William F. Whyte. *Street Corner Society: The Social Structure of an Italian Slum.* Chicago: University of Chicago, 1943.

PART III

The Nuclear Family

LIKE ALL SYSTEMS operating in a community, the nuclear family must overcome two problems. First, it must adapt to other systems in the community—kin, market, government, school. Secondly, it must integrate its internal activities.

We might illustrate the "outside" aspects of family life by imagining the times in which members of a family in an urban setting are dispersed outside the home. The father goes to work to secure provisions or to secure money to exchange for provisions; the mother also goes to work, or shops, or attends to other family and community matters; the children go to school or go out to play. While the members of the family are about their tasks—working, shopping, playing, or studying—their concentration is on the task at hand and emotional feelings toward each other are largely set aside or inhibited.

Of course, if family members did not ever again reassemble, the family would cease to exist. But family members do reassemble at the end of the day, and attention then shifts from the tasks that occupied attention outside the home to the "inside" aspects of family life. Behavior changes. In a well-ordered home there may be "laughing, playing, release of inhibited emotions, the expression of affection for each other, a warmth and a symbolization of common membership through supportive, accepting behavior."[1] The family cannot continue in this latter state indefinitely either. Again with a new day its members must disperse to carry on the outside activities that the household members may be fed, clothed, and educated.

In overcoming these problems of adaptation and integration, the nuclear family would appear to be badly handicapped organizationally when compared with other small groups. First of all, the members of the family, unlike the members of most other functioning groups, differ markedly in age, with dependents weighing heavily in the composition of the family. Unlike other groups, the family cannot freely reject any of its members or recruit more competent ones; tradition and values forbid such free interchange. The members are also involved with each other emotionally; this affects the efficiency of the group.

[1] Talcott Parsons and Robert F. Bales, *Family, Socialization and Interaction* (Glencoe, Ill.: Free Press, 1955), pp. 310–311.

The family also suffers in comparison with other groups when it comes to specificity of operation. The family carries on a great variety of activities, and its activities are characterized by diffuseness rather than specificity. It does not specialize in one or a small number of activities as do most other functioning groups, such as a children's play group, or a planning committee. In the mother-child relationship, for instance, the mother reacts to all behavior of the child and even anticipates his needs—her concern is all-inclusive. She is cook, waitress, nurse, protector, and giver and receiver of affection. The relationships in the family are characterized by emotional or affective behavior, and the relationships themselves, rather than impersonal goals, determine what is done.

Members of the leadership coalition (mother and father) do not think of the family in terms of specific functions—as a consumption unit or a child-training unit, for instance. The family is different from other groups in that there is variety in its activities as well as in the roles that its members play.

The family is also at a disadvantage in comparison with other groups because its success or failure is largely tied in with the activities of only one of its members, the major breadwinner. If the major breadwinner loses his job, the family is in jeopardy. In sum, the family, when compared with other groups, is intrinsically "a puny work group and an awkward decision-making group."[2]

If the family is viewed as a functioning system, for whom does it function? It carries on activities that are functional for its members, for other persons, and for the society as a whole. It performs such general functions as supplying or replacing members for the society (the birth function), preparing children to take their place in society (socialization), and maintaining and motivating both parents and children for participation in society. Each individual family impinges only slightly upon the larger society. It is through the impact of millions of families, each organized in much the same way and carrying on similar activities, that we can speak of the family as performing functions for the society.

[2] Reuben Hill, "Social Stresses on the Family: Generic Features of Family Under Stress," *Social Casework,* XXXIX (February–March, 1958), 139–140.

CHAPTER 6

Family Organization and Activities

CERTAIN ACTIVITIES are carried on within the nuclear family in consequence of its participation in interchanges with other social systems. Certain other of the family's activities are carried on for the family's own benefit or for the benefit of its members. What the family receives from interchange with other systems affects its internal activity; what the family supplies to other systems affects their activity. For example, in interchange with the economic system, the family supplies socialized and disciplined laborers; the economy in exchange supplies wages to purchase goods and services utilized by the family.

A productive economy abundantly cares for the material needs of the majority of American families. In 1960 the median number of persons per dwelling unit was 3.0; the median number of rooms in the dwelling unit was 4.9, or better than an average of one and one half rooms per family member.[1] The striking difference between housing in the United States and housing in many other parts of the world reflects the affluence of American society. In contrast to the many societies in which people keep their bodies warm primarily by the wearing of clothing, Americans keep their bodies warm by the expensive method of heating the dwellings in which they live. The same abundance characterizes the American food supply. Food takes the largest part of the family budget next to shelter. Recent computations show the average American consuming 3,200 calories daily. People in northwestern Europe, on the other hand, consume an estimated 2,000 to 3,000 calories, while in many parts of the world daily consumption drops well below 2,000 calories per day.

Despite the general affluence, there is "an unseen America, a land of limited opportunity and restricted choice."[2] There are nearly ten million American families—forty-five million people—who try to provide for their basic needs on less than forty dollars a week. These deprived families include families of workers displaced by technological change, rural families,

---

[1] U.S. Bureau of the Census, *Statistical Abstract of the United States: 1963* (Washington, D.C.: 1963), p. 762.
[2] *The War on Poverty: The Economic Opportunity Act of 1964* (Washington, D.C.: United States Government Printing Office, 1964).

fatherless families, the aged poor, and the families of persons with less than an eighth-grade education. About one-half of the black and Indian families in the United States have incomes below the so-called poverty line—three thousand dollars—as do about a third of the Puerto Rican and Mexican families. Less than one-fifth of the white families fall in the poverty category.[3] In total as many as one-fifth of the nearly fifty million families in the United States have incomes of less than three thousand dollars. The hardest hit by poverty are the nonwhite fatherless families; their median annual income is under two thousand dollars, and the average size of these families is nearly three children per family.

DIFFERENTIATION OF ROLES IN THE FAMILY

To be of maximum service to itself, to its own members, and to society, the family must be a relatively orderly system. Role differentiation is necessary to the performance of tasks even in systems with small membership. What activities are to be carried on in the home? Who is to be responsible for them? How are members of the family to be motivated to cooperate with each other and to do their part? We have referred to the family as a "puny work group and an awkward decision-making group." Be that as it may, it still *is* a working and a decision-making unit.

Systems which endure over a period of time are characterized by the fact that roles within the system become differentiated from each other. When roles are differentiated, acts of certain kinds are expected of certain persons at certain times, while acts of other kinds are expected of other persons at other times. A major part of the way of life of any family that lasts over a period of years is made up of expectations specifying how each member of the family should behave. These expectations become fixed and apply over extended periods of time.

Father and mother in a nuclear family tend to constitute a leadership coalition, but they also enact roles differentiated from each other. Since there is variety in the activities engaged in by the family, variety in the competencies of the members is called for. The two basic problems of the family system—adapting to other social systems and integrating inside activities—call for different kinds of leadership. The family must allocate roles to its members in such a way that both its outside and inside responsibilities are met. The outside activities in large measure determine how the family survives in the community; the inside activities are concerned with integrating the group behavior that arises out of the external system and reacts upon it.

---

[3] Catherine Chilman and Marvin B. Sussman, "Poverty in the United States in the Mid-Sixties," *Journal of Marriage and the Family*, XXVI (November, 1964), 391–392.

How Roles are Allocated Within the Family

The age of some of the family members—infants and young children—precludes their sharing equal responsibility with the adult members of the family. Only if the family setting is such that a large amount of unskilled labor is called for can young children take an active part in major family activities.

The function of bearing and giving early care to children establishes a strong presumptive primacy for the mother as integrative-emotional leader in the family. She becomes the focus of gratification as the source of security and comfort not only for the newborn but for all members of the family. One of the internal activities of the family is the disposing of negative feelings which to some degree are inevitably generated in family living. For instance, if the husband-father, the person who symbolizes the demands of the major tasks outside the home, presses for changes in the goals of the family or in the ways of achieving its goals, he becomes a deviant in the family. If he accepts a new job, for instance, changes occur in the way of life of the family; and in suggesting change, he may incur hostility from other family members. Centering positive feelings on one adult, presumably the mother, who in turn supports the father as the task specialist, is one possible way of easing the tension created by change. The mother becomes "a kind of symbolic transmuter of negative affect into positive affect." Her support of her husband becomes a critical condition of the stability of the family.[4] If the family is to maintain itself through the efforts of at least one of its members in the occupational world, reason must be used, emotions must be suppressed, and decisions must be made even at the expense of some hostile reactions from other members of the family.

Norms Supporting Traditional Family Roles

Married women in America continue to expend the greater share of their energy in the home. Traditionally, the father is regarded as the head of the family, its main economic support, and its representative in the community. These are widely accepted cultural patterns despite the social and economic ferment that has characterized relations between the sexes in America and despite the fact that before the law women have achieved near equality with men, may seek gainful employment, may retain their earnings, and may have equal rights with men to education.

American family norms continue to affirm that the American male should take responsibility for the support of his wife and children. He is expected to give his major performance in his occupational role; his primary function in the family is to supply an income.

[4] Talcott Parsons and Robert F. Bales, *Family Socialization and Interaction Process* (Glencoe, Ill.: Free Press, 1955), *passim*.

Task Performance in the Home

The American family is essentially a consumption unit. The fact that the basic necessities of life are met with relative ease for the majority of families has to be a factor in assaying life inside the contemporary American family.

Since the family is no longer a major production unit, the processing of raw materials into useable goods has passed out of the home. Food as well as other material goods are purchased rather than home-produced. This is strikingly apparent particularly for urban homes, as shown in the accompanying table.

TABLE 6.1. SUBSISTENCE PRODUCTION IN CITY AND FARM FAMILIES
IN THE DETROIT AREA

*Families Producing "Most" or "All" of Each Item**	*Place of Residence*	
	City	*Farm*
Baked goods	55%	79%
Canned, frozen foods	7	74
Summer vegetables	9	87
Dresses	7	15
Number of families	(731)	(178)

* Reciprocal percentages of families produce half or less of the same item: e.g., the remaining 45 percent of city families bake half or less of their cakes, cookies, and pies.

SOURCE: Robert O. Blood, Jr., and Donald M. Wolfe, *Husbands and Wives: The Dynamics of Married Living* (Glencoe, Ill.: The Free Press, 1960), p. 82.

If there is financial need, women in urban families seek employment outside of the home to bring in income rather than reducing the financial drain through home production. Going to work outside the home increases purchasing power while at the same time lessening the time available for home production. For the urban wife, home production has become an optional rather than a necessary activity. If home production is valued, it is valued not primarily because of the money saved, but out of a desire to be personally creative or to provide superior cuisine for the family or guests. Home production becomes a creative art or recreation rather than filling a primarily economic need. The way for the wife to achieve a high level of living for her family is not to produce consumer goods, but to participate in the labor force and to earn a salary.

Socialization in Family Tasks

The pattern of task performance in the American family is one of fairly marked differentiation. Husbands and wives complement rather than duplicate each other's tasks. The division of labor in the modern family tends to coincide with the division of labor in the traditional family. Most fathers do the lawn-mowing, snow-shoveling, and repairing, while mothers do the dishes, housecleaning, and cooking. The family makes a definite allocation of tasks.

Seeley and his colleagues found that even in affluent families the man was at least ritually responsible for tasks regarded as requiring physical strength —gardening, putting on storm windows, and so on. In practice, however, these duties were often delegated to commercial firms. Success in a career sets up something of a vicious circle for the father. As he spends more time away from his family, he has to buy more services to replace the work he once did himself. In buying these services, he also needs more income. To make more money, he must spend even more time away from home.[5]

Household duties are commonly associated with the role of the mother. Johannis, in a study of families in which half the working parents were in blue-collar or service occupations, found mother taking the child-care and control roles that they have traditionally taken—nursing, teaching right from wrong, seeing that the children get enough to eat, have fun, and get up in time for school. Participation by other members of the family was low in these traditional areas. Where the father did help it was frequently in activities for which fathers have probably assumed considerable responsibility in the past—teaching right and wrong, imparting knowledge, teaching skills, helping the child choose a vocation, and taking care of matters of discipline.[6]

In addition, women specialized as consumers—a necessary step, perhaps, because the world of the American consumer is one of profusion and variety. The woman became the central figure in family purchases. And although she may have been encapsulated and something of a household drudge before the "kitchen revolution," the application of technology to the kitchen and its activities has freed her from much drudgery. As both children and parents participate more and more outside the home, household activities are correspondingly lightened too. The mother who has many community responsibilities tends to select food which can be quickly and easily prepared, rather than painstakingly planning meals to build a reputation as an excellent cook. Despite the reduced volume of work within the home itself, however, Seeley and his colleagues found that there was an incredible increase in what had to be done if the home was to be a proper exhibit of status and thus an aid to the male career. The house cannot be decorated once and for all time, or the furniture be finally placed and remain there for the period of one's married life. Also, development in the domestic

[5] John R. Seeley, R. Alexander Sim, and Elizabeth W. Loosley, *Crestwood Heights: A Study of the Culture of Suburban Life* (New York: Basic Books, 1956), p. 190.

[6] Theodore B. Johannis, Jr., "Participation by Fathers, Mothers and Teenage Sons and Daughters in Selected Child Care and Control Activity," *The Family Life Coordinator,* December 6, 1957, pp. 31–32.

arts has shown signs of a general humanizing trend that expresses convenience in the home while at the same time leaving room for changing interests and experiences that provoke new tastes.[7]

Specialization has led in the direction of the professionalization of the mother's functions. She no longer learns all her tasks from her mother's teaching and example. Housekeeping and child-care functions are rationalized. Intuitive processes give way to formal rules and special technical knowledge. Women's functions are seen as susceptible to greater finesse in their accomplishment, as the very instruments used are subjected to critical appraisal and functional selection. In the words of Miller and Swanson, "The women's magazines provide a kind of in-service training, supplemented with the post-graduate work of the mothers' study clubs, the meetings with the specialists at the nursery schools, the cooking classes, and the growing number of handbooks for preparing unfamiliar or exotic foods."[8] Specialization or professionalization of role starts with the elementary matters of child feeding and physical care. Attempts are made to rationalize aspects of child care with the help and encouragement of child-care experts.

The application of applied science to aspects of the intimate life of personalities (as in the mother's care of her children and in the marriage relationship) is especially crucial for women since women have specialized in the expressive tasks. In specializing in the expressive tasks, the American woman does not necessarily sacrifice the rationality so highly prized in our society, for she is heavily involved in the attempt to rationalize her role in relation to her husband and to her children. She is consciously aware of her love for her spouse and her children, but beyond loving she attempts to understand rationally the nature, conditions, and limitations of love and the ways in which its deviant forms might injure rather than benefit her loved ones.

Wife's Supportive Role and Multiplicity of Roles

In marriage the wife is supportive of the husband's tasks. This is particularly true of the woman who "has her wagon hitched to a fast-rising star." In this case the husband is typically a professional man or a corporation executive whose career line is relatively clear and promising. The wife in this case plays her role by being sympathetic and not too demanding. She is not herself economically productive either through working outside the home or producing goods at home. She pays close attention to her own grooming and behavior and to the decor of the home, entertains her husband's clients on occasion, and perhaps gives advice. Her role is differentiated from the husband's but supportive of it. He carries an instrumental

---

[7] Daniel R. Miller and Guy E. Swanson, *The Changing American Parent* (New York: Wiley, 1958), p. 201.

[8] *Ibid.*

role—that is, he is responsible for the family's standard of living and sets the pace in upward mobility. Ideally, he has the interest, moral support, and appreciation of his wife.[9]

Caught up with the American premium placed on equality and self-fulfillment, it is not surprising to find that wives of successful men resent being regarded as merely supportive of husband and children, or as decorative or useful adjuncts to their husbands' careers. As a mother, a woman is expected to provide an atmosphere of warmth, security, and unconditional love for her children. But her education and premarital life experiences usually do not prepare her particularly well for this role. Furthermore, it is expected that a woman in an advantaged family will carry on extra-familial activities that are socially useful though unpaid. This may account for the considerable amount of participation in clubs and charitable associations and in philanthropic activities; no woman could become outstanding simply by being a brilliant hostess or by being selected as one of the ten best-dressed women of the city.

Nondifferentiated Family Tasks

Not all family tasks are clearly differentiated between the two major performers, the father and the mother. As practiced by the middle class, democratic family norms dictate the cooperative spending of the family income although an air of secrecy often surrounds the actual amount of that income. Johannis found that though fathers played a more active part in purchases of items which required a relatively large expenditure at one time (automobiles, furniture, large appliances), these large purchases were shared by mothers and fathers. Sons and daughters were more apt to participate in purchases for their own use, clothing and food, than in larger purchases. In many of the families in which activities were shared, the sharing was between fathers and mothers rather than between parents and their teenage offspring. More mothers than fathers, more fathers than teenage daughters, and more teenage daughters than teenage sons participated in child-care and control.

Despite the kind of role differentiation outlined above, Americans maintain a somewhat flexible pattern both within and outside the home. Fathers may set the table, help with the dishes, and make formula for the baby; mothers may supplement the family income by working outside the family. Paying the bills and shopping for groceries are neither exclusively husband's nor wife's jobs in many families, though they tend to be done more by wives. Keeping track of the money and the bills also lacks a generally accepted pattern of allocation. Among the shared activities, Johannis found that grocery shopping was a shared activity in over half the families in his sample.

9 Robert O. Blood, Jr., and Donald M. Wolfe, *Husbands and Wives: The Dynamics of Married Living* (Glencoe, Ill.: The Free Press, 1960), pp. 95–97.

Both fathers and children "pitch in" to help the mother, particularly in emergencies. Sometimes the emergencies are prolonged; with the woman's growing activity outside the home, the husband is much more deeply involved in routine household tasks and child care than he was in earlier times. To be able to help at home, a man must be at home; but more than time is needed. Blood and Wolfe found that for most husbands, a wife's shortage of time was enough to get them to respond with help; but some husbands failed to respond despite clear evidence of need. Many of these husbands appeared to have no excuse for not helping out and wives resented their inertia correspondingly. Unresponsive husbands were concentrated primarily in working-class nonwhite communities.

Blood and Wolfe point out that two-income families are not necessarily more companionable than one-income families in their division of labor. They share the breadwinning responsibility, and they also share the feminine tasks; but they do not share the masculine tasks as much as do single-income families.

Changing Family Tasks and the Family Cycle

Specialization of tasks with the family varies with the family cycle. The honeymoon period, a period of role experimentation, involves more sharing of tasks than any later period. For most couples, the wife retires from work outside the home during the child-bearing and child-tending period. On the other hand, as the child-tending period comes to an end, role differentiation between husband and wife increases at an accelerated pace, reaching its peak either when the wife has trained children to help her with her tasks or when the husband, now retired, has unlimited time to perform his own tasks.[10]

The wife-mother role therefore goes through two marked phases before ending in a more indeterminate one. If first pregnancy is postponed she may at first work along with her husband, helping to get the new household off to a good start financially. With the coming of children her role shifts dramatically to that of housewife and mother. As children grow in independence and are launched from the home she acquires several options. She may continue to attempt to make a career of homemaking while enjoying increased leisure, she may return to work outside the home, or she may concentrate on social life and volunteer activities in church, club, and community.

In a sense men suffer even more in the realignment of roles with increasing age than do women. As long as a wife keeps house she does not experience the trauma of sudden transition from daily work to enforced idleness so characteristic of retirement for men.

[10] Blood and Wolfe, *op. cit.* (see above, fn. 9), p. 71.

FAMILY LEADERSHIP: POWER AND AUTHORITY

A condition of family stability is the maintenance of order. Certain members of the family are granted more power than are other members; power carries responsibility and authority in family activities.

Maintaining the motivational level of family members is important and the wise authority figure makes efforts to handle power in such a judicious way that the motivation of family members is not impaired. If the goal is to break the will of family members, then heavy-handed methods are in order; but in most societies, and particularly in democratic societies, autocratic methods of maintaining order are viewed with disapproval.

Parental Leadership Roles

If American families were ever patriarchal, they have moved a long way from it today. In the Detroit study the groups which would be expected to most closely resemble the patriarchal pattern—farm families, immigrant families, old couples, uneducated couples, and Catholic families—did not confirm expectations. Families on the whole were extraordinarily alike when it came to the balance of decision-making.[11]

In interviews with fifty upper middle-class families, Lynn reports that the men reject decisively the patriarchal, authoritarian father role. They neither owned it for themselves, nor would they tolerate the associate who would embrace this idea of headship for himself.[12]

This does not mean that there are no American families in which the husband makes the decisions. In fact, Straus found that during attempts to solve a laboratory task husbands tended to predominate in both instrumental and expressive roles, particularly in middle-class families.[13] But it does appear that where husbands do exercise authority today, it is not because they subscribe to a patriarchal belief system. Blood and Wolfe prefer the term "husband-dominant" since it does not imply the supporting sanctions implied in the term "patriarchate." They found that the more successful the husband in the eyes of the community, the more dominant his part in family decision-making. Generally speaking, the higher the husband's occupational prestige, the greater his voice in decisions in the home. The husband's earnings were an even more sensitive indicator of his power than

11 *Ibid.*, pp. 23–27.

12 Robert W. Lynn, "Fifty Church Families and Their Role Expectations." An unpublished paper presented to the Consultative Conference on Theology and Family, Atlantic City, October 17–20, 1957; as reported in Ray W. Fairchild and John Charles Wynn, *Families in the Church: A Protestant Survey* (New York: Association, 1961), p. 30.

13 Murray A. Straus, "The Influence of Sex of Child and Social Class on Instrumental and Expressive Roles in a Laboratory Setting," *Sociology and Social Research,* LII (October, 1967), 7–21.

was his occupation. His power was also directly related to his social status; the higher his social status, the greater his power. White husbands were more powerful than their nonwhite equals. This was true within each occupational stratum, each income bracket, and each social-status level. The largest percentage of nonwhite families were dominated by the wife.

Families living in Detroit suburbs were more husband-dominated than were those living in the city of Detroit. This observation calls into question the notion that the absence of the father from the suburban home during the day leads to a matricentric form of marriage. Also, the more education the husband has, the greater his power, while the more one partner's education exceeds that of the other, the larger that person's share in decision-making. Generally, the partner who belongs to more organizations also takes a more active part in family decisions. Blood and Wolfe found that husbands who attended church more regularly were also those with more power than were those who did not attend as regularly.

Whichever partner works more outside the home appears to gain power. The power to make decisions appears to stem primarily from the resources which the individual can provide to meet the needs of his family and to upgrade his decision-making skill.[14]

Seeley and his colleagues point out that the father's authority in the home is often present in latent form. The paternal role has symbolic significance and might become highly active in conditions of strain and uncertainty. The father's participation in family discipline in Crestwood Heights tended to the peripheral and variable, but his nonparticipation did not negate his potential authority, which existed even when it was not exercised. Seeley compares the father to the president who, it is well understood by all in the organization, sits over the general manager even though he delegates authority and responsibility. The day-to-day situation within the family might suggest a father-controlled matriarchy with the father's dominance being latent rather than manifest. Some family life experts point to such a wife-dependent authority pattern as important to good family organization.[15] Thus power and the division of labor are aspects of family life that can coexist in almost any combination.

Children and Family Authority Patterns

Children have attained a respected and sometimes feared position in the family authority pattern. Free discussion between parents and children has to a considerable extent replaced arbitrary decision-making. There is an emphasis on respect for the person coupled with the expectation of responsible behavior toward oneself and others for all members of the family.

[14] Blood and Wolfe, *op. cit.* (see above, fn. 9), p. 40.
[15] William A. Westley and Nathan E. Epstein, "Family Structure and Emotional Health: A Case Study Approach," *Marriage and Family Living,* XXII (February, 1960), 25–27.

Parents have mixed feelings about disciplining their children and concerning what their attitude should be toward their children. In the battle of wills that sometimes occurs, parents are anything but confident about what their own behavior should be. They are torn between "giving in" and dominating the child.

Fairchild and Wynn[16] found that one facet of parental motivation that appeared with surprising regularity was the fear of alienating children. In suburban interviews especially, the researchers formed the impression that parents were often "cowed" by their offspring and earnestly sought their good will and approval.

This fear has important implications for family government. Riesman analyzes the problem in terms of the concepts of the inner-directed and the other-directed parent. The other-directed parent has to win not only his child's good behavior but also his child's good will. He is tempted to use his superior didactic skill to reason with the child. And when the child learns to argue, too, the parent is undecided—should he give in or fall back on the sterner methods of discipline used by inner-directed parents.[17] The parent who wants to be liked by his child is not content with cringing obedience on the child's part. As one parent put it, "With the children now, we yell and they don't listen to us, and our voices get louder, and still they like us. There is really a genuine affection and they talk to me about things I wouldn't have discussed with my parents."[18]

Strommen found that youth do not appear to be as sharply critical of their parents or teachers as adults supposed them to be; however, youth appear to be less concerned over adult authority and more concerned over the social distance between themselves and adults.[19] Adults are inclined to rate the family as an obstacle to the development of youth in certain areas of their lives, responding as though youth are more troubled by their family relationships than by other concerns. Youth, on the contrary, respond as though they had fewer concerns in the area of family relationships than in other areas. Their responses indicate a greater closeness with the family unit than has been supposed.

FACTORS RELATED TO INTEGRATION AND SOLIDARITY IN THE FAMILY

The chances of a family being maintained as a functioning system over a period of time are enhanced if the members of the family are committed to each other, have common goals, and share a feeling of solidarity. There are

[16] *Op. cit.* (see above, fn. 12), p. 142.

[17] David Riesman, Nathan Glazer, and Reuel Denney, *The Lonely Crowd* (New Haven, Conn.: Yale University, 1950), p. 72.

[18] Fairchild and Wynn, *op. cit.* (see above, fn. 12), p. 142.

[19] Merton Strommen, *Report on Lutheran Research, Introductory Volume* (Minneapolis: Lutheran Youth Research, 1959).

a number of factors contributing in various ways to the establishment of a setting within which family integration and solidarity can be developed and maintained.

Common Values

Maintaining order in a family is simplified if there is such a high degree of acceptance of common values on the part of all family members that decisions can be reached with only a minimum of conscious decision-making and without the threat of force or coercion. In families possessed of consensus, suggested changes in family goals or procedures, or even a call for the accommodating of personal goals is not resented or viewed as threatening by family members.

Common values and norms guard the family from the divisive tendencies that follow from specialization of roles. A family cannot maintain the intimate relationships that family living entails with equanimity solely through the application of discipline. Members must feel personally committed to the family and its goals. Behavior is influenced by the values they hold in common. A system of values held in common can give meaning and purpose to specific family activities and make effortless the execution of them.

Yet no two families are alike. Despite common cultural expectations, the specific expectations guiding the corporate behavior of family members are individualized and based on a combination of personal idiosyncrasies and family experiences. The family's unique cultural pattern involves shared feelings of rightness and wrongness. To the extent that a family's unique culture is consistent and integrated, to that extent it may contribute to consistent and orderly family activity.

Leadership, task performance, and differentiation of roles all take place within the context of the family's overall value system. The effect of an integrated family culture is conservative. A culturally integrated family can be expected to be less receptive to innovation than one lacking integration. Proposed changes are evaluated not only as to their appropriateness as norms guiding family activities, but also as to their consistency with prevailing beliefs and values.

Nevertheless, family culture is modified by interaction in time and space, and reflects the impact of environing physical, social, and general cultural conditions as well as the changing needs and demands of the various family members. The problem of guiding activity successfully in a changing family situation becomes, in part, a problem of extending the family culture. In general, the need for modification in the family culture is apparent to some member of the family before it is apparent to other members. For instance, the adolescent boy or girl may see the need for extending his away-from-home privileges more urgently than does any other member of the family. There is apt to be a time lag between recognition of a problem, a proposed solution, and consensus on the solution constituting an extension of the family culture.[20]

Community Solidarity

A feeling of need for solidarity helps to develop and maintain a family culture. This feeling of need may reflect the external environment in which the family finds itself. If the community is closed and possessed of solidarity based on a common culture, there is less need of a family maintaining its own distinct way of life. In an integrated community the development of the individual is unconsciously adapted to the expectations of the community, rather than being exclusively adapted to the expectations of the family. Conversely, modern open communities with their plurality of cultural patterns encourage a closed type of family and a unique family solidarity. Closed families make for a more varied development of citizens since each person is nurtured in the unique culture of his own family.[21]

As a manifestation of the closed character of the American nuclear family living in an open or pluralistic community, each family normally lives within an apartment or separate dwelling; others cannot enter except as they are invited. Individual members leave the "inner sanctum" to carry on various transactions, and the home and family are selectively opened so that others may be admitted for various purposes and for varied lengths of time. These privileged outsiders can be ranked on their accessibility to the family; immediate family friends are first to be admitted, followed by certain professional persons, such as the family physician, a clergyman, a lawyer, and so on. Others enter the home with greater difficulty and with greater need to justify their reasons for entry to it.[22]

Family Status

If the community and the society generally give high priority to the family, persons are stimulated toward favorable attitudes toward their own families. More particularly, if a specific family enjoys high status in the community its members may be induced to have feelings of pride toward the family and toward involvement in it. Families are constantly being evaluated by the community. One criterion for evaluation is the occupational role of the father, and in American society it is largely this criterion that establishes the social class position of the family. The way in which the family members perform their functions *vis-à-vis* one other and the kinds

[20] Parsons and Bales, *op. cit.* (see above, fn. 4), p. 301.

[21] C. D. Saal, "Causes of the Delay in Western European Family Research and Some Notes on the Investigation of the Dutch Rural Family," *Studies of the Family,* ed. Nels Anderson (Tübingen: V. C. B. Mohr [Paul Siebeck], 1956), p. 235.

[22] Reuben Hill, "Sociology of Marriage and Family Behavior, 1945–56," *Current Sociology,* VII (1958), 1–33.

of contributions that members of the family make to their community and
to the nation are other criteria. A "good" family may have a social identity
and a family solidarity that extends through generations in a heritage of
responsible citizenship.[23]

Activities Within the Family

There are family activities with potential for the development of family
solidarity. One group of such activities is family ceremonials or rituals,
such as weddings and christenings. Less formalized activities with potential
for developing family solidarity are family meals, attendance at religious
worship as a family, outings, picnics, and family vacations. Persons who
report most ritual and feel this ritual to be important in their lives tend to
perceive a comparatively high degree of family solidarity.[24] Many families
try to get together on weekends for Sabbath observance or Sunday dinner.
Birthdays and anniversaries are occasions for family celebration, with
friends and relatives often included, especially for children's birthday parties.
Religious festivals such as Christmas, Purim, Easter, or Bar Mitzvah provide ritual occasions on which families are drawn together for observance
of the day, for reaffirmation of kinship ties, and for a revival of mutual obligations symbolized by gift giving.[25] At all these celebrations, Seeley found
that the mother was the central figure. It was she who made the preparations,
sent out the invitations, and created a suitable atmosphere with decorations,
flowers, table settings, and emotionally appropriate symbols.

Berger found that what industrial workers in his sample did in their
spare time was to watch television.[26] Television appears to be both part of
the solution and part of the problem in family integration and solidarity.
Television programming effects changes in household routines. Fairchild
and Wynn found that in an essentially middle-class sample, television was
viewed by the youngsters for an average of twenty-four hours per week,
and ninety-three percent of the families owned one or more sets.[27] While
most parents put up with television, they were found to be ambivalent
about it. They credited television with being an excellent "mechanical
sitter" for children, a relaxer for parents, and, occasionally, a first-rate edu-
cator; but they also decried quarrels caused by program conflicts, undesirable programs that majored in themes of violence, and interference with

[23] Bernard Barber, "Family Status, Local-Community Status, and Social Stratifica-
tion: Three Types of Social Ranking," *The Pacific Sociological Review,* IV (Spring,
1961), 3–10.

[24] Orrin E. Klapp, "Ritual and Family Solidarity," *Social Forces,* XXXVII (March,
1959), 212–214.

[25] Seeley, Sim, and Loosley, *op. cit.* (see above, fn. 5), p. 207.

[26] Bennett M. Berger, *Working-Class Suburb: A Study of Auto Workers in Suburbia*
(Berkeley and Los Angeles: University of California, 1960).

[27] Fairchild and Wynn, *op. cit.* (see above, fn. 12), p. 145.

family meals. The claim that television keeps the family at home was not considered an asset by most parents. What family members do and how they relate to each other was seen as more important than just being at home together. In some families, however, television was seen as helping to keep peace or at least helping to avoid conflict.

Families complain that the shortage of time available and conflicting schedules affect the amount of time which family members spend together. While breakfast and lunch are likely to be at the convenience of the individual family members, dinner is more frequently a family occasion. Some families try to keep the evening meal a purely social affair with only light talk exchanged, while others make it a time for family discussions and decisions. In a few, the presence of all members opens up so many conflicts that it is felt to be preferable to have the family members eat separately.

While the importance of formal and informal activities is recognized, there are many other potential symbols of family solidarity, for example family movies, slides, or photographs; vacation mementos; the outdoor barbecue; as well as incidents of successes or crises in the life of the family recalled and recounted.

Expressions of affection involving the embrace, words of approval, and appreciation also can enhance family solidarity. The very process of interaction may result in a feeling of family unity.

Closeness of Family Members

When children participate actively in social activities within the home, there appears to be no clear-cut distinction between the child's status and that of the adults around him. The old notion that children should be seen and not heard does not hold as a general principle. Seeley and his colleagues found that young children joined in the conversation of their elders at the dinner table and remained in the living room, frequently interrupting the talk of the grown-ups, demanding attention for their play. More rarely, the child was formally included in the social activity, perhaps helping to serve at a tea or cocktail party.[28]

Landis hypothesized that a child's feeling close to his father is a more accurate index of family relations than his feeling close to his mother and that the way a child feels toward both parents is a more accurate index of family integration than the feeling he has toward either the mother or father separately. To test the hypothesis, 3,000 college students were asked to rate their feelings of closeness to or distance from each parent. The ratings were then related to a series of family variables such as parents' marital happiness, parents' divorce or nondivorce, and a series of self-appraisals. The mother-distant relationship was more predictive of negative family

[28] Seeley, Sim, and Loosley, *op. cit.* (see above, fn. 5), p. 207.

values than was the father-distant relationship. A close relationship with the father usually indicated the highest type of family solidarity. Children tended to report close feelings to the mother in all types of homes, happy or unhappy, married or divorced. They reported a close relationship with the father in happy homes only. A father-distant relationship did not indicate a distant relationship from the mother, although a distant relationship from the mother usually indicated a father-distant relationship. In a few cases children reported that they were distant from both parents and yet reported that their parents had a happy marriage.[29]

Fairchild and Wynn found that sibling tension ranked high among problems bothering parents: discussion of sibling rivalry came up often in their interviews with city and rural parents but not in interviews with suburban parents. The highly organized life outside the home in the suburbs might reduce such friction within the home, the study suggested, as might the more spacious suburban living quarters. Crowded housing conditions in the city, on the other hand, were seen to contribute to dissension among offspring.[30]

Family Crises as a Basis of Family Solidarity

Family solidarity need not be based simply upon the sharing of pleasures. The family may derive solidarity from a sense of standing together to meet economic difficulties or other crisis situations. Strengths in the families of the poor may be seen as arising out of their efforts to cope with an environment that is essentially negative.[31] For example, the difficulties of the non-white male finding employment is compensated for in part by the women of the family—mother, grandmother, aunts—and other members of the family banding together to share the responsibilities of earning a living, caring for the children, and managing the home. Poverty and hardship can contribute to family solidarity though they may more often lead to apathy and disorganization. Strengths among the poverty-stricken include cooperativeness and mutual aid among family members, the avoidance of the strain that can accompany competitiveness and individualism, freedom from parental overprotection, lessened sibling rivalry, and time to enjoy leisure-time activities such as music, games, sports, and cards.[32]

Different Levels of Solidarity Within the Family

There is much interaction in the family and not all of it involves all of the family members. Each interacting subgroup has different solidarity

[29] Judson T. Landis, "A Re-examination of the Role of the Father as an Index of Family Integration," *Marriage and Family Living*, XXIV (May, 1962), 122–128.

[30] Fairchild and Wynn, *op. cit.* (see above, fn. 12), p. 147.

[31] Frank Reissman, "Low-Income Culture: The Strengths of the Poor," *Journal of Marriage and the Family*, XXVI (November, 1964), 418.

[32] *Ibid.*

tendencies. The husband-wife relationship has a tendency toward increased solidarity though it may not appear so during the child-rearing phase of family life when children make almost total demands on the wife's time. The parent-child relationship moves in the direction of decreased solidarity, culminating in the launching of children from the parental home. The sibling relationship also tends toward decreasing closeness as brothers and sisters are occupied with individual careers and their own marital families,[33] with some inclination for siblings to revitalize the bonds between themselves in the later years of life.[34]

SOCIETAL VALUES AND THE FAMILY VALUE SYSTEM

Individualism

The American family aims to serve persons within the family and particularly its younger members. Relatively speaking, passing on a family tradition is of less importance to parents than is freeing their children to create their own patterns of life both within the family or orientation and when they marry.[35]

Individual security based on a sense of belonging is highly regarded as a family goal. Family life for the nuclear family is a short-term present; the feeling of family security tends to have a short-term referent. Despite this, many families, even socially-mobile families, are able to produce stable children. The security given by the family may take the simple form of providing food and shelter or the more complicated form of an integrated system of emotional involvements.

Children are not the only ones expecting to be served by the domestic American family. The idealized pattern calls for a person-centered, as well as a child-centered family. If the home is to produce achievement-oriented, future-oriented, independent persons, it must permit and foster individualistic expression. An important consequence of the stress on the person is belief in the fullest development of his personality consistent with his potential for development. The point of emphasis is on a collection of discrete family members, each being served by the family without being unduly restricted by its demands. The family is seen as existing for its members, not the members for the family. As family members strain to achieve individualistic goals, their sense of obligation to each other and to the family *per se* may be blunted.

---

[33] Otto Pollak, "Family Diagnosis: Commentary," *Social Casework,* XXXIX (February–March, 1958), 83–85.

[34] Elaine Cumming and David M. Schneider, "Sibling Solidarity: A Property of American Kinship," *American Anthropologist,* LXIII (1961), 498–507.

[35] Gerhard Lenski, *The Religious Factor* (New York: Doubleday, 1961), pp. 221–226; Fairchild and Wynn, *op. cit.* (see above, fn. 12), pp. 139 ff.

Companionship or Togetherness as Family Values

Along with the emphasis on the person in America runs a secondary and sometimes conflicting emphasis on the importance of family life *per se*. This latter emphasis supports a strong and cohesive family; marriage and parenthood are both highly valued. The family is founded on the affection and compatibility that draws people into marriage, and ideally the growing child becomes conditioned to a way of family life wherein affection and compatibility are practiced, sought, and expected. In family-life education this doctrine reflects itself in an emphasis on family recreation, on father's not being preoccupied with his business, on parents learning to play with their children—getting down to the child's level, literally, if this appeals to the child.[36]

Much family literature pressures the male to be more of a family man than he is. He is urged to be a better companion to his wife and children, and to share in the activities and education of his children. Other voices warn that this emphasis on the domestic qualities of the male role is overdone and that men of adventure and daring, willing to give of themselves in the public good, are being inhibited by an emphasis on family living.

Some years ago, Burgess pointed to a process of change from the "institutional" family toward an emerging type of family which he described as the "companionship" form.[37] He emphasized that the essential bonds in the companionship family are in the interpersonal relationships of its members, as compared with the bonds in the older institutionalized forms of the family, bonds which were created by the external pressures of law, custom, public opinion, and duty. The central objectives of the institutional family were children, status, and the fulfillment of its social and economic function in society.

It is in the nonwork, recreational context rather than in the work area that the companionship family can have "togetherness." For most families, togetherness has to be an evening and weekend endeavor when families can spend time together exploring their potential for comradeship and learning patterns of getting along together that are mutually satisfying. Attempts at family participation are at times uncertain, misdirected, and fumbling; yet participation is important in that it may serve as something of a counteractant to marked individualism.

Good family life is sometimes equated with life in a family in which family members do things together and are happy while doing them. With such an image of the good life, it is understandable why "inadequate recreation

---

[36] Joseph K. Folsom, "Health, Society and Envy," *Marriage and Family Living*, XX (February, 1958), 5–10.

[37] Ernest W. Burgess, "The Family in a Changing Society," *American Journal of Sociology*, LIII (May, 1948), 417–422.

and leisure time" was checked as a problem by almost half of the families in the Fairchild and Wynn sample.

Happiness as a Goal of Family Living

Happiness is often mentioned as a goal of family living. What is the nature of this happiness? Seeley and his colleagues see it as "a blend of material well-being, success, social status, good physical and mental health," with family life as essential to its attainment.[38] It is regarded as more important for the person to find happiness than for the family to do so, though it is debatable whether or not personal happiness can be achieved at the expense of the family. The majority of respondents in the Seeley, Sim, and Loosley study described themselves as happy and attributed their happiness largely to the family.

A fun morality has emerged in America; people worry about not having enough fun just as they formerly worried about having it. It is now quite acceptable to urge that adequate facilities for leisure-time activity be provided for all. The 1960 White House Conference on Children and Youth recommended that federal, state, and local governments utilize every opportunity to acquire and develop new land, buildings, and water resources; that existing facilities for leisure-time use be preserved and safeguarded from encroachment; and that large natural areas—such as forests, reservoirs, and defense areas—be developed for multiple recreation purposes. The Conference also recommended that diversified community recreation programs, including both physical and cultural activities and provided with adequate leadership, be an integral part of every community.[39] The vast expenditures for the equipment needed to utilize family leisure time—for boats, cabins, cars, trucks, and trailers; equipment for fishing, hunting, swimming, water skiing, and camping, for instance—attest both to affluence and to the fact that American families pursue leisure-time activities with a vengeance.

Confusion Over Family Values

The good family may be the happy family, and doing things together may be indispensable to this happiness, but there appears to be some ambivalence regarding these values. Fairchild and Wynn found a strong desire for togetherness; side by side with this desire there appeared to be a fear of close family relationships. Parents wanted togetherness, or thought they should want togetherness, but found it unnatural and unpleasant. It is not strange that togetherness is an awkward posture especially in the nuclear family, where the age spread and the differences in maturity and interests of family members are so great.

[38] Seeley, Sim, and Loosley, *op. cit.* (see above, fn. 5), p. 218.
[39] *Conference Proceedings,* Golden Anniversary White House Conference on Children and Youth, March 27–April 2, 1960, Washington, D.C.

It has been suggested that families turn in upon themselves and toward family togetherness not because it is their conscious choice but partly as protection against the increasing complexity of society. The family can become the small, meaningful community where each person finds a sense of his own identity and function.[40]

SUMMARY

Adaptation of the American family to its environmental milieu is simplified by the abundance of material resources available. The majority of American families live in relative comfort; the income of one-fifth of all families falls below the poverty line, however.

The American family is essentially a consumption rather than a production unit. The woman who needs to contribute to the support of the family is more likely to take a position outside the home than to engage in homebound industry.

Internally, the family is concerned with the problem of allocating roles to the various members and maintaining order without impairing the motivational level of its members. The acceptance of common goals and values on the part of family members greatly aids in the integration of the family.

Differentiation of roles within the contemporary American family tends to be along the lines characteristic of the traditional American family but with some differences. One change in family tasks has been the professionalization of the wife's functions. Both husbands and children help around the home, particularly in emergencies.

There are various authority patterns in today's families. There are many husband-dominated families, but husbands do not aspire to the status of patriarch. Whichever partner works more outside the home tends to gain power within the home. The father's authority—since he is absent from the home so much of the time—is apt to be latent but nevertheless real.

Regarding parent-child authority relations, the modern parent finds the conflict between having to govern his children and the desire to be liked by them a difficult problem to resolve. Children have gained increasing status in decision-making within the family and in regard to the supervision of their own activities.

Family ritual is important to the establishment of family solidarity. The ritual frequently centers around having fun together as equals. There are family strengths in the poverty-stricken community; poverty is apt to contribute to apathy and family deorganization, however.

As a society has values so do its social systems. The American family is more inclined to cater to the needs and desires of its members than it is to

[40] Lawrence LeShan and Eda J. LeShan, "Some Recent Trends in Social Science Research Relevant to Parent Education," *Marriage and Family Living,* XXIII (February, 1961), 31–37.

ask the members to subjugate their needs and desires to those of the family. The somewhat contradictory value of togetherness has also received considerable emphasis in the contemporary American family, not without some confusion and embarrassment, however. The family aims to keep its members happy.

BIBLIOGRAPHY

Wendell Bell. "Familism and Suburbanization: One Test of the Social Choice Hypothesis," *Rural Sociology,* XXI (September–December, 1956), 276–283.

Bennett M. Berger. *Working-Class Suburb: A Study of Auto Workers in Suburbia.* Berkeley and Los Angeles: University of California, 1960.

Jessie Bernard. *Marriage and Family Among Negroes.* Englewood Cliffs, N.J.: Prentice-Hall, 1966.

Robert O. Blood, Jr., and Donald M. Wolfe. *Husbands and Wives: The Dynamics of Married Living.* Glencoe, Ill.: Free Press, 1960.

Elizabeth Bott. "A Study of Ordinary Families," *Studies of the Family,* ed. Nels Anderson. Tübingen: J. C. B. Mohr [Paul Siebeck], 1956. Pp. 29–68.

Marie S. Dunn. "Marriage Role Expectations of Adolescents," *Marriage and Family Living,* XXII (May, 1960), 99–104.

Roy W. Fairchild and John Charles Wynn. *Families in the Church: A Protestant Survey.* New York: Association, 1961.

Joseph K. Folsom. "Health, Society and Envy," *Marriage and Family Living,* XX (February, 1958), 5–10.

Reuben Hill. "Social Stresses on the Family: Generic Features of Families Under Stress," *Social Casework,* XXXIX (February–March, 1958), 139–150.

Theodore B. Johannis. "Participation by Fathers, Mothers, and Teenage Sons and Daughters in Selected Child Care and Control Activity," *The Family Life Coordinator,* December, 1957, pp. 31–32.

Orrin E. Klapp. "Ritual and Family Solidarity," *Social Forces,* XXXVII (March, 1959), 212–214.

Judson T. Landis. "A Re-examination of the Role of the Father as an Index of Family Integration," *Marriage and Family Living,* XXIV (May, 1962), 122–128.

Lawrence LeShan and Eda J. LeShan. "Some Recent Trends in Social Science Research Relevant to Parent Education," *Marriage and Family Living,* XXIII (February, 1961), 31–37.

Daniel R. Miller and Guy E. Swanson. *The Changing American Parent.* New York: Wiley, 1958.

Margaret Park Redfield. "The American Family: Consensus and Freedom," *American Journal of Sociology,* LII (November, 1946), 175–183.

Peter H. Rossi. *Why Families Move.* Glencoe, Ill.: Free Press, 1955.

John R. Seeley, R. Alexander Sim, and Elizabeth W. Loosley. *Crestwood Heights: A Study of the Culture of Suburban Life.* New York: Basic Books, 1956.

Murray A. Straus. "The Influence of Sex of Child and Social Class on Instrumental and Expressive Roles in a Laboratory Setting," *Sociology and Social Research,* LII (October, 1967), 7–21.

William A. Westley and Nathan E. Epstein. "Family Structure and Emotional Health: A Case Study Approach," *Marriage and Family Living,* XXII (February, 1960), 25–27.

CHAPTER 7

Procreation and Socialization

THE MARRIED COUPLE is the social unit responsible for having children. Most couples accept this function; an extremely small percentage of couples choose voluntarily to remain childless. The regulation of family size is also a responsibility of the married couple, though public responsibility for family planning has been developing.

The bearing and rearing of children, particularly among the advantaged classes, is not characterized by impulsive action followed by neglect. Rather, the approach to procreative activity is a rational one. The majority, but by no means all, of married couples decide whether or not they want children, whether or not they can afford to bring them into the world, and whether or not they can provide them with an atmosphere in which to grow and develop.

There was a marked decline in the size of completed families from the year 1700 to 1954. Since 1954 there has been a trend toward increase in average size of the completed family, and family size is expected to continue to increase to about 3.2 children per completed family in 1970. The increase is due in large part to an increase in the proportion of families of moderate size (three and four children) rather than to increase in the proportion of large families. The situation is not comparable to what it was in 1910, for instance, when the average family had about five children and nearly half of the families had five or more children.

Overall, the population of the United States has been increasing at a decreasing rate. There has been a decline in the birth rate since the peak of 4,308,000 births in 1957[1] as shown in Figure 7.1. It is too soon to tell whether the reduction reflects a trend toward a smaller average family size or a postponement of childbearing. There has been a slight increase in age at marriage and some evidence of postponement of childbearing within marriage. On the other hand, there is some evidence that women who put off having children or who space their children at longer intervals end up with fewer children.

---

[1] Department of Health, Education, and Welfare, Public Health Service, *Vital Statistics of the United States* and *Monthly Vital Statisics Report*.

FAMILY PLANNING

Largely through the influence of one man, Anthony Comstock, contraceptives came in the late 1800's to be classified legally with the obscene and the pornographic; legislation gave to the birth-control movement an evil reputation that it has had difficulty overcoming.[2] However, certain events, mainly court decisions, facilitated the change to a status of respectability

FIGURE 7.1. BIRTH RATE, UNITED STATES, 1910–1967

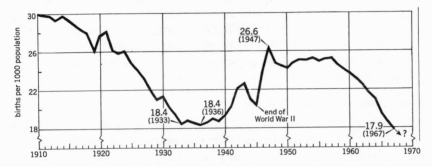

SOURCE: Population Reference Bureau, *Population Profile*, February, 1968.

for contraceptive methods and materials. The most celebrated court case was that of *United States* v. *One Package* (1936), which came to court because customs officials had confiscated a shipment of contraceptive materials addressed to a physician. A federal judge ruled that a provision in the Tariff Act of 1930 should be construed to permit importation of contraceptive supplies by physicians. This meant that for the first time in the twentieth century contraceptives and information about them could be passed through the mail. In the next year, 1937, the first state (North Carolina) pioneered by incorporating birth control into its public health program. Yet, as late as May of 1941, United States postal authorities ruled that a contraceptive report which had been selectively distributed since 1937 could no longer go through the mails. After an appeal to postal authorities was denied, the matter was appealed to the courts. In February of 1945, the United States District Court in Washington issued a permanent injunction preventing the Postmaster General from barring the report from the mails.

The birth-control movement, which had been largely a women's volunteer movement viewed variously as inconsequential, embarrassing, or illegal, has

[2] Alvah W. Sulloway, *Birth Control and Catholic Doctrine* (Boston: Beacon, 1959), p. 16.

only gradually become a significant and respectable movement with substantial public support. In 1942, the changing of the name of the major organization in the movement from the Birth Control Federation of America to the Planned Parenthood Federation in itself heralded a new acceptance and a new emphasis. In 1943, a public opinion poll found 85 percent of American women agreeing that birth control should be available to all married women. The results of a 1955 study using a national sample show that 94 percent of all white couples in the reproductive ages were either trying to or intending to regulate conception, or that they were not sufficiently fertile to require such regulation. Many urban couples wait until after their first pregnancy before starting conception practices; only about 10 percent have yet to adopt contraceptive practices after a second birth.[3] Two, three, or four children are the most popular family size, accounting for more than 90 percent of preferences reported by wives; spousal consensus is substantial.

Social Class and Family Planning

Many low-income families, and a disproportionate number of nonwhite families, remain outside the population that practices effective fertility control. However, a number of recent studies have shown that working-class Americans want as few children as, or fewer children than, those of higher socio-economic status. This is demonstrated in the 1960 Growth of American Families (GAF) study, which is a replication of the 1955 study of a representative national sample of white wives in their childbearing years. Lower-income couples wanted somewhat smaller families than did higher-income families. Nonwhite couples wanted a significantly smaller average number of children than did white couples. White wives wanted a minimum of 3.1 and a maximum of 3.5 children, while nonwhite women wanted a minimum of 2.7 and a maximum of 3.0 children.[4] There is some evidence that these findings apply to the most impoverished American families—those on relief and those who depend on public help facilities. A study of aid to dependent children clients in Chicago reports that ninety percent of the mothers of out-of-wedlock children did not want to have the children. In 1963, data from the Florida State Health Department indicates that seventy percent of nearly 3,000 women attending maternity clinics wanted to have no more children. Two-thirds of the group were nonwhite; they expressed a consistent desire to have fewer children than did white clients. But the wish is not the deed, and in 1962, 34 percent of the families with

[3] Charles F. Westoff, Robert G. Potter, Jr., Phillip C. Sagi, and Elliot G. Mishler, *Family Growth in Metropolitan America* (Princeton, N.J.: Princeton University, 1961), p. 152.

[4] Frederick S. Jaffe, "Family Planning and Poverty," *Journal of Marriage and the Family*, XXVI (November, 1964), 467.

five children and 44 percent of those with six children had incomes below four thousand dollars. By comparison, 22 percent of the families with three children were in the same income bracket.[5]

The 1960 GAF report indicates that one out of five couples with children have excess fertility—excess fertility being defined as the last child being unwanted by either husband or wife. The problem of unwanted pregnancies is most severe in the low-income and low-education groups. Some of them have more children because they do not use contraceptives regularly and effectively. If the wife has a grade-school education and if the husband has an income of less than three thousand dollars a year, 39 percent have excess fertility as judged by their own opinion.

The increase in contraceptive use over 1955 is greater among the couples in the lower socio-economic group, and the proportion of users with only a grade-school education increased from 49 percent in 1955 to 66 percent in 1960. There is evidence also of acceptance of the newer conception control methods—the oral pill and the intrauterine contraceptive devices—by the lower class as well as by the advantaged classes. A study of women coming to a birth-control clinic in Charlotte, North Carolina, found the desired number of children to be one or two as opposed to the actual number of four or five. The Charlotte Health Department added oral contraceptives to its clinical services in 1960 and intrauterine devices in 1964. The better-educated clients in the lower-class families accepted the new devices quite readily; the less-educated clients were somewhat fearful.[6]

Social Mobility and Fertility

Westoff tested the hypothesis that upward social mobility is inversely associated with fertility; the hypothesis was not consistently supported.[7] Families appeared, rather, to be fashionable. By contrast, family sociologists reacting to 1940 census data had seen a trend toward a rising feeling that parenthood was becoming unfashionable. Childlessness, for instance, was most prominent among the educated, the urban, and the well-to-do classes. Married couples in these classes were seen as either not wanting children or as postponing childbearing until they could not have children.

Miller and Swanson have suggested that the assumption that most parents would desire to keep the number of their children to a minimum was rooted in observations of earlier middle-class families in a predominantly "free enterprise-entrepreneurial" society; the greater security of the present "bureaucratic" middle-class families (especially of the lower middle class),

---

[5] U.S. Census Bureau, *The Current Population Reports—Consumer Income,* P-60, October 21, 1963.

[6] Elizabeth C. Corkey, "A Family Planning Program for the Low-Income Family," *Journal of Marriage and the Family,* XXVI (November, 1964), 478–480.

[7] Westoff *et al., op. cit.*

together with lesser opportunities for social advance through individual enterprise, may take away some of the reasons for not having larger families. Parents in "bureaucratized" families, like those in the older agricultural families, may find children more of a fulfillment than a burden.[8]

Religious Identification and Family Size

Compared to religion, influence of social class on family size appears to be negligible. Studies have shown religion to be a better predictor of fertility.[9]

With respect to family size there are significant differences between religious groups, but from some points of view the similarities are more striking than the differences. For example, families in none of the major religious groupings can be characterized as having very large or very small families. Both Catholics and non-Catholics have moderate sized families (two to four children). A large majority of Catholics as well as Protestants and Jews use some form of conception control sometime during the childbearing period. Virtually all Jews start contraception before first pregnancy. Catholic and mixed Catholic–non-Catholic couples delay longer in beginning contraceptive practices than do Protestants. Jewish couples utilize effective methods almost exclusively. This is less true of Christians, particularly Roman Catholics and mixed Catholic–non-Catholic couples.

One might ask if differences between the religious groups are not really socio-economic differences. Sixty-six Jewish couples on a national survey of fertility were matched with Catholic and Protestant couples on duration of marriage and five socio-economic characteristics. These socio-economic controls eliminated most of the Protestant-Jewish differentials for the fertility variables. However, the Catholic-Jewish differentials were not reduced. The distinctive Catholic fertility pattern could not be explained by a combination of socio-economic characteristics. Comparisons between the matched groups indicated that the fertility complex for Protestants was very much like that for Jews when they had similar social and economic characteristics; this was not true for Catholics. On almost all of the comparisons, the difference between Jews and Catholics was as great or greater when the social and economic characteristics were controlled as when they were not. The expected direct association of religious affiliation with number of children desired prevailed only for Catholics.

In general, Catholics educated in secular schools and colleges behave more like Protestants in their fertility behavior than they do like Catholics with parochial education. There are some differences within the Catholic group when differentiated by ethnic background. Catholics of Irish back-

---

[8] Daniel R. Miller and Guy E. Swanson, *The Changing American Parent* (New York: Wiley, 1958), p. 204.

[9] Westoff *et al., op. cit.,* p. 152.

ground have the highest fertility; Catholics of Italian background have the lowest.

The factors affecting fertility are not necessarily the same in the three religious groups. In the case of Jews, careful analysis of the data clearly points up the importance of education in the fertility pattern. Perception of

TABLE 7.1. FERTILITY BEHAVIOR OF PROTESTANT AND CATHOLIC COUPLES WHO MATCH THE JEWISH COUPLES ON DURATION OF MARRIAGE AND SELECTED SOCIO-ECONOMIC CHARACTERISTICS

Fertility and Demographic Characteristics	Protestants 66	Catholics 66	Jewish 66
Mean expected number of births, when family completed	2.4	3.4	2.4
Attitude towards use of family limitation methods Percentage expressing:			
Unqualified approval	92%	18%	89%
Qualified approval	4	12	5
Qualified disapproval	2	58	3
Unqualified disapproval	2	9	—
Percentage who have already used contraception (including rhythm)	83	59	86
Percentage who planned number and spacing of all pregnancies	33	14	47
Methods of Contraception			
Ever used an appliance or chemical method	78	15	83
Only used rhythm	3	44	1

SOURCE: Ronald Freedman, Pascal K. Whelpton, and John W. Smit, "Socio-Economic Factors in Religious Differentials in Fertility," *American Sociological Review,* XXVI (August, 1961), 610.

finances as relevant in decisions about having children is another component of their rational behavior. Most of the remaining explained difference in family-size preference can be covered by the factor of aspirations to send children to college. Only among Jews is there evidence of perceived incompatibility between wanting to send children to college and wanting large families.

Sixty-four percent of the variance of family-size preference of Catholics is accounted for by perception of the relevance of finances in family-size decisions. The second factor is clearly that of their religious affiliation.

Protestant reformers of earlier centuries were no less pro-fertility than were their Roman Catholic counterparts. But Protestants have interpreted the relationship between marriage and family in a way that constitutes a markedly different approach toward family planning. Protestant groups have gone on record as viewing the unitive relationship of man and wife as more important or at least of equal importance with the procreative aspects of marriage. For example, the Episcopal Lambeth Conference of 1958 reported as a result of its deliberations that the procreative and unitive functions of marriage are not to be subordinated one to the other, either procreative to unitive or unitive to procreative.

Historically, Catholic pronouncements on marriage have been more proscriptive, with emphasis on the primary function of marriage being the bearing and rearing of children. Nevertheless, there have been marked changes in attitude toward the unitive and procreative functions in the writings of Roman Catholics. The year 1932 marked something of a turning point in the attitude of Roman Catholic writers toward birth control. In that year the so-called safe period of rhythm method of birth control was first widely publicized in the United States. The method required no mechanical or chemical applications and came to be viewed by some as a natural method and hence acceptable, together with absolute continence, as a conception control method for Catholics. Earlier Roman Catholic writers impugned the birth-control movement as antisocial, unpatriotic, a symptom of religious decay, fraudulent, and hypocritical. In contrast, since the widespread acceptance of the rhythm method, handbooks instructing in the use of rhythm have come from Catholic authors. The support given the rhythm method in Pope Pius XI's 1930 encyclical, *Casti Connubii* (On Christian Marriage), provided major support for the change noted in Catholic literature. Pius XII in 1951 further expressed the hope that science might succeed in providing this licit method (rhythm) with a sufficiently secure basis for reliable conception control. In a second address in the same year, he further elaborated on the possible use of rhythm when he said that a couple might be exempt from the duty of parenthood for a long time, even for the duration of married life, if there were serious medical, eugenical, economic, or social reasons. But for Pope Pius XII's caution in 1951 that matrimony as a natural institution does not have the personal improvement of the couples concerned as its primary end, the unitive function in marriage might be as strongly upheld by Roman Catholics as it is among contemporary Protestants and Jews; for Pius XI had unequivocally spoken of the "mutual inward molding of husband and wife, this determined effort to perfect each other" as "the chief reason and purpose of matrimony" in the encyclical *Casti Connubii.*[10]

There is a similarity in the sexual norms of the secular culture, of Protestantism, and of Judaism. Will the future bring Catholic changes consistent with these norms? This problem has received thorough, scholarly analysis by Roman Catholic family sociologists. As John L. Thomas, a Roman

[10] Pius XI, *Christian Marriage* (*Casti Connubii*), 5th ed. (New York: American, 1943), p. 71.

vented, or at least minimized, if parents had been instructed in the proper care of children.

A continuing high rate of death in infancy during a period in which the death rate of the general population declined caused additional concern and stimulated inquiry. The conclusion reached was that infant mortality was a complex problem and that several measures had to be taken: expectant and nursing mothers had to be cared for; mothers of young babies who could not feed their infants at the breast had to have an adequate supply of clean milk; and infants needed medical attention. Above all, it was realized that the cooperation of enlightened mothers was needed. The ability to bring a baby successfully through the first year of life was seen not as a feminine characteristic with which all women were endowed, but as a skill requiring a technique which, like any other technique, had to be acquired.[15] Converging trends of thought in child psychology, psychoanalysis, social psychology, social anthropology, and psychopathology all contributed to an increasing emphasis on the importance of parents in the mental development of their children.

In the United States, well-baby clinics were set up and the situation began to improve. The resulting decline in infant mortality and the general improvement of child health could not be attributed to educational measures alone, but there is little doubt that—in addition to better hygiene, better medical care and nutrition—greater health knowledge and good child care practices played a considerable part in the improvement.

Organized parent education in the United States dates back to the last decades of the nineteenth century. The earliest date usually recorded is 1888, when the association that later became the Child Study Association of America was formed by parents who wanted to make use of help and knowledge of experts in the upbringing of their children.

In the 1920's, research on child development was initiated at a number of universities and at the Merrill-Palmer School at Detroit. By 1932, professional courses in parent education were offered in many American colleges and universities, and between 1928 and 1932 a number of widely read books for parents on child management, child psychology, and child guidance were published. Publications made the findings of research accessible to those involved in parent education.[16]

Radio broadcasting on parent education began in the United States in 1923. Institutes of child welfare have for many years since conducted radio

15 G. F. McCleary, *The Early History of the Infant Welfare Movement* (London: H. K. Lewis, 1933), p. 7.

16 See, for example, *Child Development Abstracts and Bibliography,* published by the Society for Research in Child Development for more than 30 years; also *Research Relating to Children* (U.S. Department of Health, Education, and Welfare, 1955).

programs over university radio stations. Tape recordings on child care and development are broadcast or used by local groups, and dramatic sketches followed by discussion have been televised.

Well-baby clinics are now widespread. Mothers take their babies for examination at regular intervals. Mothers are also given individual instruction by a doctor and nurse who will also visit the home in case of an emergency.

One of the most common and popular ways of providing parent education is the informal study or discussion group led either by a trained specialist or by a lay leader. In recent years there has been a tendency to arrange these discussion circles with particular groups in mind, for example, for parents of young children, of school-age children, of adolescents; for fathers only; for mothers only; for mothers and daughters, for fathers and sons; for widowed or divorced parents and parents of handicapped or delinquent children. In Flint, Michigan, for example, a private foundation has pioneered in offering courses and discussion groups for expectant parents as part of a larger educational program designed to further the welfare of mothers. Expectant mothers can attend a series of mothercraft classes as well as training classes for pregnancy; there is also a men's forum for fathers and a couples' club if husband and wife wish to attend jointly.

Sometimes this work is sponsored by a university. For example, the Institute of Child Welfare of the University of Minnesota worked for over thirty years with parents' groups in Minnesota. A staff of specialists gave talks on child development and family life and led group study discussions on behavior problems, parent-child relations, and other aspects of child development. Among the organizations taking advantage of the services provided by the Institute were women's associations, parent-teacher organizations, organizations responsible for adult and rural education, radio stations, churches, and social services.[17] In other parts of the country a local authority may be responsible for such activities. In Baltimore, for example, a parent education program that has been conducted by the Department of Education provides meetings arranged in such a way that people whose children are in different stages of development can find one suitable for their needs. Some of these groups meet year after year and deal with new problems as they arise according to the increasing age of the children concerned, finally dealing with the parents' own problems of adjustment to middle age and beyond.

Where parent education is carried out under the auspices of adult education departments of the school administration of a city or state, the responsibilities of the specialist concerned with it are broadly interpreted and are usually wide enough to include programs at various levels. For example, the Bureau of Adult Education of the California State Department of Edu-

[17] The Institute, now called the Minnesota Institute of Child Development, has withdrawn from this particular program of services.

cation suggests a program of family life education under the following headings:

Prenatal Counseling
Counseling During Infancy
Parent-Child Study Groups
Kindergarten Teachers with Half Time for Parent Contacts
Parent and Teacher Co-operation
Study of Family in Junior High School
Emphasis on Family Life in High School
Courses in College
Courses in Teacher Training Institutions
Family Service (i.e., an agency for individual advice)
Education for Family as a Lifelong Process

In about forty cities there are full-time supervisors, consultants, or specialists under a department of education concerned with education for family life and with parent education.

That the approach is multiple and comprehensive is apparent in the number of different organizations concerned with parent education and the varied activities they undertake. Mental health and casework agencies have added parent education to their activities; the Cooperative Extension Service of the Department of Agriculture now includes specialists on problems of family life in home demonstration agencies; university activities include—besides courses and group discussions—research, publication of monographs, training of professional workers and group leaders, and consultation services.

The educational approach to parenthood has not been without its critics; even some of its supporters have mixed feelings. Faced with concrete examples of parental stupidity or mismanagement, one is inclined to be wholeheartedly in favor of parent education, though further reflection gives rise to doubts. There is a fear that parent education might become a naive didactic attempt to tinker with superficial details of parental care, or that it could develop into a crude intervention into family life. Parental common sense is mistrusted, but the popular books on child-upbringing to which people take refuge are apt to be an inadequate substitute. The experts who are said to be replacing the folkways, habits, and customs passed on and sanctioned by grandmothers are criticized on the grounds that their advice may lead to misunderstanding; their demands may surpass what parents can achieve; their help may create the impression that society wants to relieve parents of their obligations. Mother-blaming on the part of psychologists and the illusion of omnipotence of parent educators have also been attacked.[18] This

18 J. Loevinger, "The Mother-Blaming Complex Among Psychologists," *The American Psychologist*, VIII (1953), 748–750; H. Bruch, "Parent Education or the Illusion of Omnipotence," *American Journal of Orthopsychiatry*, XXIV (October, 1954), 723–732.

criticism is significant, for social compulsions and cultural pressures can raise the responsibilities and anxieties of parenthood to an excessive degree.

What is being criticized is not the attempt to provide parent education, but its excesses. The movement has been strengthened by a more cautious and discriminating attitude in dealing with parents, in recommending practices, and in popularizing the results of research.

That there is still much to be done in the area of improved child care in the United States is attested to by the data reported in Figure 7.2. In 1965

FIGURE 7.2.   THE U.S. RANKED 15TH IN INFANT MORTALITY RATES IN 1965.

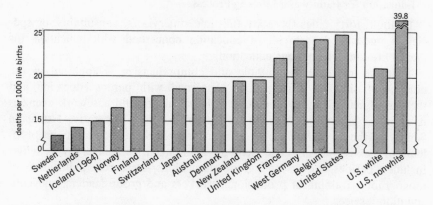

SOURCE: Population Reference Bureau, *Population Profile,* September, 1967.

the United States ranked low among so-called developed nations in infant mortality. The rate of infant mortality is particularly high in the American nonwhite population, 39.8 deaths per 1000 live births in 1965.

SOCIALIZATION

If we view marriage and the nuclear family as separate systems, then there is no nuclear family until the birth of a child to a married couple. Prior to that there is only a marriage, for a marriage is a heterosexual system of two (monogamy) or more than two (polygamy) adults. With the birth of a baby the status of one or more adults must change drastically. Someone must be alert to the dependent child's needs and ready to discontinue other activity to respond to them. The infant on his part contributes nothing or almost nothing to the interaction. So far as the orderly routines of living are concerned, the infant's value is primarily "nuisance" value. Since the infant lacks internalized discipline and is not conscious of himself or of others, he ushers in an "anomic stage," a stage of normalessness in the family.

The human infant is an individual rather than a person if we equate the individual with the behavior of the human biological organism and equate the person with the individual shaped in the socialization process. ("Socialization" is a term used to denote the process by which an individual learns to adjust to life in society by acquiring behavior of which his associates approve.) The human infant is in a "pre-personality" stage; for personality is a system of activities, orientations, and motivations with some internal cohesion. The infant is born with potential personality but only gradually develops it in interaction with children and adults. The infant, as a result of relations with others, develops both self and social responses. In the process of developing a personality, the most significant interpersonal contact of the newborn is with the mother or mother surrogate who meets his physical and emotional needs.

The basic and most pervasive activities of the family on behalf of persons are those provided on behalf of the newborn. It is only through prolonged guidance that the "naive, impulsive mammalian organism" is finally transformed into a participant member of society. This begins with a series of activities aimed at organizing and regulating the infant's eating and sleeping, and continues with the patterning of his overt impulsive behavior. We refer to this child-rearing process, or this process of creating a socially-acceptable individual, as the socialization process. The child's role is primarily that of one being socialized as he gives approved responses to the cues of the socializing agent, an older child or adult. But he is far from passive in the interaction with the socializing agent. He brings his own psychological makeup to bear on the situation and reacts to the efforts of the socializing agent to modify his behavior.

The Individual and Instrumental Control

In order for the individual to maintain himself and to participate in group life, it is necessary that he learn certain skills. As the society must master nature in order to provide food, clothing, and shelter for its members, so the individual must master skills and techniques of getting on as an individual and as a member of society. Some of these skills are acquired without conscious effort on the part of others to teach or the child to learn. This is true of basic language skills, for instance. The child imitates language used by others as they converse with one another and as they speak to him.

Some learning takes place through direct experience as the family carries out its tasks. In preparing the individual to take his place, the family attempts to give him opportunities for involvement in tasks consistent with his capacity to carry them out and consistent with his capacity to learn from the experience. Only in the simpler societies can most of the skills needed by the individual be learned directly through participation. In an agricultural economy or in a hunting or gathering economy the child does learn how to carry on these skills in association with older children and adults. The more complex the society and the more differentiated the functions performed by the various systems of society, the less the family is able through task performance to contribute to the skills necessary for the individual to maintain himself in society. A dramatic example is an urban family living in an apartment building with no responsibility for garden or yard and with father carrying out his major tasks in an occupation which requires him to spend most of his working hours outside the home. There are not many tasks to assign, and what tasks there are do little to prepare a child for his adult roles. The urban family's adaptive activity, since it is so largely concentrated in the breadwinner's job, may have become so remote and technical or require so little effort from other family members that there is little opportunity for the child to learn either by doing or by observing. This is not to say that he does not learn skills in a complex society; it is to say that the development of skills for task performance has been largely transferred to agencies performing specialized functions which the family with its diffused and relatively untrained personnel cannot perform. The major agency for the development of skills in the complex society is the school.

The Individual Must be Motivated

Unsatisfied individual needs do not necessarily provide sufficient motivation for the individual to act in behalf of himself or in behalf of society. If we assume that the development of personality, self-preservation, and the preservation and advancement of the group are goals to be sought, then the individual must be motivated to learn necessary tasks, to adapt to the outside world, to integrate his personality and his social roles, and to express himself in ways that are not destructive of himself or of the group to which he belongs. Not all accept these goals. Some Americans, for instance, feel that the world they have come to know and experience is hardly worth preserving and maintaining. If large numbers of individuals acquire motivations inconsistent with the apparent goals of society, its functioning will, of course, be thwarted or impaired.

One of the first things the child learns is behavior appropriate to the world immediately outside himself—that is, the world outside his own being. The child does not instinctively know what it means to be motivationally committed to maintaining the family and meeting its requirements. This must be learned. He first experiences this learning in relatively sympathetic surroundings, that is, among adults and older children who are concerned about him and responsible for his care.

Respect for group goals, and respect for the property and person of others, depends upon how the child learns to recognize and respect these goals and on whether or not group-inspired prohibitions are transformed into self-administered inhibitions. The family acts as a cultural agent transmitting to the young child ideas, beliefs, values, and norms, inducting him into a symbolic world that hopefully will give meaning to his life. Preparing the child to accept the rewards as well as the frustrations entailed in the proscriptions and prescriptions of society is in large measure the responsibility of the family.[19]

The Integration of Personality

The very need of the family to maintain some integration of the activities and sentiments of its members influences the individual personality and, in turn, is affected by it. Influences from outside the nuclear family—from kinsmen, neighbors, and peers—have impact on the personality structure depending upon the extent to which the family mediates these influences. In simpler societies, community influences are quite direct. In such societies the family as a system within society will have a value system of its own more or less consistent with the values of the environing community. To the extent that the values in the family culture are consistent with each other and are consistently affirmed, the child can be expected to sustain a consistent value system within his own personality system. Should the child be socialized into a family value system that is rigid or at odds with the value system of the environing society, socialization to society outside the family will be rendered difficult.

The Problem of Maintaining Personality

The individual must have opportunities for expression; there must be opportunity for tension release; and if personality is to be integrated there must be order in the hierarchy of values and in the roles he plays. There must be outlets for negative feelings. Some types of behavior might be valuable to the person but have negative consequences if carried on without regard to the consequences for other persons.

To maintain the person, the structure of the family must be such that it sustains and renews both the physical and mental health of family members. No other agency provides the daily care provided by the homemaker. It is the daily tasks of selection and preparation of food, and the cleaning of house, clothing, and utensils that provide the nutrition and sanitation important to physical health. Contributions to mental health are likely to result from the provision of an orderly home life and the affection, reassurance, and feeling of belonging that it can offer. The older child or adolescent relies upon the family for the encouragement, reassurance, and some of the basic skills he needs in undergoing the transition from childhood to adulthood.

To the extent that we recognize the person as an independent system in society, all social systems are conditions to his personality and not a part

[19] Lawrence K. Frank, "What Families Do for the Nation," *American Journal of Sociology*, LIII (May, 1948), 471.

of it. The family becomes a condition once the individual develops a personality of his own. Yet it is also correct to say that the family becomes incorporated within the personality of the individual as his character-structure is formed through example, training, and precept. When a person is socialized into a way of life it is not correct to say that a role is something he has or plays; it is something that he is.[20]

In America, it is generally affirmed that the family is the unit of society responsible for developing values, initiative, and self-discipline in children. The nature and quality of family relationships are seen as vitally affecting the development of the child's potential. The most direct function of the American family is on behalf of family members. Despite some loss of functions, child rearing is still the responsibility of the family; parents assume the dependent child's economic support as well.

Social Class and Socialization

What are parents' expectations for their children? Kohn made a study of 200 families randomly selected from among the white-collar class and 200 from among families with fathers having a manual occupation.[21] Families were of the stable working class rather than the lower class; the men had steady jobs. Inquiry was limited to values that parents would most like to see embodied in their fifth-grade children. Middle- and working-class mothers shared a broad set of values, but not an identical set. There was considerable agreement among mothers that happiness and such standards of conduct as honesty, consideration, obedience, dependability, manners, and self control are highly desirable for both boys and girls of this age. Popularity, being a good student (especially for boys), neatness and cleanliness (especially for girls), and curiosity were next most likely regarded as desirable, with relatively few mothers choosing ambition, ability to defend one's self, affectionate responsiveness, being liked by adults, ability to play by one's self, or seriousness as highly desirable for either boys or girls of this age. These latter values might be valued for children of other ages.

Middle-class mothers' conceptions of what is desirable for boys were much the same as their conceptions of what is desirable for girls. But working-class mothers made a distinction between the sexes; they were more likely to regard dependability, being a good student, and ambition as desirable for boys and to regard happiness, good manners, neatness, and cleanliness as desirable for girls. Fewer working-class mothers regarded happiness as highly desirable for boys.

The higher a mother's status, the higher the probability that she would choose consideration, curiosity, self-control, and (for boys) happiness as

---

[20] Talcott Parsons and Robert F. Bales. *Family Socialization and Interaction Process* (Glencoe, Ill.: Free Press, 1955), p. 107.

[21] Melvin L. Kohn, "Social Class and Parental Values," *American Journal of Sociology,* LXIV (January, 1959), 337–351.

highly desirable. Working-class mothers were more likely to value obedience. They wanted their children to be responsive to parental authority. In fact, the lower the mother's status, the higher the probability that she would select not only obedience, but also neatness and cleanliness. Mothers in the lowest stratum also appeared to be more likely than were those in the highest stratum to value honesty.

A significantly larger proportion of middle- than of working-class parents valued self-reliance or independence. Friendliness, cooperativeness, or ability to get along well with others were also a predominantly middle-class concern.

Thus middle-class parents appear to be more attentive to the child's internal dynamics, while working-class parents appear to want the child to conform to externally imposed standards. Middle-class parental values appear to center on self-direction, while working-class values seem to center on conformity to externally-imposed standards. To middle-class parents it is the child's motives and feelings that appear to be more important than rote conformity to externally-imposed roles.

Middle-class parents read what the experts say on child rearing; they also search for additional sources of information and advice. More than working-class parents, they discuss child-rearing with physicians, friends, and neighbors, as well as with the child's teacher. Middle-class parents seem to regard child-rearing as more problematic than do working-class parents. They turn outward for relevant information and serviceable techniques for carrying out their values. The middle-class child in contrast to the lower-class child lives in a parent-dominated world.[22]

Social class analysis cannot be used to predict child-rearing practices with confidence, however. Behavior and personality are influenced by social class, but researchers are not prepared to say that they are determined by social class.

American parents appear to be quite optimistic over their child reaching a desirable occupational level once he completes his education. This is true not only of white-collar but also of blue-collar parents. Miller and Swanson report that only thirteen percent of a sample of mothers thought that their child would have a factory job—this in a population of parents in which sixty-five percent of the fathers had blue-collar jobs and sixty-nine percent of the grandfathers were similarly employed. This optimism held true for mothers' guesses about both boys and girls.[23]

About eighty percent of the respondents preferred to have their children involved in activities which would teach them to think, plan, or organize, while seventeen percent favored activities which would develop the child's

[22] James Walters, Ruth Connor, and Michael Zunich, "Interaction of Mothers and Children from Lower-Class Families," *Child Development*, XXXV (June, 1964).
[23] Miller and Swanson, *op. cit.* (see above, fn. 8), p. 229.

physique or give him plenty of exercise. Only eleven percent saw personality as most important for monetary success in the factory, while thirty-nine percent chose it for office situations. Over sixty percent of the mothers said they would encourage the child to do what he liked, while thirty-seven percent said they would try to get him to go along with others' wishes. It would seem from this study that parental hopes are higher than can be realized, particularly by children of blue-collar parentage. Miller and Swanson suggest that there must be marked frustration for blue-collar workers who do not succeed in having occupations different from those of the parent generation.

Theories of Socialization

Child rearing has been complicated by the fact that the advice given by the experts has been subject to dramatic changes in a relatively short period of time. In 1928, behaviorists were telling parents always to be "objective and kindly firm" in dealing with their children, never pampering them with sentimental expressions of love. Thirty years later parents were told that the youngster would be in better mental health if he experienced "a warm, intimate, and continuous relationship" with his mother.[24] A current best seller purports to offer "concrete suggestions and preferred solutions for dealing with daily situations and psychological problems faced by all parents." It also sets forth basic principles "to guide parents in living with children in mutual respect and dignity."[25]

The permissive approach which grew out out of behavioristic and Freudian theory saw the home as child-centered, with the needs of the child as paramount to those of the father and the mother. But the permissive approach is challenged by the developmental approach, which sees the child-centered home as undemocratic. The developmental family is person-centered; the parents as well as the children are seen as flexibly capable of change. The family and its individual members must be ready to adapt and adjust to the changing needs of all members of the family, old and young alike. The cult of the child appears to have given way to a perspective which sees both parents and child as worthy of attention from each other, resulting in a reassertion of the personality of the parents.

The developmental approach is in some ways supportive of groupism—belongingness or togetherness—the approach emphasizing the importance of being and doing together in the family across age, status, and interest differences. It is an unfamiliar posture for family members nurtured on a philosophy of self-assertion. The child under a family philosophy of togetherness needs to see his superiors as nurturing, friendly, and supportive

[24] Glenn R. Hawkes, "The Child in the Family," *Marriage and Family Living,* XIX (February, 1957), 46–51.

[25] Haim G. Ginott, *Between Parent and Child: New Solutions to Old Problems* (New York: Macmillan, 1965), *passim.*

—not as hateful people—so that he will in turn love them and be friendly, cooperative, and supportive. Ideally, children are not subordinate in such a household. As equals, they join their parents in decision-making. They are "junior partners" whose opinions are sought and honored, though as junior partners they may not be admitted to full participation in deciding the family's course until they have attained proper seniority.[26]

Socialization in a Changing Society

It is generally accepted that the difficulties in child-rearing are magnified in a society and in a time of rapid social change. The problem might be eased if parents could better understand the society into which they are about to launch their children. Miller and Swanson suggest that if parents knew that bureaucratization, not some immutable natural law, was what created their concern that children be able easily to make numerous friendships, they might be more tolerant of the child's desire to spend some of his time alone. If parents knew that the way of life they develop is a means of solving particular problems, rather than all problems, they might find themselves freed from excessive restraints and pressures. They might be able to grant their children similar freedom.

While the socialization of the child is not exclusively the responsibility of the family, generally speaking, enough of a cultural heritage is usually transmitted by parents to children to equip them for independent existence in the world outside the home. The family, in conjunction with the school and other institutions, produces nondependent, achievement-oriented adults in enough numbers to insure the continuance of the culture.

The child must develop a balance between competition and cooperation, both of which are needed to succeed in modern urban society. Contemporary urban society calls for a kind of covert competition or the abandonment of competition altogether. The child must learn to compete, but he must act as though he is not competing. The ambitions and desires for independence which many authorities see as having prevailed earlier in our history would not fit the child for later participation in contemporary American society as an adult—a society that requires him to be relaxed, to cooperate, and willingly to subordinate his wishes to the policies of some bureaucratically-structured organization. In the past, when children were prepared for free enterprise, values of self-control and a posture that called for an actively manipulative orientation toward the world were more in keeping with the times.

Child Discipline

The problem of discipline confuses American parents. It was concerning this point that Fairchild and Wynn found confusion and dissatisfaction to be

[26] Miller and Swanson, *op. cit.* (see above, fn. 8), pp. 201–202.

most apparent.[27] Parents appear to lack the self-assurance that successful inner-direction gives. The inner-directed parent is not particularly worried if his handling of the child causes some resentment or hostility on the part of the child or on the part of others.[28]

Seeley and his colleagues found that the whole area of child care and control in a state of flux in Crestwood Heights. Fathers might differ from mothers at almost every point in the complex socialization process; families were divided between permissive and authoritarian ways of handling children, as were individuals at different times or at the same time. The Crestwood Heights child was not receiving the same consistent direction where discipline was concerned that he received in learning to earn and to spend money.[29]

Disciplinary actions differ somewhat by social class. Working-class parents are more likely to employ physical punishment, while middle-class families rely more on reasoning, isolation, appeals to guilt, and other methods employing loss of love. Kohn found a distinct difference in the conditions under which middle- and working-class parents resorted to physical punishment. Parents of both social classes reserved physical punishment for what they regarded as fairly extreme circumstances, however.

Kohn concluded that mothers of neither social class are especially quick to resort to physical punishment or to other forms of coercion.[30] But when their children persist in wild play, fighting with their brothers or sisters, or displays of temper, both working- and middle-class mothers are apt to turn to one or another form of punishment. The more extreme forms of wild play and fighting are particularly intolerable to working-class mothers and less so to middle-class mothers. Middle-class mothers are far more likely to punish their sons physically for what they call loss of temper than for behavior defined as wild play. They appear to find the child's loss of temper but not his wild play to be intolerable.

The most marked differences in working-class mothers' response to boys and to girls occur when the child defiantly refuses to do as he is told. Boys are permitted to have their own way, while girls are punished physically. In fact, working-class mothers are less likely than middle-class mothers to punish their sons for refusing to do things they have been told to do.

The major conclusions about the conditions under which mothers of the two social classes punish their children physically also apply to fathers.

[27] Roy W. Fairchild and John Charles Wynn, *Families in the Church: A Protestant Survey* (New York: Association, 1961), p. 140 ff.

[28] David Riesman, *The Lonely Crowd* (New Haven: Yale University, 1950), p. 72.

[29] John R. Seeley, R. Alexander Sim, and Elizabeth W. Loosley, *Crestwood Heights: A Study of the Culture of Suburban Life* (New York: Basic Books, 1956), p. 203 ff. This study of Crestwood Heights, a suburb of a Canadian city, is one of the best studies of the contemporary family in a differentiated, urban-industrial society.

[30] Kohn, *op. cit.* (see above, fn. 19).

Working-class parents are more likely to respond in terms of the immediate consequences of the child's action, middle-class parents in terms of their interpretation of the child's intent in acting as he does. This should not be interpreted as implying that middle-class parents act on the basis of long-range goals for their children's development, while working-class parents do not. On the contrary, Kohn is of the opinion that parents of both social classes act on the basis of long-range goals—but that the goals are different. In the case of working-class parents, desirable behavior consists essentially of not violating proscriptions; in the case of middle-class parents it consists in acting according to the dictates of one's own principles. Here the act becomes less important than the actor's intent. Middle-class parents appear to make little or no distinction between what they regard as desirable for boys and for girls—the issue for both sexes is whether or not the child acts in accordance with internalized principles. The working-class orientation, since it excludes or minimizes considerations of subjective intent, places fewer restraints on the impulse to punish the child when his behavior is out of bounds. Instead, it provides a positive rationale for punishing the child in precisely those circumstances when the parent might most like to do so.

Kohn and Carroll,[31] examining middle- and working-class parents' conceptions of the relative importance of support and constraints in child rearing and of how parental responsibilities for the two should be allocated between mother and father, found that middle-class mothers emphasized the father's obligation to be as supportive as the mother herself, his role in imposing constraints being of only secondary importance. Working-class mothers wanted their husbands to be more directive; the father's responsibility to play a major part in the imposition of constraints assumed far greater importance.

Middle-class fathers shared their wives' conception of how responsibilities toward sons should be allocated and seemed to act accordingly. They did not appear to be as supportive of daughters; apparently they felt this to be more properly in the mother's domain. Working-class fathers seemed to play neither the directive role their wives would have them play, nor a more highly supportive role. Rather, they appeared to see child rearing as more completely their wives' responsibility. McKinley found that lower-class fathers are strict with their sons while upper-class fathers give their sons more freedom.[32]

Seeley and his colleagues found that the father in an advantaged family appeared to enjoy his children, but that their care and control did not con-

[31] Melvin L. Kohn and Eleanor E. Carroll, "Social Class and the Allocation of Parental Responsibilities," *Sociometry*, XXIII (December, 1960), 372–392.

[32] Donald G. McKinley, *Social Class and Family Life* (New York: Free Press, 1964), pp. 104–105.

cern him directly.[33] His participation in the family's activities and his emotional ties with wife and children were largely symbolic. The child-rearing theories which his wife espoused might seem arrant nonsense to him; and the male experts from whom she derived her information frequently appeared to him, unless they were doctors, as inadequate men who had not been able to make the grade in the really masculine world. In the office, whatever his private reservations, the Crestwood Heights man was prepared to go quite a distance along the personnel-directed path for the sake of production and industrial peace. At home, he was under no such obligation to moderate his views; he could give vent to his feelings unopposed. Seeley observed that out of love for wife and children, he might, in time, be persuaded to take an interest in the newfangled notions; but rarely would he come wholeheartedly to endorse democratic and permissive norms seeping into the family.

The number of advantaged Crestwood Heights children who mentioned spanking and strapping as most-feared experiences was rather large in view of the prevalent views in the community against these practices. Seeley concluded that fathers reached the point of corporal punishment early in the disciplinary process. The mother, with her greater inclination to absorb the theories of the child-rearing experts, might be opposed to authoritarian discipline. Most families apparently arrived at some kind of compromise solution to the discipline problem.

Recent findings suggest that corporal punishment may not be uncommon. A study by Kempe and his colleagues[34] based on documentation gathered from seventy-one hospitals, indicates that there is no cessation of child beating in spite of contemporary theories of child raising. To many doctors the incidence of child beating is becoming distressingly familiar. Despite parental protests, X-ray and experience often lead the doctor to conclude that a child brought to him for treatment has been beaten by his parents and is suffering from "the battered child syndrome." Kempe reported 302 battered-child cases in a single year. Thirty-three of the children died, and eighty-five of them suffered permanent brain damage. The beating of children is not confined to people of any particular social class or to people with psychopathic personalities. According to Kempe, the beatings are an indication of psychologically disturbed parents.

Finally, it should be noted that the mother's disciplinary capability decreases and the father's increases somewhat as the children enter their teens, particularly where boys are concerned. Access to the family car, for instance, is customarily controlled by the father.

[33] Seeley, Sim, and Loosley, *op. cit.* (see above, fn. 29), pp. 194–202.
[34] C. Henry Kempe, Frederick N. Silverman, Brandt F. Steele, William Droegemueller, and Henry K. Silver, "The Battered-Child Syndrome," *Journal of the American Medical Association,* CLXXXI (July 7, 1962), 17–24.

Community Participation of Child Dependents

The relationship between the character formation of the child and the life-history of the family is extraordinarily close because of the isolation of each nuclear family. Parents are convinced that their children need activities outside the home, and they want their children to be a part of such activities. On the other hand, they complain that tension mounts, that communication in the family deteriorates, and that family freedom is crowded out in a seemingly relentless schedule of outside activities. In the midst of a desire for their children's social acceptance, some parents are aware of dangers. They raise questions about dances for fifth graders, for example, feeling that growing up too early may be associated with an increase in adolescent sex problems, teen-age marriages, and premarital pregnancies.

FAMILY-SCHOOL INTERCHANGES

The family is not alone in carrying the burden of socializing the young child. Other social systems feel responsibility for socialization in general and for family-life education in particular. At the 1960 White House Conference on Children and Youth, a proposal that family-life education be part of the school curriculum at all age levels drew some opposition but when put to a vote, the resolution passed overwhelmingly.

The school has become involved in traditional family functions. Sex education and family-life education materials are being introduced into the offerings of more and more schools. In many communities, sex and family-life education deemed appropriate to the age and maturity of the child is begun in the early grades and continued throughout the high school years. To meet the need for teachers, schools provide in-service training for their own staffs, and teacher-training institutions offer workshops and summer institutes. Indeed, the number of teachers wishing to register often exceeds the capacity of the institutes.[35] As Seeley has observed, the school has shifted from "curriculum" to "customer" in that it is concerned with the socialization of the whole child (the customer) and not only with the teaching of the traditional curriculum.[36] Obviously, the relatively simple job of transmission of factual knowledge alone is a thing of the past. The American school is now attentive also to the social experiences of children in the school communtiy as a preparation for future citizenship and family life. Family-life education in the school includes sex education; it also includes developmental changes in the child and problems of early adolescence. Thus, beyond basic socialization, the school program includes education in

[35] Esther D. Schulz and Gilbert M. Shimmel, "Teacher Preparation Programs— Summer '68," *SIECUS Newsletter,* IV (December, 1968), 1–2.
[36] Seeley, Sim, and Loosley, *op. cit.* (see above, fn. 29), pp. 238–245.

personal relations, marriage preparation, and preparation for parenthood. The educational program in child development and family life is coupled with a counseling service in many schools. Furthermore, the White House Conference suggested that trained social workers be added to school staffs to provide counseling and guidance to families.

In an undifferentiated society, education is a function of the kinship system. The child learns all he needs to know to survive and succeed in the society from parents and other kinsmen. In a highly differentiated society such as ours, however, the school assumes the educative function; and, as we have seen, it would appear to be assuming more and more of the overall socializing of the child. The establishment of the school as the principal, if not the only, system preparing the individual for successful achievement in society is a major factor in emancipating the person from the family. It is possible that the higher the educational achievement of the person, the less he feels the need to depend on the kinship system for assistance in securing employment or assistance in selecting a mate.[37] The fact that the median number of years in school for Americans is constantly rising gives mute testimony to the fact that education more and more is replacing kinship as the system saddled with the responsibility of preparing the person for adult life, as well as for "retooling" the mature adult who is not satisfied or is unsuccessful in his career.

In the total socialization process of the American child, the sphere of ethical and religious training is not clearly assigned territory, though, superficially, recent action to further separate church and state (especially the public school) in the United States would seem to indicate a clear differentiation of functions. Seeley and his colleagues found little conflict over religion between home and school.[38] Both parent and teacher appeared to view religion as a means to other, more important ends such as happiness, peace of mind, and mental health. Parents asked whether a given theological teaching was "bad for the child," that is, whether it might be damaging to his personality or to his likeliness of success. The impression of the Seeley study was that if the school felt that the religious teaching were detrimental, "religion would have to be reluctantly sacrificed in favor of health or success, as the case might be." To the extent that this is a valid assessment of the situation, it would mean that the church and the school have reversed their former stance. It was at one time true that the church made a major impact on the views of the child and that the parent in turn dominated the teacher. In fact, the church often established and operated the schools. In the emerging pattern, the teacher influences the child and the parent. They also mutually influence each other and unite in influencing the church. According to the Seeley study, "the school, with the support of 'the human

---

[37] Paul Jacob Reiss, *The Extended Kinship System in American Urban Middle Class* (Cambridge, Mass.: Harvard University, unpublished Ph.D. thesis, 1960).

[38] Seeley, Sim, and Loosley, *op. cit.* (see above, fn. 29), p. 240 ff.

relations experts and their institutions,' has largely replaced the church as an ideological source." Stern observes that it is increasingly taken for granted that certain aspects of education of the child are the exclusive domain of the school, and parents are sometimes bluntly told not to interfere in the education of their children.[39]

This is not to suggest an alienation of the school and the home. Far from it. Recent research has shown the close relationship between home influence and school attainment. A clear distinction between the home and the school is no longer considered feasible or advisable. The school, from the strength of its dominant position, actively seeks the cooperation of parents, for without the intelligent support and cooperation of the parents children do not do as well. Parents are expected to maintain their children "in a state of scholastic receptiveness," since the school is ineffective if families are hostile or indifferent.

TABLE 7.2.   COOPERATION BETWEEN HOME AND SCHOOL IN 33 COUNTRIES

No organized cooperation—in 3 countries	Cambodia, Nepal, Thailand
Limited or slight—in 16 countries	Australia, Belgium, Cuba, Egypt, France, Federal Republic of Germany, Haiti, Israel, Italy, Jordan, Luxembourg, Mexico, New Zealand, Portugal, South Africa, Switzerland
Moderately developed; some Parent-Teacher Associations—in 9 countries	Austria, Brazil, Ceylon, India, Japan, Netherlands, Norway, Sweden, United Kingdom
Widespread Parent-Teacher Associations; Parents' Committees—in 5 countries	Canada, Poland, Turkey, United States of America, Yugoslavia

SOURCE: H. H. Stern, "Parent Education: An International Survey," *Studies in Education, Journal of the Institute of Education* (Hamburg: Special Monograph published jointly by the University of Hull and the UNESCO Institute of Education, October, 1960), p. 43.

Close, organized cooperation between home and school of the kind that exists in the United States is not common in most nations. Remove the close neighbor, Canada, from the list, and there are only three countries in which there is widespread organized cooperation between home and school.

To promote this close cooperation, there have been three significant trends in the area of parent education. First, the school makes a concerted effort to keep parents informed of activities of the school. Besides circulars

[39] Stern, *op. cit.* (see above, fn. 15), p. 13.

and letters, teacher-parent consultation and home visits are arranged. In some cases the teacher-parent consultation takes the place of the formal report card. Secondly, the school, the Parent-Teacher Association, or some other organization is used as a vehicle for parent education with open meetings, discussions, and reading groups. The National Congress of Parents and Teachers, an organization with over 10,000,000 members, works with parents as an essential element of its program. Third, stress is laid on the teacher and the parents learning together rather than the teacher educating the parent. Together teachers and parents study problems facing the school, the home, and the child.

The modern American family has become a specialized system partly by legislative design. There are laws preventing parents from assuming major responsibility for educating their own children, this regardless of the knowledge or capacity to teach possessed by the parents. However, laws to protect the child from working when he should be in school have not been altogether effective. The Fair Labor Standards Act of 1938 established a minimum employment age of sixteen years (and in particularly hazardous occupations eighteen years) for the production of goods for interstate or foreign trade. A 1950 amendment also established sixteen as the age under which children are not to be employed in agriculture during school hours.

SUMMARY

Planning of family size is an established part of the American pattern of family life. Birth control is generally accepted, and improved methods of control make planning feasible. There has been a noticeable increase in family planning and use of birth control among lower socio-economic classes. There is also greater rapprochement between the major religious groups as to the desirability of family planning.

Parents, as well as the school and other supporting social systems, emphasize the need to give the child opportunities for self-realization and self-expression. There is some variation in child-rearing practices between the socio-economic classes. There is also some uncertainty as to what the specific goals of child rearing should be and as to what methods can best be employed to reach the goals.

Professionalization of the child-rearing practices has gone on apace. Both private and public agencies have programs designed to help parents in the job of child rearing. The public school has increasingly broadened the scope of its concern for the well-being of the child and his family.

BIBLIOGRAPHY

Grace F. Brody. "Socio-Economic Differences in Stated Maternal Child-Rearing Practices and in Observed Maternal Behavior," *Journal of Marriage and Family*, XXX (November, 1968), 656–660.

Thomas J. Casey. "Catholics and Family Planning," *The American Catholic Sociological Review*, XXI (Summer, 1960), 125–135.

Catherine S. Chilman. "Poverty and Family Planning in the United States: Some Social and Psychological Aspects and Implications for Programs and Policy," *Welfare in Review*, V (April, 1967), 3–15.

Catherine S. Chilman and William T. Liu (eds.). "Family Planning and Fertility Control," special issue of *Journal of Marriage and the Family*, XXXVI (May, 1968), 189–366.

Robert C. Cook (ed.). "New Trends in Roman Catholic Opinion," *Population Bulletin*, XVII (November, 1961), 129–138.

Edward Z. Dager. "Socialization and Personality Development in the Child," *Handbook of Marriage and the Family*, ed. Harold T. Christensen. Chicago: Rand McNally, 1964. Pp. 740–781.

Kingsley Davis and Judith Blake. "Birth Control and Public Policy," *Commentary*, XXIX (February, 1960), 115–121.

Ronald Freedman, P. K. Whelpton, and Arthur Campbell. *Family Planning, Sterility, and Population Growth*. New York: McGraw-Hill, 1959.

Ronald Freedman, P. K. Whelpton, and John W. Smit. "Socio-Economic Factors in Religious Differentials in Fertility," *American Sociological Review*, XXVI (August, 1961), 608–614.

Hiam G. Ginott. *Between Parent and Child: New Solutions to Old Problems*. New York: Macmillan, 1965.

Alan Guttmacher, Winfield Best, and Frederick S. Jaffe. *The Complete Book of Birth Control*. New York: Ballantine, 1961.

Glenn R. Hawkes. "The Child in the Family," *Marriage and Family Living*, XIX (February, 1957), 46–51.

Joseph M. Jones. *Does Overpopulation Mean Poverty?* Washington, D.C.: Center for International Economic Growth, 1962.

C. Henry Kempe, Frederick N. Silverman, Brandt F. Steele, William Droegemueller, and Henry K. Silver. "The Battered-Child Syndrome," *Journal of the American Medical Association*, CLXXXI (July 7, 1962), 17–24.

Richard K. Kerckhoff. "Family Life Education in America," *Handbook of Marriage and the Family*, ed. Harold T. Christensen. Chicago: Rand McNally, 1964. Pp. 881–911.

Clyde V. Kiser. "Is the Large Family Coming Back?" *Child Study*, Fall, 1958, pp. 23–25.

Clyde V. Kiser and P. K. Whelpton. "Resumé of the Indianapolis Study of Social and Psychological Factors Affecting Fertility," *Population Studies*, VII 1953), 95–110.

Melvin L. Kohn and Eleanor E. Carroll. "Social Class and the Allocation of Parental Responsibilities," *Sociometry*, XXIII (December, 1960), 372–392.

Melvin L. Kohn. "Social Class and Parental Values," *American Journal of Sociology*, LXIV (January, 1959), 337–351.

Philip R. Kunz. "The Relation of Income and Fertility," *Journal of Marriage and the Family*, XXVII (November, 1965), 509–513.

Rose Reimann-Hunziker and Gottfried J. Reimann-Hunziker. "Twenty Years' Experience with Vasectomized Patients," *The Journal of Sex Research,* II (July, 1966), 99–109.

Arthur B. Shostak. "Education and the Family," *Journal of Marriage and the Family,* XXIX (February, 1967), 124–139.

H. H. Stern. "Parent Education: An International Survey," *Studies in Education, Journal of the Institute of Education.* Hamburg: University of Hull and the UNESCO Institute of Education, October, 1960.

Alvan W. Sulloway. *Birth Control and Catholic Doctrine.* Boston: Beacon, 1959.

John L. Thomas. *The American Catholic Family.* Englewood Cliffs, N.J.: Prentice-Hall, 1956.

Glenn M. Vernon and Jack A. Boadway. "Attitudes Toward Artificial Insemination and Some Variables Associated Therewith," *Marriage and Family Living,* XXI (February, 1959), 43–47.

Charles F. Westoff, Robert G. Potter, Jr., Phillip C. Sagi, and Elliot G. Mishler. *Family Growth in Metropolitan America.* Princeton, N.J.: Princeton University, 1961.

P. K. Whelpton, Arthur A. Campbell, and John E. Patterson. *Fertility and Family Planning in the United States.* Princeton, N.J.: Princeton University, 1966.

PART IV

The Family and Other Social Systems

THE CONTEMPORARY PERIOD in America is a period of bigness and bureaucratic structure in many areas of organized societal life—particularly in business, industry, and government. The corporation, the most important form of modern business organization, accounts for more than eighty percent of the total number of workers employed, wages paid, and goods produced. The tendency is in the direction of greater concentration of power, as small units are consolidated into larger ones. On the other hand, the nuclear family is a smaller unit in terms of number of family members than it was in any of the historical epochs considered in Part II. Contemporary family interaction and interchange with the economy, social class and community, kinsmen, the state, and the church is the subject matter of Part IV.

CHAPTER 8

The Family and the Economy

THE FAMILY AS A PRODUCTIVE ECONOMIC SYSTEM

IN THE PAST a major function of the family has been the production of goods. As late as the time of the Civil War, besides the many farms that were operated as family enterprises, new enterprises in business and industry often began as family enterprises. Capital came to be drawn from family holdings and business expanded by family financing. Most of the middle-sized industries in the country have been family enterprises. This has been true of textiles, brewing, packing, chemicals, soap, newspapers, banking, and shipping. Names of many American industries reflect family ties: Armour, Dow, DuPont, and Ford.

The social position of the family rested on property, and the dynastic marriage. Property meant power and, through marriages between families with large economic assets, holdings were preserved or built up, and the family enterprises passed on to succeeding generations. In a day when families were large it was possible to draw on a variety of skills needed in the growth of an industry or business; the decline of the large family narrowed the choice of heirs competent for the various phases of the industry. This was a factor in the decline in family control of large industries.

The Corporation Replaces the Family

The corporation, not the family, has now become the responsible functioning entity in the economic system. The rate of technological change and the need for workers with technological expertise continue to increase. This break up of family capitalism began around the turn of the century when American industry overextended itself. As a result of the ensuing financial crisis many of the country's leading enterprises were reorganized and came under the control of investment bankers. Investment bankers installed professional managers who were skilled as managers but had no proprietary stake in the enterprise, hence they were unable to pass along their power to their sons as was true of family-controlled enterprises. Reorganization motivated by the desire for economic efficiency brought a radical separation of property and family; affluent families continued to

162

assert themselves in the business world mainly through control of some middle-sized enterprises. Performance for its own sake rather than family ties has come to be the major justification for economic power. The architects of the modern corporation were not family entrepreneurs but specialists, often engineers, whose task it was to guide a new economic form. Few accumulated the fortune of a Carnegie, a Rockefeller, or a Harriman family. The majority of family businesses today are not on a continuum with the corporation; they are laundries, insurance agencies, restaurants, drugstores, bottling plants, lumberyards, and automobile dealerships. They are vital in that they service an economy, but they are rarely engaged in primary industry. American families live more derivatively than they once did; few have direct control over a business or industry.[1]

American industry can produce beyond what can be consumed. Families engaged in wholesaling and retailing became a drag on efficiency and profit since there is no profit to be made from large-scale production unless an efficient marketing system exists. Many family businesses were concentrated in the distribution end of the economic system, and it was here that from a purely economic point of view the economic system was least efficient. Pressures within the economic system resulted in more and more retail and wholesale businesses—formerly owned and controlled by family capital and family enterprise—passing under corporate ownership and control. The family as an economic force had to retreat.

The Removal of Family Entrepreneurial Risk as An Outcome of Family-Economy Interchange

One of the advantages of employment in America's present economic system is that entrepreneurial risk has been largely eliminated. That is, the family head does not take the risk of having to show a profit. Entrepreneurial risk was inherent in the life of a proportionately greater number of American families in the pre-corporation era. Not only is there entrepreneurial risk for fewer families, but technological advances have made work less physically strenuous. Many hours per week have been added to the free time of the man who is not an entrepreneur, and he is in better physical condition to enjoy that time. In 1850 the work week is estimated to have averaged nearly seventy hours, or the equal of seven ten-hour days.[2] During the seventy hours the workman produced only thirty cents worth of goods in terms of present purchasing power. The modern family has in a sense traded the economic influence of the entrepreneurial family for the greater leisure time and less risk of a family in a bureaucratic system.

[1] William H. Whyte, Jr., *The Organization Man* (Garden City, N.Y.: Doubleday, 1957), pp. 21–22.

[2] John Kenneth Galbraith, *The Affluent Society* (Boston: Houghton Mifflin, 1958), p. 334.

Modern Merchandising and the Family

More efficient wholesaling and retailing were not in themselves adequate solutions to the problem of overproduction. Producers found it necessary to contrive wants through advertising, and the home became a primary target of the professional advertiser. For production to increase it was necessary that advertising become big business as a builder of consumer demand. When supply outstrips demand, the limitation of further expansion lies not in productive capacity but in success in selling what can be produced. In a society of abundance, in which new kinds of goods are created and produced ahead of any felt need for them, the need must be created.

One way to create new markets is by changing the habits of the consumer, and the family is one of the major consuming units in American society. To induce the homemaker and other members of the family to spend rather than to save, or, better yet, to spend what they have not yet earned, required a change in values as well as in overt behavior for Americans reared on some version of the Puritan ethic of hard work and frugality. Untrained and often unskilled family members as consumers were pitted against skilled staffs in motivational analysis and research.

Along with advertising based on careful motivational analysis and research and prices lowered through efficient marketing methods, installment buying is an important aspect of family-economy interchange. Installment buying is used extensively by American families.

Most young couples carry life insurance but the actual cash value of their policies is small. They appear to have faith in their capacity to borrow. They are budget conscious but not in the old sense. Rather they practice what William H. Whyte calls "budgetism." They do not keep formal budgets. Quite the contrary; they are precommitted to regular, unvarying monthly payments on all major items of purchase. Total cost of an item becomes a less important consideration than the monthly payments on it. Planned obsolescence is also used in appealing to the homemaker to buy new things for the home and family. The store that used the slogan "Your Home is not a Home unless it is Changing" was not encouraging the development of a sense of the enduring value of the old and the familiar.[3]

Criticisms of advertising have been legion. It is sometimes referred to as an irresponsible social system, a deterrent to prudent family financial planning. It has been compared to such social systems as the school and the church in the magnitude of its influence. Furthermore, it inclines toward domination of the communications media, and in its vast power to shape popular standards, it has become one of that limited group of social systems

[3] Margaret Park Redfield, "The American Family: Consensus and Freedom," *American Journal of Sociology*, LII (November, 1946), 182.

which exercise social control.⁴ It is suspicion of lack of responsibility and lack of inherent social purpose to balance social power which creates concern over the role advertising plays in the interchange between the family and the economic system.

Abundance—Reward of Economic Efficiency

In evaluating the effects of the contemporary economic system on family life, the abundance it has provided must be regarded as a major factor.

FIGURE 8.1.   THE REVERSING PYRAMID OF INCOME

Distribution of families by income group (*in constant dollars*)

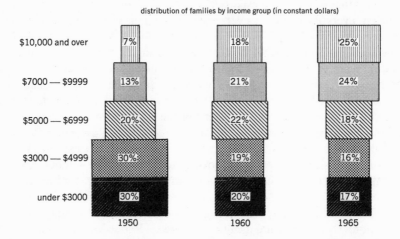

distribution of families by income group (in constant dollars)

	1950	1960	1965
$10,000 and over	7%	18%	25%
$7000 — $9999	13%	21%	24%
$5000 — $6999	20%	22%	18%
$3000 — $4999	30%	19%	16%
under $3000	30%	20%	17%

U.S. consumer markets of the future will increasingly be dominated by the effects of the powerful ongoing trend illustrated in these charts—the reversal of the income pyramid that has been typical of human societies through the centuries. To cancel out inflation, the charts show the changing distribution of income in constant 1965 dollars.

Seen in perspective, the evolutionary shift in the income structure seems revolutionary in its cumulative effect. In 1950 three out of five families in the U.S. had incomes of less than $5,000, and only one in five had an income of $7,000 or more. By 1965, virtually half of all families had incomes of $7,000 or more, and only one-third were below $5,000. In the years ahead, the $7,000-or-more families will make up an increasing majority. By 1970, or soon after, $10,000-or-more families will outnumber those with incomes of less than $5,000.

SOURCE: William Bowen, "The U.S. Economy Enters a New Era," *Fortune,* LXXV, No. 3 (March, 1967).

⁴ David M. Potter, *People of Plenty: Economic Abundance and the American Character* (Chicago: University of Chicago, 1954), pp. 166–177.

Americans are a people of plenty in an affluent society. With approximately six percent of the world's population and only seven percent of its land area, the people of the United States produce and consume one-third of the world's goods and services.

From 1900 to mid-century the scale of living of Americans increased by two and one-half times. While the population doubled, real national production increased five times.

There are still American families living in poverty, however. Their poverty is of two kinds. There is first what has been called "case poverty." Case poverty is related to some characteristic of the individuals afflicted. Nearly everyone else has mastered the environment but they have not, showing that the environment is not necessarily tractable. Secondly, there is insular poverty—that which manifests itself as an island of poverty. In the area in question, everyone or nearly everyone is poor, indicating a situation which is not readily transformed into one of abundance. With the production-population ratio being what it is, however, bringing these families out of a state of poverty would not require taking goods and services away from others; American business and industry can produce the additional goods and services needed. This is a point worth noting for it is unique to modern times; throughout much of the history of the West the relationship between various levels of society could not be altered without assuming that class struggle would ensue as limited resources were redistributed. In America today it is possible for economic poverty to be alleviated without any class becoming a victim of another class or without class antagonism over the distribution of resources—although such antagonisms, undeniably, do now exist. The same is largely true in regard to the benefits of education, police protection, recreation, and health measures.[5] Reduction in economic inequality would in itself remove some of the differences between American families.[6]

THE OCCUPATIONAL ROLE IN A CORPORATE ECONOMIC SYSTEM

In an industrialized corporate system the major point of articulation between the family and the economic system is through the family member who is both a member of the family and a member of the economic system. It is the individual breadwinner's job and not the products of the cooperative activities of family members that produces the primary source of income for the family. The breadwinner's job is a boundary role between the

[5] David E. Lilienthal, *Big Business: A New Era* (New York: Pocket Books, 1956), p. 197.

[6] Robert E. L. Faris, "The Middle Class from a Sociological Viewpoint," *Social Forces,* XXXIX (October, 1960), 1–5.

two systems. The husband-father, in holding a job and earning an income, performs an essential role for his family and an essential role in the economic system.

The Nature of Available Employment

What kinds of employment does an economy dominated by the corporation offer the employable person? There has been a shift in the nature of employment with corporate consolidation in business and industry. There has also been a shift because of the contemporary emphasis on the saleability of services as well as products. In 1870, three-fourths of all workers in the labor force were engaged in the production of physical goods—manufacturing, agriculture, forestry, fishing, mining, construction. At the turn of the century, more than one-half (53 percent) of the labor force was engaged in the production of services in the professions, transportation, communication, white-collar and service businesses and industries.[7] Below the top executive class there has grown up a large number of junior executive, technical, and service positions. Such jobs absorb the person's energy and emotional interest while his cognitive role is relatively narrow. This restricts the area in which a worker can share common interests and experiences with family members and with others not in the same occupational specialty.[8]

Employment and Family Mobility

Mobility denotes movement. Movement through physical space is called "physical or geographic mobility." If movement represents change in status, particularly in the occupational system, it is called "social mobility." If the move changes one's social class position, it is called "vertical social mobility."[9]

Employees, in the sense that all corporations require some of the same specialties, are interchangeable and hence mobile. Engineers, managers, and technicians can shift from one industry to another and thus are most representative of the mobile families of American society.

In a system that fosters mobility of the worker, we cannot ignore the fact of downward mobility as well as of upward mobility and the effect that it may have on the person and on his family. Wilensky and Edwards report that the person who is upwardly mobile in industry represents but a tiny fraction of the population. The skidder, as they define the downwardly-

[7] U.S. Department of Labor, Bureau of Labor Statistics, *Economic Forces in the USA in Facts and Figures* (Washington, D.C.; U.S. Government Printing Office, June, 1955), pp. 24–25.

[8] Talcott Parsons, "Age and Sex in the Social Structure of the United States," *American Sociological Review*, VII (October, 1942), 604–616.

[9] Julius Gould and William L. Kolb, *A Dictionary of the Social Sciences* (New York: The Free Press of Glencoe, 1964), pp. 434–435.

mobile man, represents perhaps a fifth of the working class of urban background, almost a tenth of all urbanites in the labor force and, in time of recession, more.[10]

Occupational Role and Family Interaction

Entrepreneurial families of the past had considerable freedom in running their own businesses, but they had constantly to deny themselves for the sake of future gain. Easy relations with other people were hindered by the kind of control and manipulative activity fostered by the entrepreneurial pattern; entrepreneurial conditions fostered a kind of egocentricity in outlook. The entrepreneurial family is often closed in and withdrawn into itself, thus encouraging strong intimacies and strong feelings toward one another. Deprivations for the sake of business are justified in terms of the future success of the children, who must give up things now, but who, by doing so, may legitimately claim the rewards of deference and gratification in the future.

There are also other aspects of the relationship between occupational role and family behavior. There is a relationship between satisfaction in the major breadwinner's job and behavior within the family, for instance. Eighty-seven families were interviewed in a recent study. The top and bottom thirds were labeled "satisfied" and "less-satisfied," respectively; and comparisons were made of responses to items concerning feelings of satisfaction. The "less-satisfied" father felt that his wife and children were not satisfied with his job and that family members were not satisfied with the prestige level of his job. His work was a cause of family disagreement, and he less often wanted to see his children follow his line of work. His occupation also affected the relationships of his wife both within and outside the family. The "less-satisfied" wife had more feelings of dissatisfaction in her relations outside the family. She had more negative responses regarding in-family factors as a result of the influences the job had on the father and the family. Like the father, the "less-satisfied" mother did not want to see her children follow in the father's line of work. "Less-satisfied" children responded negatively more often to both in-family and out-family items. They were not proud of the father's job: they considered it not as good as the jobs of their friends' fathers, and they wished he would change jobs. Within the family, the children were aware of aspects of the father's job that had an adverse effect on him.[11]

[10] Harold L. Wilensky and Hugh Edwards, "The Skidder: Ideological Adjustments of Downward Mobile Workers," *American Sociological Review,* XXIV (April, 1959), 215–231.

[11] William G. Dyer, "A Comparison of Families of High and Low Job Satisfaction," *Marriage and Family Living,* XVIII (February, 1956), 58–60.

Occupational Role and Social Participation

The family man who struggles to get ahead does so in part at the expense of his participation in family life.[12] The man who has achieved a good status, on the other hand, can afford to devote time to the enjoyment of family life, though he does not necessarily choose to do so. Men who are entrepreneurs and not bureaucratic technicians—businessmen, doctors, lawyers, consultants—often work extremely long hours. If having control of one's own work schedule and working at least fifty-five hours a week is an indication of preference for income over leisure, then most of these men have such preference.[13] Wilensky found small proprietors leading the list, with 59 percent working at least a fifty-five hour week; lawyers who worked without

TABLE 8.1. MEAN NUMBER OF YEARS IN WORK FORCE, BY OCCUPATIONAL CATEGORY

Major Occupational Category	Mean Number of Years in Working Force	Average Age of Entry	Average Retirement Age
Professional, technical, and kindred workers	40	Late	Early
Managers, officials, and proprietors— except farm	41	Late	Early
Craftsmen, foremen, and kindred workers	44	Late	Average
Operatives and kindred workers	45	Early	Early
Sales workers	47	Early	Average
Clerical and kindred workers	47	Early	Average
Farmers and farm managers	48	Late	Late
Laborers, except farm and mine	51	Early	Late
Farm laborers and foremen	52	Early	Late
Service workers	52	Early	Late

SOURCE: A. J. Jaffe and R. O. Carleton, *Occupational Mobility in the United States, 1930–1950* (New York: Columbia King's Crown, 1954), pp. 49–50.

a partner were next, with 38 percent logging such a heavy work week. Wilensky found that a third of the high-income men worked at least fifty-five hours a week compared to about a fifth of the less affluent. There was a general tendency for higher occupational strata to work long hours. Only about a fifth of all lawyers and one-fourth of the professors worked fewer than forty-five hours per week. Were these high-income men working long hours because they were driven by a religiously-oriented ethic? Wilensky

[12] Daniel R. Miller and Guy E. Swanson, *The Changing American Parent* (New York: Wiley, 1958), p. 208 ff.
[13] Harold L. Wilensky, "The Uneven Distribution of Leisure: The Impact of Economic Growth on 'Free Time,'" *Social Problems*, IX (Summer, 1961), 32–56.

indicates that if this was true anywhere, it was true among the Jewish professionals and white-collar workers. Catholics and Protestants, while they were unevenly distributed among occupational groups, were virtually identical to each other in their propensity to work.

Taking into consideration the number of years in the work force (people in the higher strata occupations tend to enter their field of work at an older age and retire at an earlier age) and the length of the work week, the average man's gain in leisure perhaps has been exaggerated. There appears to be a slowly increasing minority of the male urban labor force working fifty-five hours a week or more.

Orderliness of Career and Social Participation

Wilensky has investigated the orderliness of career of the family head in relation to social participation. (What Wilensky means by "orderliness of career" is a succession of related jobs arranged in a hierarchy of prestige through which a person moves in an orderly and more-or-less predictable sequence.) He hypothesized that by holding out the prospect of continuous, predictable rewards, careers foster a willingness to train and achieve, to adopt a long-time perspective and to defer immediate gratifications for later ones. Careers lead to the creation of a life plan.[14]

In the study—which represented a cross section of upper-working class and lower-middle class men at the bottom of various ladders leading upward, and some on their way down—47 percent were classified as white-collar and 53 percent as blue-collar. Nearly three in five lived in the suburbs. Most men did not experience the joys of a life plan because most work situations did not afford the necessary stable progression over the work life. Rather, a majority experienced various degrees of disorder in their work histories. If the lower class had been added to the sample, it would appear that a vast majority of the labor force was not progressing in an orderly way and could expect a work life of unpredictable ups and downs.

Except for regular church services, almost four in ten men spent less than thirty minutes a month on all organizational activity. The median time was about two hours, as compared with their median estimated time of about forty-eight hours per month watching television.

Men whose careers were orderly had stronger attachments to formal associations and the community than did men whose job histories were disorderly. Men with orderly careers had memberships in formal associations and attended more meetings than did men with disorderly work histories. Men with orderly careers averaged more hours a month in all activities of formal associations, excluding church, than did men with disorderly work

[14] Harold L. Wilensky, "Orderly Careers and Social Participation: The Impact of Work History on Social Integration in the Middle Mass," *American Sociological Review*, XXVI (August, 1961), 521–539.

histories. Men with orderly careers ranged widely in their secondary attachments and were exposed to organizations representing a greater variety of values, interests, and status levels. The memberships of men with orderly careers offered greater opportunity for interacting with persons who differed from themselves in important social characteristics.

The memberships of men with orderly careers exposed them to more of the major systems in society, and they had stronger attachments to the community than did men with disorderly work histories. Men with orderly careers more often supported local schools; they remembered the last school election; and they reported that they voted in favor of increased school taxes. They more often reported a contribution of one hundred dollars or more to churches and charities in the past year. They also evidenced greater vitality of primary relations (with kin, friend, and neighbor) ranging into a wider community than did men whose work histories were disorderly. The range of primary contacts of men with orderly careers was wider—going beyond family and relatives in the same income bracket, and beyond others in the same neighborhood or type of work—though their best friends were more often persons in the same work place or the same line of work, and they more often saw work associates socially.

Men whose careers were orderly integrated work and nonwork roles to a greater extent than did men whose work histories were disorderly. They had more long-lasting friendships than men with disorderly work histories, and they had best friends in clubs and organizations more often than those with disorderly work histories. Men who had predictable careers for at least a fifth of their work lives belonged to more organizations, attended more meetings, and averaged more hours in organizational activity. Their attachments to the local community were stronger.

According to Wilensky's conclusion, "If we give a man some college, put him on a stable career ladder, and top it off with a nice family income, he will get into the community act. Give a man less than high school, a thoroughly unpredictable sequence of jobs, a family income of five to eight thousand and it is very likely that his ties to the community will be few and weak."[15]

FAMILY INFLUENCE ON OCCUPATIONAL ROLE

How does the family affect a person's chances in the occupational world?[16] There is evidence that the motivation to achievement is a person-

[15] *Ibid.*, p. 535.

[16] The following draws on Lipset and Bendix's analysis of social mobility. See Seymour Martin Lipset and Reinhard Bendix, *Social Mobility in Industrial Society* (Berkeley and Los Angeles: University of California, 1959); see also Neil J. Smelser and Seymour Martin Lipset, eds., *Social Structure and Mobility in Economic Development* (Chicago: Aldine, 1966).

ality component that stems in large part from early childhood experiences. Early training for independence related to high achievement motivation is more characteristic of middle-class than working-class families. Eighty-five percent of a sample of New Haven high school boys from the two highest social classes scored high on an achievement scale, compared to only 32 percent of the boys from the three lowest classes.

Douvan and Addelson, investigating the occupational aspirations of 1,000 high school boys, found that those whose aspirations were upward tended to come from warm, permissive families that encouraged the development of achievement and autonomy and realistic attitudes toward parents and self. The boys with the higher aspirations were more likely to share leisure-time activities with parents than were boys without high aspirations.[17]

The relationship between family and motivation is not a simple one, however. There are other factors related to motivation of offspring than those analyzed by Douvan and Addelson. For example, Dynes, Clarke, and Dinitz found in a study of 350 university students that the high aspirers had experienced feelings of rejection more frequently than had those with lower aspirations; the high-aspiring persons also indicated less attachment to their parents and had experienced a lesser degree of happiness during childhood. The authors concluded that unsatisfactory interpersonal relations in the family of orientation were significantly related to high aspirational levels and that satisfactory relationships were related to lower aspirational levels.[18] The apparent contradiction between the findings of the two studies indicates something of the complexity of the factors contributing to the motivation of offspring and the difficulty of isolating and establishing their effect on motivation.

During any period of marked change characterized by the creation of new enterprise, persons will rise to positions of importance, influence, and wealth in relatively short periods of time. To what extent is advancement due to one's own efforts and to what extent is it due to family? American folklore is inclined to overemphasize spectacular careers; however, the spectacular careers of a few individuals do not necessarily reflect the characteristics of the business elite as a whole.[19] Freedom of the person to rise is often facilitated by the family; yet the person who rises economically or socially must be willing to break with some previous patterns. The process of social mobility requires the capacity to leave earlier environments behind and to adapt to new ones. Socially mobile business leaders show an unusual

[17] As reported by Lipset and Bendix, *ibid.*, pp. 250–251.

[18] Russell R. Dynes, Alfred C. Clarke, and Simon Dinitz, "Levels of Occupational Aspiration: Some Aspects of Family Experiences As a Variable," *American Sociological Review*, XXI (April, 1956), 212–215.

[19] This section follows the analysis of the mobility of business elites in Lipset and Bendix, *op. cit.* (see above, fn. 16), p. 117 ff.

capacity to break away from persons who are liabilities to their mobility and to form relationships with those who can help them. On the other hand, it is likely that success of a person of the business elite is based upon and facilitated by the gradual advance of his family in preceding generations; the successful business leader is often a member of a relatively well-to-do family. His career is an extension of the step-by-step advances of the many. The typical sequence appears to consist of the slow buildup of an enterprise in the first generation, a consolidation and expansion of the business by the second generation, and the successful or unsuccessful efforts of subsequent generations to maintain and strengthen the position of the family. Since 1801 a majority of prominent businessmen have come from families already well-established economically. If the businessmen whose fathers were gentry farmers are included, about two-thirds of each generation of successful businessmen had a very favorable family background. The proportion of business leaders coming from well-to-do families has remained relatively stable, varying between 63 and 64 percent. The evidence points strongly to the favorable social and economic background of a great majority of those whose later careers placed them in the American business elite. The validity of the doctrine that the successful businessman has proved himself to be the fittest in the struggle for survival can be questioned since his success in the majority of cases has been so greatly facilitated by the influence of favorable family background.

That family influence has remained a very significant factor in the recruitment of American business elite bears on a larger issue. Sir Henry Maine advanced the theory a century ago that modern society is a society of contract rather than of status. This distinction was defined by Maine in the following terms: "the individual is steadily substituted for the Family, as the unit of which civil laws take account. . . . Nor is it difficult to see what is the tie between man and man which replaces by degrees those forms of reciprocity in rights and duties which have their origin in the family. It is Contract. Starting, as from one terminus of history, from a condition of society in which all the relations of Persons are summed up in the relations of Family, we seem to have steadfastly moved towards a phase of social order in which all these relations arise from the free agreement of Individuals."[20] American social scientists have perhaps erred in misinterpreting Maine's major point to mean that in the course of the nineteenth century the autonomy of the person had developed *de facto* rather than *de jure,* and in attempting to demonstrate that modern society was on the way to developing a status society out of a contractual society. The *de jure* autonomy of the person never implied that the person would willfully divest himself of the advantages which the status of his family afforded him. Rather the con-

[20] Henry Maine, *Ancient Law* (New York: Dutton, 1927), p. 99.

tractual autonomy of the person enabled him to escape many of the family liabilities which were his merely by virtue of his birth.

Families have continued the practice of conferring as many advantages upon their individual members as they can, even though reciprocal duties to the family have become in some measure discretionary acts. The families of America's business elite persist in preserving for their descendants as much of their economic success and their social status as they are able to and pass it on to them.

Conformity to the standards of a family system with higher status than one's family possesses may facilitate upward mobility. Coming from a lower-class family with good work habits, cleanliness, concern for personal appearance and for following rules of middle-class morality is more likely to influence one's move up in the social system than is the rejection of these norms.

Economic Advancement and Family Formation

The practical test of the achievement motive comes when its satisfaction requires the deferring of other gratifications in favor of occupational achievement. The desire for advancement has a restrictive effect on fertility in times of economic disadvantage, but it may not be restrictive in times of affluence. Boggs found that, on an average, upwardly mobile men of a metropolitan suburb had slightly more rather than fewer children than did nonmobile families. Also, white-collar men with several children had higher levels of aspiration than did those with fewer children.[21] Similarly a study of 2,205 bureaucratic technicians, salesmen, engineers, and bank employees shows no differences between mobile and nonmobile men in such indices of familism as number of offspring, age at marriage, and childless span. The men who had risen from humble origins were as family oriented as men with white-collar backgrounds.[22]

MARRIED WOMEN IN THE LABOR FORCE

Some important interchanges between the family and the economic system are occasioned by the high incidence of employment of married women outside the home. In 1890 less than 5 percent of wives in America were in the labor force; in 1940 15 percent were employed; in 1950 the figure rose to 20 percent; and by 1960 one-third of American married women were in the labor force. It is expected that the proportion of married women in the labor force will continue to rise. It was during World War II that Amer-

[21] Stephen T. Boggs, "Family Size and Social Mobility in a California Suburb," *Eugenics Quarterly*, IV (1957), 208–213.
[22] Seymour Yellin, *Social Mobility and Familism* (Evanston, Ill.: Northwestern University, 1955, unpublished Ph.D. dissertation).

ican mothers moved into paid employment in significant numbers. It was generally believed that with the end of hostilities they would return to the home. Contrary to expectations, the number of women in the labor force continued to increase rapidly during the postwar period.

In the 1960's two out of every five families in the United States had more than one wage earner; and it is expected that by the early 1970's half of all American families will have double incomes, mainly though not entirely due to the number of wives working for pay. It is possible to predict that nearly all wives will work after marriage until their first pregnancy; that a few mothers of preschool children will work part-time; and that when the last child is in school, employment will rise sharply and continue to increase until the youngest child leaves home or reaches adulthood, when employment will reach a second peak.[23] Nye found a sizable minority of non-employed mothers who said they would like to have a job, and a smaller proportion of working mothers who said they would like to quit work.[24]

Young women in 1940 were just as likely as are mothers today to work for pay for a few years and then quit when children come; however, once out of the work force they were not as likely to return to it again. In each five-year age group over twenty-five, the proportion of women in the labor force declined gradually but steadily from a high of 46 percent of those in their early twenties to 15 percent of those in their early sixties. By 1960 this pattern had changed radically. Women who had quit work when the first child was born came back into the labor market in large numbers a few years later. In each five-year age group the proportion of women employed rose, from 35 percent of those in their late twenties to 47 percent of those in their late forties. For women in their fifties the proportion tapers off, though many continue to work into their sixties. Almost 30 percent of those sixty to sixty-four years of age are working, whereas only half that many were working in 1940.[25]

The reasons why women enter the labor force are numerous. It was once the case that married women commonly entered the labor force out of necessity—the husband's income was not adequate to meet basic needs. With greater affluence and with increasing numbers of middle-class wives entering the labor force, the factor of necessity becomes less significant; the desire to earn money does not necessarily decrease in significance, however. Technological advances are a factor; the work of the home has been simpli-

---

[23] Robert O. Blood, Jr. and Donald M. Wolfe, *Husbands and Wives: The Dynamics of Married Living* (Glencoe, Ill.: The Free Press, 1964), p. 104 ff.; Jean A. Wells, *15 Years After College: A Study of Alumnae of the Class of 1945*, U.S. Department of Labor, Women's Bureau Bulletin, CCLXXXIII (Washington, D.C., 1962), 1–26.

[24] F. Ivan Nye and Lois W. Hoffman, *The Employed Mother In America* (Chicago: Rand McNally, 1963), p. 390.

[25] "Marriage and the American Woman," *Population Profile* (Washington, D.C.: Population Reference Bureau, Inc., June, 1963), pp. 1–5.

fied by the addition of mechanical gadgets. Moreover, many of the jobs in society that recently called for brawn can now be performed by anyone capable of controlling power tools.

Smaller families and the spread of an equalitarian family ideology are also factors in women's entry into the labor force. Since the average American woman has her last baby when she is about twenty-seven years of age, she has her youngest child in school by the time she is thirty-three years of age. The full-time child-tending period is then at an end, and after such a period of intensive activity she is apt to want something to do during the forty or more remaining years of her life.

It was once thought that married women would confine their out-of-home activity to community volunteer work. Many are so engaged (eighty-three to 91 percent of women in the Women's Bureau study of 1945 college alumnae), but others who have been involved in both volunteer work and paid employment tend to report that volunteer work is less attractive. Employees receive more recognition than do volunteers. The paid person appears to receive the more respectable assignments and to have more incentive, interest, and satisfaction. Married women could not work outside the home if the sentiment of employers was strongly opposed.[26]

One study indicates that employers share the traditional view that a mother's place is in the home, but they still do not hesitate to employ women. They define the same job responsibilities for mothers as for anyone else; but, in practice, they are inclined to allow mothers to take time off for emergencies related to their children. They are inclined to rationalize this practice by stating that mothers are better employees in other respects.

The most important change in the type of work of women in the labor force in the past half century is their movement from unskilled and semi-skilled manual work to clerical and sales employment. Clerical and sales work is a most popular type of employment; it avoids the unpleasant conditions of factory work and, on the other hand, does not require the preparation required for professional work. The occupations which employ the largest number of women are principally those involving traditional functions, however; caring for the sick, training the young, making and caring for clothing, preparing and serving food, and keeping house.[27]

The large number of women in the labor force raises the question of the effect of wives' and mothers' working on their marriages and on their families. There has been an avalanche of empirical research on questions relating to the employment of married women. No very definitive conclusions

[26] Nye and Hoffman, op. cit., p. 385 ff.
[27] Roland R. Renne, "Woman Power and the American Economy," Journal of Home Economics, XLIX (February, 1957), 83–86; Blood and Wolfe, op. cit., pp. 83–86.

as to the effects of employment can be arrived at, however; there is a multiplicity of factors affecting relationships within the home, and whether or not the wife is employed outside the home is only one of the factors. Other factors are the nature of her work, the number of hours she works, the age of the children, the reaction of the husband to her work, the quality of the babysitting services employed, and others.[28]

Effect on the Marital System

When only one spouse is employed outside the home, there is apt to be differential personal growth, with the husband and wife having less and less satisfying interaction with each other. The husband is involved in more stimulating activity in adult concerns and with adults, while the woman in the home is involved with small children and with the routines of the home and has less opportunity for adult relationships. On the other hand, it seems reasonable, as Litwak has suggested, that it is only when personal creativity takes place within the overall marriage system that it is likely to lead to marital adjustment. If it takes place outside of that context, it is apt to have a disorganizing or disintegrating effect.[29]

Traditionally, the roles of husbands and wives tend to follow a sex-linked division of labor. The wife takes more of the integrative and expressive roles and the husband takes the instrumental ones. The integrative activity in the family system has to do with the development and maintenance of the family as an orderly system within which compatible interaction of family members centers around the goals and purposes of the family and the needs and desires of each person in the family.[30] Expressive activity has to do with mediation and conciliation in the family; smoothing out disputes and resolving hostilities as well as comforting and consoling individual family members. The instrumental function relates to the future-oriented rather than the immediate goals of the family. Immediate goals relate to integrative-expressive functions—orderly and gratifying interaction in the family; future-oriented goals relate to the overall planning for the future well-being of the family and its members and to acquiring the resources to assure a future for the family as an on-going social system. The occupation of the major breadwinner falls in this category, as does financial planning, making and managing investments, purchasing insurance, and others. Litwak tested the

[28] Marian R. Yarrow, Phyllis Scott, Louise de Leeuw, and Christine Heinig, "Child-rearing in Families of Working and Nonworking Mothers," *Sociometry*, XXV (June, 1962), 122–140; Nye and Hoffman, *op. cit.*, p. 191 ff.

[29] Eugene Litwak, Gloria Count, and Edward M. Haydon, "Group Structure and Interpersonal Creativity as Factors Which Reduce Errors in the Prediction of Marital Adjustment," *Social Forces*, XXXVIII (May, 1960), 308–315.

[30] Talcott Parsons and Robert F. Bales, *Family Socialization And Interaction Process* (Glencoe, Ill.: The Free Press, 1955), p. 22 ff.

hypothesis that marital adjustment is greater for both husband and wife where the husband has more creativity than the wife in the instrumental areas of life, and found the data confirming the hypothesis.

The findings of a number of studies indicate that the marital relationship tends to contain more negative elements among couples when the wife is employed.[31] Not only do men believe that children will suffer if the wife is employed; they also fear that the wife will increase her independence, thereby threatening the husband's culturally-defined dominance, particularly if she enjoys greater economic success than he does. Fairchild and Wynn found that the heaviest burden was carried by the wife whose activity outside the home did not receive the wholehearted support of her husband. If the husband did not share her attitude toward her work, troubles of a more serious kind were almost always in evidence. Axelson found that the husbands of working wives seemed to hold less tenaciously to the historical masculine prerogative of greater economic advantage and sexual predominance. A next problem for the researcher is to demonstrate empirically whether the poorer marital adjustment found in working-wife families is the effect or the cause of her decision to enter into the labor force. In general, women's jobs tend to be of a qualitatively different type from those of men and not of a status which seriously competes with that of the husband as the primary breadwinner and status-giver.

Effect on Parent-Child Relationships

Nye found that adolescent children of part-time working mothers had better relationships with their parents than did children of either full-time working mothers or mothers who did not work outside the home. In 1957, the Glueck's reported that maternal employment was not related to juvenile delinquency, and that where there was such a relationship the data seemed to indicate that it was not employment that was the important factor but the existence of an erratic household.[32]

The employed mother is more likely to encourage independence on the part of her children than is the mother who remains in the home. It is possible that part-time employment might help the mother of an adolescent to move from the roles of protector and nurturer to that of a trainer in independence, thus enabling both mother and child to adapt more easily to the child's growing independence. Yarrow and others found that working mothers had firmer control over children and assigned them greater respon-

[31] Nye and Hoffman, op. cit. (see above, fn. 24), p. 385 ff.; Leland J. Axelson, Jr., "The Marital Adjustment and Marital Role Definitions of Husbands of Working and Nonworking Wives," Marriage and Family Living, XXV (May, 1963), 189–195.
[32] Sheldon and Eleanor Glueck, "Working Mothers and Delinquency," Mental Hygiene, XLI (July, 1957), 347–348.

sibility.[33] Part-time employment is a less abrupt change for both the parent and the child than full-time employment would be, yet it may be less of a psychological change for the mother than nonemployment would be as she sees her child-tending period draw to a close.

The positive relationships found between part-time employment and parent-child adjustment cannot be generalized to younger children; more empirical research is needed. It is reasonable to assume that the effects of maternal employment would be more dramatic and perhaps more detrimental where young children are involved: the guilt reaction of the mother appears to be greater if younger children are involved.

The findings of studies to date suggest that a daughter's admiration of her mother may be greater if the mother is employed. The mother's working also presents to the daughter an image of the female role that includes less restriction and a wider range of activities. For boys, the mother's employment might influence concepts of the mother's role, but what the nature of the influence is on their attitudes towards themselves and toward their fathers depends on the circumstances surrounding the mother's employment. Hoffman suggests that a reasonable hypothesis would be that maternal employment is negatively related to achievement for boys.

Findings from several studies show that mother's motivations regarding work and her attitudes toward it are important factors. If the mother's employment is gratifying to her, the mother-child relationship is apt to be good. If a mother's employment is not satisfying, the parent-child relationship is also likely to be unsatisfactory. But the same can be said of women who want to be employed but do not do so out of a sense of duty to the family; Yarrow and others found that these mothers had lower scores on "adequacy of mothering" than did employed mothers. These women had more difficulties in the area of child control, less emotional satisfaction in relationships with their children, and less confidence in their functioning as mothers.

The addition of provider role may actually act to reduce family tension by restoring the economic contributions of the wife and reducing the burden of the provider role for the husband. Furthermore, it helps the family implement the dominant American values of upward mobility and a higher standard of living.

Personal Adjustment of the Employed Mother

In regard to the employed mother's personal adjustment, Nye found that she showed significant satisfaction with her work and with the community as a place to live. Factors related to recreation, income, house, and furni-

[33] Nye and Hoffman, op. cit. (see above, fn. 24), p. 191 ff.; Yarrow et al., op. cit., pp. 137–138.

ture showed no significant difference between employed and nonemployed mothers. Concerning organizational participation, fewer differences were found than anticipated; there were no significant differences in the number of organizations to which the two groups belonged or in the frequency with which they attended meetings. Fewer employed mothers held offices or committee chairmanships, however.

Employed mothers tended toward higher self-esteem as individuals than did the nonemployed, but in situations in which there was conflict between the roles of employee and homemaker they often felt inadequate. Working mothers also tended to be bothered less by pains and ailments of the body and by not feeling healthy enough to do the things they would like to do. They did not appear to suffer from the dual roles of employee and home-maker. The "stereotype of the employed mother as an exhausted, 'bedrag-gled,' physically debilitated 'wreck' can be safely stowed in the intellectual garbage can along with an increasing number of common sense myths."[34]

The great increase in the number of women working outside the home should not be taken to mean that women are finding their major functions to be outside the home. The number of mothers in the labor force who have small children is still quite small and has not shown a marked tendency to increase. The homemaker role is still the overwhelmingly predominant one for the married woman with small children.

Generally it would appear that the adult female role has not ceased to be anchored primarily in the internal affairs of the family—as wife, mother, and manager of the household. It appears too as though more women will play the employed role noncontinuously than will be continuously em-ployed. Despite consideration from employers, the employee role is an in-flexible and dominant one, representing a major structural change in a woman's way of life.

SUMMARY

As industry became impersonally corporate instead of existing as a family affair, persons, not families, became the important units so far as the eco-nomic aspects of society were concerned. The primary source of family income came to lie in occupational earnings. It is above all the presence of the modern occupational system and its mode of articulation with the family which accounts for the difference between the modern, especially American, family system and any found in nonliterate or peasant societies.

Through the history of much of the world, a very large proportion of the world's work has been and still is performed in the context of family units. Occupational organization as we know it in America today is the socio-

[34] Nye and Hoffman, *op. cit.* (see above, fn. 24), p. 388.

logical antithesis of this. The primary responsibility for support comes to rest on one adult male member of the nuclear family. It is clearly the exceptional male who can occupy a respected place in American society without having a regular job. In this sense a married woman has more freedom than a married man; she can choose to be employed or not to be employed.

As the prospect of the family head, personally, to supervise a family industry has decreased, so also has his economic risk and his direct responsibility for the output of economic activity. His freedom and his responsibility, economically speaking, have been curtailed; his leisure time has been increased. The chief economic roles of the family are the preparation of the individual for his occupational role, the sustaining of him in that role, and the purchasing and consuming of the products of a corporate productive system. In an era of abundance of goods and services and relatively high wages most but not all American families are able to maintain themselves on the salary of the major breadwinner. For the majority of American families the entry of the wife-mother into the labor force is more by choice than by dire economic necessity. Her earnings increase the prospects of establishing a higher material standard of living and expanding the family's educational and cultural horizons. Whether her entry into the labor force will markedly alter other aspects of marriage and family life depends upon the influence of a number of related factors.

Economic well-being is not the heritage of all American families. A relatively high incidence of both case and insular poverty is still a fact of American economic and social life in the twentieth century.

BIBLIOGRAPHY

Bert N. Adams and James E. Butler. "Occupational Status and Husband-Wife Social Participation," *Social Forces,* XXXXV (June, 1967), 501–507.

Leland J. Axelson, Jr. "The Marital Adjustment and Marital Role Definitions of Husbands of Working and Nonworking Wives," *Marriage and Family Living,* XXV (May, 1963), 189–195.

Daniel Bell. *The End of Ideology.* Glencoe, Ill.: The Free Press, 1960.

Peter M. Blau and O. Dudley Duncan. *The American Occupational Structure.* New York: Wiley, 1967.

Stephen T. Boggs. "Family Size and Social Mobility in a California Suburb," *Eugenics Quarterly,* IV (1957), 208–213.

Glen G. Cain. *Married Women in the Labor Force: An Economic Analysis.* Chicago: University of Chicago, 1966.

William G. Dyer. "A Comparison of Families of High and Low Job Satisfaction," *Marriage and Family Living,* XVIII (February, 1956), 58–60.

Russell R. Dynes, Alfred C. Clarke, and Simon Dinitz. "Levels of Occupational Aspiration: Some Aspects of Family Experiences as a Variable," *American Sociological Review,* XXI (April, 1956), 212–215.

Robert E. L. Faris. "The Middle Class from a Sociological Viewpoint," *Social Forces,* XXXIX (October, 1960), 1–5.

John K. Galbraith. *The Affluent Society.* Boston: Houghton Mifflin, 1958.

Eli Ginzberg and Alice M. Yohalem. *Educated American Women: Self-Portraits.* New York: Columbia University Press, 1966.

Suzanne Keller. *The American Lower Class Family.* Albany, N.Y.: New York State Division for Youth, 1965.

Hazel Kyrk. *The Family In The American Economy.* Chicago: University of Chicago, 1953.

David E. Lilienthal. *Big Business: A New Era.* New York: Pocket Books, 1956.

Seymour M. Lipset and Reinhard Bendix. *Social Mobility in Industrial Society.* Berkeley and Los Angeles: University of California, 1959.

Daniel R. Miller and Guy E. Swanson. *The Changing American Parent.* New York: Wiley, 1958.

C. Wright Mills. *White Collar: The American Middle Classes.* New York: Oxford, 1951.

M. F. Nimkoff and Russell Middleton. "Types of Family and Types of Economy," *American Journal of Sociology,* LXVI (November, 1960), 215–225.

F. Ivan Nye and Lois W. Hoffman. *The Employed Mother in America.* Chicago: Rand McNally, 1963.

Roland R. Renne. "Woman Power and the American Economy," *Journal of Home Economics,* XLIX (February, 1957), 83–86.

Walter L. Slocum. *Occupational Careers: A Sociological Perspective.* Chicago: Aldine, 1966.

Marvin B. Sussman (ed.). "American Poverty in the Mid-Sixties," *Journal of Marriage and the Family,* XXVI (November, 1964), 389–498.

William H. Whyte, Jr. *The Organization Man.* Garden City, N.Y.: Doubleday, 1957.

Harold L. Wilensky. "Orderly Careers and Social Participation: The Impact of Work History on Social Integration in the Middle Mass," *American Sociological Review,* XXVI (August, 1961), 521–539.

Harold L. Wilensky. "The Uneven Distribution of Leisure: The Impact of Economic Growth on 'Free Time,' " *Social Problems,* IX (Summer, 1961), 32–56.

Harold L. Wilensky and Hugh Edwards. "The Skidder: Ideological Adjustments of Downward Mobile Workers," *American Sociological Review,* XXIV (April, 1959), 215–231.

Marian R. Yarrow, Phyllis Scott, Louise de Leeuw, and Christine Heinig. "Child-rearing in Families of Working and Nonworking Mothers," *Sociometry,* XXV (June, 1962), 122–140.

CHAPTER 9

Family, Class, and Community

A COMMUNITY can be viewed as a collectivity of families sharing a limited territorial area as a base for carrying out many of the activities of family members. While the United States was essentially an agricultural society, local community served as the center of man's concerns. The community as a definite social and economic unit with a locale whose boundaries were coterminus with the homes of the people who produced and used its goods and services.

The elements associated with family organization in the traditional small, self-contained community were a large family attached to a homestead; a rich heritage of tradition; a degree of isolation from others, so that something of a distinct form of life developed with freedom from rapid change. People could be identified by naming the local community in which they lived. Status and prestige were bestowed upon worthy citizens. Competition within the community whetted the individual desire to stand well in the eyes of fellow citizens. Acquaintance was widespread within the limited area and neighbors depended upon one another. Participation of citizens in community affairs established a pattern of social behavior expected of local residents.

THE SPATIALLY-ORIENTED LOCAL COMMUNITY

Local communities made up of people living in the same spatial area, people with the same interests and common concerns, develop within the modern industrial city, though these communities are not self-sufficient local units. The presence of local community within the city has been demonstrated as an empirical reality. Within a city there are communities in which home-and-family-committed people have many relationships that are particular to the area, such as neighboring and participating in various organizational activities. These intracity communities provide the market for an urban press which emphasizes the small-scale worlds within the metropolis. The press is in itself an active agent reinforcing and extending the mutual recognition of interdependence and identification within the aggregate and moving it further toward the conditions of community.[1] The urban weekly newspaper is an effective instrument for developing, reinforcing, and extending local community identification and involvement.[2]

Local communities also develop within some suburbs.[3] Whyte found in one suburb in the United States that each court or block had unity and a special spirit.[4] In trying to explain this special block spirit, Whyte came to the conclusion that the character of the original settlers in the court or block was most important. He concluded that in the emergent phase of the suburb the impact of families with strong personalities, whether good or otherwise, was magnified. The presence of children had much to do with the continuing community system that developed. Children's friendships were translated into mothers' friendships, and these, in turn, into family friendships. "Find where the flow of wheeled juvenile traffic is and you will find the outlines of wives' kaffeeklatsch routes."

THE COMMUNALITY

The spatially-oriented local community is not the only kind of community that the family has interchanges with within the city and within the suburb. There is also what McClenahan has labeled "communality."[5] Communality refers to the sentiment of community solidarity without a spatial referent. People gravitate together across locality lines in congenial groupings. The place where they meet need have no special relation to their place of residence. The communality is made up of persons or families characterized by their social nearness regardless of the fact that their homes may be in separated localities. The communality system may be formal or informal, its members belonging simply because they share life interests, ranging from the ephemeral to the relatively permanent. They meet together whenever they find it convenient, but usually not by accident or without some previous

[1] Morris Janowitz, *The Community Press in an Urban Setting* (Glencoe, Ill.: The Free Press, 1962).

[2] Otto N. Larsen and Alex S. Edelstein, "Communication, Consensus and the Community Involvement of Urban Husbands and Wives," *Acta Sociologia*, V, Fasc. 1 (1960), 15–30.

[3] Clark reports that people in the Toronto area moved to the suburbs in search of space. Families were in search of houses, and the place they could find houses was in the suburbs. The emerging suburban community which made demands upon the new residents was a community they often sought to avoid rather than to become a part of. See S. D. Clark, *The Suburban Society* (Toronto, Canada: University of Toronto, 1966).

[4] William H. Whyte, Jr., *The Organization Man* (Garden City, N.Y.: Doubleday, 1957), p. 368.

[5] B. A. McClenahan, "The Communality: The Urban Substitute for the Traditional Community," *Sociology and Social Research*, XXX (March–April, 1946), 264–271. The concept "communality" parallels the concept "social network" developed by Bott. See also Elizabeth Bott, *Family and Social Network* (London: Tavistock, 1957).

planning. Communalities can be as varied as the interests of people. Their activities involve social, economic, political and religious concerns, and they are not limited by neighborhood boundaries.

While Seeley, Sim, and Loosley found a lack of strong local friendships, a communality system was common to Crestwood Heights (though it should be noted that this is a Canadian suburb). Friends of the family were scattered all through the metropolitan area and even beyond it. The Crestwooder thought little of driving thirty or fifty miles to spend an evening with friends. Distance, while it could be obliterated to some extent by car and telephone, dictated a formalized system of interaction which was very different from the casual dropping in of neighbors at unheralded times throughout the day.[6]

EXTENT OF MOBILITY

Mobility, both spatial and social, is antithetical to development of a sense of community; Americans tend to hold both spatial immobility and rigidity of social status in disrepute. American society has been committed to the almost impossible ideal of horizontal and vertical mobility for everyone; consequently there is tension and insecurity in the society. Families are deprived of the psychological values inherent in a stable, unchanging status in society.[7] However, Fairchild and Wynn report that moving as a part of the pattern of young executives in the American corporate economic system has apparently become accepted and is not regarded as a problem for the family. Mobility is taken as a matter of course.[8]

American economic life is fully intelligible only when viewed as a national economy.[9] The fact that America is a national community, that life is much the same throughout the country, explains why persons and families in moving about the country make physical moves, but essentially not cultural moves. As family heads are transferred about the country from one installation to another of some business or governmental establishment, the decor, the architecture, the faces, and the names may change, but the type of people, the conversation, and the values do not. Organization people talk the same language everywhere;[10] they understand each other.

[6] John R. Seeley, R. Alexander Sim, and Elizabeth W. Loosley, *Crestwood Heights: A Study of the Culture of Suburban Life* (New York: Basic Books, 1956), p. 206.

[7] David M. Potter, *People of Plenty: Economic Abundance and the American Character* (Chicago: University of Chicago, 1954), p. 108.

[8] Roy W. Fairchild and John Charles Wynn, *Families in the Church: A Protestant Survey* (New York: Association, 1961), p. 157.

[9] For development of the concept of nation as community we are indebted to Don Martindale, *American Society* (Princeton, N.J.: Van Nostrand, 1960).

[10] Whyte, *op. cit.* (see above, fn. 4), pp. 305–306.

National Community and Family Mobility

If local communities within the nation were unique one from another in basic cultural patterns, business transfers would render transient families rootless as they broke old community ties and moved to new communities. But they are not left rootless by transfer. Children have shown themselves to be especially adaptable to a mobile way of life. Teachers note that the children of transient families are more socially responsive than are those from the stable type community. A national community makes it easier for people to move since the national economy is a unity and the head of a family who has a business or industrial skill can find his place in the economic structure almost any place in the country. In turn, mobility of families helps make for uniformity of cultural patterns across the nation.

Mobility and Extent of Family—Community Interchange

Community commitments must be tenuous if the head of the house is to be free to move according to the demands of his occupational role. Involvement with the occupational system primarily through the role of the adult male reduces the number of family-community commitments. If the wife is also employed, the mobility of the family is to that extent further circumscribed.

An important feature of the American family that makes it mobile and adaptive is its accent on affectivity, with affect to be shown primarily within one's family and not toward one's fellow workers. This has partly the effect of inhibiting the development of some of the kinds of affectional community involvement which are a threat to the operation of an economic system wherein employees are employed as individuals recognized for their competence rather than for their affectional, familial, or other ties. The emphasis on affection within the nuclear family serves as a counterbalance to this inhibiting of affection for the community and a network of friends in the community. Because of the dominance of the economic system, the family must be adaptive.[11] There is bound to be strain between the economic system and the family, nevertheless, as nonemployed members of the family make commitments to other community systems—the market, the school, clubs, the church, and other persons.

Why Families Move

There have never been so many people moving in so many different ways in America as there are today. About one person in every five shifts residence over a year's time, and about three-quarters of the urban population was living in 1950 in places in which they did not reside in 1940. Migration

[11] Talcott Parsons, *The Social System* (Glencoe, Ill.: The Free Press, 1951), p. 182 ff.

of individuals and families from the farms and small towns to the city continues, and families, particularly white families, continue to leave the central
city for the suburbs. The population of the suburbs is growing five times
as fast as is the population in the central cities. (see Figure 9.1). America's
city dwellers appear to change their housing almost as often as they trade
cars.[12]

FIGURE 9.1   SUBURBS GROWING FASTEST

SOURCE: Wilbur J. Cohen, "Social Planning and Urban Development," *Health, Education, and Welfare Indicators,* October, 1966.

Of studies of reasons why American urban families move, the most comprehensive is that by Rossi.[13] Two samples were taken from two stable areas
of an eastern city, each of contrasting socio-economic status; and two
samples were taken from two mobile areas, also of contrasting socio-
economic status. The two stable areas contained large proportions of households in the child-rearing phase of the family system. The two mobile areas,
on the other hand, contained larger proportions of single-person households
and families without children (presumably either before or after the child-
rearing stage). Both stable areas were characterized by high proportions of
home ownership, while only three out of twenty in the two mobile areas

[12] Peter H. Rossi, *Why Families Move* (Glencoe, Ill.: The Free Press, 1955), p. 1.
[13] *Ibid.*

were home owners, and many of the latter were rooming-house landlords living on the premises.

It is commonly assumed that families move primarily for economic reasons; but Rossi found that the stage of a family in the family life cycle and its attitudes toward its home and neighborhood were extremely accurate predictors of a householder's desire to move. In those cases where a move was voluntary—that is, where the household had a clear choice between staying and moving—the most important factor impelling families to move was dissatisfaction with the amount of space in the present dwelling. Other factors were complaints about neighborhoods and about the cost of rent and maintenance.

Mobility was greatest in the period when families were experiencing greatest growth, with most of the moves taking place within a decade after the formation of the family. Young families with children were those most likely to move.

The social environment of the dwelling was also important. When both space and acceptable social environment were found to be inadequate, a family was especially likely to move.

Houses vary in the extent to which they can be adjusted to life-cycle changes, with large houses being more flexible than smaller ones. Home owners are in a better position to modify their homes, particularly in making changes in the interior characteristics of the house. It is renters living in small dwelling units who are most inclined to move.

Mobile areas derive their mobility primarily from the type of housing they offer. The small dwelling units found there are unsuited to the housing needs of expanding families, who use mobile areas only as stations on the way to residential areas where larger dwellings offer more congenial housing.

The younger the head of a family, the greater the inclination to move; the larger the household, the higher its mobility. Both age of family head and size of family are independently related to mobility, although age is somewhat more strongly related than household size. Families which were ten or more years old had completed an average of 3.16 moves during their lifetimes. On the average, during the first decade of their existence they completed 2.80 moves. In other words, most of the moves undertaken by a family throughout its entire existence took place in the first decade of its existence.

Five out of seven complaints of respondents referred to characteristics of the structure or dwelling unit itself (e.g., amount of room, closets, etc.); one referred to characteristics of the surrounding environment (street noises); and one referred to the location of the dwelling in relation to friends and relatives. Factors which play a prominent role in the discussions of city planners and housing experts—distance to work and conditions of the schools were relatively infrequent complaints.

TABLE 9.1. COMPLAINTS ABOUT AND INDIFFERENCE TO SELECTED
ASPECTS OF HOUSING

Housing Characteristics (Arranged in rank order of complaints)	Proportion Complaining	Proportion Indifferent*
Amount of closet space	33%	0%
Open space about the house	28	6
Street noises	23	16
Amount of room	22	2
Heating equipment	16	0
Rent (or maintenance)	15	1
Nearness to friends and relatives	15	15
Amount of air or sunlight	14	2
Kind of people around here	13	9
Amount of privacy	12	1
Nearness to church	9	8
Travel to work	8	10
Kind of schools around here	6	41
Shopping facilities	6	1

* "Indifferent" is used to indicate that a particular housing aspect didn't matter too much to the respondent.

SOURCE: Peter H. Rossi, *Why Families Move* (Glencoe, Ill.: The Free Press, 1955), p. 82.

One might expect that mobility would be lessened when families had developed strong interpersonal ties, but the data of Rossi's study do not support this generalization. By and large, it made little difference whether or not the family was integrated into the community in the sense of having close friends living nearby. Persons whose closest kinsmen were located nearby in the community moved nearly as much as persons whose kinsmen resided at some distance. This finding applied both to renters and owners. Lack of concern with kin when considering a move may reflect the fact that short moves were contemplated or that modern means of overcoming distance made mobility appear not as a threat to continued relations with kinsmen and others.

A second study of family mobility focuses on a relatively new urban subdivision in a diversified, industrial city of approximately 40,000 population.[14] In a sample of restricted age range and household composition, the life-cycle variables found to be reliable predictors of family mobility in the Rossi study were not useful in predicting family mobility. Forty-four of the forty-seven upwardly-mobile families planned to move within a year, while only twenty of the 154 non-upwardly-mobile families planned to do so. Of

[14] Gerald R. Leslie and Arthur H. Richardson, "Life Cycle, Career Pattern, and the Decision to Move," *American Sociological Review*, XXVI (December, 1961), 894–902.

forty-four upwardly-mobile households that moved during the year, forty-two were judged to have done so as part of the processes of upward social mobility, while only two moves were judged to have occurred independently of upward mobility. Four variables—expectations of upward social mobility, perceived social class differences between self and neighbors, attitude toward the present dwelling, and education of the household head—produced an extremely accurate predictive equation. Pursuing the link between career pattern and residential mobility, upward social mobility far outweighed all other considerations in producing residential mobility.

Berger found in a study of automotive workers living in a suburb that very few, if any, social-mobility attitudes were in evidence. Although their lives had been bettered as a result of a collective residential shift to the suburb, they had achieved a standard of living beyond which most of them did not expect to rise.[15]

Differences in the populations in the three studies cited do not require that their findings be considered as contradictory. It does mean that an adequate explanation of the reasons for family mobility must encompass factors within the family system and factors in the interchange between family and community.

Effect of Family Mobility on Other Families

What effect does family mobility have upon those who remain in the community? According to Rossi, the negative impact of mobility upon the residents who remained in mobile areas came about through their perception of new residents as undesirable neighbors. Change was regarded as bringing about a deterioration of the population composition of the area. But only one out of every three families perceived the incoming residents as different from present residents; hence the unfavorable impact of mobility affected only a small number of the inhabitants of mobile areas. Whatever other effects mobility had upon households, its direct impact upon them was slight. Rossi found the greatest awareness of mobility in areas where mobility was least, but even in these areas there was a substantial proportion who felt they knew too little about local mobility to estimate the proportion of movers in their areas.

More striking than the awareness of mobility was the lack of personal concern with it. Most saw no difference between the mobile portions of the population of their area and the stable portions and perceived no unfavorable effects of mobility. Where mobility was perceived, perception was not accurate. The turnover of residents in their neighborhoods was apparently a social phenomenon below the threshold of attention of many families.

15 Bennett M. Berger, *Working Class Suburb: A Study of Auto Workers in Suburbia* (Berkeley and Los Angeles: University of California, 1960).

There was greater awareness of mobility in areas where there was the least mobility. One of the reasons for this awareness is that awareness of mobility depended on a family's involvement in the community. Families who had been long residents of an area and had many local ties were the most aware of mobility. Yet, most families were neutral in their feelings about the moving of other families. Mobility was not seen as altering the essential elements of the community's social composition. Only a small minority of families approved or disapproved of residential turnover. The search for the major effects of mobility on a community must proceed along other lines of investigation.

Effect of Family Mobility on Organizations Within the Community

Rossi anticipated that organizations within the community would be more sensitive to residential mobility than would families. The family's existence by and large is not threatened by changes in the population resident in its community. Friends and relatives entering a home may be persons from outside the community; families are under no obligation to associate more than in a casual manner with other residents in the community. By contrast, some local organizations are directly dependent on the maintenance of relationships within the community. Business organizations must have customers; clubs, churches, and other organizations need members. The turnover of population can affect the operation and the very existence of an organization.

Interviews showed organization personnel on the whole to be quite sensitive to the existence of mobility. Virtually every one of the organizational personnel knew that this area was either mobile or stable, and many could pinpoint quite accurately the amount of mobility not only during the present but going back over several decades. Yet there were striking differences between organizations, and quite a few persons had distorted perception of mobility or evidenced a lack of concern with the problem. These differences were closely related to differences in the activities and structures of the organizations involved.

There are variations in the ways in which mobility affects organizational life. Some types of organizations were apparently exempt from its effects; others were so seriously affected by mobility as to have their very existence threatened. Some were sensitive to any amount of mobility among any groups, while others were affected only when certain types of residents moved. One unanticipated finding was that some organizations considered mobility an asset rather than a liability, and several businesses complained that they were suffering because of the stability of the area.

There were two characteristics of organizations which by and large determined what the perception of and the reaction to mobility would be: both had to do with the nature of interchanges between the organization and the people. Some of the organizations were not located directly in the area to which they were oriented or were interested in that area plus others; the latter are referred to as metropolitan-oriented organizations. These were by and large exempt from the impact of mobility because their population base was not experiencing turnover to the extent involved in one specific area. For example, an electric company, although very much aware of the mobility taking place in the study area, was not particularly concerned because the area it served included a considerably larger area than the census tract studied. Locally-oriented organizations, concerned with the population inhabiting the census tract or some subportion of it, were much more sensitive to mobility. In fact, the smaller the area served, the more vulnerable the organization appeared to be. What makes the finding in regard to population served particularly important is the finding that a typical successful adjustment to the impact of mobility is to shift from a local to a metropolitan orientation. Some of the smaller stores, ethnic-style bakeries, for example, survived the loss of populations they once served by developing a clientele that was metropolitan in character. This was also a typical survival mechanism for organizations which suffered because the area was so stable. A realestate broker and a moving company survived stability by enlarging the base of their operations to include other neighborhoods.

There was also a distinction in awareness and adjustment between client-oriented and member-oriented organizations. A client-oriented organization is one in which the major interaction is between the persons served and the organization personnel, with relatively little interaction between the clients; clerks and customers in a retail store would be an example. The chief concern of client-oriented organizations is with the maintenance of these relationships; it has no direct concern with any interaction that might exist between customers.

Membership-oriented organizations, on the other hand, constitute social systems with the populations they serve. Members have relationships with each other as well as with the organizational leaders or other organization personnel. Successful functioning of such an organization depends not only on the maintenance of organization-member relationships but also on the maintenance of member-member relationships. Hence, there are many more relationships which must be maintained by member-oriented organizations than by client-oriented organizations. Examples of member-oriented organizations are social clubs, church groups, and fraternal groups.

Generally speaking, client-oriented organizations were not so strongly affected by mobility as were member-oriented organizations. To survive, the organizations had to find replacements for clients who had left. The loss of members in a member-oriented organization was more serious. Not only was the relationship to the organizational personnel disrupted, but in addition all the relationships which the lost members had to other members were broken. Recruiting new members meant inducting them into a system and hence the task was difficult. The membership-oriented organizations particularly felt the loss of active members, those well-integrated into the system.

One of the more successful adjustments to mobility was enlargement of the area from which members were solicited. Some organizations hard hit by the mobility of the populations they once served modify their structure, and sometimes their function. A store owner, finding his old clients gone and the new residents trading at the chain stores, changed his store into a restaurant and catered primarily to clerks from the local chain stores. The local movie house became a third-rate cinema, though it had once offered first-run movies and before that had been a vaudeville theater.

Still another mode of adjustment involved the establishment of special procedures. The grammar school, for instance, instituted several new procedures for the induction of new students into the student body, some of which were very successful. The program made older pupils responsible for the initiation of the new. Each teacher appointed "Big Brothers" and "Big Sisters" who were put in charge of new children to help them get around and to influence their acceptance by others.

Not all organizations made a successful adjustment to population mobility. According to the local retail-trade association, there was a seventy-five percent turnover in retail establishments attributable to problems occasioned by population mobility.

SOCIAL CLASS DIFFERENCES IN FAMILY-COMMUNITY INTERCHANGE

By social class we mean all persons or families in a community or society who possess relatively equal status or prestige.[16] Social organization in American society is immensely complex, and not all persons have acquired equally the ability or the desire to carry the higher levels of responsibility.[17] Experience, intelligence, and education are necessary for the more complex levels of organization. Those having greater ability for abstraction, classification, and organization seem to find organized social activity more to their liking.

It has been said that it is through association that Americans avoid the excesses both of state worship and complete individualism. If this is true, it is most true of socially-responsible families. Whatever the basic motives of these families, a contributing factor to increased participation seems to

[16] Julius Gould and William L. Kolb, *A Dictionary of the Social Sciences* (New York: The Free Press of Glencoe, 1964), pp. 648–650.

[17] Robert E. L. Faris, "The Middle Class from a Sociological Viewpoint," *Social Forces,* XXXIX (October, 1960), 5.

be a community pattern that proliferates subsystems, including systems devoted to the welfare of offspring of these families. Keeping up with community work has become one of the new imperatives of families. Busyness has been characteristic of socially-responsible families in earlier decades as well; what is new is the lure of community activities for each member of the family.[18]

Havighurst and Feigenbaum,[19] in a study of social activity among people aged forty to seventy, found that community-centeredness was the favorite leisure style of upper-middle class people. Community-centered individuals tended not to have young children at home, suggesting that it was not only in the service of their offspring that middle-class adults engaged in community activity, or that once begun the activity persisted beyond the time when children are the cause of it.

In contrast to the upper-middle class, Havighurst and Feigenbaum found that the people who enjoyed home-centered leisure engaged in most of it around their own residence. This style of life was stronger in lower-middle class and upper-lower class individuals. Perhaps the family-centered style of life was not entirely one of choice but of necessity, for the home-centered families had more children to care for at home.

Seeley, Sim, and Loosley[20] also found that the upper-middle class participated a great deal in community activities, particularly in impersonal, highly structured systems. Clubs and associations were marked features of life in the Crestwood Heights suburb for both children and adults. These relationships served a definite purpose. Just as it appeared that it was becoming less common to take a trip of any length merely for pleasure and without some ulterior business or professional motive, so it was also less usual for people to meet each other purely on a basis of affection or of liking to be together. Human contacts were more generally organized around some activity or cause, preferably one which would also advance or make plain the social standing of the participating persons.

Warner found a direct correlation between the height of the class level and the propensity to join associations. Moreover, each of the classes tended to join different kinds of groups and for what appeared to be different reasons. The middle classes seemed to use associations as a way of improving their social status and for training themselves in articulateness and leadership.[21] Among the upper class, on the other hand, he found the associations being used chiefly as instruments for the strategic manipulation of the life of

[18] Fairchild and Wynn, *op. cit.* (see above, fn. 9), p. 132.
[19] Robert J. Havighurst and Kenneth Feigenbaum, "Leisure and Life-Style," *American Journal of Sociology,* LXIV (January, 1959), 396–404.
[20] Seeley, Sim, and Loosley, *op. cit.* (see above fn. 6).
[21] William Lloyd Warner, *Social Class in America* (Gloucester, Mass.: Peter Smith, 1957), pp. 12–13, 242–248.

the community—through their control of the country clubs, the eating discussion clubs, the civic association, and the fund-raising drives. Among the
lower classes, what group activity there was centered mainly on the
church.

Low status people belong to relatively few associations partly because
their work leaves them with less free time, partly because they lack the
money for membership, and partly because their interests and perspectives
are limited. The lower class even over against the lower-middle class is more
concrete in its outlook; there is a greater tendency to live on the surface and
in the present, to move in a narrow circle of kinsmen and friends, and to
have few organizational contacts. Both community-centeredness and home-
centeredness fall off in the lower-lower class, where family values lose some
importance and the few pastimes engaged in became sex-differentiated, with
the men going fishing alone or to the bar or to the poolroom with the "boys."

In the advantaged classes it is the women who carry much of the responsibility for community participation. In view of the importance of social
activities for family status and for the man's career, it may seem surprising
that women usually are the initiators of social activities. There are reasons,
however, why cultural interests, interest in social welfare, and community
activity are particularly prominent in the activities of women rather than of
men in urban communities. On the one hand, the masculine occupational
role tends to absorb a very large proportion of the man's time and energy
and to leave relatively little time for other interests. Unless his position is
such as to make him particularly prominent, his primary orientation is to
those elements of the social system which divide the community into occupational groups rather than to those which unite it in common interests and
activities. The woman's major responsiblity for her children, on the other
hand, draws her into a great variety of school, church, and club activity.

Part of the emancipation from domesticity on the part of middle- and
upper-class women lies in the emphasis placed on the humanistic elements
of life. This takes a variety of forms, with one of them being a relatively
mature appreciation and systematic cultivation of cultural interests and
educated tastes, extending from the intellectual sphere to matters of art,
music, and house furnishings. A second consists in the cultivation of serious
interests and humanitarian obligations in community welfare situations and
the like.

In regard to her relationship to her husband, the middle- or upper-class
woman can be expected to be an equal and a good companion, putting less
stress on the exploitation of sex-defined roles as such and more on that
which is essentially in their common interest.

The means used in child-centered, adult-controlled organizations among
the advantaged classes to ensure that the child learns skills are strikingly

similar to those employed by the school in formal instruction.[22] The child is encouraged to compete in excellence with his age mates, and rewards are given for outstanding performance. While the child is urged towards competition with others in the community, he is also taught that he must cooperate with and be accepted by his peers—the dilemma of achieving and at the same time looking to one's social acceptance rating. The adult-controlled children's groupings share a common orientation toward the future—they regarded themselves as preparing the child for the life that, hopefully, he is going to lead as an adult. Parents regard the Scouts, Little League, children's clubs, Sunday School, 4-H, and other adult-controlled, child-centered systems as a means of socializing their children. Parents are liberal in providing their children with associational activity. This is not mere generosity on the parent's part; it is a way of ensuring the child's social status and of forcing the child to organize his leisure rigidly, thus grooming him for later adult status in his kind of community.

Parents in advantaged classes are frank to say that it is the children's organizations which contribute most to family disorganization and busy-ness.[23] The adult-centered organizations to which so many belong are rarely mentioned as culprits. Some adults, however, feel that they come to know their children better as a result of their endless chauffeuring and participation in youth activities; for this they are grateful. They leave the impression that the desire to be good parents, community members, persons active in civic affairs is the motive for the rigorous organization life they lead.

Both working-class husbands and wives find the world around them confusing and chaotic according to findings of Rainwater's study of forty-six working-class men and fifty working-class women. They did not feel that they understood their world, and they felt that what went on was essentially unpredictable, up to fate. Women were part of that world to working-class men and were characterized by the same unpredictableness and confusing qualities as the rest of their world. Both men and women found it difficult to think of themselves as effective, mastering agents; they simply hoped things would go well and did their best with the resources they had.[24]

Working-Class Families in Suburbs

The suburban community has been characterized as a place with a special propensity for social life and community activity. But not all suburbs are of this type. It is useful to distinguish between two main types of suburbs—employing and residential. Residential suburbs have considerably more of

[22] Seeley, Sim, and Loosley, *op. cit.* (see above, fn. 7), p. 305.

[23] Fairchild and Wynn, *op. cit.* (see above, fn. 9), p. 133.

[24] Lee Rainwater, *And the Poor Get Children: Sex, Contraception, and Family Planning in the Working Class* (Chicago: Quadrangle, 1960), p. 77.

their population who have completed high school. They also have more in white-collar occupations, higher median family incomes, markedly higher median rates of population increase, and markedly fewer places losing population through migration out of the suburbs.[25] Do working class people who move to a suburb take on the style of the suburban middle class or extend their own style of life to the suburbs? The data indicate that the latter is closer to the truth.[26]

Berger found no evidence that participation in formal associations had increased since the respondents moved to the suburb. Indeed, he found very little formal participation at all; seventy percent of the respondents belonged to no clubs, organizations, or associations; only eight percent belonged to more than one.

The wives of the workers, like their husbands, tended to have few memberships in organizations, but there was, for them, a noticeable increase in their memberships since moving to the suburbs. Community activities, such as those represented by P.T.A., Girl Scouts, and Campfire Girls, commanded most of their organizational participation time. It seemed to be the women who, in the daytime, engaged in most of what sociable behavior there was; evening visiting between couples was rare.

With the exception of daytime women's kaffeeklatsches, organizational participation and mutual visiting of a semiformal sort among friends and neighbors was slight. Neighboring of an extremely casual sort, and usually of short duration, was more frequent; but the fact that people did not appear to invite each other to their homes suggests either that they had not as yet mastered middle-class, sociable know-how or that the home was conceived in working-class terms as a place for the family.

CONTROLLING FAMILY-COMMUNITY INTERCHANGE

Family interchanges in the community can be a source of tension for parents; there are other complicating factors, too. Parents are often disturbed by values prevailing in the community, values that clash with their own. The home is a major locality system for family members if they do not choose to associate with other people in the vicinity. To the extent that the family as a residential system can close out the community and allow only the interchanges that it wants, it controls its environment and preserves a unique family culture. On the other hand, if the community system is acceptable, the family opens up and encourages interchanges in the community. What seems to characterize some urban areas is a constellation of

[25] Leo F. Schnore, "The Social and Economic Characteristics of American Suburbs," *The Sociological Quarterly*, IV (Spring, 1963), 122–134.

[26] Berger, *op. cit.* (see above, fn. 15).

closed nuclear families. While local community has to some extent dis-
integrated as national community has emerged, so also families of parents
and children with strong affectional ties have emerged.

One way families have found for preserving influence and control is to
isolate their children from interaction with other children. This has had
some notable effects. Studies of scientists, gifted children, and geniuses show
that families of those who become exceptional keep their children isolated
from other children. There are implications for social mobility here. It would
seem that factors which intensify the involvement of a child with his parents or other adults, and reduce his involvement with other children, increase the likelihood that he will be upwardly mobile.[27]

Isolation is a method by which "successful" and "good" families maintain
themselves and their integrity in unfavorable community settings.[28] High
school seniors filled out questionnaires concerning their own families and
friend-families. "Successful" and "good" families were divided from the
"ordinary" families based on whether or not the family had been disrupted
by divorce or desertion, had avoided interference by the police, and had
kept its children in school. The most successful families met all of these
tests; families meeting a lesser number were considered good families.
Families in which the child dropped out of school as soon as it was possible
for him to take a job were called "ordinary." The researchers reasoned that
"civilization-adequate" families in modern American cities might be achieving their aims in the control of the minds of their teen-agers by surrounding
themselves with similar families having like ideals and values.

The successful American families did allow into their homes and circles
of intimacy only other families remarkably like themselves. This was shown,
first of all, by the larger proportion of kinsmen among the friend-families.
Secondly, the friend-families were of the same background as the parent
families. Successful families had more intimate family friends and had more
in common with their friends than did unsuccessful families.

Five friend-families were generally the important ones in the mind of
the child; personal interviews further confirmed a figure of five or six friend-
families. Beyond these were the more-or-less casual visitors who were not
permitted to penetrate very deeply into the family's intimate affairs. Most of
the acquaintancesehips had lasted more than ten years, and two-fifths of
them had lasted more than fifteen years; this would suggest a "psychological
wall" around the child that began early in his life and lasted through his
teen-age years. The friend-families gave the student a panorama of the

[27] Seymour Martin Lipset and Reinhard Bendix, *Social Mobility in Industrial
Society* (Berkeley and Los Angeles: University of California, 1959), p. 240.

[28] The following account is based on Carle C. Zimmerman and Lucius F. Cervantes,
Successful American Families (New York: Pageant, 1960).

traditional "good" family life cycle; the friends were at various stages in the family life cycle-stages that the teenager had not yet lived through but which he would soon approach.

Intact families avoided broken families and families marked by "lack of determination, defectism, and poor fortune." It seemed to be a case of keeping unacceptable personal and family models away from the home so that the child would not be distracted in his efforts to reach high goals. In 1960, Zimmerman studied the family and family friend background of college seniors, graduate students, and professional students, as well.[29]

The similar-friend device had also been used by these families. The more rigidly they used the similar-friend device, the further their children went up the educational ladder. The upper elite did not even let kinsmen into their homes very often if these persons did not measure up to the expected standard. Old friends who did not measure up to the newer standards were seen fewer and fewer times, and the children forgot them. This lack of entertainment of old friends was in part due to the fact that in these elite families one-fourth of the mothers worked in gainful employment away from home when the children were in college. Most of them had to do this in order to help pay the educational expenses.

The educated woman or the education of women must not be underestimated as a factor in the production of a creative elite, according to Zimmerman. In the elite group, fathers classified as fairly well educated not uncommonly had wives with more formal education. These educated women, ambitious for their children, made their tastes dominant in the kinds of persons allowed the intimacy of their homes.

SUMMARY

The type of community in which the American family lives has changed markedly from what it was a century or more ago. Gone is the small self-contained rural community; America's population has been more urban than rural since the census of 1920. The growth of the economy, mobility, the mass media—among other factors—have created a mass society, a national community. The locality communities that still exist are not self-contained and self-supporting. Some local communities have no territorial base as such but exist because of other interests; these have been labeled "communalities."

The extent of family-community interchange varies with social class and with attitude toward the community. Middle- and upper-class families participate more extensively and intensively in community life. If families

[29] Carle C. Zimmerman, *The Family as a Creative Unit of Our Society* (Mimeographed).

regard the community as hostile to the interest of family members, the family may be closed to interchange or selectively opened to allow what is regarded as proper interchanges.

BIBLIOGRAPHY

Bennett M. Berger. *Working Class Suburb: A Study of Auto Workers in Suburbia*. Berkeley and Los Angeles: University of California, 1960.

Elizabeth Bott. *Family and Social Network*. London, Tavistock, 1957.

Ruth Shonle Cavan. "Subcultural Variations and Mobility," *Handbook of Marriage and the Family,* ed. Harold T. Christensen. Chicago: Rand McNally, 1964. Pp. 535–581.

S. D. Clark. *The Suburban Society*. Toronto, Canada: University of Toronto, 1966.

Roy W. Fairchild and John Charles Wynn. *Families in the Church: A Protestant Survey*. New York: Association, 1961.

Herbert J. Gans. *The Levittowners: Ways of Life and Politics in a Suburban Community*. New York: Pantheon, 1967.

Nathan Glazer. "Housing Policy and the Family," *Journal of Marriage and the Family,* XXIX (February, 1967), 140–163.

Sidney M. Greenfield. "Love and Marriage in Modern America: A Functional Analysis," *The Sociological Quarterly,* VI (Autumn, 1965), 361–377.

Robert J. Havighurst and Kenneth Feigenbaum. "Leisure and Life-Style," *American Journal of Sociology,* LXIV (January, 1959), 396–404.

A. J. Jaffe and R. O. Carleton. *Occupational Mobility in the United States, 1930–1960*. New York: Columbia King's Crown, 1959.

William H. Key. "Urbanism and Neighboring," *The Sociological Quarterly,* VI (Autumn, 1965), 379–385.

Otto N. Larsen and Alex S. Edelstein. "Communication Consensus and the Community Involvement of Urban Husbands and Wives," *Acta Sociologica,* V, Facs. 1 (1960), 15–30.

Gerald R. Leslie and Arthur H. Richardson. "Life Cycle, Career Pattern, and the Decision to Move," *American Sociological Review,* XXVI (December, 1961), 894–902.

Seymour Martin Lipset and Reinhard Bendix. *Social Mobility in Industrial Society*. Berkeley and Los Angeles: University of California, 1959.

Robert S. Lynd and Helen Merrell Lynd. *Middletown: A Study in Modern American Culture*. New York: Harcourt, 1929.

Don Martindale. *American Society*. Princeton, N.J.: Van Nostrand, 1960.

C. Wright Mills. *White Collar: The American Middle Classes*. New York: Oxford, 1951.

John Mogey. "Family and Community in Urban-Industrial Societies," *Handbook of Marriage and the Family,* ed. Harold T. Christensen. Chicago: Rand McNally, 1964. Pp. 501–534.

M. F. Nimkoff and Russell Middleton. "Type of Family and Types of Economy," *American Journal of Sociology,* LXVI (November, 1960), 215–225.

F. Ivan Nye and Lois W. Hoffman. *The Employed Mother in America*. Chicago: Rand McNally, 1963.

Talcott Parsons. *The Social System*. Glencoe, Ill.: The Free Press, 1951.

Roland R. Renne. "Woman Power and the American Economy," *Journal of Home Economics*, XLIX (February, 1957), 83–86.

Peter H. Rossi. *Why Families Move*. Glencoe, Ill.: The Free Press, 1955.

Leo F. Schnore. "The Social and Economic Characteristics of American Suburbs," *The Sociological Quarterly*, IV (Spring, 1963), 122–134.

John R. Seeley, R. Alexander Sim, and Elizabeth W. Loosley. *Crestwood Heights: A Study of the Culture of Suburban Life*. New York: Basic Books, 1956.

Aida K. Tomeh. "Informal Participation in a Metropolitan Community," *The Sociological Quarterly*, VIII (Winter, 1967), 85–102.

Carle C. Zimmerman and Lucius F. Cervantes. *Successful American Families*. New York: Pageant, 1960.

CHAPTER 10

Family and Kin

IT HAS BEEN SAID that the only American kinship unit of significance is the nuclear family, but empirical evidence would suggest that the concept of a modified extended kinship system or kin network may serve as an alternative to the isolated nuclear family as more accurately describing the overall American kinship system.[1] A kin network differs from a classical extended family as we find it in some primitive societies in that it is not necessarily characterized by geographical propinquity, kinship occupational involvement, or nepotism; nor does it have a hierarchical authority structure. There need not be hierarchical authority; a kin network can consist of a series of nuclear families bound together on an equalitarian basis with an emphasis on kin family interchange as an end value.

THE PRIMACY OF THE NUCLEAR FAMILY

The isolated nuclear family is the typical household unit in America. It is the unit of residence and the system whose members pool a common basis of economic support, especially money income. In the typical case neither the household arrangements nor the source of income bear any direct relationship to the family of orientation of either spouse, or, if there is any relationship, it is about as likely to be to the one family of orientation as to the other. The typical family of procreation lives in a dwelling unit separated from those of both pairs of grandparents and may be economically

---

[1] Litwak suggested the term "modified extended kinship system" to describe the American kinship situation. More recently Sussman suggested the use of the term "network." The term "network" has one advantage in that it does not suggest a hierachy of authority, as the term "extended kinship" might. The term "kin family network" would cover nuclear families bound together by affectional ties and choice, performing supportive and not coercive roles. See Eugene Litwak, "Occupational Mobility and Extended Family Cohesion," *American Sociological Review*, XXV (February, 1960), 9–12; Eugene Litwak, "Geographic Mobility and Extended Family Cohesion," *American Sociological Review*, XXV (June, 1960), 385–394; and Marvin B. Sussman and Lee Burchinal, "Kin Family Network: Unheralded Structure in Current Conceptualizations of Family Functioning," *Marriage and Family Living*, XXIV (August, 1962), 231–240.

independent of both. In many cases the geographical separation between the homes is considerable.

The residential pattern of independent dwelling units is a major determinant in interaction between kinsmen. Marriage is monogamous, residence is neolocal, and inheritance is by testamentary disposition.

The marriage bond is the main structural keystone of the American kinship system largely because of the principle governing the choice of marriage partners. It is an open system; there are no prescribed matings on a kinship basis, and newly married couples are not incorporated into an already existing kinship unit.

The absence of any structural bias in favor of solidarity with the ascendant or descendant families in either line of descent increases the structural isolation of each nuclear family.[2] People do not generally identify with their relatives beyond the circle of grandparents, cousins, aunts, and uncles.[3] The pattern of inheritance of property allows for equal division between children regardless of birth order or sex. Hence, the expectation of inheritance does not typically bind certain children to their families of orientation more closely than it does others.

To measure the extent of involvement with kinsmen, Reiss asked respondents to diagram relationships with kin.[4] Most respondents appeared to stop naturally at first cousins, nieces, nephews, grandparents, and grandchildren, due not only to lack of knowledge but also to lack of contact and concern for more distant relatives. Interest in kin tends to increase with age, however. Cumming and Schneider, working with an older group of informants, found them able to recognize a larger number of relatives.[5]

THE TEMPORAL NATURE OF AMERICAN KIN NETWORKS

A peculiar set of temporal and accidental factors in each generation results in the formation of solid kin systems; these go out of existence or change with the next generation, for collective solidarity in the American kinship system is noncontinuous, shifting its structure with each succeeding family cycle and generation. Solidarities made up of relations with kinsmen are established not directly on kinship considerations, but rather on the same basis as friendship relationships. The prior existence of a kin linkage

[2] Talcott Parsons, "The Kinship System of the Contemporary United States," *American Anthropologist*, XLV (January–March, 1943); reprinted in Talcott Parsons, *Essays in Sociological Theory Pure and Applied* (Glencoe, Ill.: The Free Press, 1949), pp. 233–250.

[3] Helen Codere, "A Genealogical Study of Kinship in the United States," *Psychiatry*, XVIII (1955), 65–79.

[4] Paul Jacob Reiss, *The Extended Kinship System in American Urban Middle Class* (Cambridge, Mass.: Harvard University, 1960, unpublished Ph.D. thesis).

[5] Elaine Cumming and David M. Schneider, "Sibling Solidarity: A Property of American Kinship," *American Anthropologist*, LXIII (1961), 498–507.

may provide the initial basis for the development of the relationships, however.

The Typical Kin Network

Extended kinship solidarity is most commonly based upon relations between parents and children and between siblings. A relatively high level of solidarity among certain kinsmen is constantly being created. Solidarity is attenuated with the formation of new family units, but it is rejuvenated again in the next generation of that kinship system. Thus it is that the solidarity of the nuclear family does bring about at least a minimal solidarity within an extended kinship system; factors which cause solidarity in the nuclear family result in increased solidarity within extended kinship systems in successive generations.

Different Types of Family Solidarity

It is well to make a distinction between family solidarity as nuclear family integration and family solidarity as kinship orientation. Family solidarity is possible either within the nuclear family or within the kin network; the two may act independently. The attitude of family solidarity expresses itself differently in the nuclear family and in the kin network.[6] Familism (signifying the subordination of personal interests to family interests) directed toward the nuclear family has little overlap with familism directed toward the kin network. Rogers and Sebald define the concept of family integration as the degree to which a family member is oriented toward optimizing rewards and satisfactions for other family members—in other words, familism toward a nuclear family system. Kinship orientation is defined as the degree to which an individual fulfills the expectations of the kin network. It is likely that an individual with a high degree of kinship orientation will have considerable contact with his kin, even at the expense of his nuclear family. Persons high in family integration are not necessarily high in kinship orientation and vice versa.

Intimate Solidarity Systems

The marriage relationship is the most intimate solid relationship in the American kinship system. The parent-child relationship is after marriage the second most intimate relationship. Whether one's parents are considered as family or as relatives depends on whether or not one perceives himself as a member of the family of orientation after he has acquired marital status. Looked at from the viewpoint of the parents, the relationship to their children is considered as a family relationship throughout the entire life

[6] Everett M. Rogers and Hans Sebald, "A Distinction Between Familism, Family Integration, and Kinship Orientation," *Marriage and Family Living*, XXIV (February, 1962), 25–30.

cycle. But the children do not necessarily reciprocate; they may not continue to consider the relationship to the parents as a family relationship.

This lack of reciprocity in the parent-married child relationship is apparently a condition of the two family statuses which each married person holds. The married child assumes a new and superceding status, while his parents continue from the position of their marital family status to define their relationships to him as a family relationship.

A family relationship is a more solid one than are relationships to other kinsmen (relatives), and differences in the classification of the relationships amount to differences in role expectations. The married child sees relative-type behavior as appropriate to the relationship to his parents, whereas the parents expect family-type behavior.

The mother-married daughter relationship appears to be a closer relationship than that between any other combination of parents and children.[7] A mother's children play a vital part in her life not only during the child-rearing period but also as a part of her future happiness.

The sibling relationship is the third and last kin relationship frequently classified as a family relationship. This relationship is normally attenuated by two marital relationships as each sibling takes a spouse, each of which takes precedence over the sibling relationship. In this case, unlike the parent-married child relationship, the relationship is reciprocal, with neither sibling defining the relationship as a family relationship. Difference of opinion over the nature of the relationship between them is more likely to develop if one of the siblings is not married. The unmarried sibling is more likely to regard the relationship as family and not as relative. As pointed out earlier, sibling solidarity appears to increase with age. This phenomenon is perhaps in part a characteristic of the stage of family development of people in the older age bracket. The sibling bond may have been reinvoked initially to manage a crisis, but ultimately it may have acted as a fundamental axis of socio-emotional interaction. Sibling or generational solidarity seems to be a very important relational tie of the last twenty or thirty years of life.[8]

In-Laws

"In-law" is a term used to refer to certain types of kinship relationships; most frequently mentioned as in-laws are mothers, fathers, brothers, and sisters of one's spouse. Reiss found that parents of the spouse were almost

[7] Robert Winch, "Further Data and Observations on the Oedipus Hypothesis," *American Sociological Review*, XVI (1951), 784–795; Sheldon Stryker, "The Adjustment of Married Offspring to their Parents," *American Sociological Review*, XX (1955), 149–154; Mirra Komarovsky, "Functional Analysis of Sex Roles," *American Sociological Review*, XV (1950), 508–516; Paul Wallin, "Sex Differences in Attitudes Toward In-Laws: A Test of a Theory," *American Journal of Sociology*, LIX (1954), 466–469; Reiss, *op. cit.*

[8] Elaine Cumming and David M. Schneider, *op. cit.*, p. 501.

always thought of as in-laws. On the other hand, since parents continue to think of their children as family and not as relatives and because of a heavy emphasis on marriage as a real bond, their children's spouses were assimilated as family and were not regarded as in-laws.

Spatial Distance and Kin Network Interchange

The high rate of mobility of the American people disperses kin. Nevertheless, only one-fourth of the wives interviewed in the Detroit area Study had no siblings or siblings-in-law in the Detroit area. About one-half had uncles, aunts, cousins, nephews, or nieces and about 45 percent had parents in the metropolitan area; only 11 percent had no relatives at all in the Detroit area.[9] Of a total of something over 2,000 kin mentioned by respondents in the Reiss study,[10] 254 or slightly more than 12 percent were residing in the same suburban town or immediately adjacent towns, 755 or roughly 36 percent were in other sections of the metropolitan area, 445 or 21 percent lived throughout the remainder of New England; 8 percent of these were in other sections of the world.

Distance between kin, physically speaking, is not necessarily related to degree of kin relationship. Reiss found that although parents and children did live closer to each other than did other relatives, there was no difference between the percent of siblings and the percent of cousins who lived in the same metropolitan area. Although frequency of interaction may increase solidarity between kin and thus be a reason for kin to reside closer to each other, location of residence is likely an independent variable in reference to interaction frequency.

Distance of residence and type of relationship together appear to account for a large portion of the variation in interaction frequency. They are the most important determinants of frequency in interaction with specific kin. Reiss found that the single most important reason for change in interaction patterns was a change of residence of some individual. Geographic mobility of nuclear families, which has the overall effect of putting greater distance between kin, led to an attenuation of kinship interchange more than any other factor.

Reiss asked his respondents what they thought it was that prevented a greater frequency of kin contact among those who felt that they had not been able to see their relatives as much as they would like. Seventy-three percent replied that the primary reason was distance, while 10 percent felt a lack of time to be the important reason; an additional 12 percent apparently thought back a step further, believing that they and their relatives had drifted

[9] Detroit Area Study, *A Social Profile of Detroit, 1955* (Ann Arbor: Survey Research Center, Institute for Social Research, University of Michigan, 1956), p. 22.
[10] Reiss, *op. cit.* (see above, fn. 4).

apart socially through the years, with the consequent lack of desire to meet being the inhibiting factor.

They were also asked, if they had it within their power to have their family and relatives reside where they wanted, which they would set up as the most ideal arrangement. The answers show a desire to have family and relatives reside in the same city; about half of the respondents chose this alternative. There was a definite tendency to desire that kinsmen live closer than they actually did live. About half the kinsmen did not live in the same city, but only 23 percent of the respondents preferred that kinsmen not live in the same city.

Not many respondents desired that kinsmen should live in the same neighborhood. The only exception to this was found for respondents in the late part of the family cycle. This is another indication of the desire of older persons, as contrasted to younger persons, for more kinship interaction.

Reiss found that females were in contact with only 8 percent of the in-laws daily or weekly but with 20 percent of their own relatives. Females tended to favor their own kin, whereas males did not favor theirs. Since women are in charge of kinship relationships, a part of the difference in frequency of contact is explained. The greater activity in extended kinship on the part of the women may also reflect the greater specialization of extended kinship interaction in the expressive area, since this is an area in which women are likely to be the family's representatives. The siblings with the least contact with each other turn out to be two brothers, the only ones with the same last name. This demonstrates how defunct the patrilineal tradition is.

Both husband and wife were in contact with their own relatives on their own. For the husband this additional contact on his own was just sufficient to provide him with equal contact with relatives and in-laws. For the wife, however, additional contact on her own with her own relatives magnified the already greater contact she had with her relatives as compared to her in-laws when in company with her husband.

Significant changes in interaction were related to family cycle changes. Marriage, the birth or growth of children, or the death of a kinsman brought important changes. The death of a connecting relative, for instance, reduced the interaction between kin. The death of a parent or a grandparent was an important influence on the interaction between siblings or cousins.

Personal Mobility and Family Solidarity

Persons with close family identification are as likely as others to move for occupational reasons. (A major conclusion of Strodtbeck's comparative study of Italian, Catholic, and Jewish families in New Haven, Connecticut, was that the economic success of the Jews was in part a function of their greater willingness to leave their kin. However, Jewish boys were much more likely than Italian boys to agree with the statement that "nothing in life is worth the sacrifice of moving away from your parents.[11]) Those on the upswing of their careers are especially apt to move; those on a career plateau are not likely to move or if they move they move toward their kinsmen. The member who has moved can serve as an outpost for other kinsmen and can communicate with them regarding opportunities or difficulties at a new location.

Kinsmen are less apt to object to a move on the part of a family member today than in the past partly because it is the accepted thing to do and partly because the vast technological improvements in transportation and communication and affluence make it possible to keep in touch. Geographical distance is less socially inhibiting than it once was.[12]

Early Marriage, Longevity, and Kinship Solidarity

With marriages occurring at younger ages and with increased longevity, family unity is affected by the increasing overlap of years in the three generations of grandparents, parents, and children. For example, in a study of one American family from 1635 to the present, it was found that in the 1600's, grandparents often did not live to see their grandchildren born. As the expectation of life increased, grandfathers overlapped their grandchildren by two years in 1712, by three years in 1772, by ten years in 1843, and by 27 years in 1941. This overlap should support the continuity of family traditions and hence family unity. In the particular case cited, the home of the grandparents in each three-generation overlap was often a central rallying point. It is reasonable to expect that this pattern may characterize many other families as well.[13]

THE MULTI-GENERATIONAL HOUSEHOLD

It is not uncommon to find a parent of one of the spouses or even a sibling or cousin residing with the family, though common residence is not a generally accepted feature of kin family network relations in the United States. Young people are expected to break away from their parental families and

[11] Fred Strodtbeck, "Family Integration, Values, and Achievement," in A. H. Halsey, Jean Flood, and C. Arnold Anderson, *Education, Economy and Society* (New York: Free Press, 1961), Chapter 26.

[12] Eugene Litwak, "The Use of Extended Family Groups in the Achievement of Social Goals: Some Policy Implications," *Social Problems,* VII (Winter, 1959–60), 177–187.

[13] Stuart F. Chapin, "Explaining Consumer Behavior–On What Level?" in Nelson N. Foote, ed., *Household Decision-Making,* Consumer Behavior, IV (New York: New York University Press, 1961), 306.

not to do so is looked upon as a failure to live up to expectations, an unwarranted expression of dependency.

The three-generation household does not last very long. It is usually a temporary arrangement; Koller found that most multi-generational households lasted for one to five years. One possible explanation for the short duration is that grandparents do not move in with relatives until they are quite old.[14] Koller found as many households not favoring bringing aged parents into their homes as he did households favoring such an arrangement. Many people expressed themselves as wanting to do the right thing with respect to their parents and their own families. Since the means by which this is to be accomplished is not clearly defined in our society, each family has to explore or to experiment with its own methods of solving the problem. A sample of the principles that might support their decisions in regard to the care of aged parents can be gleaned from some of the statements of the respondents. They spoke of treating grandparents as equals; keeping them well separated from the rest of the family; agreeing beforehand who is boss; giving them control at times; understanding their personalities; and keeping away from them if possible, for there is bound to be trouble.

The three-generation household was recognized by most as a hazardous type of family living, calling for the combined virtues of the diplomat, statesman, and saint. The elders, having had considerable authority in the past, do not find it easy to relinquish power to their children. The husband and wife in the receiving family who are becoming accustomed to living their lives independently and liking it resent the intrusion of a threat to their authority.

Life Within the Multi-Generation Household

With the eldest generation facing constant problems associated with failing health and loss of status and the youngest generation constantly pressing for more freedom of thought and action, it is the second or middle generation which is caught between the pressures from above and below. Koller found that the second generation generally demonstrated an ability to solve the numerous problems associated with multiple-family living. Where this quality was limited or absent, household accord was not likely to ensue.

Where the wife is responsible for expressive-integrative functions, the brunt of responsibility for redefining and clarifying role expectations for the older person in such a way that he can accept and find his role satisfying falls upon her. In a large sense the task of the wife in this situation is a

[14] Marvin R. Koller, "Studies of Three Generation Households," *Marriage and Family Living*, XVI (August, 1954), 205–206.

socializing one, since there is a great deal of learning involved in the acceptance of secondary as opposed to primary roles by the older person. He must accept new and less important role performances bringing changes in the organization of his personality if he is to find secondary-role performances gratifying.

If we assume that the functions of the family were being adequately accomplished within the nuclear family before the advent of the aged person, a strain is put upon the system by the intrusion of the aged person as a functionless member, a member who is not necessary to the processes of the stable family system. The structure of the system has to be changed to include him; if re-equilibrium cannot be accomplished in this way, the system is likely to exclude him either literally or figuratively.

The three-generation family has an additional function, that of replacing or incorporating the family of gerontation, or the terminal family, for the aged person. The nuclear family continues to perform its direct functions on behalf of the personalities of its family members, including now the personality of the aged person.

Scott found that male instrumental leadership was deflated when the family system had an aged female member for a long period of time.[15] There appeared to be male abdication of this role in the face of a prolonged coalition of females. An avoidance pattern existed between adult male and aged female; conversely the large number of activities involving adult female and aged female underscored the suspected coalition between adult female and aged female within the family system.

A socio-economic factor is also important in the functioning of the multi-generation family. Scott found that when the aged person's income was higher, he assumed an important instrumental or expressive primary or secondary role. This would appear to be in line with a conclusion by Stone that a situation in which elderly parents live with their grown children is a satisfactory arrangement if it is not a result of necessity but rather of a willing, mutual agreement between the parties.[16]

In an attempt to ascertain the effect of the multi-generational family system on the younger generation, Stone matched high school students living in multi-generation households with a control sample of students not in multi-generation homes.[17] The two groups were then compared on several

[15] Francis Gillespie Scott, *The Urban Three-Generation Family, Role Structure, and Interaction Process* (Los Angeles, Calif.: University of California, June, 1960, unpublished Ph.D. thesis).

[16] Carol L. Stone, "Living Arrangements and Social Adjustments of the Aged," *The Family Life Coordinator,* VI (September, 1957), 12–14.

[17] Carol L. Stone, "Three Generation Influences on Teenagers: Conceptions of Family Culture Patterns and Parent-Child Relationships," *Marriage and Family Living,* XXIV (August, 1962), 287–288.

items concerning family interaction patterns. There were some differences between the two groups, but none of the differences were statistically significant. The teen-agers in the three-generation families appeared to be slightly more socially minded and to spend more time in activities outside the home and in running around with or talking to friends than was true of those in two-generation households.

There are varied values at work in the forming of multi-generation families. Kosa and others, working with a population of Catholic undergraduate college students, distinguished two family types—one oriented toward traditional-religious values and another oriented toward success. The former was characterized by large family size, positive religious attitudes, low levels of aspiration, and little desire for higher education; the latter by the opposite traits. Three of the four factors (number of children, religious attitude, and college expenses) appear to be significantly related to multi-generation families. Families having many children or having a child with high scores on a religious test were more willing to share their homes; families paying college expenses were less willing to do so. Kosa concludes that the tradition-oriented family is more likely than the success-oriented family to provide a home for kinsmen. Kosa sees the practice of taking in kinsmen as a conspicuous feature of family solidarity, the frequency of the practice not being associated with socio-economic or ethnic status but with the value orientation of the family.[18]

FUNCTIONS OF THE KINSHIP SYSTEM

The functions of the kinship system are on behalf of nuclear families and more specifically on behalf of personalities. Zimmerman and Cervantes put it bluntly when they stated that the nuclear family uses what kin relations it feels are sympathetic with its purposes and supplements these with nonkin friends.[19]

The American kin family system insofar as it has functions must of necessity have specialized functions. Because of social differentiation there exist specialized systems covering economic, political, educational, and religious functions. As an example, the kin family system does not generally provide employment for the employable adults within the kin system; this is provided within the economic structures of society. Yet kin may perform the more limited economic function of making cash gifts or small loans to kinsmen in time of need.

[18] John Kosa, Leo De Rachiele, and Cyril O. Schommer, "Sharing the Home With Relatives," *Marriage and Family Living*, XXII (May, 1960), 129–131.
[19] Carle C. Zimmerman and Lucius F. Cervantes, *Successful American Families* (New York: Pageant, 1960), p. 41.

Social Activities

The major activities linking families in the kinship network can be classified under two headings: mutual aid and social activities.[20]

In regard to social activities, kinship visiting is a primary activity of urban dwellers and outranks visitation patterns found for friends, neighbors, or co-workers. With from 70 to 86 percent reporting about five or more family-group friends, Zimmerman and Cervantes found that kindred constituted from 30 percent to almost half of the family friends.[21]

Most kin interaction takes place in the context of social visits or gatherings of kinsmen on the occasion of some event or holiday to be celebrated. Hence it is primarily expression-oriented, directed toward the gratification of the individual members, rather than toward the attainment of any kin system goal. It is at such times that a solidarity with kin is reaffirmed through ritualistic practices. Being without status in a kin system is most noticed on holidays.

Cumming and Schneider[22] found that among older persons no class of kindred was specifically favored for interaction. There appeared to be a selection of people who lived close by on the grounds of personal compatibility, although in some cases this seemed less apparent because all kin were described as close. Kindred who were geographically distant were in an available pool; intimacy would come with opportunity. This is in a sense an equalitarian attitude, since it does not prescribe any set modes of deference between people of different generations. The naturally equalitarian relationship with collaterals would probably be more comfortable and be seen as more appropriate and, therefore, selected where there was a choice.

The expressive nature of extended kin contact is clearly seen in the large family gathering. Sixty-five percent of Reiss's respondents reported such gatherings.[23] They occurred either on a holiday or on the occasion of a family event, with no particular preference for either. Two-thirds were on a regular basis, and one-third were irregular.

Do people have an obligation to keep in touch with their kinsmen? About half of Reiss's respondents believed that there was such an obligation while only eleven percent definitely stated that there was none. The remaining answers were qualified. The most frequent qualified answer was one which admitted an obligation to keeping in touch with some relatives, usually the ones closer in relationship, but not others. Perhaps most striking is the small

[20] Based on the findings of a number of studies of kinship functions as reported in Sussman and Burchinal, *op. cit.* (see above, fn. 1), pp. 320–332.

[21] Zimmerman and Cervantes, *op. cit.,* p. 38.

[22] Cumming and Schneider, *op. cit.* (see above, fn. 8).

[23] Reiss, *op. cit.* (see above, fn. 4).

number who did not admit any obligation to keep in touch with relatives. The obligation to keep in touch may not have entailed any significant burden, but it did at least imply that a minimum kinship obligation was held by about 90 percent of the respondents.

There was a significant difference in the responses of men and women to this question of obligation to keep in touch with relatives. Women had a greater tendency than men to give a yes answer. In fact, without the greater concern of women for keeping in touch with kin, many relationships would not be maintained. The minimum in keeping in touch was fulfilled through letters and cards. Correspondence and notification of family events was allocated to the wife. Some men admitted that they would be completely out of touch with some of their relatives if it were not for the activities carried on by their wives.[24]

Conferral of Status

One of the most commonly perceived functions of kin is the conferral of status. Status denotes a position in a social system involving reciprocal expectations of actions with respect to occupants of other positions in the same system. Ascribed status is status a person has because of some quality or qualities which he possesses. Achieved status is status received as a result of what one does—one's performance.[25] Membership in a kin family network means that an individual's status is enhanced or degraded according to the statuses and actions of other members. Some respondents in the study by Reiss mentioned the pride one could have in relatives and their accomplishments, while several mentioned the disgrace which kin could bring. People not only achieve status by associating with others of equal or greater social rank; they also attain it through deference from others; a person can achieve status by gaining deference from his family.

The American kinship network does not have as great a status-conferring power as kinship systems do in societies in which social position is primarily based on ascription. In such societies all the members of the kinship system have a similar status, and the kinship unit and its members rise and fall as a unit. In an achievement-oriented society like the United States, on the other hand, status is based upon the separability of the individual nuclear family from kinsmen and the separability of the person from the nuclear family. The person is not as dependent upon kin for status in highly differentiated societies nor do his achievements necessarily reflect upon his relatives.

[24] Reiss, *op. cit.;* see also Lee N. Robins and Miroda Tomanec, "Closeness to Blood Relatives Outside the Immediate Family," *Marriage and Family Living,* XIV (November, 1962), 340–346.

[25] Julius Gould and William L. Kolb, *A Dictionary of Social Sciences* (New York: The Free Press of Glencoe, 1964), pp. 292–293.

Socialization

The kin family network can have significant functions for the personalities of kin family members even in the American system. The kin family network is a larger unit than the nuclear family, and one with more personal and material resources; it can support the nuclear family in the performance of its principal socializing functions. These functions of kin can have particular importance in an achievement-oriented society, for there are few systems in which a person can feel that he has a secure, ascribed status, where he is sure of belonging. Except for the network of kinsmen the maintenance of a stable, secure, social context for the person falls almost exclusively to the nuclear family. The nuclear family can perform this function intensively but not extensively. It is in the latter respect that the kin family network can function, widening the basis of ascribed status and thereby providing additional, though less intensive, relationships.

Mutual Aid

In interchanges between kin and nuclear family, kin provide aid for the mobile nuclear family without interfering with its mobility of occupational efficiency. One of the principal ways in which the network remains viable is by providing support to its mobile members. In fact, the kin network provides aid to those who are upwardly mobile, to those who are downwardly mobile, and to those in the initial stages of their career. This aid is frequently provided in other ways than by providing jobs, thus obviating the charge of nepotism.

The nuclear family which is part of a kin family system is more likely to achieve its goals than the nuclear family which is not. Money, a generalized means to many goals, can be transferred easily; family aid can be given promptly over great distances.

Only 38 percent of Reiss's respondents stated that kinsmen had not been of any assistance to them, financially or otherwise, in recent years; and considerably less, about 20 percent, answered that they had not been of any assistance to kinsmen during the past several years.

Data from a study of a small number of Jewish families that came to a civil agency for health care supports the hypothesis of a kinship family network of need.[26] Among the 120 cases, 45 of the elderly were living with their children; 61 were receiving financial assistance from their children; 27 of the aged were living with their children and receiving financial assistance from them; and 77 were receiving financial aid from their children or living with their children. The authors expected that they would find con-

[26] Paul H. Glasser and Lois N. Glasser, "Role Reversal and Conflict Between Aging Parents and Their Children," *Marriage and Family Living*, XXIV (February, 1962), 46–51.

flict between striving to get ahead by children and having to care for their aged parents. This did not turn out to be so. The hypothesis which states that the greater the cultural difference between the older and the younger generation, the greater will be the distance and points of conflict between them, also was not supported by the data.

The help patterns take many forms, including the exchange of services, gifts, advice, and financial assistance.[27] Financial aid patterns are direct or they are indirect and subtle. There is mixed feeling about giving and receiving financial aid within the kinship system. The exchange of aid flows from parent to children, children to parent, among siblings, and, less frequently, from more distant relatives.

Financial assistance from parents to children may take various forms—substantial sums of money, valuable gifts given at the time of marriage, at the time of birth of children, at Christmas, anniversaries, or birthdays.

In the parent-child relationship the aid is primarily in one direction, with the direction depending on the phase of the family cycle. Young people are more in need of assistance when establishing a family; the parents in turn are more apt to need assistance in the late stages of the family cycle.

Aid functions of the kin network include services performed regularly throughout the year or on occasions. These include shopping, escorting, care of children, advice giving, and counseling. Services for older kinship members include the giving of physical care, providing shelter, performing household tasks, and sharing leisure time. Families or individuals on the move are serviced by family units of the kin network. These services include motel-type accommodations for vacationing kin, scouting for homes and jobs, and providing supportive functions during periods of in-migration and in the transition from rural to urban patterns of living. Services on occasion include those performed at weddings, during periods of crisis—such as death, accident, disaster, or personal trouble of family members.

A major function of kin is that of providing security. This security may seldom be tested and may serve more as an impression of solidarity than for the actual provision of physical aid. Kin help out in time of disaster, despite the fact that the protective or security function in time of crisis is one that is frequently cited as having been largely relinquished either to social workers or to some private or governmental agencies. Quarantelli has summarized data of what approximately fifty different reports have observed concerning the protective function of the family.[28] He points out that the extended family was the major source to which disaster victims turned for help. Much assistance of both a material and a nonmaterial sort was generally obtained. In the vast majority of disasters it appeared that any-

---

[27] Sussman and Burchinal, *op. cit.* (see above, fn. 1), pp. 231–240.
[28] Enrico L. Quarantelli, "A Note on the Protective Function of the Family in Disasters," *Marriage and Family Living,* XXII (August, 1960), 263–264.

where from two-thirds to three-fourths of the victims received the substantial part of their relief and rehabilitation aid from relatives. Even when a considerable part of the assistance was obtained from nonfamilial sources, it was rare for victims of disasters not to have received at least some sort of aid from their kin.

Formal welfare agencies were the last source from which help was sought and obtained. There was a fairly discernible hierarchy of orientation in seeking help. Victims first sought aid from family members and close friends; secondly, from other friends and neighbors. They then turned to anonymous local community residents and to various systems of which they were members, such as unions and churches. Lastly, and only if familiar systems such as the police and the mass media agencies proved unrewarding, was there any turning to public agencies specifically organized to deal with problems of disaster relief.

The smaller the scope of the community disaster, the more probable were kin to be the major source of help. In large urban centers where most disasters were likely to be relatively localized in space, assistance of all sorts was generally asked for and obtained from kin sources, first in the neighborhood and second in the city at large. Even when a disaster was extensive, as in the instance of floods which inundated a city, considerable aid was still sought and obtained from kinsmen even though spatially located at some distance. The physical dispersion of kin families is functional in preventing crises from incapacitating all members of the same kin family network simultaneously. Some families remain intact outside the impact area to assist those involved in disaster.

Reiss found that help during illness was the major form of assistance provided by members of kin-related families.[29] If there is so much kinship interchange around protective and security functions, why have we emphasized the independence of the nuclear family as a system isolated from its kin? Apparently, one important reason is that it is a part of the American family ideal. Each man is expected to succeed, and a part of this success is demonstrated in his ability to support his family. No prestige accrues from the knowledge that his family has received or is receiving support from kinsmen. This reluctance to accept the fact of kin support was clearly shown in the Cumming and Schneider interviews with older people.[30] Their respondents were reluctant to discuss instrumental kin activities or mutual aid but eager to discuss socio-emotional and ritual activities. Initial questioning about financial aid among kinsmen elicited responses that indicated that borrowing and lending among kinsmen were seen as a mistake. Even exchange of services was discussed reluctantly. Kinship interchange ideally did not include services or financial help although the latter might be necessary.

[29] Reiss, op. cit. (see above, fn. 4).
[30] Cumming and Schneider, op. cit. (see above, fn. 8).

KINSHIP SYSTEM DYSFUNCTIONS

Reiss found that respondents saw the kin network as more functional than dysfunctional, though a sizable percentage listed dysfunctions. The most commonly mentioned dysfunction was competition and jealousy. A sizable minority felt that their kin took advantage of them, and one-third of the respondents rated the obligation to supply residence and financial aid as a disadvantage of kinship relations.

Interference, when perceived as a dysfunction of kin, occurs when kin disagree on the relative status of extended kin in relation to nuclear families. Most of the interference which was mentioned as dysfunction by Reiss was reported as a potential difficulty which had not been a problem for the respondent's own family. Many respondents immediately answered in terms of in-laws when asked about difficulties in connection with relatives. Their concern over potential interference is one of the factors indicating a very respectful attitude toward the integrity and privacy of the nuclear family.

TABLE 10.1. FUNCTIONS AND DYSFUNCTIONS OF KIN

Response	Percentage
Functions	
sense of belonging	64
affection	30
companionship	39
security	63
advice	43
help	22
none	11
Dysfunctions	
taking advantage of people	24
obligations to supply residence	
and financial aid	32
competition and jealousy	37
interference	34
none	08
N	161

SOURCE: Paul Jacob Reiss, *The Extended Kinship System in American Urban Middle Class* (Cambridge, Mass.: Harvard University, 1960, unpublished Ph.D. thesis).

THE KINSHIP SYSTEM AND MAJOR SOCIAL SYSTEMS

The kinship system when compared with other systems in society is both structurally and functionally weak. Since kinship tends to be sharply divorced from other systems, the effect is to make kinship appear insignificant beside such complex and ramifying systems as the economy and the government.[31]

There is little direct articulation between the kin family network and other systems in American society. Rather, each person is independently related to or involved in these other systems; and the nuclear family is related to these other systems through the members they have in common. The prime example is the relationship between the family and the economic system through the father's occupational role.

Large societal systems that the nuclear family can articulate with include (besides the kinship system), the economic system, the political system, and religious systems. Historically, in Europe the state and the church fought over which should dominate the family. But the principle of a free nuclear family not directly articulated under any larger system prevailed. In a sense, however, the family of the American comes to be articulated under some larger system. The economic bureaucrat tends to be integrated into the economic system; the family of the clergyman into the religious system; the family of the career diplomat or military man into the political system. In each case, it is an occupational system (not the kinship system), that assumes preeminence in integrating the nuclear family into the larger society. Kinship systems continue to exist despite the absence of direct functional relationships of the kinship system with other societal systems. The fact that they do exist suggests that they are not without function. Whether they exist because of their functions, or have functions because they exist depends on one's frame of reference.

SOCIAL CLASS DIFFERENCES AND KIN FAMILY INTERCHANGE

Sussman, comparing working-class and middle-class help patterns, found that all families of the middle class and ninety-three percent of the working class were actively involved in a network of giving help to kinsmen or receiving help from them on one or more items of assistance within a one-month period preceding the interview.[32] He found significant differences in four items of interchange by social class—middle class more than working class gave and received financial aid, more middle-class grandmothers were called on to take care of the grandchildren, and middle- more than working-class families exchanged advice and gave valuable gifts to one another.

[31] David M. Schneider and George C. Homans, "Kinship Terminology and the American Kinship System," *American Anthropologist,* LVII (December, 1955), 1194–1208.

[32] Marvin B. Sussman, "The Isolated Nuclear Family: Fact or Fiction," *Social Forces,* VI (Spring, 1959), 333–340.

Seventy-four percent of the working and 81 percent of middle-class families had large family gatherings at least once a year.[33]

Blumberg and Bell found that during and after migration lower-class migrants turned to relatives whenever possible.[34] If no relatives were available, the lower-class migrant turned to people from the old home area, feeling that they were like him and were therefore people that he could trust— i.e., he established pseudo-kin relationships with them. Lower-class activity appears to be more direct and less ritualistic and encompasses more of the total number of interpersonal relations than is true of middle-class activity.

In the lower-class are found the largest concentrations of first- and second-generation immigrant groups. These groups, although differing culturally among themselves, are commonly characterized by close relationships to extended kin. The doubling-up of families with relatives is also more common in this class.[35]

Regarding social activities, extended family get-togethers and joint recreational activities with kin dominate the leisure-time pursuits of the urban working class. And among urban middle classes there appears to be an almost universal desire for interaction with kin; distance being a limiting factor.

In the old upper-class families in the United States kinship relationships beyond the nuclear family are maintained to a great extent.[36] There are reasons for the greater extended kin activity in this social class. The first, and perhaps the most important reason, revolves about the possession, management, and inheritance of property. In the absence of a system of primogeniture and entail, it is through kin family support that an economic basis for family continuity is possible. A second factor which serves to reinforce upper-class kin ties is the prestige derived from them.

In the upper class, status is ascribed to a larger degree according to the status of the extended kinship system rather than on personal achievement alone, and the individual member has something to gain in terms of status by maintaining an attachment to the wider kinship group. The nuclear family may be seen as part of the larger kinship system and as a temporary partaker of its enduring tradition and prestige more reminiscent of the classical extended family. In addition to the family name, a coat of arms, the

[33] See also Earl L. Koos, "Middle Class Family Crises," *Marriage and Family Living*, X (1948), 27–40; and Earl L. Koos, *Families in Trouble* (New York: King's Crown Press, 1946).

[34] Leonard Blumberg and Robert R. Bell, "Urban Migration and Kinship Ties," *Social Problems*, VI (Spring, 1959), 328–332.

[35] Paul C. Glick, *American Families* (New York: Wiley, 1957), pp. 687–693; and Floyd Dotson, "Patterns of Voluntary Association Among Urban Working-Class Families," *American Sociological Review*, XVI (1951), 687–693.

[36] See also Cleveland Amory, *The Proper Bostonians* (New York: E. P. Dutton, 1947); and Allison Davis, *Deep South* (Chicago: University of Chicago, 1941).

oldest living family member, a business, or an estate and mansion may serve as symbols of collective solidarity. The older generation, as a depository of tradition and social prestige, possesses an authority not characteristic of older people in the other classes.

The new upper class, in contrast to the old upper class, possess the kinship pattern characteristic of the middle class from which they come. They lack the kinship traditions and authority patterns of the older upper class.

SUMMARY

The nuclear family is the primary kinship unit in the American social system. It has historical antecedents, but there are also important on-going reasons why it has persisted as the kin unit. First, since jobs are provided by other organizations than the family, the worker and his immediate family have to be prepared to go where the job is. Secondly, a dynamic, affluent society offers opportunities for independent individual and nuclear family social mobility.

Even in a society of high mobility a kinship network does exist. The components of the system are neolocal nuclear families in a bilateral or generational relationship. The system functions to give financial aid, to aid in disaster, to give status, and to provide social interaction. Occasionally three or more generations will live within one household, but it is not the common residential pattern.

BIBLIOGRAPHY

Bert N. Adams. "Occupational Position, Mobility, and the Kin of Orientation," *American Sociological Review,* XXXII (June, 1967), 364–377.

Ruth Albrecht. "The Parental Responsibilities of Grandparents," *Marriage and Family Living,* XVI (August, 1954), 201–204.

Felix M. Berardo. "Kinship Interaction and Communications Among Space-Age Migrants," *Journal of Marriage and the Family,* XXIX (August, 1967), 541–554.

Felix M. Berardo. "Kinship Interaction and Migrant Adaptation in an Aerospace-Related Community," *Journal of Marriage and the Family,* XXVIII (August, 1966), 296–304.

Leonard Blumberg and Robert R. Bell. "Urban Migration and Kinship Ties," *Social Problems,* VI (Spring, 1959), 328–332.

Allen D. Coult and Robert W. Habenstein. "The Study of Extended Kinship in Urban Society," *The Sociological Quarterly,* III (April, 1962), 141–145.

Elaine Cumming and David M. Schneider. "Sibling Solidarity: A Property of American Kinship," *American Anthropologist,* LXIII (1961), 498–507.

Floyd Dotson. "Patterns of Voluntary Association Among Urban Working-Class Families," *American Sociological Review,* XVI (1951), 687–693.

Paul H. Glasser and Lois N. Glasser. "Role Reversal and Conflict Between Aging Parents and Their Children," *Marriage and Family Living,* XXIV (February, 1962), 46–51.

A. O. Haller. "The Urban Family," *The American Journal of Sociology*, LXVI (May, 1961), 621–622.

Marvin R. Koller. "Studies of Three Generation Households," *Marriage and Family Living*, XVI (August, 1954), 205–206.

Earl L. Koos. *Families in Trouble*. New York: King's Crown Press, 1946.

Earl L. Koos. "Middle Class Family Crises," *Marriage and Family Living*, X (1948), 27–40.

John Kosa, Leo De Rachiele, and Cyril O. Schommer. "Sharing the Home With Relatives," *Marriage and Family Living*, XXII (May, 1960), 129–131.

Eugene Litwak. "Geographic Mobility and Extended Family Cohesion," *American Sociological Review*, XXV (June, 1960), 385–394.

Eugene Litwak. "The Use of Extended Family Groups in the Achievement of Social Goals: Some Policy Implications," *Social Problems*, VII (Winter, 1959–1960), 177–187.

Talcott Parsons. "The Kinship System of the Contemporary United States," *Essays in Sociological Theory Pure and Applied* (Glencoe, Ill.: The Free Press, 1949), pp. 233–250; first appeared in *American Anthropologist*, XLV (January–March, 1943).

Enrico L. Quarantelli. "A Note on the Protective Function of the Family in Disasters," *Marriage and Family Living*, XXII (August, 1960), 263–264.

Paul Jacob Reiss. *The Extended Kinship System in American Urban Middle Class*. Cambridge, Mass.: Harvard University, 1960, unpublished Ph.D. thesis.

Lee N. Robins and Miroda Tomanec. "Closeness to Blood Relatives Outside the Immediate Family," *Marriage and Family Living*, XXIV (November, 1962), 340–346.

Everett M. Rogers and Hans Sebald. "A Distinction Between Familism, Family Integration, and Kinship Orientation," *Marriage and Family Living*, XXIV (February, 1962), 25–30.

David M. Schneider and George C. Homans. "Kinship Terminology and the American Kinship System," *American Anthropologist*, LVII (December, 1955), 1194–1208.

Harry K. Schwarzweller and John F. Seggar. "Kinship Involvement: A Factor in the Adjustment of Rural Migrants," *Journal of Marriage and the Family*, XXIX (November, 1967), 662–671.

Ethel Shanas and Gordon F. Streib (eds.). *Social Structure and the Family: Generational Relations*. Englewood Cliffs, N.J.: Prentice-Hall, 1965.

Sheldon Skryker. "The Adjustment of Married Offspring to Their Parents," *American Sociological Review*, XX (1955), 149–154.

Carol L. Stone. "Living Arrangements and Social Adjustments of the Aged," *The Family Life Coordinator*, VI (September, 1957), 12–14.

Carol L. Stone. "Three Generation Influences on Teenagers: Conceptions of Family Culture Patterns and Parent-Child Relationships," *Marriage and Family Living*, XXIV (August, 1962), 287–288.

Marvin B. Sussman. "The Isolated Nuclear Family: Fact or Fiction," *Social Forces*, VI (Spring, 1959), 333–340.

Marvin B. Sussman and Lee Burchinal. "Kin Family Network: Unheralded Structure in Current Conceptualizations of Family Functioning," *Marriage and Family Living*, XXIV (August, 1962), 231–240.

Paul Wallin. "Sex Differences in Attitudes Toward In-Laws: A Test of a Theory," *American Journal of Sociology*, LIX (1954), 466–469.

CHAPTER 11

The Family and Systems of Control

SOCIETY must have some administrative system responsible for seeing that goals of society are attained. "Polity" is the term applied to these systems charged with administrative functions. In complex differentiated societies, the primary system charged with administrative function is government. Other public systems (such as the school) and voluntary systems (such as the church) perform administrative or polity functions for those under their jurisdiction.

Historically, the family has had interchanges with the two major systems that impose control. Both presume to some knowledge as to what the structure and function of the family should be. As we have pointed out, the control of one, the state, is now mandatory; the control of the other, the church, is now voluntary. The family cannot choose to disassociate itself from control by government and remain within the good graces of the society. It can disassociate itself from the discipline of the church, though a majority of American families have at least a nominal affiliation with it.

The history of western societies has evidenced an ever increasing intervention of the state into the structure and activities of family life. This increasing intervention of the state in the affairs of the family is not unique to the family; it represents the extension of state responsibility generally. The state conceives of few domestic or foreign affairs as beyond its interest and concern.

> The increase of state authority, however, has not in itself signified that the total control over the family has grown; for the family, relative to other elements of society, has never been free of social controls, and the growth of state responsibility has in some measure represented a substitution of state authority for other previous forms of control. The shift from spiritual to temporal values, paralleled by the transfer of authority from the sacred to secular authorities, has resulted in replacing in the modern era earlier religious controls by the legal structure of the state.[1]

In interchange with polity systems the family contributes loyalty in exchange for leadership. In return the family receives a number of advantages,

[1] Samuel Mencher, "Social Authority and the Family," *Journal of Marriage and the Family*, XXIX (February, 1967), 166.

such as protection, order, and legitimacy. Loyalty goes beyond the mere passive acceptance of the validity of the polity system's claim to legitimate power. It includes commitment to the policies the polity system is administering.

THE FAMILY AND THE STATE

Since the family is one of the structures of society having to do with disciplining sexual behavior—the control of sex expression, reproduction, child rearing, and relationships between age, sex, and generational system—it stands in a special relationship to the state, society's ultimate agency of discipline.

Family Law

Family law reflects values of the society. To insure that those who marry are competent to make a decision to marry and competent to fulfill family functions, and to insure that the participants are making the decision to marry voluntarily, the state asserts its authority. Age at marriage is controlled by law, with eighteen years for males and sixteen years for females most widely established by the states as minimum age at marriage with parental consent. There are laws preventing marriages of those physically or mentally unfit. Persons who are feebleminded or insane are barred from marrying, and most states refuse marriage licenses to persons with active cases of venereal disease.

Laws serve to prevent the formation of bigamous and incestuous unions; monogamy and family exogamy[2] are values in American society. All states prohibit marriage of close relatives—parent and child, siblings, grandparent and grandchild, uncle and niece, aunt and nephew. Marriages of first cousins are also forbidden in a majority of states.

The state is also concerned with marriage procedures and behavior. The state grants the sanction of society to a sex relationship between husband and wife; the marriage unit is the only unit to which this privilege is legally given. The state supervises the contract between a man and a woman since the law states that contract is not to be revoked by either partner or even by the partners acting together; it is the state that determines grounds for annulment or divorce. Property rights and inheritance are of vital importance in a free-enterprise, moneyed economy, hence government regulates economic transactions, even within the kinship system and between family members.

The state protects family dependents. It is concerned with the legitimacy of children and the privilege of family support and protection that accompanies legitimacy. There are laws to prevent the exploitation of wives and

[2] Exogamy denotes the principle of prohibition of marriage within certain systems; in this case with close relatives within the kin family network.

children. If the male head of the family is not held legally responsible for the support of dependents, the burden ultimately falls upon the state, for in America the state rather than the kinship system is ultimately charged with the care of persons.

Since family law is enacted by the separate states rather than by the federal government, there are variations in statutes and enforcement from state to state. In some cases the variations reflect regional differences as to what marriage and family procedures and activities are considered advantageous to persons and to society. Prohibition of interracial marriages falls in this category. At one time a majority of the states had statutes that prevented the marriage of persons of different races. In 1967 the United States Supreme Court ruled that such laws are unconstitutional.

Completely effective control of sexual behavior by the state is not possible; coitus and reproduction are biological processes and not dependent on state sanction for their performance. Legal obstacles can be evaded. Enforcement depends on the loyalty of the participants and of the general public to the law and to the authority of the state. Some persons engage in illegal sexual acts outside of wedlock, applications for license to marry are kept secret, minors desiring to marry falsify their ages, couples go to neighboring states with less stringent marriage laws or to states with lax enforcement.

Any basic changes in the status of persons or families show up in the statutes, for customs and values highly prized by the people are reflected sooner or later in the legal system.[3] Legal sources reflect the fact that the structure of the family has changed from a patriarchal authority system to a bilateral system based on equality of the spouses.[4] Traditionally, under common law, the husband-wife relationship was defined by suspending the legal personality of the wife. Upon marrying, the wife lost ownership of her personal property and control of her real property. She also lost her ability to make contracts and to use the courts. The unquestioned legal superiority of the husband is shown, for example, in the fact that if both husband and wife were in an accident in which both were injured and rendered incapable of marital intercourse, the husband would have the right to an action for the loss of consortium, but the wife would not. Also, if the wife was enticed away from the husband by a third party, the husband could bring action because of alienation of his wife's affections; similar relief would not be available to the wife under like circumstances. Lastly, the husband had the right to choose the family domicile and mode of living. It was his duty to

---

[3] This section based on Herma H. Kay, "The Outside Substitute for the Family," *Man and Civilization: The Family's Search for Survival,* eds. Seymour M. Farber, Piero Mustacchi, and Roger H. L. Wilson (New York: McGraw-Hill, 1965), pp. 3–14.

[4] Patriarchal denotes the governing of a family system by the father; bilateral denotes the governing of a family by a leadership coalition of father and mother.

support his wife, and he could select the means and place at which his duty should be performed.

The husband's paternal authority over his children further demonstrated his legal primacy over his wife. During his lifetime the father had virtually an absolute right to the custody and control of his minor children. He could designate a guardian whose right to custody of the children upon his death would be recognized as superior to the rights of the mother. If the father did not appoint a guardian, the mother succeeded to his parental rights. The father was entitled to both his child's services and his child's earnings. On the other hand, the father's duty to support his children was held in some American states to be only a moral obligation not directly enforceable by the child. If he refused to provide for his child, the poor laws authorized the municipal authorities to provide and then to demand reimbursement from the father to the extent of his ability to pay.

Traditionally, immunity from suit for wrongful acts between husband and wife and between parent and child obtained. The wife could not sue the husband because she was not legally a person.

In the case of the parent and the child, there was no legal merging of the child's personality with that of his parent. The child's inability to sue the father was based on an unwillingness to permit such a direct challenge to the father's authority over his family.

Development of American family law from 1850 to the present reflects the emergence of the married woman as a legal personality. In general, the disabilities imposed upon her by the common law have been removed by legislation or judicial option. Her rights as a mother have become equal if not superior to the parental rights of her husband. Beginning with Mississippi, in 1839, every state has enacted statutes known as Married Women's Acts which alleviate the restrictive property rules of the common law. Subsequent reforms have had the effect of permitting the wife to resort to the courts as freely as an unmarried woman can, without the necessity of her husband joining with her as a party to an action. Married women may now contract freely with their husbands as well as with others. Many states have abolished not only the husband's rights to action for alienation of affections but also his rights to action for loss of consortium.

Recent changes in the law in regard to parent-child relations also attest to the mother's strengthening legal position. In nearly all states the mother's right to custody of her child has been made equal to that of the husband.

The husband still retains his titular position as head of the family and retains also his right to choose a domicile for the family. But this right is also being challenged. A number of cases declaring it unreasonable for the husband to expect his wife to share a home with his mother, for instance, indicates the law's preference for equality between the spouses in the choice of domicile.

The child still occupies nearly the same status he has traditionally held. There are indications, however, that future legal developments will contribute to the emergence of the child as a person in his own right. Exceptions to his inferior legal status are already found in support laws. The child's legal right to support from both his parents is now recognized, and in some cases he may compel support from his parents' estate. Furthermore, the prevailing standard for awarding custody in child-custody cases is the best interest of the child.

Toward a National Family Policy[5]

Despite accumulated regulatory and welfare legislation passed by the various state legislatures and by the Congress over the years, the United States has not come readily or unequivocally to a national family policy—consensus on a core of family goals toward the realization of which national programs and policies are directed. The law nowhere defines family.

One major factor standing in the way of the development of a national family policy is a strong cultural commitment to individualism. America's goals are stated mainly in individualistic terms. The dominant democratic political theory, *laissez faire,* the emancipation of women, and the securance of the rights of children have been major contributions to a principle of individualism. The full realization of the self is the desired end; the family and other social systems are means to that end. There is a strong current of feeling that the family is a private venture for the personal satisfaction of the persons involved in it; a man's family is his own business, not the government's.[6] The government, it is held, should not interfere unless behavior in the home is hindering the chances of self-realization for one or more of the family members, particularly a child dependent.

This distinction between concern for individual and concern for family can be observed at the national level. For example, there have been White House Conferences on Children in each decade since President Theodore Roosevelt called the first one in 1909; there has been only one National Conference on Family Life (held in 1948) and it was not held on the call of the President. The federal government has a Children's Bureau and a Women's Bureau; there is no Family Bureau.[7] A kind of double talk has wittingly or unwittingly crept into many public pronouncements, indicating

---

[5] This section based on Alvin L. Schorr, "Family Policy in the United States," *International Social Science Journal,* XIV (1962), 452–467.

[6] J. Douglas Brown, "The American Philosophy of Social Insurance," *Social Service Review,* XXX (March, 1956), 1–8.

[7] There is a Bureau of Family Services in the Department of Health, Education, and Welfare, but its concern is with meeting the needs of persons not families *per se.* It coordinates the administering of grants to help the states provide services on behalf of old persons, dependent children, the blind, and permanently and totally disabled persons.

an ambivalence between values regarding the centrality of the individual and values regarding the centrality of the family. The President's Commission on National Goals affirmed that the family is the heart of society, but the report addresses itself to the citizens, each of whom sets his own goals. More explicitly, the report affirms that all American systems—political, social, and economic—must enhance the dignity of the individual, promote the maximum development of his capacities, stimulate responsible exercise of these capacities, and widen the range and effectiveness of his opportunities for individual choice.

A subtle but telling effect on the balance of individualism versus familism in public policy resulted from the shift of social work as a profession away from its orientation in the familism of sociology to its preoccupation during the 1940's and 1950's with the individualism in theory and research characteristic of psychology, psychiatry, and psychoanalysis. Family sociology contributed to the individualistic orientation when family sociologists focused on the person and on marriage in preference to the family as a system and wrote textbooks and taught courses in the personal preparation-for-marriage vein.[8] The current attempt to orient the social work profession to the family as the unit of analysis and therapy may reflect a nascent development of a unitary concept of the family.

The church is another deterent to the development of national family policy. A national family policy would come into conflict with the major religious systems—Roman Catholic, Jewish, and Protestant. On the national level, compromises are often feasible in practice which would not be made if the decision turned on an agreement on underlying principles, for all the major religions are more or less united in giving an important position to the family both in doctrine and in practice. They are led to an interest in national family policy, but they could not be expected to agree on what the details of the policy should be.

The diversity of family types resulting when a society is committed to the nuclear family as the only recognized family system complicates the formation of national family policy. There are married couples, nuclear families, three-generation households, broken nuclear families, widows and widowers, and some extended families. This wide variety raises problems for the formulation of broad policies. Policies and programs must be formulated that support broken families without discriminating against intact families, that assist old people who want to live with their children as well as those who do not. If the American people were committed, for instance, to a patriarchal-patrilineal-extended family as the basic familial system, all policies and programs could be formed in terms of it.

[8] Family sociologists with so-called functional textbooks to their credit include Robert Blood, Ruth Cavan, Reuben Hill, Paul Landis, Floyd Martinson, Atlee Stroup, and others.

Under the influence of the traditions of individualism, *laissez faire,* and the diversity of religious traditions, national planning to meet the goals of families and persons in families has taken a peculiar course. Schorr has delineated three propositions that have guided national planning on its uncertain course in planning for families. First is the principle of coherence; since the family is an instrument, sometimes an indispensable one, in the development and self-expression of persons, policies and programs in behalf of the family are most readily accepted if they are defended as necessary to or at last consistent with the needs of persons. It has also been assumed that if persons are served, families will automatically be served.

The second proposition guiding national planning is the pickaback principle. According to this principle it is assumed that change designed to achieve family goals is most likely to succeed when it is coincidental with other developments—for example, resolving some social issue or meeting an economic crisis. In part this reflects the fact that there are no specific governmental agencies supporting organized efforts in the interests of the family.

Lastly, there is the principle of direct response; action taken explicitly in pursuance of narrowly defined family objectives. In lieu of an overall national family policy, it is on specific issues that agreement can most readily be reached. Not infrequently such action is taken to correct the inadvertent effect on families of programs designed for other purposes; it may also tend to be regulatory rather than preventive.

The developments in social insurance and public assistance programs have followed these principles; legislation has been for individuals, with amendments covering family members tacked on later. The original Social Security Act passed in 1935 had family benefits added in 1937; disabled workers were covered in 1956, their dependents in 1958, and others later. In the aid to dependent children program, federal participation was at first limited to children in a family; participation in aid to mothers was added fifteen years later. Fathers in need because of unemployment were added after another eleven years, in circumstances consistent with two of the guiding principles. First, they were added in connection with legislation designed to meet the economic necessity, the pickaback principle. Second, they were added after two successive secretaries of the Department of Health, Education, and Welfare had defined the precise issue that exclusion of fathers from the program might lead to the exclusion of some fathers from their own families, the principle of direct response.

An element of national family policy appears in the general consensus that children are cared for best in their own families. This principle is as clear in aid given to dependent children as it is in insurance benefits paid to a surviving parent. Yet the defense of such programs rests on the principle of coherence and on the undergirding and primary conviction that unnecessary barriers must not be allowed to stand in the way of the development of persons.

So far as the aid to dependent children program is concerned, the decisions of public bodies so far have been essentially regulatory rather than preventive. Legislation concerned with bringing negligent fathers to judicial attention or with ways of requiring them to meet their responsibility require only the common-denominator agreement that fathers should be responsible; broader differences affecting the nature and function of marriage need not be resolved. The fact that efforts to enforce responsibility have not been notably successful may be one of the factors leading to a change.

There is a growing movement aimed at treating the family as a unit and its problems as group problems. The notion of a family court, with jurisdiction over all affairs of the family, has emerged. The idea for the new approach grows out of experience with the juvenile court and its philosophy of protecting and rehabilitating children instead of punishing them. The family court would handle juvenile court matters as well as cases involving paternity, child custody, child support, adoption, consent to marry below the legal age for marriage, annulment of marriage, divorce, and alimony. The court's legal staff would be assisted by a staff of social workers, psychologists, psychiatrists, and medical doctors in gathering the necessary data on which to base a judgment. It is conceivable that the family court, like the juvenile court, would not employ the adversary process, with its tendency to bring hostilities out into the open and to produce additional basis for hostilities, particularly in divorce and child custody cases.

There is then a tendency in the law to emphasize the individuality of the persons who make up the nuclear family, while at the same time treating their specific problems as problems of the family as a system. In this way, the law provides one more foundation for the building of the kind of family relationship that considers the needs of each person without losing sight of the importance of the interaction of each with the others. Nevertheless, a national family policy has not been developed, and the *de facto* policies that meet family goals still can, in large part, be described in terms of the coherence, pickaback, and direct response principles.

FAMILY-CHURCH INTERCHANGE

The state presumes to interpret and administer the law of the land and the will of the people in regard to family life; the church presumes to interpret and administer what it conceives to be the law and will of God in regard to the family. Judaic-Christian policy and polity is based on "the Word of God," the interpretation of the Word, and on church tradition.

The voluntary nature of church control is relatively clear-cut in a society built on the principle of separation of church and state. Whether American families affiliate with the church because they appreciate its discipline (polity function), because of its service functions, or for other reasons will become more clear as we review some of the empirical studies of the relationship between the family and the church.

Historically, the church has regarded the patriarchal type of nuclear family organization as proper, with the male head also serving as spiritual leader of the family. In recent years, there has been some departure from defense of the patriarchal family and more recognition of the family system as a democracy of equals.[9]

The Church and Control of Marriage

The churches in America have felt it within their province to exert influence over marriage and the family by promulgating doctrine or at least guidelines on the marital relationship, by encouraging marriage of believer with believer, by establishing rules for the marriage ceremony, by fixing permissible grounds of separation and divorce, by prescribing regulations as to the remarriage of divorced persons, by the exercise of discipline upon those guilty of irregularities in their sex lives. Family policy of the state and family policy of the church are not always in agreement. For example, the state has allowed some grounds for divorce not recognized by church policy.

Not only has the church aspired to influence directly the families of its members, measures have also been taken to secure regulations or provisions regarding marriage and divorce by bringing pressure to bear on civil authority.

To what extent is Judaic-Christian policy and polity reflected in American family life?

The presence of three major religious groups and a multiplicity of denominations, along with the American spirit of individualism, work to break down the religious particularity of American families. Not uncommonly husband and wife belong to different denominations, and, on occasion, children assert their freedom and join still other groups.

As further evidence of religious particularity, students of religion and society see a tendency to regard faith in the American way of life as synonymous with religious faith.[10] As one interviewee in the Fairchild and Wynn study queried, "What's the difference between being a Christian and being an American? Is there any difference?" Many parents assume that happy relationships and religious faith are identical. Many identified religion with congenial personal relationships, faith with self-sufficient confidence, and service with occasional generosity. One hundred suburban

[9] John R. Seeley, R. Alexander Sim, and Elizabeth W. Loosley, *Crestwood Heights: A Study of the Culture of Suburban Life* (New York: Basic Books, 1956), pp. 212–214.

[10] Martin E. Marty, *The New Shape of American Religion* (New York: Harper, 1959).

parents reported that growth in religious faith (as they conceived it) was best stimulated within their families by recreation together, vacations, grace at mealtime, and discussion of behavior problems of the family. Bible reading and worship were placed far down the list.[11]

Seeley and his colleagues were impressed by a rational concern for the child's religious life among Crestwood Heights parents. Religious activities, like those of the school, appeared to serve to gird the child with a minimum of spiritual armor which he could shed easily in favor of other defenses should it seem to become obsolete or cumbersome for him. He needed to be free to follow his life course; he should not be held back by old-fashioned ideas. "Like a new and finer house, a new and advanced religion can be a powerful source of reassurance to the Crestwooder that he has escaped his hampering past and can now grasp at a more alluring and dazzling future."[12]

Studies have shown that denominational distinctions mean little to parents who seek a congenial fellowship. An apparent tolerance appears to minimize the basic differences between faiths. Church members find it convenient to unite with whichever congregation has its building located along their traffic pattern. In this way they can most easily join friendly neighbors who gravitate to the same church for the same reason. Of all the factors that weigh in the choice of a church home, denomination is relatively unimportant.[13]

Parents appear to be most willing to join a church where their children feel at home. They appear to move with ease from one church to another. Even Jewish and Roman Catholic parents, as well as Protestant parents, sometimes send their children to the nearest Sunday church school regardless of its creed, because it is conveniently located.

The posture of disregard of religious particularity is not universal, however; Fairchild and Wynn found that many families take a stand. Protestant families feel the tension of living in areas that are overwhelmingly Roman Catholic, Mormon, or Jewish, for instance. Their struggle to keep their distinctive form of faith alive precludes any easy syncretism. Fairchild and Wynn found that some, but not many, described the church as a redemptive society; their understanding of normative religious doctrine, a view of the church as the people of God sharing a redemptive mission to the world, stands out because of its rarity.

It is the institutional view of the church that prevails. People see the church primarily as a building with an employed staff and a scheduled program. The church means a bundle of organizations, a mass of activities, and

---

[11] Roy W. Fairchild and John Charles Wynn, *Families in the Church: A Protestant Survey* (New York: Association, 1961), p. 138.

[12] Seeley, Sim, and Loosley, *op. cit.*, p. 216.

[13] William H. Whyte, Jr., *The Organization Man* (Garden City, N.Y.: Doubleday, 1957), pp. 407–422; Fairchild and Wynn, *op. cit.*, p. 177.

a crew of volunteer workers who engage in about the same basic activities as other character-building agencies.

Not infrequently the church is seen as a corporate, and usually authoritarian, teacher of morality; character building in this context means being told about high moral standards and good character. Many a Sunday school teacher teaches every lesson moralistically. Justification by faith might be propounded from the pulpit, but righteousness by works is taught in the classroom.[14] Viewed as a policing organization, the church appeared to many as a good thing to have, "like substantial banks, swimming pools, or a city dump."

Some families view the church as instrumental, as useful chiefly for other things over and beyond itself. This utilitarian idea of the church is expressed in a variety of ways. Church membership can improve one's mental health; it might open the way to a desirable social status in the community, to job advancement, or to the developing of a more desirable neighborhood. Church life might play its part in helping family unity or in helping persons to fill out their lives. "You have to have some activities of all kinds and try to keep the thing balanced."[15]

There is a different outlook on the part of fathers and mothers in regard to the church. One of the most striking differences found by Fairchild and Wynn was in the greater church interest manifested by women. Many wives complained of the lack of religious interest of their husbands, while husbands seldom entered such a complaint against their wives. In a study of a Roman Catholic parish Fichter also found a predominance of women involved in church activities. Out of every one hundred persons who went to confession, only thirty-six were males; of those attending evening services, thirty were males; and of those attending special Lenten services, twenty-four were males.[16]

Religion and the Family

Many clergymen indicate their feeling that sheer ignorance of the meaning of religious family life and how to practice it characterizes their parishioners. Few mothers or fathers accept easily the role of religious director in the family, though they feel that the child should be exposed in some form or other to some religious training from which the parents might or might not hold themselves aloof.

Only a minimum of families worship at home as families; Fairchild and Wynn found that more than half of the active church families report that they have worship at home less than once a year, if at all.[17] They seldom

---

[14] Fairchild and Wynn, *op. cit.,* p. 175.

[15] *Ibid.,* p. 176.

[16] Joseph H. Fichter, "The Profile of Catholic Religious Life," *The American Journal of Sociology,* LVIII (September, 1952), 145–149.

[17] Fairchild and Wynn, *op. cit.,* p. 185.

utilize church literature on the family, and tend to a vagueness in theological understanding that pervades their household conversation and common life. When parents do read church literature they do not read it for the joy of reading; they read it with a function in mind—a problem to solve, a class to prepare for, a discussion in which they expect to share. The man reads religious literature less than his wife, whether it is denominational magazines or parents' materials published by church educational boards.

American families go to church in large numbers, though church attendance has declined and fluctuated somewhat since the revival of religious interest around the turn of the century. Apparently worshipping together in a church, along with face-to-face relationships with friends, is regarded as important to many families. It is difficult to ascertain the extent to which religious participation is valued as sociability. Fairchild and Wynn found that personal friendship within the congregations was rated second only to sermons and congregational worship in a checklist of church-related experiences in rank order of their helpfulness. It has not occurred to many clergymen and church members that religion could inform family life at such points as sexual behavior or family planning. Although the Roman Catholic Church is outspoken and specific on these questions, many a Protestant pastor contents himself in speaking of them only in reaction.

Some parents express themselves as expecting the minister to be a leader of young people. They hope that the minister will be able to hold the interest of their young people. Feeling their own authority for this age group slipping as the adolescents gain greater emancipation, they welcome additional support from the church. Some parents express themselves as feeling that the last vestige of parental control, indirect though it is, is to be found in a young people's fellowship group at church.

Parishioners show an interest in the pastor as a counselor over others from the helping professions. Even if a personal or family problem becomes too involved for a clergyman to work with, many parents want to take a problem to a psychiatrist or other counselor only upon recommendation of their clergyman. Strommen, in his study of several thousand church-related young people, found that parents were much more concerned about the poor relationships between the adolescents and the family than were the young people themselves. The young people felt that family relations were reasonably good.[18]

Church youth are receptive to guidance from the church in the area of boy-girl relations, an area where insufficient help is being given by the church and where the pastors and youth workers do not feel competent to help.[19] A large percentage expressed themselves as bothered by the fact that they do not feel free to discuss intimate problems with their pastor. Most of

[18] Merton Strommen, *Report on Lutheran Youth Research*, I (Minneapolis: Lutheran Youth Research, 1959), 24.

[19] Strommen, *op. cit.*, p. 9.

the major church bodies are attempting to correct this situation. Programs of the Roman Catholic Church are illustrative. Family-life courses, including instruction in preparation for marriage, are taught in Roman Catholic high schools, and most dioceses have either a Catholic Youth Organization or Catholic Youth Council clubs. Youth clubs or groups in contiguous communities sponsor workshops on marriage and family living.[20]

Besides youth organizations, churches sponsor Cub Scouts, and Boy and Girl Scout groups. A large part of these activities is secular in nature and does not differ from activities that might be offered by the school or other community agencies. Thus the major competition between these two groups of activities appears to be between auspices, not between content.

The major religious bodies—Roman Catholic, Protestant, and Jewish—all support special family service agencies, apart from the work of local congregations and synagogues. Family agencies under church auspices also carry on casework services, homemaker services, and home nursing services.

Family Criticism of the Church

When institutional aspects of the church prevail in the thinking of parishioners, they are apt to be most concerned about keeping the organization going. Thus, parents often complain about being loaded with too much church responsibility. They speak of being caught in a veritable beehive of activity, all aimed at nurturing the organization rather than ministering to the world.

To parents, the church often resembles a three-ring circus in which father and mother are separated from each other as well as from their children by the numerous specialized groups in the frenetic activity of something called "the program." Among unhappy comments about the church are complaints about ill-conceived family nights that promote more confusion than fellowship, or infant days at church that fulfill promotional plans to gather babes in arms but end in upsetting both babies and their parents. Other complaints cite poor planning of the many events that make Sunday not only the busiest but also the most tension-fraught day of the week. Parents plead in various ways to have the hyperactivity reduced. They feel pushed or exploited by their churches. They see activities, once planned to nurture church people, now requiring people to nourish them.

Fairchild and Wynn found the most frequent complaint of clergymen similarly to be one of too much activity. Pastors were critical of the plethora of outside-the-home activities that competed to separate family members and fan domestic friction. Pastors were well aware of the multiple activities in community life that divided households and dissipated their sense of unity. Besides church activity, pastors report that Little League, drama

[20] Lawrence J. McNamara, "A Digest of Some Family Life Projects Under Catholic Church Auspices," *The Bulletin on Family Development,* II (Spring, 1961), 25.

groups, extracurricular school activities, ski clubs, dances, garden groups, and bowling teams cut into family morale until it is all but impossible for fatigued parents and children even to be civil to each other, let alone live in a spirit of charity.

Pastors also cast an introspective look at their own parsonage families. They were given the opportunity to rank a series of categories in their order of importance when asked what family problems ministers most frequently had. First by a clear lead was their opinion that too many demands on the pastor left him without time for his own family.

Not all families feel plagued by the hyperactivity in the church. Berger found a low percentage of church attendance in a working-class suburb. Participation in church activities other than church attendance was practically nil; eighty-one percent said that they never participated. Despite the complaint of some ministers about the amount of time that they must devote to family and marital problems, ninety-three percent of these automotive workers reported that they had never spoken to their clergyman about any of their family problems.[21]

The Church and the Family—A Sociological Critique

The concern of the church for the family has not diminished over the years; if anything it has increased. The church has traditionally taken an equivocal stance in its relationship to other systems of society, particularly political and economic systems, but not to the family. Berger[22] sees the church's concern over the family as accompanied by a full-blown ideology, the attributing of extraordinary sanctity to the family system. The sociological aspect of the ideology which the church traditionally has accepted is the proposition that the family is the basic unit of society. If this is true, it would follow that if the church works for a religiously-oriented family it is thereby working for a religiously-oriented society. Implied in this view is more than the unverified axiom that the family that "prays together stays together"; there is also the implication that the totality of religious homes constitutes a religious nation. The level of sociological sophistication involved in this ideology is comparable to a view which would hold that the fiscal policies of the national government should adhere to the same economic principles on which the family budget is operated.

The family can be regarded as a basic social unit mainly in a psychological sense. In the life of the individual, both the family of orientation and the family of procreation are of vital importance, but this psychological fact cannot be transferred to the sociological level of analysis. On the contrary,

21 Bennett M. Berger, *Working Class Suburb: A Study of Auto Workers in Suburbia* (Berkeley and Los Angeles: University of California, 1960), p. 46.

22 Peter L. Berger, "The Second Children's Crusade," *The Christian Century*, LXXVI (December 2, 1959), 1399–1400.

in society the family is in a dependent relationship to some other system; in a highly differentiated society the family is dependent upon political, social, and economic systems.

By concentrating on the family to the exclusion of other systems, Berger contends that the churches are not at work where important societal decisions are made but where the effects of these decisions are experienced. To the extent that the churches are linked intimately with the family system to the exclusion of other systems, to that extent they are impotent in society. Family-centeredness has helped to confine the understanding of religious ethics to personal relations only, ignoring the policy-making, social systems.

The Detroit Surveys

That religious affiliation is related to difference in patterns of family life has been empirically demonstrated. Results of the University of Michigan Detroit surveys are to the point.[23] Lenski found marriage relationships to be less durable among Protestants than among Catholics in the Detroit area. Also, Catholics remarry after divorce much less readily than do Protestants. According to Lenski, this means that Catholics are under greater pressure than are Protestants to make the first marriage work.

Findings from the Detroit surveys suggest that white Protestant churches contribute to the weakening of kinship ties, at least ties with the extended family. For example, in the 1952 survey data Lenski found that only 43 percent of the active Protestant churchgoers reported visiting their relatives at least once a week, while 51 percent of the marginal church attenders visited relatives. Other evidence suggests that activity in Protestant churches is linked with an extrafamilial orientation. Churchgoing Protestants were more likely to be involved in voluntary associations than were marginal Protestants. The 1958 survey demonstrated that church-related organizations play a much more prominent role in Detroit Protestantism than in Detroit Catholicism. Fifty-four percent of the active, churchgoing, white Protestants were currently active in some such organization, compared with only 24 percent of the active, churchgoing Catholics. Whereas the Protestant churches appear to stand in a somewhat competitive relationship with the kin group, the Catholic Church stands in what might be classified as a complementary relationship. That is, the church and the kin group appear more often to be mutually reinforcing organizations in the lives of devout Catholics. In the 1952 Detroit survey, for instance, 60 percent of the Catholics who reported weekly attendance at mass reported visiting relatives at

---

[23] Gerhard Lenski, *The Religious Factor: A Sociological Study of Religion's Impact on Politics, Economics, and Family Life* (Garden City, N.Y.: Doubleday, 1963). Lenski surveyed 656 families in Detroit in 1958. For the analysis of religion and family life he also used data from the 1952, 1953, 1955, 1956, and 1957 surveys.

least once a week, whereas the same was true for only 45 percent of those reporting irregular attendance at mass. The pattern for white Protestants was the reverse of this. While 60 percent of active Catholics visited relatives weekly, 43 percent of the active Protestants visited relatives weekly.

On the basis of the evidence, Lenski concludes that church and kin group stand in one relationship to each other among Catholics and another among Protestants. The Catholic pattern appears to be one devoted to transforming the world gradually through an evolutionary process. To achieve its ends it seeks to use, rather than to destroy, existing systems such as the family. According to empirical evidence, the Protestant church appears to treat the family as something of a competitor.

SUMMARY

Certain interchanges of the family with government are of a mandatory nature. The family cannot completely separate itself from the authority of the state. The state controls entry into marriage and departure from it through its administration of marriage and divorce law. It also exercises control over relations between spouses and between parents and children. Laws reflect and are an embodiment of some of the major values and customs of the people. As values and customs change, change is reflected in legal sanctions. The law reflects changes in the structure of the family from a patrilineal to a bilateral system over recent decades.

Despite a growing body of family law, America has not developed a national family policy. Reasons why a national family policy has not developed include the commitment to individualism in policy and polity, *laissez faire,* and respect for family policy and polity of the various church denominations. There is, however, a growing tendency on the part of the courts to treat the family as a system and its problems as system problems.

Whereas the state presumes to interpret the law of the land and the will of the people insofar as family is concerned, the church presumes to reflect the word and will of God. In America, many families voluntarily affiliate themselves with the policy and polity of the church. Church policy on marriage, divorce, and other aspects of family life is not consistent in all respects with state policy.

There is some evidence to suggest a decrease in religious particularism as families move with apparent ease from one denomination to another. A secular rather than a religious polity appears to characterize much of American family life. Furthermore, Protestant families complain that church-related activities contribute to an overorganized way of life that is in itself a threat to family life.

238   THE FAMILY AND OTHER SOCIAL SYSTEMS

BIBLIOGRAPHY

Bennett M. Berger. *Working Class Suburb: A Study of Auto Workers in Suburbia*. Berkeley and Los Angeles: University of California, 1960.

Peter L. Berger. "The Second Children's Crusade," *The Christian Century*, LXXVI (December 2, 1959), 1399–1400.

Arthur W. Calhoun. *A Social History of the American Family: From 1865 to 1919*. New York: Barnes and Noble, 1946; first published in 1917.

Nathan E. Cohen and Maurice F. Connery. "Government Policy and the Family," *Journal of Marriage and the Family*, XXIX (February, 1967), 6–17.

Roy W. Fairchild and John Charles Wynn. *Families in the Church: A Protestant Survey*. New York: Association, 1961.

Joseph H. Fichter. "The Profile of Catholic Religious Life," *The American Journal of Sociology*, LVIII (September, 1952), 145–149.

E. Franklin Frazier. *The Negro Family in the United States* (revised and abridged ed.). New York: Dryden, 1948.

John D. Hogan and Francis Ianni. *American Social Legislation*. New York: Harper, 1965.

Paul H. Jacobson. *American Marriage and Divorce*. New York: Rinehart, 1959.

William M. Kephart. *The Family, Society, and the Individual*. Boston: Houghton Mifflin, 1966.

William M. Kephart. "Legal and Procedural Aspects of Marriage and Divorce," *Handbook of Marriage and the Family*, ed. Harold T. Christensen. Chicago: Rand McNally, 1964. Pp. 944–968.

Hope J. Leichter and William E. Mitchell. *Kinship and Casework*. New York: Russell Sage Foundation, 1967.

Gerhard Lenski. *The Religious Factor: A Sociological Study of Religion's Impact on Politics, Economics, and Family Life*. Garden City, N.Y.: Doubleday, 1963.

Richard V. Mackay. *Law of Marriage and Divorce*. New York: Oceana, 1959.

Lawrence J. McNamara. "A Digest of Some Family Life Projects Under Catholic Church Auspices," *The Bulletin on Family Development*, II (Spring, 1961), 24–29.

Martin E. Marty. *The New Shape of American Religion*. New York: Harper, 1959.

Samuel Mencher. "Social Authority and the Family," *Journal of Marriage and the Family*, XXIX (February, 1967), 164–192.

Dennison Nash and Peter Berger. "The Child, the Family and the 'Religious Revival' in Suburbia," *Journal for Scientific Study of Religion*, II (Fall, 1962), 85–93.

Harriet F. Pilpel and Theodora Zavin. *Your Marriage and the Law*. New York: Rinehart, 1952.

Morris Ploscowe. *Sex and the Law*. Englewood Cliffs, N.J.: Prentice-Hall, 1951.

Morris Ploscowe. *The Truth About Divorce*. New York: Hawthorne, 1955.

John Scanzoni. "Resolution of Occupational-Conjugal Role Conflict in Clergy Marriages," *Journal of Marriage and the Family*, XXVII (August, 1965), 396–402.

Alvin L. Schorr. "Family Policy in the United States," *International Social Science Journal*, XIV (1962), 452–467.

John R. Seeley, R. Alexander Sim, and Elizabeth W. Loosley. *Crestwood Heights: A Study of the Culture of Suburban Life.* New York: Basic Books, 1956.

Richard V. Sherwin. *Sex and the Statutory Law.* New York: Oceana, 1949.

John L. Thomas. *The American Catholic Family.* Englewood Cliffs, N.J.: Prentice-Hall, 1956.

Chester G. Vernier. *American Family Laws.* Stanford, Calif.: Stanford University, 1931–1938.

Stephen L. Wasby. "The Impact of the Family on Politics: An Essay and Review of the Literature," *The Family Life Coordinator,* XV (January, 1966), 3–23.

William H. Whyte, Jr. *The Organization Man.* Garden City, N.Y.: Doubleday, 1957.

PART V

The Individual and Socio-Sexual Systems

ONLY THE INFANT has all of his needs met within the family. As the child emerges into adulthood, more and more of his needs are met by persons and systems in the community. Leaving home does not usually come about as an abrupt and sudden departure initiated solely through the efforts of parents or child. The child begins his break with the family early in life. Parents are aware that the process of leaving home has started the day the child begins to attend school (if they were not aware of it even earlier): it is a portent of things to come. The child may first leave home for a few hours of kindergarten; however, for several hundred thousand American children it begins earlier in day-care, nursery facilities. Next he is in school for a full day; high school adds evening extracurricular participation and keeps the adolescent out of the home beyond his "normal" bedtime. Peer-group loyalty, dates, conflict of schedules between the family and the adolescent all prepare for the break with the family of orientation that comes with marriage—or which may come before marriage as college, a job, or military service breaks up the family as a face-to-face functioning unit.

To the extent that society provides systems to facilitate transfer and systems that make leaving home seem right, the separation of the child from the parental home is more easily accomplished. The child has incentive to change if things happen to reduce the rewards he receives from activity in the family and if things happen to increase his estimate of the rewards he receives from activities outside the home. Having incentive to change is not changing, however; the means for change must be provided. The means are dramatized in rituals known as rites of passage. One rite that helps to launch the adolescent into adulthood in primitive societies is the puberty rite or initiation that comes approximately at the time of pubescence. Margaret Mead contrasts the pubescent experience for girls in our society with that of girls in societies possessing puberty rites. The California Indians, the Thompson River Indians, the Gilbert Islanders, and others prescribe a ritual —a series of definite, easily comprehended acts, "often exacting, often boring, but not baffling."[1] Although rites help to alleviate indecision and anxiety, we have no specific rite to signify the passage from dependent childhood to independent adulthood.

Puberty is hardly an age for assuming adult roles in urban-industrial society, however. Exercises at the time of graduation from high school and college are examples of rituals that fill part of the need for rites of passage in American society.

At first when the child goes out from the family he continues to identify with the family and its values, and he is motivated to implement these values as a representative of the family and, with familial support, to learn new values in interaction with persons outside the family. Gradually, his sensitivity to the approval of new socializing agents, such as peers and teachers, increases. He comes more and more to represent himself rather than his family. His parents alter their roles, too; during childhood the norms his parents used in judging his behavior were centered in the family. As they come to accept his involvement outside the home they utilize community norms in appraising his behavior. The parents react more and more as members of the community rather than as parents of a particular child as their child becomes more and more a part of the community.

Theoretically, it is useful to view the period between the time the young adult leaves the parental home (the family of orientation) and formation of his own family (the family of procreation) as a period of freedom from family during which the person is without intimate attachment to any nuclear family. He is relatively free from the supervision of his parents, and he has not yet committed himself to form a family of his own. It is a period in which the person interacts less with his family and relatives than with other persons. In urban-industrial societies the family-free period is often a time in which the young adult lives apart from his parents in a rented room, an apartment, or a college domitory, and is a period in which he associates with peers of both sexes.

Young men commonly have a greater degree of freedom from parental domination than do young women and for a longer period of time, since they gain freedom from parental supervision at an earlier age, and, on the average, do not marry at so early an age. The person's family-free period varies in length from little or no real emancipation from the family of orientation for girls in some families to a matter of years of family-freedom for both young men and young women in some urban communities.

Sooner or later pressures latent or manifest, subtle or direct, personal or social, come to bear, and the person enters a family again—his marital family or family of procreation.

In various ways society encourages the formation of new family units, but encouragement is not enough. Society must provide systems to facilitate the passage from single to married status. There is variety in these enabling systems. In some societies professional matchmakers are employed by the

[1] Margaret Mead, "Adolescence in Primitive and Modern Society," in *The New Generations,* eds. V. F. Calverton and S. D. Schmalhausen (New York: Macauley, 1930).

family to find a spouse for the eligible son or daughter, to arrange a meeting between a family representative of each, and even to supervise the details of the agreement and the subsequent marriage ritual. In other societies a kinsman—father or an uncle—may be charged with the responsibility. In still other societies family-free adults are permitted to make their own choice of marriage partners and to negotiate directly with each other. In American society choice of a mate is by this method of personal confrontation.

After the necessary personal commitments and social arrangements have been made, some rite of passage marks the changed status of the marrying partners. This is the function served by the wedding ritual.

The birth of a child signals another change in status for the person. The newly married person now faces the same general problem that he had in his parental home, namely, working out an accommodation with other members of an intimate family unit; thus he returns again to a family unit calling for integration. In the family of orientation his responsibility was limited; in the family of procreation he is a member of the leadership coalition, with the successful integration of the family falling to his charge. This new leadership coalition has the responsibilities of adapting the new family to the outside world—providing sustenance and maintaining the kinds of relationships outside the family that will reflect creditably upon the family and make it possible to survive. All the situations of an intimate, diffuse family system are present for him again but with the newly married person in a new status and with new roles; the cycle is complete.

Once again he is being socialized in a family system; socialization in the family is not by any means restricted to the development of the personalities of children. In the family, adult men and women ideally speaking find fulfillment of their basic needs and desires, the expression of sentiment, the release of tension, and the encouragement they need to face the responsibilities of adult life. Personality development and increase in emotional stability are possible outcomes for adults experiencing the socializing process of the family of procreation.[2] Adult socialization may well be one of the basic functions of the family, along with the primary socialization of the child.

There is another marked difference between a person's relationship to his family of procreation and to his family of orientation. With marriage and the birth of children he is for the first time a part of both a marriage system and a family system. During his childhood phase he was a member of the family but an outsider to his parents' marriage. Now he has roles in both systems. The distinction between marriage and family may not be a significant distinction in primitive societies, where differentiation between nuclear and extended family and between marriage and nuclear family is not clear-cut, but it is significant in differentiated societies where nuclear family is differentiated from extended family and marriage is differentiated from nuclear family. The significance of this differentiation will be elaborated in chapters to follow.

[2] Robert M. Gomberg, "Family Diagnosis: Trends in Theory and Practice," *Social Casework*, XXXIX (February–March, 1958), 73–83.

CHAPTER 12

Youth, Socio-Sexual Norms
and Systems: I

IN AMERICAN SOCIETY the child gradually changes his major reference system from one of the major socio-sexual systems—the family of orientation—to playmates, to school peers, and to other persons and agencies in the community. A gradual transfer of personal allegiance from the family to other persons and systems is to be expected in a society with a nuclear-family system. As the child grows, increasingly he seeks to find peers as colleagues whose favor he courts and whose respect he solicits.

YOUTH AND THE FAMILY OF ORIENTATION

The problem of leaving home is complicated by the fact that the period of nonage, which was twelve and fourteen years under common law, has practically doubled in two generations or less. The adolescent has his residence and his identity as a part of his family of orientation.

When the child leaves home, there is a relationship between the quality of the parent-child relationship and the adjustment of the child to persons and situations outside the home. Boys from homes characterized as friendly and cooperative are held in higher esteem by their classmates;[1] higher socio-economic class of the home is reflected in greater adolescent participation in the life of the community;[2] parental support of upward mobility is reflected in the upward mobility of boys;[3] parental interest in the child is reflected in his self-esteem in school;[4] adolescents are more likely to accept their parents as models and to associate with parent-approved peers if their parents explain their rules of procedure and discipline when asked to do so:

[1] Charles F. Warnath, "The Relation of Family Cohesiveness and Adolescent Independence to Social Effectiveness," *Marriage and Family Living*, XVII (November, 1955), 346–348.

[2] August B. Hollingshead, *Elmtown's Youth* (New York: Wiley, 1949), p. 358.

[3] Richard L. Simpson, "Parental Influence, Anticipatory Socialization and Social Mobility," *American Sociological Review*, XXVII (August, 1962), 517–522.

[4] Morris Rosenberg, "Parental Interest and Children's Self-Conceptions," *Sociometry*, XXVI (March, 1963), 35–49.

democratic parents are more attractive as models than are either authoritarian or permissive parents;[5] adolescents' personality characteristics are significantly related to the emotional relationship and the disciplinary patterns experienced in the home.[6]

The age of transfer and the extent of transfer of loyalty from parents to peers and others also reflects the quality of the parent-child relationship.[7] In homes where relationships were satisfactory, Bowerman and Kinch found that the family could maintain a close relationship with the child in terms of affection, identification, and acceptance of family values, even though the child indicated a preference for association with his peers. Low adjustment to the family and low family orientation appeared to be results of the way in which the family reacted to the child during his period of increasing peer orientation.

The extent to which the adolescent's orientation is split between family of orientation and peers becomes apparent when he is asked to choose between parental approval and the approval of his peers. Brittain asked 280 girls in grades nine through eleven to indicate what choices young persons would make in twelve hypothetical situations involving given alternative courses of action, knowing that the counsel of their parents and their peers would be in disagreement.[8] In only three of the twelve hypothetical situations did the girls definitely reflect the decision that their peers would make in the face of parental disapproval. Girls who most frequently chose peer-favored alternatives tended not to be as well accepted by their peers as did those who chose parent-favored alternatives.

The responses of the adolescents reflect their perceptions of peers and parents as competent guides in different areas of judgment. In other words, the social orientation of adolescents appears to be of a dual nature. Choices vary depending upon which reference group the adolescent has confidence in. In choices where their immediate group status or identity is at stake, students tend to favor the judgment of peers. They want to avoid decisions that make them appear noticeably different from their peers or that separate them from their friends. In choices where they are concerned with status positions to which they might aspire as adults, they are inclined to accept their parents as guides. In Brittain's sample population there was another

---

[5] Glen Elder, Jr., "Parental Power Legitimation and Its Effects on the Adolescent," *Sociometry*, XXVI (March, 1963), 50–63.

[6] Robert F. Peck, "Family Patterns Correlated with Adolescent Personality Structure," *The Journal of Abnormal and Social Psychology*, LVII (November, 1958), 349–350; Bernard C. Rosen and Roy D'Andrade, "The Psychosocial Origins of Achievement Motivation," *Sociometry*, XXII (September, 1959), 185–218.

[7] Charles E. Bowerman and John W. Kinch, "Changes in Family and Peer Orientation of Children Between the Fourth and Tenth Grades," *Social Forces*, XXXVII (March, 1959), 206–211.

[8] Clay V. Brittain, "Adolescent Choices and Parent-Peer Cross Pressures," *American Sociological Review*, XXVIII (June, 1963), 385–391.

distinction; conformity to parental wishes was prevalent in response to dilemmas posing difficult choices, indicating greater trust in parental than in peer judgment. One device which these adolescent girls used to cope with areas in which there was disagreement between peer and parental values was secrecy. That is, they avoided conflict by not communicating with parents on a particular issue.

The high school teacher rates a poor third to parents and peers as a referent for the adolescent.[9] Over 50 percent of the students in the Coleman study and 80 percent of the students in the Epperson study indicated concern over parental reaction to their decisions, and 40 percent and 15 percent respectively indicated concern over the reaction of respected peers, while less than 4 percent of the boys and less than 3 percent of the girls indicated concern over a teacher's reaction, even a favorite teacher.

ATTENUATION OF PARENT-YOUTH RELATIONS

There are relatively few but intense emotional relationships in the American family, and it is necessary to attenuate these relationships as the child is launched from the home.

The rate of attenuation of parental attachment, as well as the extent of such attenuation, may reflect the sex of the offspring. According to Parsons,[10] the stressful combination of short-lived and intense ties in the family of orientation, along with the necessity of transferring reference-group orientation, gives rise to a "weaning mechanism" helpful in the emancipation of the adolescent, namely, the romantic youth culture carried by one's peers. Peers encourage orientation toward peer rather than toward parental norms and expectations and intensify certain kinds of parent-adolescent tensions. These tensions can help to facilitate the emancipation of the adolescent from his family. Hobart put Parsons hypothesis to a test using undergraduate students as his sample population.[11] Findings support the hypothesis with regard to males, but point in the direction of its rejection insofar as females are concerned. In other words, peer culture as a "weaning mechanism" serving to ease emancipation of the adolescent from heavy dependence and involvement with family of orientation may be valid for males but is probably not valid for females.

Sons are given earlier and more frequent opportunity for independent action and are allowed more privacy in personal affairs than are girls.

[9] James Coleman, *The Adolescent Society* (Glencoe, Ill.: Free Press, 1961), p. 5; David C. Epperson, "A Re-Assessment of Indices of Parental Influence in *The Adolescent Society*," *American Sociological Review,* XXIX (February, 1964), 93-96.

[10] Talcott Parsons, "The Kinship System of the Contemporary United States," *Essays in Sociological Theory* (Glencoe, Ill.: The Free Press, 1949), pp. 233-250.

[11] Charles W. Hobart, "Emancipation from Parents and Courtship in Adolescence," *Pacific Sociological Review,* I (Spring, 1958), 25-29.

Daughters are held to a stricter code of family and kinship obligations.[12] Komarovsky suggests that girls are perhaps unable to achieve stable emancipation from the family of orientation in adolescence. Dating depends upon the boy severing his attachment to his mother, while girls are involved in dating without emancipation from their parents.[13]

A girl's involvement in serious dating does not require the same degree of independent action or initiative as this behavior requires of the boy. Dating norms in American society presume that it is the boy who will take the initiative in asking a girl for a date. Likewise, proposing marriage requires greater readiness to assume independent action on his part than it does on hers. In other words, the requirements of the girl's status have not asked that she make a transition from the passivity and compliance in childhood in the same degree that this has been expected of the boy.[14]

Perhaps it is as a consequence of family training or of family of orientation protectiveness that the female offspring in the past have transferred dependence directly from parents to husband without an intervening interval of independence. A period of relative freedom from dependence on family of orientation may accompany a girl's attendance at college, depending somewhat on the nature of the college and its location,[15] or may accompany gainful employment away from the home community.

Once a young lady is engaged to marry, her life orientation may again undergo change as her attention shifts from job to marriage or from job to job and marriage. No comparable change in the life orientation of the male accompanies marriage.[16] Recent changes in the relationship between the sexes in regard to responsibility for the support of home and family have been markedly in the direction of equalitarianism, however.

YOUTH SOCIETY

What is the nature of the society into which the adolescent moves as he makes his choice of friends outside the parental home?[17] Every society has systems structured to implement social functions. When social functions are

[12] Mirra Komarovsky, "A Functional Analysis of Sex Roles," *American Sociological Review*, XV (August, 1950), 508–516.

[13] Robert F. Winch, "Courtship in College Women," *American Journal of Sociology*, LV (November, 1949), 269–278.

[14] Arnold W. Green, "The Middle Class Male Child and Neurosis," *American Sociological Review*, II (February, 1946), 31–41.

[15] Benjamin Morse, *Sexual Behavior of the American College Girl* (New York: Lancer, 1963), pp. 60–100.

[16] Margaret Mead, "The Contemporary American Family as an Anthropologist Sees It," *American Journal of Sociology*, LIII (May, 1948), 453–459.

[17] Ernest A. Smith, *American Youth Culture: Group Life in Teen-Age Society* (New York: Free Press of Glencoe, 1962); Robert C. Baeler and Fern K. Willits, "Rural Youth: A Case Study in the Rebelliousness of Adolescents," *The Annals of the American Academy of Political and Social Science*, CCCXXXVIII (November,

not met or are impeded by the existing systems, new or alternative systems emerge to carry out the obstructed functions. Applying this to the situation faced by American youth, education is the primary function of the school, and the school is the primary social system designated to meet the needs of youth. However, the school is not primarily designed to satisfy youth's desire for direct expression and immediate reward, though the extracurricular program in part meets these needs. Nor is the school primarily designed to facilitate the development of peer loyalty; school officials frown on fraternities and sororities, for instance. Nor is the school primarily designed to facilitate the development of boy-girl relationship. It can be argued that it is for these reasons that youth tend to develop their own systems. A set of norms, albeit informal and sometimes vague, does inform behavior of a sizeable proportion of American youth. Some of these norms operate in the area of boy-girl relations, and hence are related to the process of mate sorting and mate selection that is part of the prelude to marriage.

Informal youth groups exist in conjunction with the formal structure of education in junior high school, high school, and college. Strictly speaking, the role of student is not a part of youth society in that the school and its activities are established and maintained by adults rather than by youth. Education is not necessarily the predominant activity involving the emotions and imagination of youth.

The habitat of youth groups is the hallways, classrooms, and extracurricular rooms of the school, but it is also the drugstore, the cafe, the movie house, the automobile. In other words, youth cliques and boy-girl relationships are carried on in conjunction with facilities borrowed from social systems established for other purposes. The school buildings are a part of the educational system, the drugstore and cafe a part of the adaptive system, the movie house a part of the recreational system, the automobile a part of the transportation system. Few facilities are structured specifically to promote the activities of youth cliques or of the dating pair. Only an occasional dance hall or teen-age canteen may have the servicing of these activities as a primary goal.

Since youth society uses facilities designed primarily for other purposes; since its members are dependents rather than independent citizens with authority; and since the span of membership in youth society is short (they grow up to be adults), youth culture does not become highly structured. Both childhood and adulthood have been more highly structured status categories than is adolescence. Behavioral scientists speak of the adolescent's status as marginal. He is too old to be accorded the privileged status

---

1961), 63–69; Jessie Bernard, "Teen-Age Culture: Foreword," *The Annals of the American Academy of Political and Social Science,* CCCXXXVIII (November, 1961), viii–ix.

of the child, and yet he is not accorded the rights and responsibilities of an adult.[18]

Not all teen-agers subscribe to the norms of teen-age culture, and not all teen-agers who do subscribe to teen-age culture do so in the same degree. In some rural areas there is no teen-age society. In a rural community the teen-age population is relatively small, time and facilities are limited, and children move almost directly from childhood expectations to adult expectations. Some teen-agers do not choose to belong to a teen-age system; others are not eligible since they are in the armed services, are working, or are married.[19]

Teen-age society is in many respects a society of the leisure class. Children of lower socio-economic class parentage are in teen-age groups only during their early teens. Most American youth are a part of youth society during the early teens; less than half are in teen-age society in the late teens. Since teen-age society is comprised more of youth of middle and upper class parentage, teen-age culture is marked by the paraphernalia that money can buy—distinctive clothing, cars, records, and cosmetics.

Teen-age society has been characterized as having norms that place a high premium on activistic hedonism, social irresponsibility or nonresponsibility, and peer acceptance. Primary importance is placed on the teen-ager having a good personality, being accepted, and being popular. Acceptance is important in adult society also, but youth appear to pursue acceptance with less subtlety and with a passion. How to be attractive, in order to be popular, in order to have fun is a major theme.[20] They want to know how to be attractive, how to overcome shyness, how to deal with problems with the opposite sex.[21]

It is a moot question whether or not youth society should be characterized as irresponsible. It is true that when the adolescent male is compared with the adult male he comes off second best on any test of social responsibility.[22] But in his own world and according to the norms of his own society he is no anarchist; he is responsible and conforming. To be personally responsible for one's part, particularly in the extracurricular activities of the school, is highly prized among his peers—to be a good basketball player, to be an enthusiastic, acrobatic cheerleader—these are prized. Rebelliousness does not characterize the majority of youth. The great majority of American

[18] Albert J. Reiss, "Sex Offenses: The Marginal Status of the Adolescent," *Law and Contemporary Problems*, XXV (Spring, 1960), 309–333.

[19] Jessie Bernard, "Teen-Age Culture: An Overview," *The Annals of the American Academy of Political and Social Science*, CCCXXXVIII (November, 1961), 1–32.

[20] Bernard, "Teen-Age Culture: An Overview," *op. cit.*

[21] Charles H. Brown, "Self-Portrait: The Teen-Type Magazine," *The Annals of the American Academy of Political and Social Science*, CCCXXXVIII (November, 1961), 13–21.

[22] Talcott Parsons, "Age and Sex in the Social Structure of the United States," *American Sociological Review*, VII (October, 1942), 604–616.

youth behave either in the conventional manner subscribed to by adults or participate in conventional versions of deviant youth behavior prescribed by the youth[23] culture.

The great majority, if influenced by norms of rebelliousness and irresponsibility, return to the society of the majority (that lived by adults) once they attain adulthood.

Dating

Youth society manifests itself in the dating behavior of young people and in its eventual effect upon mate selection and marriage. Teen-agers like to date. In a study of high school dating,[24] teen-agers were asked to rate dating in comparison to other types of social activity, such as recreation with their own sex and recreation with members of their own family. These young people preferred dating as a type of social activity. When they were asked how often dates turned out to be dull, about three-fourths of both boys and girls indicated that dates were seldom or never dull, and only about a fourth reported that dates were sometimes dull. Very few reported dates usually or always dull. In general, those who went steady rated steady dating more interesting than "playing the field," while those who did not believe in steady dating said that casual dating or "playing the field" was the more interesting. Less than a fourth thought going steady should be reserved for those seeking a marriage partner. In other words, most teenagers valued steady dating as an end in itself and not as a stage in the mate-selection process. Thus dating is a major part of the interpersonal and recreational systems of youth society.

According to one estimate, as high as one quarter of persons in their early teens go steady.[25] Group activities preparatory to dating begin even earlier. Prior to junior high school, some children are involved in mixed parties and sex games such as "spin the bottle," "post office," and "flashlight." It used to be commonly believed that boys and girls passed through a stage of withdrawal from each other, and perhaps it was true in an earlier day.[26] At present it is not uncommon to find fifth- and sixth-grade youngsters interested in one another and dating beginning as early as ten or eleven years of age.

[23] David Matza, "Subterranean Traditions of Youth," *The Annals of the American Academy of Political and Social Science,* CCCXXXVIII (November, 1961), 102–118.

[24] Paul H. Landis, "Research on Teen-Age Dating," *Marriage and Family Living,* XXII (August, 1960), 266–267.

[25] Ira L. Reiss, "Sexual Codes in Teen-Age Culture," *The Annals of the American Academy of Political and Social Science,* CCCXXXVIII (November, 1961), 53–62.

[26] For a review of findings on sexual behavior of pre-adolescents and a bibliography see Carlfred B. Broderick, "Sexual Behavior Among Pre-Adolescents," *The Journal of Social Issues,* XXII (April, 1966), 6–21.

In keeping with the observation that it is higher status groups that engage in the patterns of youth society, Lowrie found that daughters of parents with at least some college education tend to begin to date at earlier ages than do those of parents with a high school education or less; students from homes of higher economic and social status appear to initiate dating at earlier ages than do those from lower status homes.[27] One must be cautious in generalizing, however, for the dating patterns of youth differ from decade to decade, from region to region, and from community to community. Lowrie found girls in the South beginning to date at earlier ages than did girls in other regions of the country. Those who began dating early also began going steady early. On the other hand, those who were late in beginning to date appeared to be more likely to marry someone they have dated for a short period of time.

Some fairly well crystallized values and norms have emerged in contemporary American youth society insofar as dating is concerned. Dating is a valued activity; the experience is usually regarded as enjoyable; and dating is valued as an end in itself without regard to its established place as the mate selection method of American culture.

Since dating is valued in youth culture, it follows that one who seeks status in youth society must contend with group pressures to date. Whatever becomes a fashion also puts pressure to comply on those for whom the fashion does not have an appeal,[28] on those who are not permitted to date by their parents, and on those who have difficulty attracting partners. Their peers may not permit them the freedom of enjoying being nondaters. The acceptance of a common set of norms compromises the freedom of individuals to proceed at their own idiosyncratic rates.

The Problem of Attraction

A fundamental problem facing the teen-ager is the problem of attraction. The dilemma between commanding respect (which implies a superordinate relationship) or disrespect (which implies a subordinate relationship) and winning friendly acceptance (which implies an egalitarian relationship) is deeply rooted in democratic group life and is an essential part of the situation involved in attracting desirable dating partners and repelling undesirable dating partners, as well as in controlling behavior during the dating experience.[29] The social life of the teen-ager abounds in such dilemmas as he seeks to attract and be attractive to peers of both sexes. Every person has

[27] Samuel H. Lowrie, "Early and Late Dating: Some Conditions Associated with Them," *Marriage and Family Living*, XXIII (August, 1961), 284–291.

[28] David Riesman, "Permissiveness and Sex Roles," *Marriage and Family Living*, XXI (August, 1958), 211–217.

[29] Peter M. Blau, "A Theory of Social Interaction," *American Journal of Sociology*, LXV (May, 1960), 545–556.

a wide repertory of qualities, and which of these qualities win favor in a given situation is not a matter of chance. Persons seek to control the image they present and thus the impressions they make.[30]

A mark of the highest status is acceptance into the leading crowd or clique in one's age-sex category. The clique sets the norms that are the highest authority for members of that age-sex category, norms that may take precedence over family, school, and adult norms.

Coleman[31] asked high school students what was most important in getting into the leading teen-age crowd. For boys, personality ranked first followed in order by a good reputation, being an athlete, having good looks, getting good grades, having a car, having good clothes, having money, coming from the right neighborhood. For girls, having a good personality ranked highest followed by good looks, nice clothes, good reputation, being neat and dressing neatly, having money, getting good grades, and coming from the right neighborhood.

Insofar as youth culture is cultic, its heroes outside the culture include the young and handsome popular musicians, movie stars, and television stars. Good looks are important, and to have a weight problem (either underweight or overweight), acne, or crooked teeth are causes for grave concern on the part of those so burdened.

When asked how they would like best to be remembered, the image of the star athlete was most attractive to boys, while girls preferred the image of activities leader and being most popular. Values were in keeping with a tendency to underplay the skills of intellect and overplay activity skills, gregariousness, and amiability; young people chose these images to be remembered by rather than the image of the brilliant student.

Acceptance is the primary reward of possessing the valued traits. Much of teen talk is directed toward making invidious distinctions among people and their activities. The highly normative content of teen-age language makes it admirably suited for use in applying sanctions. It approves the teen-ager who conforms to youth standards and condemns the one who deviates. Just to be the object of favorable rather than unfavorable gossip is a reward of no small significance.

Coleman found that brilliant girl students fared poorly as prospective dates for boys. Less marked but still evident was a poor showing by the brilliant boy student as a date for girls. For both boys and girls, the movement over the school year was away from the brilliant student as someone to date. The "best looking" boy or girl gained at the expense of the best student.

---

[30] Erving Goffman, *The Presentation of Self in Everyday Life* (Garden City, N.Y.: Doubleday, 1959).

[31] Coleman, *op. cit.* (see above, fn. 9).

The young person in youth society is not entirely "on his own" in the procedures involved in making himself attractive to his peers. He may be helped or hindered by both parents and peers. He may be aided or handicapped by relevant ascriptive qualities and by parents who are or are not knowledgeable or sympathetic to youth norms. Peers prod him on; they also provide a sense of security for him as he attempts to establish dating relationships. Peer cliques and crowds provide settings wherein he gets to meet and associate with persons eligible as dates.

Peers exert control over dates through their ability positively or negatively to influence a person's reputation. Also, peer groups are strategically situated to play a role in the socialization process of their members. The person ready to begin dating has arrived at one of the teachable moments of life. He is eager to make good and is motivated to receive whatever help is proffered by his peers as well as by older and more experienced teen-agers. Youth groups connected with the school, church, or other community organizations also serve to introduce the teen-ager to paired association with the other sex.

Group Dating

In a survey of middle-class parents, 84 percent reported that their adolescents had passed through a stage which could be described as group dating.[32] Group dating may begin when the child is a pre-teen under the auspices of parents or some other adult group. Individually paired dating usually begins a little later. For some young people dates first grow smoothly and almost imperceptibly out of group activities. For others, getting the first date is a traumatically memorable experience.

Steady Dating

There is a progression in teen-age dating. After one or more dates, two teen-agers dating each other are apt to decide that they should "go steady." Generally speaking, steady dating does not involve commitments other than that neither will date anyone else during the period that they are going together. Peer expectations play a part in steady dating. Young people asked to reflect on their reasons for going steady claim that they do it in part because it brings peer group recognition and acceptance; going steady is also a means of providing date security or participation insurance.

Dating as Socialization

Early dating tends to be fun-oriented, but it may have broader, long-range functions not perceived by the participants. Every society must have

32 E. E. LeMasters, *Modern Courtship and Marriage* (New York: Macmillan, 1957), p. 96.

structures to facilitate the passage of young people from the single to the married state. Since American society does not provide an adult-supervised pattern that all single persons are expected to follow but depends instead on the initiative of the youthful participants, early, uncommitted dating provides a way for the inexperienced in heterosexual relationships to gain experience. Dating is one of the activities that introduce young people to sex-differentiated society, a type of society they will participate in for the rest of their lives. At the same time, dating is one of the activities that introduces teen-agers to members of the other sex as companions. Dating experience can be helpful in developing skills in interpersonal relations. Dating can also fulfill an important dalliance function. With increased demands for a highly educated, highly trained work force, marriage is often delayed until the late-teen or post-teen period. Dating can fill some of the desire for association with the opposite sex until marriage is a possibility.

AMERICAN SEX CULTURE

Before considering sexual intimacy in teen-age dating, we must look at the sex norms of adult society; youth society does not operate free of the influences of adult society.

There is no single integrated normative pattern governing American sex life today. Sex is a powerful natural urge difficult for society to control. Not all behavior is normatively sanctioned and norms antithetical to each other are extant. The silencing of responsible voices in dialogue over sexual norms during a period of Victorian prudery may not have resulted in the hoped-for gains of restraint in sexual behavior; it probably has resulted instead in a set of sex values less consistent with American democratic principles than would otherwise have developed.

One of the major events in modern times that broke the silence was the publication of the Kinsey reports.[33] These reports broke upon the scene as major events in American society. They were scholarly reports and were not sensationally written; yet the report on the American male became a best seller almost overnight. There appeared to be an inordinate backlog of interest dammed up by the silence of the past.

Sex and the Puritan Tradition

The sexual thesis of the past was conservative and restrictive of sexual outlet; emergent norms challenging tradition are more permissive and ac-

---

[33] Alfred C. Kinsey, Wardell B. Pomeroy, and Clyde E. Martin, *Sexual Behavior in the Human Male* (Philadelphia: Saunders, 1948); Alfred C. Kinsey, Wardell B. Pomeroy, Clyde E. Martin, and Paul H. Gebhard, *Sexual Behavior in the Human Female* (Philadelphia: Saunders, 1953).

cepting of sexual outlet. The traditional normative pattern reflected the significant place that the Puritanistic emphasis in the Judaic-Christian traditions played in the development of American society. The scriptures were read; preachers and religious writers admonished audiences that they should not commit adultery, that fornicators would not inherit the Kingdom of God, and that God had struck Onan down for masturbating or practicing *coitus interruptus.*

Judaic-Christian themes are invoked against open discussion of sexual matters today also, as seen in the responses to a mailing from *Eros,* a now defunct magazine devoted to the topics of love and sex. According to the editors of *Eros,* some 10,000 unsolicited letters expressing opinions on the propriety of such a magazine were received. The editors state that most of the letters were "pro-*Eros*"; of the critical letters many had religious themes or invoked religious sanctions. The following is a sample of statements from letters to the editors bearing criticism based on Judaic-Christian themes:

> It seems to me . . . after noticing that my mail indicated that I am a minister of the Gospel, that you or the imbecile who sends out your mail, would refrain from sending me such an abomination as you did. . . . Keep your wretchedness for those who have never known the saving grace of Jesus Christ. . . . I am praying that God will save your souls or else destroy your place of business and all who promote and cause it to flourish.

> What will you do on Judgment Day?

> Most *diabolical, vulgar, indecent, immoral,* and *derelict,* magazine ever *conceived* by the evil mind of Satan's Chosen People. Please cast it into the "Bottomless Pit" where it belongs before it sends thousands there.[34]

Sexual Norms and the Law

American law dealing with sexual behavior reflects a conservative public morality. There are laws interdicting petting, mutual masturbation, fornication, and adultery.[35] Two states, Indiana and Wyoming, have held it a crime to encourage a person to masturbate; no state, however, makes it a criminal offense for an individual to masturbate. Historically, within and outside of the law, premarital intercourse has been strongly condemned in America, and sex knowledge has been denied to children and young people, lest it adversely affect character and serve as a stimulus to illicit sexual behavior. According to the traditional morality, sexual outlet is permitted only to the married.[36]

---

[34] "Letters," *Eros,* I (Summer, 1962), 81–96.
[35] Morris Ploscowe, "Sex Offenses: The American Legal Context," *Law and Contemporary Problems,* XXV (Spring, 1960), 217–224.
[36] John Sirjamaki, "Cultural Configurations in the American Family," *American Journal of Sociology,* LIII (May, 1948), 450–456.

Sexual Ignorance and Empirical Evidence

Accompanying traditional norms calling for sexual secrecy, there is a great amount of sexual ignorance and naïveté in an otherwise literate society.[37] Sexual fears of an irrational nature are not uncommon to human societies, but proscriptions in American culture have tended to isolate the individual in his sexual fears. Because of the suppression of folk knowledge, American society came to rely on scientific surveys, such as the Kinsey reports, to inform its people that the solitude was imaginary. The reports surprised some parts of the population with some facts and other parts with other facts, but what the Kinsey reports said to society as a whole was that there was an almost universal involvement in the sexual life and much variety of conduct.

The Sexual Revolutions

Sexual asceticism was never without challenge from competing sex norms in America's history; an ascetic sex code was at no time the acceptable, working code of all the people. The first organized challenge came in the first half of the nineteenth century. This challenge accompanied the establishment of Oneida, New Harmony, Brook Farm, and other experimental communities. This nineteenth century revolt spent itself largely in isolated experimental communities. The second attack on the traditional sex code came in the 1920's. This revolt was less organized but more pervasive than that in the experimental communities of the nineteenth century in that it involved more people and more media; affected the behavior of a greater proportion of the populace; and planted a posture of cynicism, doubt, and normlessness in the minds of others.[38] Among the conditions setting the stage for the revolt were the writing of Sigmund Freud and the unrest, mobility, and anonymity accompanying World War I. Many imaginative formulations came from the pen of Freud, but one popularized idea of his that caught on with the American public was the idea that any sort of repression of sexual expression might cause grave personal and social maladjustments. Individualism, humanism, and other patterns of thought extant in American culture before the revolt provided a supportive milieu receptive to social change and freer personal expression concerning sex.

One manifestation of the revolt of the 1920's was the full flowering of a folk belief in romantic love. Romantic love was neither conceived nor born on American soil, but during a "period of innocence" prior to the depression

[37] For a perceptive analysis of secrecy and its effects upon our sexual norms and behavior, see Trilling's essay written on the occasion of the publication of the first Kinsey report in 1948 (*The Liberal Imagination* [Garden City, N.Y.: Doubleday, 1957]). The following is based in part on his analysis, pp. 216–234.

[38] Max Lerner, *America as a Civilization* (New York: Simon and Schuster, 1957), pp. 667 ff.

of the 1930's, America provided fertile soil in which romantic love could thrive. Love was viewed as a harbinger of life's fulfillment.

The ideal of romantic love provided an antithesis to ascetic strains in the Judaic-Christian tradition. At the heart of the difference between the Judaic-Christian and the romantic models of interpersonal love were radically different views on the nature of man and the nature and source of authority. In the Judaic-Christian tradition man was, as a result of the "fall," sinful, unclean, unwilling, and unable to choose the good. Only with the help of God through a process of rebirth and growth in sanctification could he make progress on the road to perfection, a perfection that he would not attain fully during his finite life. God, the authority, created various institutions, especially the family and the state, to retain the basic order of society over against the onslaughts of sinful, rebellious man. On the other hand, in the romantic, humanistic design, man was perfectible but was held back largely by ignorance and the trappings of society. In his view, he was held back by the very same system that the Judaic-Christian saw as God's creation.

The Judaic-Christian marriage model called for vows of fidelity to the object of one's affection, and marriage was seen as real—not lacking in essence or substance—rather than nominal. God's presence in the marriage resulted in a mysterious union making the two "one flesh." In the romantic model, the individual person was real; marriage was nominal and had no permanence in its own right. Man, though real, was not free; he was the "slave"of love. If gripped by passionate love, such a slave of love (the notion that man is a slave of love is inconsistent with a view of man as rational and has its roots in romantic love, not in humanism) would fall in love with his "soul mate." Whether soul mates remained true to each other was not within the control of the lovers; they could not predict whether their love for each other would flourish or die. Being in love did not necessarily call for the two to marry. Even if they did marry they had no assurance that their love would last. What both partners hoped to get from a love marriage was happiness. One could not be sure that he had found his soul mate, but if he did not find his soul mate the first time around the romantic model called for another try at love. The diversity of attitudes regarding sexual behavior extant in America and the strong emotions accompanying the different attitudes still encourage caution and conservatism in the public expression of responsible persons. Persons in positions of leadership have felt constrained to support a traditional conservative sex code.

The "New" Morality

The revolt against the traditional sex code has emphasized the right of the individual to break that code or any social code, the freedom to engage in sexual practices that the code would label as deviant, and the right to pursue the goal of personal happiness with a fully expressive sexual life as integral to happiness. There is an inclination to direct personal freedom into channels of self-expression, with self-expression being defined not in terms of success, power, and material goods, but in terms of broad personal experience, including sexual expression. This point of view was at least implicit in the two Kinsey reports; the authors made little attempt to hide their goal of "a good sexuality" for all.[39] The first Kinsey report impressed some as having as one of its goals the habituation of the reader to sexuality in all its varied manifestations—to establish a democratic pluralism of sexuality.

As one example of the liberal view, Albert Ellis, a prolific writer on the subject of sexual freedom, asserts that every human being should have the right to as much, as varied, as intense, as enduring, sex enjoyment as he prefers, as long as he does not interfere with the sexual rights and satisfactions of others.[40] A liberal view of sexual behavior brooks no legislation or invocation of social sanctions against sex acts performed by responsible adults who do not use force or duress in the course of their sex relations, do not injure their partners, and who participate in their sex activities privately. Few sex acts would be considered to be illegal or illegitimate from this point of view.

Liberal jurists assert that a rational code of sex offense laws is overdue. It is claimed that the sex-offense legislation presently on the books, apart from being unenforceable, is too inclusive, making potential criminals of most of the population. Proposed changes call for legal sanction to be applied only to a narrow range of antisocial activities, such as seduction of a minor by an adult, rape, sexual assault, and exhibitionism or other forms of public display.

Failure to achieve a successful marriage is sometimes alleged to be due to the failure to realize the importance of and the achievement of complete and mutual sexual satisfaction. Empirical studies support the fact that sexual satisfaction is related to marital happiness. The scholarly attention focused on the subject of sexual expression helped to bring discussion of the subject out into the open and to lend support to the respectability of sex as a factor to be considered in evaluating the success of a marriage.

Intergenerational Differences

Kinsey and his associates undertook to make a comparison of the older and younger generations in a male sample. They divided the sample into two groups. One group included all of those persons who were over thirty-three years of age at the time they contributed their sex histories; the

[39] Trilling, op. cit.
[40] Albert Ellis, Sex Without Guilt (New York: Lyle Stuart, 1958), pp. 188–189.

median age of this group was 43.1 years. The other group included all the persons younger than thirty-three years of age; the median age of this group was 21.2 years. The difference between the median ages of the two groups was about twenty-two years. The older group represented the generation that was in its youth and sexually most active from 1910 to 1925. The members of the younger group were at the peak of activity between 1930 and 1947.[41]

The number of persons ultimately involved, and the ages at which they became involved, were almost exactly alike for the college-educated older and younger generations in regard to the following types of behavior: masturbation, nocturnal emissions, heterosexual intercourse, total premarital intercourse, intercourse with prostitutes, and homosexual outlets. Older and younger grade school educated males were alike in number involved and age at which they became involved in intercourse with prostitutes. The same number of grade-school educated persons in both generations were ultimately involved in heterosexual intercourse and premarital intercourse, but the younger generation apparently became active a year or two earlier than the older generation.

More grade-school-level persons of the younger generation than of the older generation were involved in nocturnal emissions, masturbation, and petting experience; and they began their activity at an earlier age. Among college educated men more in the younger generation than in the older generation were involved in petting and petting to climax, and they began this activity at an earlier age than did the older generation.

In general, Kinsey found the sexual patterns of the younger generation to be so nearly identical with the sexual patterns of the older generation in regard to so many types of sexual activity that he rejected the widespread opinion that the younger generation was more active in its socio-sexual behavior. The instance in which a larger number of the younger generation were involved at an earlier age applied mainly to nocturnal emissions and masturbation, activities not ordinarily considered when the charge is made that the younger generation is becoming increasingly sexually involved. On the other hand, the increase in petting experience and petting to climax could be interpreted as supporting the contention of increased sexual involvement on the part of the younger generation. With regard to premarital intercourse with companions and prostitutes, and homosexual contacts, the records for the older and the younger generation were nearly identical. But a third to a half of the intercourse that males previously had with prostitutes had been replaced by premarital activities with other girls. A greater reliance on equals as sex partners constitutes a change in sexual patterns.

Where the younger generation became involved in sexual activity at earlier ages, it was generally the lower educational levels that were most heavily

41 Kinsey, *et at., Sexual Behavior in the Human Male, op. cit.* (see above, fn. 33), pp. 395–396.

represented. It is probable that better sanitation, better medical care, and better standards of nutrition which brought improvement in the general health of that group were contributing factors to the earlier involvement in sexual activity. There is evidence that the younger generation of the lower social level became adolescent a year or so sooner than did the boys of the same level a generation or two earlier.

What has been the direction of change since 1947 when Kinsey last collected sex histories? Unfortunately, no comprehensive survey has been made since that date; hence the data are limited and scattered. It would appear that changes in American values have been significant and pervasive enough to signal increase in sexual permissiveness. There is a difference, however, between value changes allowing freedom of discussion and changes reflecting either greater approval or a higher incidence of particular types of sex relationships. Impressionistic accounts of changes in sex norms suggest that intercourse outside of marriage meets with less negative reaction than it did formerly. But responses of national population samples to an item asked by Roper in 1937 and again in 1959 do not bear this out.[42] If major shifts in attitudes had occurred during this twenty-year period, we would expect to find them reflected in the surveys.

In both 1937 and 1959 respondents were asked, "Do you think it is all right for either or both parties to a marriage to have had previous sexual experience?" The responses are indicated in Table 12.1. The similarity in the responses on the two dates is striking. The period spanned between the first and second polls saw the publication and widespread distribution of the Kinsey reports on the male and the female.

TABLE 12.1. DO YOU THINK IT IS ALL RIGHT FOR EITHER OR BOTH PARTIES TO A MARRIAGE TO HAVE HAD PREVIOUS SEXUAL INTERCOURSE?

	1937	1959
All right for both	22%	22%
All right for men only	8%	8%
All right for neither	56%	54%
Don't know or refused to answer	14%	16%
	100%	100%

SOURCE: Stanton Wheeler, "Sex Offenses: A Sociological Critique," *Law and Contemporary Problems,* XXV (Spring, 1960), 265.

Another study designed to measure possible change in sex attitudes from one generation to the next utilized a sample population of college girls and

[42] Stanton Wheeler, "Sex Offenses: A Sociological Critique," *Law and Contemporary Problems,* XXV (Spring, 1960), 258–278.

their mothers.[43] Both groups were asked, "How important do you think it is that a girl be a virgin when she marries?" The results show statistically significant differences between the two groups. Of the mothers, 88 percent indicated that it was "very wrong" not to be a virgin, 12 percent indicated that it was "generally wrong," and no one rated it "right in many situations." Their coed daughters, on the other hand, appeared to be considerably more permissive, with percentages for the respective items of 55 and 34 percent indicating that virginity is very important and somewhat important respectively, and 13 percent indicating that losing one's virginity was "right in many situations."

When asked, "Do you think sexual intercourse during engagement is very wrong, generally wrong, right in many situations?" the differences are again statistically significant. The comparable percentages for the mothers and their daughters were 83, 15, and 2 percent for mothers, 35, 48, and 17 percent for daughters.

Bell and Buerkle caution that the seeming liberality of the college girls may be a temporary phenomenon, however. Later on in life when relating her attitudes to her own daughter, the college girl of today may respond in a manner more characteristic of the traditional sexual morality of her mother.

(For summary and bibliography, see Chapter 13.)

43 Robert R. Bell and Jack V. Buerkle, "Mother and Daughter Attitudes to Premarital Sexual Behavior," *Marriage and Family Living*, XXIII (November, 1961), 390–392.

CHAPTER 13

Youth, Socio-Sexual
Norms and Systems: II

ILLEGITIMACY

THE INCIDENCE of illegitimate births is one of the empirical indicators of the incidence of sexual intercourse outside of marriage. It is a highly inadequate indicator, however, since on the average perhaps no more than one pregnancy results from each one thousand single acts of premarital intercourse. Primary factors contributing to this relatively low incidence of pregnancy are the relative sterility of females, and perhaps males, in early adolescence—commonly referred to as "adolescent sterility" and the use of contraception by the unmarried.[1]

Between the years 1940 and 1965, there was a marked increase in illegitimacy[2] both as to rate and ratio as the following figures show:

	1940	1957	1965
Number of illegitimate births	89,500	201,700	291,200
Illegitimate births per 1,000 unmarried women 15–44 years old (illegitimacy rate)	7.1	20.9	23.4
Illegitimate births per 1,000 births (illegitimacy ratio)	37.9	47.4	77.4

The illegitimacy rate here referred to is defined as the estimated rate of out-of-wedlock births per 1,000 unmarried women in the United States between the ages of fifteen and forty-four years of age. The illegitimacy ratio refers to the estimated proportion of illegitimate live births compared to all live births in a given year. (Illegitimacy rates are based on information entered on birth certificates of states that require the reporting of illegitimate status.

[1] Paul H. Gebhard, Wardell B. Pomeroy, Clyde E. Martin, and Cornelia V. Christenson, *Pregnancy, Birth, and Abortion* (New York: Harper, 1958), pp. 30–34.
[2] Much of the following discussion on illegitimacy is based on Arthur A. Campbell and James D. Cowhig, "The Incidence of Illegitimacy in the United States," *Welfare in Review*, V (May, 1967), 1–6. See also Alice J. Claque and Stephanie J. Ventura, "Trends in Illegitimacy: United States—1940–65," Public Health Service Publication No. 1000, Series 21, No. 15, National Center for Health Statistics, U.S. Department of Health, Education and Welfare, February, 1968, pp. 1–90.

The number of states requesting such information has declined over the past twenty-five years because of concern for the protection of children. In 1965 registration was required in thirty-four states and the District of Columbia. Also, states use different definitions of the term "illegitimacy." In some states a birth is defined as illegitimate if the mother reports herself as not currently married and legitimate if she reports herself as currently married regardless of her status when the child was conceived. In other states, a birth is defined as illegitimate if the child is conceived "out of wedlock.")

The upward trend in illegitimate births divides into two time periods. During the first period (1940–57), illegitimacy rose rapidly. During the same period the number of unmarried women between the ages of fifteen and forty-four years declined from 12.5 million to 9.6 million. Hence, during the seventeen-year period, the rise in the number of illegitimate births represents a rise in the illegitimacy rate.

During the second period (1957–65), the rate of illegitimacy rose slowly (a little more than 1 percent per year, compared with over 6 percent per year during the earlier period), but the number of unmarried women in the fifteen to forty-four year age bracket increased from 9.6 million to 12.5 million.[3] Hence, during 1957–65 the number of illegitimate births increased not because of an increase in the illegitimacy rate but largely because the number of unmarried women in the population increased.

Future changes in the number of unmarried women in the population will likely affect the number of illegitimate births. If the proportion of women unmarried at each age also remains constant, the annual number of illegitimate births could be expected to rise from 291,200 in 1965 to 404,000 in 1980. This rise would be due to increasing numbers of unmarried women, not to an increased rate of illegitimate births. On the other hand, the illegitimacy rate might decline by 1980 if the control of premarital conception becomes more effective than it is at present.

The illegitimacy rate for nonwhite women in 1965 was eight times as high as the comparable rate for white unmarried women fifteen to forty-four years of age—97.7 births per 1,000 unmarried women compared to 11.6. Though illegitimacy is more common among the nonwhite population, trends for the period 1940–65 are approximately the same for both racial categories. That is, both show a rise in the rate of illegitimacy between 1940 and 1957, and both have increasing numbers of unmarried women of reproductive age since 1957. There are some differences between data for the two categories, however.

One difference is the continued rise in illegitimacy rates for young white women since 1957 and the continued decline for nonwhite women. Between

---

[3] The recent rise in the number of unmarried women is due to the exceptionally high birth rate in the early World War II period.

1957 and 1965, the illegitimacy rate for white women increased from 6.4 per 1,000 to 7.9, while the rate for nonwhite women in this age bracket declined from 81.4 per 1,000 to 75.9.

The marked differences in the illegitimacy rates between white and nonwhite in part reflects the higher proportion of nonwhite than of white women who have more than one illegitimate birth. Considering only the illegitimate rate for first births, the rate was 44.5 per 1,000 unmarried nonwhite women fifteen to forty-four years of age and 7.8 per 1,000 white women in the same age bracket. Using this comparison, the nonwhite rate is slightly less than six times as high as the white rate, as contrasted with eight times as high when total number of illegitimate births is used.

Another factor contributing to the differential in illegitimacy rate is the difference between whites and nonwhites in the proportion who marry after a premarital conception occurs. There is some empirical evidence showing that when a white unmarried woman becomes pregnant she more likely marries before the child is born than does the nonwhite woman, thereby affecting the statistics in those states where the marital status of the mother determines the legitimacy status of the child.

Further comparison of illegitimacy rates for nonwhite and white would require control of certain socio-economic factors. This has not been possible to date because of the lack of information on socio-economic status on the birth certificate. Data obtained by the New York City Department of Health on 13,500 women bearing children out-of-wedlock point to some of these differences. In the New York sample roughly 5 percent of the women had had some college training; about 9 percent were still in school. Although most unwed mothers were not illiterate or uneducated, they were not up to the level of all females in the community. Among unwed mothers twenty-five years old and older, 39 percent had not gone beyond grade school, while only about 20 percent of all females twenty-five to forty-four years of age had so limited an education. About 18 percent of the city's twenty-five to forty-four year old females had at least some college compared to only 5 percent of the unmarried mothers. Occupationally, the unmarried mothers also ranked somewhat lower than the female population generally. Only about half of them had an occupation outside the home.

The highest illegitimacy rates in the United States are not found among teen-agers. The highest rates in 1965 (see Table 13.1) are in the twenty-five to twenty-nine year age bracket (50.4 per 1,000). The next highest rates are for those between the ages of twenty and twenty-four and those between the ages of thirty and thirty-four. The rate for single girls aged fifteen to nineteen is slightly less than one-third the rate for unmarried women between the ages of twenty-five and twenty-nine. Between 1960 and 1965, the illegitimacy rate for the two youngest age categories increased only slightly (15.7 to 16.7 for 15–19 year olds) or declined (40.3 to 38.8 for 20–24

TABLE 13.1. ESTIMATED NUMBER OF ILLEGITIMATE BIRTHS PER 1,000 UNMARRIED WOMEN 15–44 YEARS OLD BY COLOR AND AGE: UNITED STATES, 1940, 1950, 1960, AND 1965

Color and age	Rate per 1,000 unmarried women 15–44			
	1965	1960	1950	1940
Total (15–44 years)[1]	23.4	21.8	14.1	7.1
15–19 years	16.7	15.7	12.6	7.4
20–24 years	38.8	40.3	21.3	9.5
25–29 years	50.4	42.0	19.9	7.2
30–34 years	37.1	27.5	13.3	5.1
35–39 years	17.0	13.9	7.2	3.4
40–44 years[2]	4.4	3.6	2.0	1.2
White (15–44 years)[1]	11.6	9.3	6.1	3.6
15–19 years	7.9	6.7	5.1	3.3
20–24 years	22.2	18.6	10.0	5.7
25–29 years	24.3	17.6	8.7	4.0
30–34 years	16.6	10.6	5.9	2.5
35–39 years	4.9	3.9	3.2	1.7
40–44 years[2]			0.9	0.7
Nonwhite (15–44 years)[1]	97.7	98.8	71.2	35.6
15–19 years	75.9	78.8	68.5	42.5
20–24 years	152.6	160.7	105.4	46.1
25–29 years	164.7	169.0	94.2	32.5
30–34 years	137.8	104.9	63.5	23.4
35–39 years	39.0	35.0	31.3	13.2
40–44 years[2]			8.7	5.0

[1] Rates computed by relating total births, regardless of age of mother, to women 15–44.
[2] Rates computed by relating births to mothers aged 40 and over to women aged 40–44.
SOURCE: *Vital Statistics of the United States,* Vol. 1, "Natality," 1940, 1950, 1960, 1965.

SOURCE: Arthur A. Campbell and James D. Cowhig, "The Incidence of Illegitimacy in the United States," *Welfare in Review,* V (May, 1967), 2.

year olds), while the rate increased substantially among unmarried women in the two age brackets from twenty-five to thirty-four years of age (42.0 to 50.4 and 27.5 to 37.1). In 1965, less than 2 percent of all unmarried girls fifteen to nineteen years old gave birth to an illegitimate child—less than 1 percent for white girls in this age category and 8 percent for nonwhite girls.

The increase in incidence of illegitimate births is difficult to explain in view of what has happened to age at marriage and to patterns of family growth in the United States since 1940. Throughout the late 1940's and the late 1950's couples married at progressively younger ages and had their first births relatively early in marriage. The proportion that married at ages twenty to twenty-nine also increased substantially. Economic conditions appeared to have been favorable to early marriage and childbearing. Under such conditions it would seem that premarital pregnancies would more commonly lead to marriage before the birth of the child than was the case in the 1930's and that the proportion of women having children before marriage would decline. But this did not happen. Further research is needed to explore the complex of factors associated with statistical trends and differentials in the incidence of illegitimacy in the United States.

YOUTH NORMS AND BEHAVIOR PATTERNS

Secrecy and lack of institutionalization characterize sexual behavior in youth society. Despite this, remarkable concurrence has been found in sex-conduct norms of youth in a variety of student populations.[4] The data in Table 13.2, based on samples from four schools in Virginia—a black college, a white college, a black high school, and a white high school—is illustrative.

TABLE 13.2. PERCENTAGE AGREEMENT OF 692 RESPONDENTS WITH 13 QUESTIONS ON A PERMISSIVENESS SCALE AT FOUR VIRGINIA SCHOOLS

Scale Types (Ranks)	Question Number	Percentage Agreeing	Brief Meaning of Questions
1	2.	91.8*	"Kissing when in love"
2	3.	89.2	"Kissing—strong affection"
3	1.	88.6	"Kissing when engaged"
4	5.	77.3	"Petting when engaged"
5	6.	68.8	"Petting when in love"
6	7.	47.8	"Petting—strong affection"
7	4.	43.9	"Kissing—no affection"
8	9.	37.6	"Coitus when engaged"
9	10.	31.5	"Coitus when in love"
10	11.	21.4	"Coitus—strong affection"
11	8.	19.5	"Petting—no affection"
12	13.	15.9	"Coitus—no affection"
13	12.	14.3	"Coitus—no affection"**

* The difference between the percent agreeing and 100 percent is not necessarily the percent disagreeing, since there were "no answer" questionnaires and ambiguous answers, also. The zero scale is omitted since none occurred.

** Differs from the one above in that the following words are added: "This type of relationship is just about as acceptable as full sexual relationships which involve strong affection as love."

SOURCE: Ira L. Reiss, "Sociological Studies of Sexual Standards," *Determinants of Human Sexual Behavior,* ed. George Winokur (Springfield, Ill.: Charles C Thomas, 1963), p. 127.

[4] Ira L. Reiss, *The Social Context of Premarital Sexual Permissiveness* (New York: Holt, Rinehart and Winston, 1967), pp. 15–37.

The differences between percentages on scale types one, two, and three are so slight that it would be unrealistic to accept the ordering as fixed on these three items. Items ranked tenth and eleventh and items ranked twelfth and thirteenth also show only slight differences in percentage. It is clear from the ranking that young people do not simply order the items as to their acceptability on the basis of the amount of physical intimacy involved in the act; the presence of affection in the relationship is of great importance. Premarital sexual standards are patterned; they are not purely individualistic. Standards exert a strong influence on sexual behavior. Male and female respondents ranked the various sexual activities in roughly the same order; they differed rather sharply, however, in the amount of approval which they gave to each of the activities.

Responses of blacks in the sample population indicated greater permissiveness than did the responses of white students. Ira Reiss found that even with socio-economic status held constant, the greater permissiveness of the black respondents persisted.

A large percentage of young people who accepted coitus outside of marriage had not experienced coitus. In fact, the group willing to accept coitus had the largest number whose standards allowed them to do more than they had done and the smallest proportion who had exceeded the bounds of their standards. On the other hand, the group that was willing to permit kissing and petting appeared to have somewhat more people in it who had exceeded their standards; meaning that they had been involved in kissing and petting in circumstances which were not acceptable to them. Kissing and petting did not always lead to fewer guilt feelings than did coitus. This would seem to support the contention that more respondents in the kissing and petting group had violated their own standards than was true of the group permitting coitus and that it was the violation of standards rather than the extent of intimacy that caused guilt feelings. The coitus-without-affection groups were more likely to be from lower educational backgrounds than were the groups permitting coitus with affection.

Ira Reiss attempted also to determine whether or not there had been change in the sexual standards of the students over time. He found that over 70 percent had held different prior standards and that in 90 percent of the cases the prior standards were more conservative than the later ones. In other words, there appeared to be a change in standards in the direction of greater permissiveness with increasing age. The very extreme groups, those very low or very high on the permissiveness scale, did not appear to have changed as consistently as had students who presently accepted coitus with affection. It may be the high value placed on affection that is the key to the shift of standards; as a love relationship develops it serves as a catalyst in liberalizing sexual behavior standards.

Norms covering sexual expectations for a particular boy-girl dating pair are not clearly defined or articulated in advance of their first date with each other, and a high level of tension exists until the couple establishes, by experience, their own rules of sexual conduct. If they continue to date each other and if their fondness for each other grows, they are faced at each succeeding phase of the relationship with the need to arrive at standards which both accept as appropriate to their new-found level of involvement.

Early dating is usually casual in the sense that neither dater is deeply involved emotionally with the other. In fact, if a person is going to enjoy casual dating, it is important that he have enough self-control to avoid becoming overly involved emotionally with persons who have no attachment for him.

Ira Reiss is of the opinion that the majority of America's teen-agers are quite conservative and restrained in dating behavior when compared with persons in their twenties. Reiss sees them desirous of striving toward the goals of the majority of adults, and that adult majority appears to be fairly conservative. Adults might easily interpret the teen-ager's desire for a good time and public show of affection as indications of laxness in sexual morality, but the evidence indicates that teen-agers on the whole are conservative and responsible.[5]

According to both Kinsey and Ira Reiss, changes in teen-age sexual behavior are more in the nature of increased body fondling (petting) than of sexual intercourse. There are teen-agers who engage in coitus, but coitus even today plays a relatively minor part in the activities of teen-agers, particularly of teen-age girls. In dating involving no formal commitment of the couple members to each other, necking is a common norm for teen-age girls while petting is more likely to be a norm for boys.[6]

A most important consideration in the behavior code of the teen-age girl is her feeling toward her date. If the girl is convinced that she loves or even strongly likes the boy, she feels greater justification to become involved in petting activity. It is highly unlikely that she will permit sexual intercourse unless she is "in love" with her date.[7] Kinsey found that of the girls in his sample born in the 1920's, almost 30 percent petted to orgasm in their teens.[8] Reiss's study[9] involving high school and college students that petting-

[5] Ira Reiss, "Sexual Codes in Teen-Age Culture," *The Annals of the American Academy of Political And Social Science,* CCCXXXVIII (November, 1961), 53–62.

[6] Robert R. Bell and Leonard Blumberg, "Courtship Stages and Intimacy Attitudes," *Family Life Coordinator,* VIII (March, 1960), 61–63.

[7] Winston Ehrmann, "Student Cooperation in a Study of Dating Behavior," *Marriage and Family Living,* XIV (November, 1952), 322–326.

[8] Alfred C. Kinsey, Wardell B. Pomeroy, Clyde E. Martin, and Paul H. Gebhard, *Sexual Behavior in the Human Female* (Philadelphia: Saunders, 1953), p. 267.

[9] Reiss, *op. cit.*

with-affection was extremely popular with girls, particularly those who were high school junior and seniors. Girls who were devoutly religious were inclined to look with disfavor on the practice, however, and were more conservative in their behavior.

Reiss found age to be a crucial factor in teen-age intimacy. Those under sixteen years of age were much more likely to accept only kissing as proper in dating.

To understand teen-age sexual norms it is crucial that one understand the custom of going steady. When the boy and girl are going steady, permissiveness-with-affection tends to become the corporate standard; both the boy and girl accept what they are doing to and for each other. Sexual behavior becomes an integral part of the giving and receiving of affection. In fact, affection becomes a key justification of the sexual act. It will be recalled that the persons in teen-age society are predominantly middle- and upper-class young people, the class that stresses greater equality of the sexes and the importance of affection in love making. Thus the couple members are not immoral in their behavior in their own eyes; their conduct is based on what they regard as affectional relationships.

Affection is not so important a prerequisite to sex play for the boy as for the girl. Teen-age boys commonly accept heavy petting and may urge coitus in a going-steady relationship. On the other hand, it is not uncommon to find a "double standard" boy who wants intercourse himself but does not think his steady should have it. In such cases the boy prefers and may actually have intercourse with a girl with permissive standards while going steady with a girl who is a virgin.[10]

When a going-steady couple appears to go beyond the apparent accepted standards of either participant and has sexual intercourse, it is difficult to determine whether both were carried away by the ardor of the moment or if one of them actually subscribed to permissive attitudes which had not been articulated to the other or even to himself. Dating couples not uncommonly practice an "art of brinkmanship" in their petting, for instance, and the sex drive being what it is, some of the "going over the brink" can be credited to the strength of the sex drive, particularly for couples willing to become involved in petting to orgasm, petting in the nude, and simulated intercourse.

Bell and Blumberg,[11] attempted to determine the feelings about dating intimacy after the intimacy had occurred. The assumption was that couples might be carried away by their ardor at the moment and might become involved in conduct not consistent with their own sex norms. Fifty-four percent of the females and 25 percent of the males reported feeling that they had "gone too far" during a date. A significantly larger number of males

---

[10] Ira Reiss points this out; it is also substantiated in sex histories in the files of the present author.

[11] Bell and Blumberg, op. cit.

than of females wished they had gone farther. There was no significant difference by sex in guilt over petting or coitus while going steady. No significant differences in guilt feelings or desire to have gone farther were found for males and females who were engaged. As the male perceived the female more and more as a potential marriage partner, he developed greater feelings of responsibility. Going steady for many males is an intermediate stage between the "exploitative" one of dating and the "responsible" one of engagement. A double standard persists in teen-age culture, as it does in adult sex culture, despite trends toward permissiveness with affection between equals and concern for the well-being of one's mate.

Practicing the art of brinkmanship is one of the things that has made dating a prized recreational activity. That young people frequently do not want to suffer the consequences of losing their balance and going over the brink is demonstrated by the fact that many teen-agers find falling in love and becoming intimate to be inconvenient and something to be avoided if they are to remain unattached until they are more nearly ready by temperament, education, and other experiences for the growing intimacy that leads to marriage.

SOCIAL CLASS DIFFERENCES IN YOUTH NORMS AND BEHAVIOR

Among lower-status adolescent boys in American society, coitus before marriage is relatively more important in securing status within the peer system than it is for the middle-class boy, though it may confer status here, too.[12] A mode of sexual behavior among young lower-status adolescent boys is the "gang-shag" or "gang-bang."[13] The girls involved in such a relationship are commonly ones with reputations as easy "pick-ups" who will consent to serial intercourse with the members of the gang. Since the girl is usually one who will give her consent, she is not forcibly raped. Being aware of the sex norms of the gang, she knows in advance that when she consents to being picked up she is to be a partner in serial intercourse. Lower-status boys are not without sex standards, however. They distinguish between "putting it to a girl" (she consents) and "making a girl" (she does not consent). They are reluctant to "make a girl," although they may have no objection to engaging in premarital coitus per se. Lower-status boys, especially those with a criminal record, are reluctant to risk a charge of rape. They need not take such a risk since the opportunities for coitus with a willing partner are present in the lower-status community. This is not to suggest that forcible rape does not also occur in such communities.

[12] Ira L. Reiss, "Sexual Codes in Teen-Age Culture," op. cit. (see above, fn. 6).
[13] Albert J. Reiss, "Sex Offenses: The Marginal Status of the Adolescent," Law and Contemporary Problems, XXV (Spring, 1960), 309–333.

The girl who is known to consent to premarital coitus with a variety of boys loses her reputation as a "nice girl," and boys in her own socio-economic class no longer consider her as a desirable marriage partner. Her status approaches that of a prostitute. A girl with a reputation as an "easy mark" reduces her chances for marriage and may have to seek associates among those not acquainted with her reputation. This is not always a possible alternative, and the girl who has lost her reputation as a desirable marriage partner may resort to bargaining on the only basis left to her, namely in the selling of her sexual favors. A major difference between lower- and middle-class females in respect to premarital intercourse is that lower-class girls appear to be more apt to perceive of "sex as sex" and to enter into sexual relationships on an impersonal basis, while middle-class girls must justify sexual relationships as involving love—it is good and proper because they are in love.[14]

Social class difference in degree of sexual involvement prior to marriage was found by Kanin in a study of wives of university students. These women composed a group recently married, above average in education, and predominantly Protestant; of the group 43.5 percent indicated having had premarital coitus with spouse. Upper-middle status women in the group reported the lowest incidence of premarital coitus, 31 percent; middle-class females were next with 42 percent; and the highest incidence was reported by lower-status females, 82.5 percent. The social status of the male, on the other hand, was not in itself significantly associated with premarital sexual behavior.[15]

INTERGENERATIONAL CONFLICT OVER YOUTH SOCIO-SEXUAL SYSTEMS

Not all adults appreciate dating as an important part of the activity of youth—feeling that the programs, projects, and social gatherings of adult-sponsored youth organizations are sufficient to meet the need for activity. Adult-sponsored youth groups include Scouts, Campfire Girls, 4-H, YMCA, YWCA, denominational youth organizations, as well as special interest and extracurricular organizations in the school. Adults sometimes attribute to youth society standards of behavior not in the best interest of boys and girls in their impressionable years and feel that dating should wait until young people are old enough to consider marriage rather than fun as the end in dating. Adults know that unchaperoned, paired dating can lead to

---

[14] Clark E. Vincent, "Ego Involvement in Sexual Relations: Implications for Research on Illegitimacy," *American Journal of Sociology*, LXV (November, 1959), 287–295.

[15] Eugene J. Kanin, "Premarital Sex Adjustments, Social Class, and Associated Behaviors," *Marriage and Family Living*, XXII (August, 1960), 258–262.

272   THE INDIVIDUAL AND SOCIO-SEXUAL SYSTEMS

both physical and emotional involvement with which teenagers may not be prepared to cope.

Young couples are not chaperoned or supervised in any systematic way in America. It is not acts of sexual involvement that bring young people to the attention of their parents or to the attention of legal authorities. It is the consequences of sexual acts rather than the acts themselves that bring cases to the attention of adults. Conesquences that bring attention may be either pregnancy or venereal disease. Girls who are taken into custody by the police or juvenile authorities are commonly given a physical examination to determine whether they have had sexual intercourse, whether they have venereal infection, or whether they are pregnant. This procedure is followed in particular with regard to runaway girls. Boys are seldom given as complete a physical examination for venereal infection or questioned as to their sex experience. Therefore, the chances of a girl being labeled a sex delinquent are greater than they are for a boy.

The sexual exploits of boys are apt to come to the attention of the court only if the morality of the girl's family is offended. The family may charge the boy with rape of their daughter, though evidence shows that in most cases the boy is not a rapist in the sense that force or coercion has been used. Available evidence suggests that most premarital coitus between adolescents occurs through mutual consent. In some cases, the girl involved has a reputation for dispensing her sexual favors, and she is sought out for this reason. No money is exchanged in these adolescent sexual relations.

So long as sexual involvement is a private affair between an adolescent boy and girl, society does little to find them out. But society does not tolerate sexual intimacy if it becomes public and thereby flouts the norms. One of the reasons for fearing a pregnancy is that it makes public socially-tabooed sexual behavior. After the first shock of revelation has been faced, the offending parties and the parents often go to extreme and sometimes illegal limits to minimize public exposure and disgrace.

The alleged father of an illegitimate child is regarded as having exploited the girl in question; it is also possible that the unwed mother exploited the alleged father during the time their relationship was active, but with a different focus. She may have used sex as a means—to dates, companionship, an expense account, upward mobility, and possible marriage. He may have dated her, provided companionship, paid the bills, courted, and expressed love as a means to another end, namely sexual intercourse.[16]

SEX EDUCATION AS A FAMILY FUNCTION

The contention that parents should educate their children in sex and family life is generally accepted today. Yet young people protest that parents

[16] Vincent, *op. cit.*

do not provide either by precept or example the instruction necessary to a mature sexuality.[17] Parents (even the best educated and most articulate ones) find it difficult to be open and communicative on sexual matters, especially in regard to conception control and the nuances of a satisfying sex life. Parents feel that some sex and family-life education should be provided, while in fact, and for a variety of reasons, they do not provide it. David Mace, a dean among marriage counselors, has said that he has for many years been puzzled about "our dismal failure to find a satisfactory way of enabling our youth to come to terms comfortably with their sexual nature.[18] He suggests that perhaps sex education is not the parents' duty after all. The problem, as Mace sees it, is not so much a problem at the intellectual level (the giving of information) as at the emotional level. The real need of youth beyond the relatively simple problem of gaining knowledge is to come to terms with their emotional posture toward sex. Mace concludes that perhaps parents are the last people who can help their own children with this.

Since sex is one of the major facets of life wherein adults attempt to dominate youth behavior, and since the schools and other community organizations must command the support and respect of major groups within the community, it is safe to assume that the sex education offered in most communities will be within the limits of a conservative morality.

SUMMARY

When the adolescent leaves home to make his way in the world, he carries with him influences of his family of orientation. The process of emancipation occurs by degrees as the adolescent changes his frame of reference from parents to peers and others outside the home. During the transition period he may rely on different reference groups for making different decisions. If he has a good relationship with his parents, their judgment continues to prevail in some important decision-making areas. The degree and extent of emancipation from home varies by sex. The young male appears more commonly to become emancipated from parental influence and restraint than does the young female.

American youth have developed some norms and behavior patterns unique to their own youth system. Not all youth participate in a youth society following youth norms, however. Some leave school at an early age and marry, some enter the armed forces, others enter the labor force. Youth society takes a relatively carefree posture, valuing popularity, acceptance by peers, and activity that is fun. Youth society is important to the development of values and norms of behavior in regard to teen-age boy-girl rela-

---

[17] Case histories in the files of the author give ample support to this statement. It is also supported by research of other family sociologists and family-life educators.

[18] David R. Mace, "Some Reflections on the American Family," *Marriage and Family Living*, XXIV (May, 1962), 109.

tionships. Group dating and paired dating are a part of the fun activity of youth society.

To adults, youth activity may appear to verge on the irresponsible if not the delinquent. Most participants in youth society eventually enter in a responsible way into adult society, however.

To succeed in youth society, the adolescent must solve the problem of attraction. Acceptance into the lead crowd of the high school can assist the individual. Crowd acceptance also helps in getting dates. Dating leads to going steady. Steady dating is related to intensive emotional and physical involvement on the part of young daters.

Adult sex norms are in a state of change, traditional morality being challenged by a more permissive, less proscribed normative system. There are also evidences of greater permissiveness in behavior with more sexual activity involving social equals rather than sexual activity involving customer and prostitute. The increase in rate of illegitimacy suggests increased sexual activity outside of marriage.

For middle-class teen-agers in youth society, the informing code of sexual morality permits an increase in permissive behavior with increase in affectional relationship between the dating partners. For the lower class, sexual activity is less likely to require an affectional relationship between the partners as justification for the activity.

BIBLIOGRAPHY

Robert R. Bell and Leonard Blumberg. "Courtship Stages and Intimacy Attitudes," *Family Life Coordinator,* VIII (March, 1960), 61–63.

Robert R. Bell and Jack V. Buerkle. "Mother and Daughter Attitudes to Premarital Sexual Behavior," *Marriage and Family Living,* XXIII (November, 1961), 390–392.

Jessie Bernard. "Teen-Age Culture," *The Annals of the American Academy of Political and Social Science,* CCCXXXVIII (November, 1961), viii–ix, 1–32.

Charles E. Bowerman and John W. Kinch. "Changes in Family and Peer Orientation of Children Between the Fourth and Tenth Grades," *Social Forces,* XXXVII (March, 1959), 206–211.

Clay V. Brittain. "Adolescent Choices and Parent-Peer Cross Pressures," *American Sociological Review,* XXVIII (June, 1963), 385–391.

Carlfred B. Broderick. "Sexual Behavior Among Pre-Adolescents," *The Journal of Social Issues,* XXII (April, 1966), 6–21.

James Coleman. *The Adolescent Society.* Glencoe, Ill.: The Free Press, 1961.

Winston Ehrmann. "Marital and Nonmarital Sexual Behavior," *Handbook of Marriage and the Family,* ed. Harold T. Christensen. Chicago: Rand McNally. 1964. Pp. 585–622.

Winston Ehrmann. *Premarital Dating Behavior.* New York: Holt, 1959.

Glen Elder, Jr. "Parental Power Legitimation and Its Effects on the Adolescent," *Sociometry,* XXVI (March, 1963), 50–63.

Albert Ellis. *Sex Without Guilt.* New York: Lyle Stuart, 1958.

David C. Epperson. "A Re-Assessment of Indices of Parental Influence in the Adolescent Society," *American Sociological Review*, XXIX (February, 1964), 93–96.

Mervin B. Freedman. "The Sexual Behavior of American College Women: An Empirical Study and an Historical Survey," *The Merrill-Palmer Quarterly of Behavior and Development*, XI (January, 1965), 33–48.

Arnold W. Green. "The Middle Class Male Child and Neurosis," *American Sociological Review*, XI (February, 1946), 31–41.

Robert A. Harper. "Marriage Counseling and the Mores: A Critique," *Marriage and Family Living*, XXI (February, 1959), 13–19.

August B. Hollingshead. *Elmtown's Youth*. New York: Wiley, 1949.

Eugene J. Kanin. "An Examination of Sexual Aggression as a Response to Sexual Frustration," *Journal of Marriage and the Family*, XXIX (August, 1967), 428–433.

Eugene J. Kanin. "Premarital Sex Adjustments, Social Class, and Associated Behaviors," *Marriage and Family Living*, XXII (August, 1960), 258–262.

Alfred C. Kinsey, Wardell B. Pomeroy, Clyde E. Martin, and Paul H. Gebhard. *Sexual Behavior in the Human Female*. Philadelphia: Saunders, 1953.

Alfred C. Kinsey, Wardell B. Pomeroy, and Clyde E. Martin. *Sexual Behavior in the Human Male*. Philadelphia: Saunders, 1948.

Samuel H. Lowrie. "Early and Late Dating: Some Conditions Associated with Them," *Marriage and Family Living*, XXIII (August, 1961), 284–291.

David R. Mace. "Some Reflections on the American Family," *Marriage and Family Living*, XXIV (May, 1962), 109–112.

Floyd M. Martinson. *Marriage and the American Ideal*. New York: Dodd, Mead, 1960.

Floyd M. Martinson. "Sexual Knowledge, Values, and Behavior Patterns of Adolescents," *Child Welfare*, XLVII (July, 1968), 405–410.

Bernice M. Moore and Wayne H. Holtzman. *Tomorrow's Parents: A Study of Youth and Their Families*. Austin, Texas: University of Texas, 1965.

Benjamin Morse. *Sexual Behavior of the American College Girl*. New York: Lancer, 1963.

Robert F. Peck. "Family Patterns Correlated with Adolescent Personality Structure," *The Journal of Abnormal and Social Psychology*, LVII (November, 1958), 347–350.

Hallowell Pope. "Unwed Mothers and Their Sex Partners," *Journal of Marriage and the Family*, XXIX (August, 1967), 555–567.

Albert J. Reiss. "Sex Offenses: The Marginal Status of the Adolescent," *Law and Contemporary Problems*, XXV (Spring, 1960), 309–333.

Ira L. Reiss. *The Social Context of Premarital Sexual Permissiveness*. New York: Holt, Rinehart and Winston, 1967.

Ira L. Reiss. "Sociological Studies of Sexual Standards," *Determinants of Human Sexual Behavior*, ed. George Winokur. Springfield, Ill.: Charles C Thomas, 1963. Pp. 101–141.

Ira L. Reiss (ed.). "The Sexual Renaissance in America," *The Journal of Social Issues*, XXII (April, 1966), 1–137.

David Riesman. "Permissiveness and Sex Roles," *Marriage and Family Living*, XXI (August, 1958), 211–217.

Bernard C. Rosen and Roy D'Andrade. "The Psychosocial Origins of Achievement Motivation," *Sociometry*, XXII (September, 1959), 185–218.

Morris Rosenberg. "Parental Interest and Children's Self-Conceptions," *Sociometry*, XXVI (March, 1963), 35–49.

Richard L. Simpson. "Parental Influence, Anticipatory Socialization and Social Mobility," *American Sociological Review*, XXVII (August, 1962), 517–522.

Ernest A. Smith. *American Youth Culture: Group Life in Teen-Age Society.* New York: Free Press of Glencoe, 1962.

Clark E. Vincent. "Ego Involvement in Sexual Relations: Implications for Research on Illegitimacy," *American Journal of Sociology*, LV (November, 1959), 287–295.

Charles F. Warnath. "The Relation of Family Cohesiveness and Adolescent Independence to Social Effectiveness," *Marriage and Family Living*, XVII (November, 1955), 346–348.

Stanton Wheeler. "Sex Offenses: A Sociological Critique," *Law and Contemporary Problems*, XXV (Spring, 1960), 258–278.

CHAPTER 14

The Choice of a Mate

SOCIOLOGICALLY SPEAKING, marriage is a process of interaction between a man and a woman who have satisfied society as to their eligibility to marry, have fulfilled certain requirements, and have exchanged vows before authorized witnesses or are otherwise accepted as married. When society is viewed as being made up of a number of interacting social systems, marriage is often subsumed as a subsystem of the family. Indeed for most societies it is correct to treat marriage as a subsystem of the family. But if a subsystem is defined as a system entirely contained within some other system and the interaction of the subgroup members is regarded as part of the interaction system of the larger group, then marriage in America is not a subsystem of the family.[1] Marriage as a unit of interaction is distinct enough from family as a unit of interaction so that we do not distort reality when we treat marriage as a distinct social system rather than as a subsystem of the family. Marriage as a social system separate and distinct from the family is a characteristic of the kinship structure common to Western societies and more specifically common to urban-industrial societies. In societies in which the person or group in authority in the kinship system decides when the single individual in the system shall marry, whom he shall marry, and the conditions of the contract, marriage can be treated as a subsystem of the family, for the newly married couple is subservient to the extended family under authority of its head.

Marriage is rightly considered as a subsystem of family also in societies in which marriage is not valid until the fertility of the couple has been established. In societies in which the procreative and child-rearing function

[1] Any definitions of what are the social systems and what are the subsystems of society are at best arbitrary, since society consists of continuous chains of interaction and interchange. There are few clearly differentiable social systems. System functions overlap and the collectivity of individuals contributing acts to a system overlaps with the membership of collectivities contributing acts to other social systems. However, to study these chains of interaction it is necessary to keep together as an object of study the interactions we are interested in and to separate them from interactions that we are not interested in or only secondarily interested in. Georg Karlsson, *Adaptability and Communication in Marriage* (Totowa, N.J.: Bedminister, 1963).

is regarded as the primary, if not the sole function of marriage, marriage is clearly a subsystem of the family.[2] In some societies the demonstrated fertility of the couple prior to marriage (that is, the bride-to-be is pregnant) is looked upon with favor.

In American society, ideally, the person determines whether or not he will marry, when he will marry, whom he will marry, and the conditions under which he will marry. Marriage brings into being a new social unit formed through the mutual agreement of two persons. In other words, it is an achieved status.[3] It is not formed by the kin family network or controlled by it, though the influence of kinsmen on choice of mate may be substantial. Loyalty to one's spouse is given precedence over loyalty to the family of orientation of either member of the marriage pair.

SOCIETAL INVOLVEMENT

When the dating relationship between couple members becomes serious— that is, when dating is not primarily fun-oriented—society views the relationship as a unit that must be responsible to society and as a potential procreative unit. American ideology is characterized by concern for the dignity, worth, and freedom of the person. There is concern lest the person be fraudulently led into a marriage union or that he otherwise enter a union that is not in his best interest. In cases where it can be demonstrated that the person has entered marriage under duress or for fraudulent reasons, provisions are made in the statutes for annulment of the marriage. Some marriages are regarded as voidable because they do not satisfy the interests of society; others are regarded as voidable because one or both of the marriage partners are victimized.[4] The conditions that make a marriage voidable include duress, misrepresentation, and failure to cohabit.

There are also situations in which society insists that a single person become married or pay a penalty for not marrying. When one has made a commitment to marry, the state may regard the commitment as a contract. If one should break the agreement, and it can be shown that the other is damaged thereby, the first party, if he refuses to marry, may have to pay damages to the injured party. Such suits are called breach-of-promise suits. A majority of states have had statutes allowing such action, but legal action does not always provide adequate recompense for the harm that has been done. Thus many persons are reluctant to use this form of redress. Furthermore, the breach-of-promise action has been subject to abuse. For these and

[2] For examples see Stuart A. Queen, Robert W. Habenstein, and John B. Adams, *The Family in Various Cultures* (Chicago: Lippincott, 1961).

[3] Talcott Parsons and Robert F. Bales, *Family, Socialization and Interaction Process* (Glencoe, Ill.: The Free Press, 1955), p. 127.

[4] Harriet F. Pilpel and Theodora Zavin, *Your Marriage and the Law* (New York: Rinehart, 1952), p. 255.

other reasons breach-of-promise action has fallen into disrepute, and many states have changed their statutes and no longer allow such action.

KINSHIP INFLUENCE AND THE INFLUENCE OF OTHERS

In the American mate-selection system the burden of making a proper choice of mate falls upon the individual. Society accepts only limited responsibility and jurisdiction.

It is generally understood that the family of orientation and other relatives will show concern over the marital choice and may do things to influence that choice, but neither the norms nor the law require it. Open interference of relatives in the choice of a marriage partner of one of their kin, though it does happen, is generally frowned upon as a violation of personal freedom and as a violation of the free expression of his love feelings. Any assistance that kinsmen give in mate selection has to be done with subtlety, unless their assistance is sought by the participants. A study of married students registered at a state university illustrates the independence of American couples.[5] Only thirty-five percent indicated that they had sought the advice of their parents before making the decision to marry. A few had consulted with older friends and six percent with friends of their own age, but fifty-eight percent reported that they made the decision to marry without outside advice. Recourse to professional advice was extremely rare, in part perhaps because such advice was not readily available. But, Chambliss concludes, "also it would seem because young people believe they should face this decision, unlike certain other major decisions in life, unaided and alone."

Other studies show the extent of family influence. Bates found that most young people regarded the direct participation of parents as moderate rather than either weak or extreme. More young women than young men reported parental influence, and more influence by mothers than by fathers. Nearly all young women (97 percent) reported influence by mother.[6] Sussman found in interviews with urban middle-class families that most parents stated that they sought to influence their children to select mates of similar background by providing a social milieu for proper dating and courtship and by using persuasion and threats to withdraw economic support should their children not comply. Out of 166 cases, 145 marriages of the children appeared to comply with parental hopes.[7]

The choice of a mate not approved by one's family may be reflected in poor adjustment between the one making a choice and his family. Heiss

[5] Rollin Chambliss, "Married Students at a State University," *The Journal of Educational Sociology*, XXXIV (May, 1961), 409–416.

[6] Alan Bates, "Parental Roles in Courtship," *Social Forces*, XX (1942), 483–486.

[7] Marvin B. Sussman, "Parental Participation in Mate Selection," *Social Forces*, XXXII (1954), 76–81.

found that in general those involved in interfaith marriages were persons who had greater dissatisfaction with parents when they were young, had greater earlier family strife, had less early family integration, and had greater emancipation from parents at the time of marriage.[8]

That young people choosing mates without consulting kinsmen might result in choices of which the kinsmen do not approve is a real possibility, but this is of secondary concern according to American libertarian values; of primary concern is that one has chosen as mate someone he loves.

PERSONAL INVOLVEMENT AND MATE SELECTION

No sex norm is more universally accepted nor more heatedly defended than the right of the person to choose his own mate in accordance with the way in which his affection leads him.[9] Persons marry because they want each other. It is widely held that this is the only right, proper, and decent reason for two persons to marry.

Burgess and Wallin asked 998 engaged men and women whether a person should marry someone with whom he was not in love. The responses of both sexes were nearly identical, about 80 percent said that one should not marry unless he was in love.[10] The authors expressed some surprise in finding that 12 percent of the men and 15 percent of the women thought it all right to marry someone without being in love with that person. Conditions listed under which the latter respondents thought persons might marry even though they were not in love included cases where older age limited chances in the marriage market, pressure from family and friends, the desire to marry and settle down, a sense of duty or honor, anticipated social disapproval if one broke a relationship, rejection by the person one regarded as one's true love. In other words, in the face of real-life situations a minority recognized the fact that some couples might marry for reasons other than affection, but the ideal still remained—love was the basis *par excellence* for marriage.

In the romantic tradition, being in love is a sufficient cause for marriage; one need give no other reasons for marrying nor present any other qualifications. It is assumed that the male will provide at least a major portion of the livelihood for the family, but he need not have demonstrated his ability to do so in advance of the marriage. It is also assumed that the female will have major responsibility for running the home and caring for any offspring born to the marriage, but it is no source of embarrassment (in fact it may

[8] Jerold S. Heiss, "Premarital Characteristics of the Religiously Intermarried in an Urban Area," *American Sociological Review*, XXV (February, 1960), 47–55.

[9] John Sirjamaki, "Cultural Configurations in the American Family," *American Journal of Sociology*, LIII (May, 1948), 464–470.

[10] Ernest W. Burgess and Paul Wallin, *Engagement and Marriage* (Chicago: Lippincott, 1953), p. 394.

be considered "smart") to enter upon marriage without having demonstrated the slightest ability for either housekeeping or for child care. Hilsdale,[11] in a study using a somewhat more representative sample than Burgess and Wallin's, found an almost infantile confidence in the powers of communication. Couples impressed him as having little or no awareness "of the deep-rooted patience, perseverance and selflessness that has to be developed before two people can really fit their lives together in harmony." It is assumed that the attraction of the couple for each other and their joy at being together will carry them over the rough spots as he becomes acclimated to his job and she to homemaking and child care. In fact, they may look forward to learning both occupational and homemaking roles together.

To marry is a dominant life-goal for Americans. This is amply demonstrated, empirically, in the fact that in a nation in which the person is free to choose the single or the married state, a high percentage—ninety percent or more—marry. In the American's pursuit of happiness, one place where happiness is expected to be found is in a love relationship in marriage with his chosen one, as well as through subsequent experiences of procreation, birth, and the rearing of children. Those who are not successful in finding the right person to marry blame themselves rather than blaming their parents or society.[12] The larger proportion are inclined to blame themselves for the fact that they are single, or they blame their singleness on the fact that they have not met the right person.

Free choice of mate can mean several things. What is generally meant is that marriage is an achieved status rather than an ascribed one. This statement is not compromised even if we recognize that in reality the pool of eligibles from which any one person will choose his mate will in the final analysis be restricted by the limits of his contacts and by other considerations.

The person's choice of mate even in a free society is not quixotic or unpredictable, but, within limits, patterned and predictable. There is organization and direction to the choices even in so-called matters of the heart. Personal decisions are conditioned by values and by behavior the person has experienced. The person has grown up in a particular region of the country, within an ethnic subsystem, or, in any event, in a community. He takes on some of the values peculiar to his community and his peer group. In the family of orientation before having reached the age of discretion, the child absorbs many of the values and norms peculiar to his family. This is not to imply that the person's behavior is determined by the values of the area or the group, but these values will almost assuredly influence him in decisions he makes.

[11] Paul Hilsdale, "Marriage as a Personal Existential Commitment," *Marriage and Family Living,* XXIV (May, 1962), 137–143.

[12] Herbert J. Miles and Ray F. Koonce, "The Attitude of Unmarried People Toward Marriage," *The Midwest Sociologist,* XXI (December, 1958), 39–43.

THE SOCIAL PROCESS OF FALLING IN LOVE

Students of human behavior attempt to understand and describe the process whereby persons in a free society move from the status of family freedom to the status of marital commitment. Why do they do it, and how does the process develop?

Burgess and Wallin set about to trace the progress of courtship.[13] They found that the love relationship that led to marriage was not the first serious affair in which the respondent had been involved. While twenty to thirty percent had not kept company with anyone before the association resulting in engagement and marriage, the great majority had one or more associations of exclusive or preferential pairing before the relationship that ended in engagement or marriage. Prior relationships had been taken seriously; some reported that they had been in love in a prior relationship. Engagement was not the culmination of love at first sight. Nearly half of the men and a third of the women reported that they were interested in their engagement partners upon initial encounter, but this does not imply that they experienced love at first sight. It suggests rather that one or both were sufficiently interested on first meeting to want to meet again. An additional 20 percent of the men and 29 percent of the women thought of themselves as friends of their engagement partners before romance began. Characteristically, the initial interest of couple members did not have a markedly physical attraction connected with it; at least respondents did not report awareness of immediate physical attraction. In the majority of cases, physical attraction followed rather quickly, however. About a third of the men and women could not recall a strong physical attraction until six months or longer after they were first interested in their partners. Once physical attraction was experienced, it was generally regarded by both men and women as increasing in strength as the relationship progressed.

Types of Courtship

Burgess and Wallin designated three patterns of courtship with respect to the rapidity with which persons went through the social process from first date to informal engagement. They refer to these three patterns as telescoped, extended, and average courtships.

The telescoped courtship was one in which dating, going steady, falling in love, and becoming engaged were compressed into a very short span of time. The couple's mutual emotional involvement was direct and rapid. In the most extreme cases there was love at first sight followed by an understanding as to marriage. It was the impression of the researchers that a not

---

[13] The sample couples were selected, not representative; the data represent the development of love and romance among a sample of urban, middle-class, engaged young persons. Burgess and Wallin, *op. cit.*, Chapters 2–7.

inconsiderable minority of couples progressed from first meeting to informal engagement in a few months or even a few weeks.

Burgess and Wallin give several reasons as to how this rapid development of love and commitment to marriage might come about. The person met someone who fit his clearly defined ideal image; a person one met had characteristics similar to a person previously loved; the person was lonely because of a lack of meaningful relationships; the person had an implusive temperament and labile emotions and was easily moved by a show of love and affection; external conditions such as prosperity or war affected behavior.

Extended courtships were defined as courtships in which a considerable interval of time elapsed between the time the couple began to date and the time they became engaged. These were courtships in which the partners were relatively slow in reaching the stage in feeling that they were sufficiently in love to get married. Extended involvement prior to marriage could indicate a high degree of self-sufficiency; deliberate, reserved and highly controlled emotional reactions; fear of sexual intimacy; the experience of having been jilted; or a strong career drive on the part of the female.

The average courtship, the one characterizing the majority of cases, was neither of the telescoped nor of the extended variety. It lacked "the catapult-like" movement of the former and the drawn-out character of the latter. Couples who fell in love and decided they wished to marry achieved this state with moderate rapidity—from six months to a year after they first began to date.

The Landises, in a study of engagements of college students, also report moderate rapidity in the development of courtships. Couples reported an average of four and one half months of casual dating with each other, and eight months of dating steadily before reaching an understanding.[14]

Love

Burgess and Wallin, in an attempt to test the extent to which "violent and emotional attachments" or "head-over-heels" love feelings were a reality, asked their sample couples, "To what extent are you in love with your fiancé(e)?" Twenty-four percent of the men and 25 percent of the women reported that they were "head-over-heels" in love; 70 percent of the men and 68 percent of the women reported that they were very much in love; and 6 percent of the men and 7 percent of the women reported themselves somewhat or mildly in love. In general, the respondents indicated a "highly unsympathetic" attitude toward the stereotyped notion of romantic love. They stated very positively that the stereotype did not apply to them, and some checked "head-over-heels" to indicate that their love was as

[14] Judson T. and Mary G. Landis, *Building a Successful Marriage* (Englewood Cliffs, N.J.: Prentice-Hall, 1958).

great as it could be but they did not mean by it the stereotyped conception. Hilsdale also found an almost total absence of "starry-eyed, Hollywood-type romantic love."

In the Landis study, two thirds of both men and women reported a gradual falling in love for both. Only 3 percent reported that both fell in love at first sight.

Since love is regarded as the rationale for becoming engaged and marrying, it is only natural that persons who have not experienced love are anxious about its nature, whether it will ever happen to them, and whether they will be alert to recognize it when it does occur. Burgess and Wallin's sample couples reported little difficulty in knowing when they fell in love. Most persons specified the exact day, week, or month, while some reported that they fell in love so gradually that they could not say with exactness just when it occurred. Only a small minority stated that they did not know whether or not they were in love, and in these cases the interviewers reported that they were reasonably sure that the persons in question were not in love.

Burgess and Wallin asked the couples to try to recall and analyze the reasons why they were in love. It is understandable that some respondents would protest that they did not know the reasons, but such persons were in the minority. The majority attributed their love to three or four factors including fulfillment of personality needs, fulfillment of the ideal image, mutuality and compatibility of interests and aspirations, physical attraction, and reciprocity of love. Of these factors, fulfillment of needs was frequently mentioned. Unless their attention was turned to it, many persons apparently did not realize that as a result of varied influences they had developed an image of a member of the other sex in which they invested positive emotional feelings. Common interests and aspirations were mentioned as reasons for love by a majority of the engaged couples, while "being loved" was less frequently mentioned than any other condition.

A commonly held assumption that extreme idealization of the loved one is associated with being in love was not supported by the findings of Burgess and Wallin. About one out of two women and four out of ten men reported that at one time or another they had not been sure of their choice. The doubts of some as to whether they had found suitable marriage partners were reflected in the fact that one out of four engaged couples stated that relations had at one time been temporarily broken off. Many young people were willing to act on the assumption that greater happiness might still await them with another person.

Interaction

The term "mate selection" may be an unfortunate choice when applied to the American system, for it could be interpreted to imply a unitary non-processual act of choice rather than being a process of building a human relationship over time.[15] In the American system there is not necessarily a conscious selection as such but rather a developing heterosexual paired relationship in which the two become more and more psychologically, socially, and physically involved and committed. Mate selection in a society where persons do their own choosing is based on a process of interaction between the parties within certain societal contexts; this interaction is determinant of turning points and commitments that either destroy the relationship or lead on to further commitment. The development of a relationship thus consists of advances and retreats along alternative paths. The development of a love relationship is problematical since it bears the stamp of what goes on between the principal actors as well as involving what they are as persons. The couple may not be conscious of growth or deterioration in the relationship since major transformations are ordinarily the result of sequences of small turning points. For instance, one change Heiss observed in a sample of dating college couples was that earlier in the relationship males tended to dominate in the task area while females tended to dominate in positive reactions (there was no significant difference between them in negative reactions). This traditional-type of male-female behavior declined as the intimacy between couple members increased.[16]

Dating, going steady, being pinned, and being engaged—these status plateaus are reinforced by certain expressions and symbols, and are reinforced by sanctions of the couple's associates. They exemplify "institutionalized escalators" in a developing relationship.[17]

One study of the involvement process utilized a sample of couples of different faiths, more specifically, pairs each involving a Jew and a gentile.[18] Adding to the unlikelihood that marriages would have resulted from such combinations was the fact that in the thirty-three combinations were twenty-nine persons who, prior to interfaith dating, were resistant to interfaith marriages, implying that the forces pushing them away from interfaith marriage were greater than those leading toward interfaith marriage.

What were the processes responsible for the subjects being drawn together against religious and cultural odds? Using a constructed case history of a Jewish boy and gentile girl, Mayer summarizes the factors. First, the setting was favorable (they were in the same class in college) and the Jewish boy was attracted to his future wife immediately because of certain features which were observable on first meeting (she was physically appealing, she had a pleasant voice). Secondly, he was not aware of her ethnic affiliation at the time they met. Thirdly, she was superior to the members of his peer

---

[15] Charles D. Bolton, "Mate Selection as the Development of a Relationship," *Marriage and Family Living*, XXIII (August, 1961), 234–240.

[16] Jerold S. Heiss, "Degree of Intimacy and Male-Female Interaction," *Sociometry*, XXV (June, 1962), 137–143.

[17] Bolton, *op. cit.*

[18] John E. Mayer, *Jewish-Gentile Courtships* (Glencoe, Ill.: The Free Press, 1961).

group in ways that were vitally important to him. Besides strength of character, kindness, and sexual responsiveness, she was active in the same extracurricular activities as he. They had the same network of mutual friends who both intentionally and unintentionally encouraged their dating. Being assigned to work together in extracurricular activities, they were forced to interact. She may have been more responsive than Jewish girls that he had dated, and, at a later period in the relationship, her responsiveness was supportive at times when he was undergoing stress over the prospect of facing his parents—a time when he was especially appreciative of her responsiveness.

In the beginning the boy felt sure that he would not become deeply involved emotionally though he had become interested in her. The relationship was also helped along if the one less committed to his faith agreed to make concessions; for instance, the gentile girl might agree to be married by a rabbi and to raise their children as Jews. Willingness to acquiesce sometimes stemmed from the fact that the one making concessions was more involved emotionally in the relationship.

Though the parents of the subjects objected, they were unable to keep abreast of the actual course of events and hence were not in any position to influence them. The dater was often insulated against parental objection by the fact that he lived away from home, by his reaction to their objections as morally offensive, and by his hope that they would become more accepting either on their own or because of steps he would take. The cross-pressures to which he was exposed drew him even closer to his partner, and the reaction of his sympathetic friends took an added importance. Hence, a variety of factors and situations contributed to the breakdown of resistance to Jewish-gentile courtship.

FACTORS RELATED TO MATE SELECTION

Propinquity

Studies have shown the importance of propinquity in mate selection. Persons who live near to each other and have greater opportunities for meeting tend to choose each other as marriage partners. Katz and Hill,[19] in a systematic review of the major studies on residential propinquity and marital selection, have synthesized the theories on propinquity and arrived at a norm-interaction theory that is helpful to an understanding of propinquity as a factor in mate selection. Marriages are not merely the result of chance meetings, for marriage is normative and not all persons are regarded as eligible partners. Within the field of persons regarded as eligible, the

[19] Alvin Katz and Reuben Hill, "Residential Propinquity and Marital Selection: A Review of Theory, Method and Fact," *Marriage and Family Living*, XXII (February, 1958), 27–35.

probability of marriage varies directly with the probability of interacting. Furthermore, the probability of interacting is proportional to the ratio of (a) opportunities to interact, to (b) the intervening opportunities.

Timing

Propinquity is not enough to insure that persons will date each other. Timing is important. It is not only important that one meet the right person but that that person come along at a time when one is susceptible to the influence of the other and ready to engage in a dating relationship.

Homogamy and Complementarity

Surveys of characteristics of persons who marry each other indicate that (based on evidence in over 150 empirical studies) like tends to be attracted to like. This is true in regard to physical traits such as stature, looks, and health, though correlations in the direction of homogamous mating by physical traits are low.

Much work has been done in regard to similarities in social characteristics of persons who marry each other. In their study of engaged couples, Burgess and Wallin found that forty-seven of fifty-one social traits showed statistically significant differences in the direction of homogamous choices. Social characteristics with the highest statistically significant preponderance in favor of homogamous unions were, in order: religious affiliations, drinking habits, church attendance, feeling on whether fiancée should work after marriage, age person began keeping company, place lived in during childhood (city, suburb, town, or village), nativity of parents (native-born, foreign-born), church membership, Sunday school attendance, number of children desired, smoking habits, and education.

It is generally assumed that rules of homogamy in regard to social characteristics will be followed in mate selection. That is, the person will "fall in love" with someone like himself in terms of race, nationality, religion, education, and socio-economic class. On the other hand, the romantic ideal is not dead in America; the public rallies to the support of a Cinderella-type love relationship wherein persons of very different backgrounds and socio-economic status are drawn to each other on the strength of their feelings for each other.

In the area of personality characteristics the evidence on homogamy is not conclusive. Of forty-two personality traits analyzed by Burgess and Wallin, only fourteen showed a greater than chance expectation for homogamous choices. Self-rating by engaged persons indicated homogamy in the degree of daydreaming, loneliness, feelings easily hurt, and touchiness, for example. But the differences in the relation between theoretical expectation of mating of like with like and actual outcome was much smaller for personality than for social characteristics.

Studies by Winch[20] and others[21] have demonstrated some tendency for the person to choose as a mate someone whose personality needs complement his own. In developing his theory of complementary needs, Winch defined love as "the positive emotion experienced by one person (the person loving, or the lover) in an interpersonal relationship in which the second person (the person loved, or the love-object) either (1) meets certain important needs of the first or (2) manifests or appears (to the first) to manifest personal attributes (for example, beauty, skills, or status) highly prized by the first, or both." Falling in love, utilizing Winch's definition, would consist in finding a person who gratifies one's conscious or unconscious needs. For example, a person with a need to sympathize with or help a person in need (nurturance) would be attracted to a person with a need to be helped (succorance). A person with a need to invite blame or punishment (abasement) might be attracted to a person with a need to fight or injure others (hostility). Attempts to demonstrate the validity of the theory of complementary needs have not been conclusive, though findings support a tendency in the direction of complementarity. Lack of conclusive results may be due to the crudity of present methods of isolating and measuring the various personality characteristics; it may also be that, in regard to some personality traits, theories of homogamy in mate selection more accurately interpret the empirical evidence. Then, too, persons are not altogether free to follow the dictates of their personal needs and desires; prior conditioning and the expectations of others influence personal choice.[22]

The Ideal Image

The values that one obtains from past experiences are shaped into what has been referred to as an image of the ideal mate. By this we mean that the person preoccupied with finding a mate may carry in his mind an image of the idealized characteristics of the person or the type of person he thinks he would like to marry, and that this image affects his choice. Strauss, in attempting to ascertain the influence of the image, asked a group of engaged and married couples to answer the question, "How important do you feel the 'ideal' was in picking your fiancé(e)?"[23] Approximately two-thirds of

[20] Robert F. Winch, *Mate Selection: A Study of Complementary Needs* (New York: Harper, 1958).

[21] Charles E. Bowerman and Barbara R. Day, "A Test of the Theory of Complementary Needs as Applied to Couples During Courtship," *American Sociological Review*, XXI (1956), 602–605; James A. Schellenberg and Lawrence S. Bee, "A Re-examination of the Theory of Complementary Needs in Mate Selection," *Marriage and Family Living*, XXII (1960), 227–232.

[22] Gerald R. Leslie and Arthur H. Richardson, "Family Versus Campus Influences in Relation to Mate Selection," *Social Problems*, IV (October, 1956), 117–121.

[23] Anselm Strauss, "The Influence of Parent-Image Upon Marital Choice," *American Sociological Review*, XI (1946), 544–559.

the respondents believed that the image of the ideal mate had been important or at least of some importance in the selecting of their marriage partners.

Whereas, Strauss' study elicited reactions to the ideal-mate image from persons who had already selected mates, Udry[24] compared personality relationships obtaining between single persons and their ideal mates to personality relationships obtaining between engaged persons and their real mates and to relationships between engaged persons and what they perceived their real mates to be. He found that the personality match of engaged couples appeared to be random. The mate perceptions of engaged persons bore little resemblance to the ideal-mate conceptions of single persons not engaged. Also, the mate actually selected had different personality relationships to the self than the ideal mate had, and was perceived as having different relationships to the self than were conceived between the ideal mate and the self. Udry concludes that mates are selected without regard to preexisting ideal-mate images. Ideal-mate images are not attributed to the selected person but probably change in response to new relationships into which the person enters. Ideal-mate images may be resultant rather than determinant in mate selection.

INTERRACIAL MARRIAGE

On two factors, race and religion, there are powerful sanctions directing persons toward endogamous marriages—that is, marrying within one's racial or religious classification. Interracial marriages are disapproved, and in over half of the states, including all of the southern states, interracial marriages were once illegal. At one time, all states with more than 5 percent black population had laws forbidding interracial marriage. Punishment for the offending party was as high as a one thousand dollar fine and/or ten years in prison. In some of the states the statutes also provided for punishment of the minister or other official who knowingly performed the marriage ceremony for a mixed-racial couple, as well as for the official issuing the license in violation of the law.[25] Even in states without a history of legal sanctions against interracial marriage, officials in governmental agencies sometimes put obstacles in the way of mixed couples who seek to obtain a marriage license. However, recent United States Supreme Court action setting aside the Florida statute provides a basis for calling in question the constitutionality of all state laws banning mixed-racial marriages. In 1967

---

[24] J. Richard Udry, "The Influence of the Ideal Mate Image on Mate Selection and Mate Perception," *Journal of Marriage and the Family*, XXVII (November, 1965), 477–482.

[25] Joseph Golden, "Social Control of Negro-White Intermarriage," *Social Forces*, XXXVI (March, 1958), 267–269.

the Court ruled that a Virginia statute banning interracial marriage was unconstitutional; the ruling set aside statutes in the fifteen other states still having statutes banning racially mixed marriages.

Black-white intermarriage has been going on in America since the 1600's. Indeed, with increasing spatial and social mobility, intermarriage has increased;[26] the actual number of interracial marriages in the United States is not known, however. It has been conservatively estimated at no more than about 2,000 interracial marriages per year, or about one in every 1,200 marriages.[27]

Burma, in a study of interracial marriages in Los Angeles County from 1948 to 1959, found that such intermarriages were increasing at a significant rate. Some 3,200 intermarriages were recorded, with black-white and Filipino-white marriages the most common. California's law against intermarriage was declared unconstitutional by the supreme court of the state. At the end of the eleven-year period, intermarriage rates were about triple the rates at the beginning of the period. Proportionately, the ethnic groups with the smallest numbers of persons intermarried much more than did persons from groups with larger populations.

Burma found that intermarried couples were on the average somewhat older than persons intramarrying, except if they were themselves products of intermarriage. Colored husband-white wife marriages outnumbered white husband-colored wife marriages.[28]

Analysis of trends in black-white marriages in all four states which have recent data (California, Hawaii, Michigan, and Nebraska) shows that the ratio of actual to expected black-white marriages appears to be rising. The increase may be due in part to recent decreases in residential and school segregation of blacks and whites; or, on the other hand, due to a reduction in status differences.[29] The changes in the rates of intermarriage in the four states cannot be accounted for merely on the basis of changing racial composition. Black-white marriage rates are relatively high in those areas where residential segregation by race is low and where status differences between the races are minimal.

Historically, cultural disparity and social prejudice have created problems for the interracially married and their children.[30]

[26] E. Franklin Frazier, *The Negro Family in the United States,* revised and abridged ed. (New York: Dryden, 1948), pp. 17, 50–69.

[27] Paul H. Jacobson, *American Marriage and Divorce* (New York: Rinehart, 1959), p. 62.

[28] John H. Burma, "Interethnic Marriages in Los Angeles, 1948–1959," *Social Forces,* XLII (December, 1963), 156–165.

[29] David Heer, "Negro-White Marriage in the United States," *Journal of Marriage and the Family,* XXVIII (August, 1966), 262–273.

[30] Ray E. Baber, *Marriage and the Family,* (New York: McGraw-Hill, 1953).

INTERFAITH MARRIAGE

Two of the major religious groups in America, the Jewish and the Roman Catholic, have strong sanctions against interfaith marriages. Among the Jews intermarriage is abhorred and even regarded as treason to the Jewish cause. The most conservative Jewish communities brand the outmarrying Jew as a renegade. They have been known to sit *shiva,* a period of mourning for the dead, in recognition of the member of the family lost through an interfaith marriage.[31] The Roman Catholic Church imposes sanctions on Catholics who engage in so-called invalid marriages. They are stigmatized as living in sin and are excluded from the sacraments.[32]

There is no reliable factual basis for determining nationwide trends in interfaith marriages, since in only two states, Iowa and Indiana, have there been official statistics on the incidence of interfaith marriages. In the author's own research on interfaith marriages and in an extensive review of the literature on interfaith marriages in the United States, only two empirical studies showed no increase in interfaith marriage over time.[33]

Canada has an annual series of statistics on religion of the bride and bridegroom going back to 1921. There has been an almost steady rise in interfaith marriages since 1927 for all three major religious groups— Protestant, Catholic, and Jewish. Generalizations about trends in Canada are not necessarily applicable to the United States, but Heer[34] is of the opinion that uniformity among the Canadian provinces lends additional support to the hypothesis that there has been an increase in interfaith marriages in the United States.

Higher rates of interfaith marriage are at least in part a function of the proportion of the given religious group in the population. An inverse relationship between intermarriage and proportion of the given religious group in the population under study has been found for both Catholics and Jews.[35] Rosenthal found the highest rate of Jewish intermarriage to be 18 percent in Greater Washington, where the proportion of Jews in the population is relatively high (this only for native-born children of native parents). On the other hand, in Iowa, where the Jewish population is small and where they

31 Mayer, *op. cit.,* p. 13.
32 John L. Thomas, *The American Catholic Family* (Englewood Cliffs, N.J.: Prentice-Hall, 1956), p. 149.
33 Floyd M. Martinson, *Interfaith Marriages in the U.S.* (A working paper prepared in connection with meetings of the Lutheran World Federation, 1954).
34 David M. Heer, "The Trend of Interfaith Marriages in Canada: 1922–1957," *American Sociological Review,* XXVII (April, 1962), 262–273.
35 Lee G. Burchinal and Loren E. Chancellor, "Ages at Marriage, Occupation of Grooms, and Interreligious Marriage Rates," *Social Forces,* XL (May, 1962), 348–354; Erich Rosenthal, "Studies of Jewish Intermarriage in the United States," Reprint from *American Jewish Year Book,* LXIV (1963).

live in relatively small communities, he found an intermarriage rate of 42 percent for the period 1953–59. The rate was almost twice as high in towns and rural areas as it was in cities of 10,000 or more population.

Burchinal and Chancellor[36] found in Iowa that interfaith marriages were greatest at the ends of the age distribution. The ages of the spouses and and status levels of the bridegrooms correlated in this fashion with the highest intermarriage rates; rates were high among couples where the spouses were eighteen years of age or younger, thirty years of age or older, and where the bridegrooms had lower-status occupations.

Jewish intermarriage is related to various social factors. Foremost is the distance in time from immigration. Rosenthal[37] found that intermarriage rates varied from 1 percent among the foreign-born immigrants, to 10 percent for the native-born of foreign parentage, and to 18 percent for the native-born of native parentage. Attendance at and graduation from college was also related to the intermarriage rate. Religious-school attendance and traditional Jewish economic activity were associated with lower rates of intermarriage.

The children in at least 70 percent of the mixed families were lost to the Jewish group. This fact takes on special significance when viewed against the fact that the fertility of the Jewish population in the United States is barely sufficient to maintain the present Jewish population size.

The occupation of Jewish grooms was an important factor bearing on intermarriage. In first marriages, grooms in white-collar occupations had an intermarriage rate of 27 percent; grooms in the blue-collar occupations had a rate of 47 percent.

MARITAL COMMITMENT

Engagement, though a practice with a long history, is not universally practiced in America and is not clearly defined as to either form or meaning.[38] Thomas found that of two thousand Catholic couples who brought their marriages to the chancery court of the Chicago Archdiocese between 1942 and 1948, 36 percent had not had an engagement symbolized by a ring or an announcement to friends and relatives.[39] Popenoe and Neptune report similar findings for a sample of unhappily married couples. Thirty-seven percent had not been formerly engaged before marriage. Couples in

[36] Lee G. Burchinal and Loren E. Chancellor, "Factors Relating to Interreligious Marriage in Iowa, 1953–57," *Iowa State University Agricultural and Home Economics Experiment Station Research Bulletin*, DX (November, 1962), 672–695.

[37] Rosenthal, *op. cit.*

[38] Floyd M. Martinson, *Marriage and the American Ideal* (New York: Dodd, Mead, 1960), pp. 184–187; Howard Becker and Reuben Hill, *Family, Marriage and Parenthood* (Boston: Heath, 1948), Chapter 9.

[39] Thomas, *op. cit.*, p. 194.

the lower classes and persons who experience a second or third marriage commonly dispense with formal engagement, while marriage customs of the middle and upper classes call for formal engagement.

Nor are there consistent norms or consistency in practice regarding length of courtship prior to a commitment. Landis[40] found that in approximately one-fourth (27 percent) of the cases less than five months elapsed from first date to engagement, in another one-fourth (26 percent) five months elapsed, while one to two years elapsed in another one-fourth (26 percent) of the cases. The remaining 21 percent reported a time lapse of upwards of three years.

The significance of the act of engagement has changed. In the Judaic-Christian tradition, engagement was regarded as synonymous with commitment to marry and faithfulness to one's vows. Now it is presented as a testing period used to determine the suitability of each for the other, and not as a commitment to marry *per se*.[41]

Engagement is seen now as the final stage in the increasingly intimate relationship that has been developing since the couple members first began to date each other. They may or may not choose to make a public announcement of their intention of marrying during this final testing period. If they accept the current, emerging view of engagement, the commitment to each other is tenuous until this last testing has taken place. If they "pass" the last "test" to their own satisfaction, they marry.

The traditional idea of engagement as a firm commitment to marry and to remain faithful was supported by both church and state. The church took its stand on theological grounds; the state favored a firm commitment on grounds of order and justice. Many states passed laws making breach of promise a legal offense. However, breach-of-promise action has not been generally used as recourse by the offended party, as was pointed out earlier, and a number of states have abolished such laws. With religious authorities agreeing or at least not taking issue with the fact that "it is generally agreed today that the engagement is a time for mutual testing,"[42] the major support for engagement as a firm commitment has been removed.

The most concise and definitive argument for engagement as a testing period before marriage comes not from the church or the state but from family-life educators. They contend that the custom of engagement is a good one, but that there are engagements based on unsound relationships and that these engagements should be broken. They reason that a high rate of broken engagements is preferable to a high rate of broken marriages. For this reason, a couple should enter engagement in the full realization that it might be broken. If couples recognize this, the break, if it comes, will

---

[40] Landis, *op. cit.* (see above, fn. 14).
[41] Martinson, *Marriage and the American Ideal, op. cit.*, pp. 188–213.
[42] Werner Elert, *The Christian Ethos* (Philadelphia: Muhlenberg, 1957).

be less traumatic than it would have been if couple members were not anticipating the possibility of a break. That there should be a tentative period before final commitment to marry is hardly debatable. Logic and empirical evidence support this view. The crucial question is not whether commitments between couple members should be tentative, but rather when, if ever, the tentative period should end. It is generally accepted in American society that the tentative period should end with the exchange of vows at marriage.

Hilsdale's[43] study sheds some light on the "tentative" or "permanent" nature of the commitment to marry as seen by the present generation of young people. He hypothesized that due to the institutionalization of divorce and to the publicity given to it in the communications media, respondents would reveal an existential commitment to a trial of marriage rather than to an unconditional acceptance of marriage as something absolute.

Of eighteen Catholics interviewed, all but one gave answers mirroring official Catholic teaching on the indissolubility of marriage. After a few initial tabulations, Catholics were dropped from the sample, and interviewing was confined to non-Catholics.

How many and what kinds of people commit themselves to marriage irrevocably and how many make a tentative commitment, agreeing only to making a serious effort at living as husband and wife? Catholics were overwhelmingly opposed to civil divorce and remarriage and non-Catholics were 84 percent in favor of permitting civil divorce and remarriage. Nevertheless, most of those who defended divorce were agreed that marriage must begin with a firm or absolute commitment. The majority, even of those who saw marriage as a trial run, appeared to intend to commit themselves to marriage without reservation. Sixty-four out of eighty non-Catholic respondents expressed themselves as not considering a trial commitment. Twenty percent of the sample had made what could possibly be interpreted as a tentative commitment. Hilsdale estimated that less than 5 percent consciously had made a trial commitment.

Hilsdale further hypothesized that trial commitment would correlate positively (1) with male sex (reasoning that women lose more in remarriage than do men); (2) with the black race (because of the effects of slavery and the subsequent period of adjustment on stable marital relations); and (3) with increasing insight and education (on the assumption that the more sophisticated members of society would be more ready to break away from traditional restraints). The data confirmed the positive correlation with regard to race but revealed no variation according to sex. The correlation with education was negative—in the opposite direction from that hypothesized. Hilsdale reasons that it is education that impresses on people the necessity of first making sure of themselves and only then

---

[43] Hilsdale, *op. cit.* (see above, fn. 11).

deciding to go ahead with marriage and that when they do finally decide, they feel sufficiently confident to make a firm commitment.

Other students of the family point to the great expectations of happiness in marriage as the ideology accompanying the high divorce rate—marriage for the duration of happiness rather than "until death do us part." In earlier generations, happiness was not so strongly asserted as a goal of marriage. If happiness failed to materialize in marriage, the marriage was not commonly dissolved.[44]

PREDICTING MARITAL SUCCESS

Behavioral scientists have not been satisfied with delineating factors associated with mate choice; science aims rather at control and prediction. Attempts have been made to delineate factors predictive of marital success. Much of this investigation was carried out in the decades of the 1920's and 1930's. The research of Terman and associates[45] in psychology and of Burgess and associates[46] in sociology was pioneering work. This research had a massive impact upon family sociology as well as on functional marriage education from the 1930's to the present. Numerous personal, cultural, familial, social, response, and sexual factors were correlated with measures of success in marriage. However, the predictive quality of the measures was less significant than their subsequent pedagogical and counseling use warranted.

Personal and socio-cultural data were gathered from reasonably large samples of married couples. Comparisons were made between data on couples whose marriages were defined as happy or adjusted and data on couples whose marriages rated low on happiness or adjustment. Successful marriages were found to be characterized by mutual affection and confidence, agreement on social norms, similar family background, better-than-average amount of education, and others. The data appeared to point to a highly socialized person characterized by traits of stability, conventionality, and conformity as the person best suited for marriage. It appeared that for a permanent and successful marriage one should marry someone who had traits similar to one's own and one who had similar family and general socio-cultural background.

The correlations between the various factors and marital success were low, however, suggesting that some commonsense method of prediction might have almost as much value. Burgess and Wallin demonstrated em-

44 W. F. Ogburn and M. F. Nimkoff, *Technology and the Changing Family* (New York: Houghton Mifflin, 1955), p. 8.

45 L. M. Terman, *Psychological Factors in Marital Happiness* (New York: McGraw-Hill, 1938).

46 E. W. Burgess and L. S. Cottrell, *Predicting Success or Failure in Marriage* (New York: Prentice-Hall, 1939); Harvey J. Locke, *Predicting Adjustment in Marriage* (New York: Holt, 1951).

pirically that forecasts by persons close to the situation (engaged persons, their parents, and close friends) were nearly as accurate predictors of success as one of the prediction instruments.[47]

Authorities on marital prediction studies conclude that prediction of success in marriage based on current research findings is not feasible within reasonable limits of reliability. Hill concluded in his summary of the marital-success studies, that "roughly seventy-five percent of the factors that count for marital success are left unaccounted for;"[48] Kirkpatrick suggests that "couples should not be counseled in terms of present forecasting scores unless they are able to take the evidence with full awareness of their limitations. . . . If marriage is recognized as still a gamble, it is proper to peek at the cards dimly lighted by present scientific knowledge."[49]

SUMMARY

Marriage is a unit of interaction distinct from other social systems. Society sets some limits as to who is eligible to marry. Within these limits marriages are brought into being through the mutual attraction and agreement of the two persons involved.

The process of falling in love involves advance and retreat as the two persons interact with each other and with others under varied conditions. Some relationships develop to a point of commitment or breakup in short order, others continue over a longer period of time. Propinquity, timing, factors of endogamy, homogamy, and complementarity play a part in the development of a relationship.

A period of engagement often precedes marriage. Couples normally conceive of this as a period of lovemaking and marriage preparations. Behavioral scientists have suggested that it might serve as a final testing period before vows of fidelity are exchanged.

In an attempt to predict the success of marital relationships, behavioral scientists have delineated and analyzed a number of social and psychological factors. Prediction is as yet crude, however, with a majority of the factors related to marital success unaccounted for.

BIBLIOGRAPHY

Jessie Bernard, Helen E. Buchanan, and William M. Smith, Jr. *Dating, Mating and Marriage.* Cleveland: Howard Allen, 1958.

Charles D. Bolton. "Mate Selection as the Development of a Relationship," *Marriage and Family Living,* XXIII (August, 1961), 234–240.

[47] Burgess and Wallin, *op. cit.* (see above, fn. 10), pp. 558–591.

[48] Willard Waller and Reuben Hill, *The Family: A Dynamic Interpretation* (New York: Dryden, 1951), p. 353.

[49] Clifford Kirkpatrick, *The Family: As Process and Institution,* second ed. (New York: Ronald, 1963), pp. 404–405; see also William Kolb, "Sociologically Established Family Norms and Democratic Values," *Social Forces,* XXVI (May, 1948), 451–456.

Charles E. Bowerman. "Prediction Studies," *Handbook of Marriage and the Family,* ed. Harold T. Christensen. Chicago: Rand McNally, 1964. Pp. 215–246.

Lee G. Burchinal. "The Premarital Dyad and Love Involvement," *Handbook of Marriage and the Family,* ed. Harold T. Christensen. Chicago: Rand McNally, 1964. Pp. 623–674.

Lee G. Burchinal and Loren E. Chancellor. "Ages at Marriage, Occupation of Grooms, and Interreligious Marriage Rates," *Social Forces,* XL (May, 1962), 348–354.

John H. Burma. "Interethnic Marriages in Los Angeles, 1948–1959," *Social Forces,* XLII (December, 1963), 156–165.

Rollin Chambliss. "Married Students at a State University," *The Journal of Educational Sociology,* XXXIV (May, 1961), 409–416.

Joseph Golden, "Social Control of Negro-White Intermarriage," *Social Forces.* XXXVI (March, 1958), 267–269.

David Heer. "Negro-White Marriage in the United States," *Journal of Marriage and the Family,* XXVIII (August, 1966), 262–273.

Jerold S. Heiss. "Premarital Characteristics of the Religiously Intermarried in an Urban Area," *American Sociological Review,* XXV (February, 1960), 47–55.

Paul Hilsdale. "Marriage as a Personal Existential Commitment," *Marriage and Family Living,* XXIV (May, 1962), 137–143.

Alvin Katz and Reuben Hill. "Residential Propinquity and Marital Selection: A Review of Theory, Method and Fact," *Marriage and Family Living,* XXII (February, 1958), 27–35.

William M. Kephart. "Some Correlates of Romantic Love," *Journal of Marriage and the Family,* XXIX (August, 1967), 470–474.

Judson T. Landis and Mary G. Landis. *Building a Successful Marriage.* Englewood Cliffs, N.J.: Prentice-Hall, 1958.

Floyd M. Martinson. "Ego Deficiency as a Factor in Marriage," *American Sociological Review,* XX (April, 1955), 161–164.

Floyd M. Martinson. "Ego Deficiency as a Factor in Marriage—A Male Sample," *Marriage and Family Living,* XXI (February, 1959), 48–52.

Floyd M. Martinson. *Marriage and the American Ideal.* New York: Dodd, Mead, 1960.

John E. Mayer. *Jewish-Gentile Courtships.* Glencoe, Ill.: The Free Press, 1961.

Margaret Mead. "Adolescence in Primitive and Modern Society," in *The New Generation,* eds. V. F. Calverton and S. D. Schmalhausen. New York: Macauley, 1930.

Herbert J. Miles and Ray F. Koonce. "The Attitudes of Unmarried People Toward Marriage," *The Midwest Sociologist,* XXI (December, 1958), 39–43.

Erich Rosenthal. "Studies of Jewish Intermarriage in the United States," Reprint from American Jewish Year Book, LXIV (1963), 3–53.

Marvin B. Sussman. "Parental Participation in Mate Selection," *Social Forces,* XXXII (1954), 76–81.

J. Richard Udry. "The Influence of the Ideal Mate Image on Mate Selection and Mate Perceptions," *Journal of Marriage and the Family,* XXVII (November, 1965), 477–482.

CHAPTER 15

Marriage

THE INCIDENCE OF MARRIAGE

MARRIAGE is popular with Americans. Indeed, it has grown in popularity over the years.[1] In 1940, 15 percent of women in their early thirties had

FIGURE 15.1. PERCENT OF PERSONS OVER 14 WHO MARRY

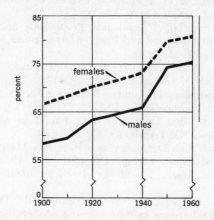

SOURCE: U.S. Bureau of the Census, *Current Population Reports,* Series P-25.

never been married; in 1960 just 7 percent of women in this age category had never been married.[2] The marriage rate (marriages per 1,000 of the

[1] While marriage continues to be the most popular way of life, a small but growing proportion of the population are living alone or with people to whom they are not related. About ninety percent of the population makes up the approximately fifty million American family units. The remaining percentage includes young people who are in the armed forces, people who are not married, and the elderly. The number of family units is expected to increase, but the number living apart from their immediate families is expected to show an even greater increase. The increasing number of older people, especially widows, is reflected in this estimate.

[2] "Marriage and the American Woman," *Population Profile* (Washington, D.C.: Population Reference Bureau, Inc., June 3, 1963), p. 1.

population) has continued to increase—from 8.5 in the early 1960's to 9.4 in 1966 (see Figure 15.2).

The popularity of marriage is further attested to by the fact that the age at first marriage moved downward for both men and women for a number of decades.

FIGURE 15.2.   SEASONALLY ADJUSTED MARRIAGES

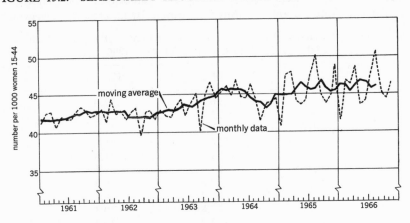

SOURCE: U.S. Department of Health, Education, and Welfare, *Health, Education, and Welfare Indicators*, February, 1967.

In 1960, the median age at marriage was 22.8 for grooms and 20.3 for brides. More men married at age twenty-one than at any other age, and more women married at age eighteen than at any other age (see Table 15.1).

The majority (about sixty-five percent) of all women are married by the time they are twenty-one years of age. Students marry while they are still in school. In 1961, nineteen percent of the women in college were married (162,000) and almost half as many (77,000) high school girls were married. At the other end of the marriage-age continuum, marriages of persons sixty-five years of age and older account for approximately 35,000 marriages per year in the United States. In other words, a long life span is partially responsible for the high rate of marriage.[3] Marriage is popular among those who are educated and capable of following an independent career as well as among the less well educated. Wells found in a survey of graduates of four colleges that at least eighty-three percent of the women graduates were married.[4]

In 1960, men were marrying about three years earlier and women about two years earlier than they were at the turn of the century. Brides and

[3] *Bulletin of the Institute of Gerontology*, IX (November, 1962), 8.
[4] Jean A. Wells, "15 Years after College: A Study of Alumnae of the Class of 1945," U.S. Department of Labor, *Women's Bureau Bulletin*, CCLXXXIII (1962), 4.

grooms are closer in age at first marriage than formerly. They are also closer in age at first marriage than are couples in other urban-industrial countries.

THE MARRIAGE RITE

All states permit the solemnizing of marriage by a clergyman and all states recognize marriage performed by civil authorities. The majority of marriages in America are performed in church, by an ordained clergyman,

TABLE 15.1. MEDIAN AGE AT FIRST MARRIAGE BY SEX, FOR THE UNITED STATES CENSUS YEARS, 1890–1967

Year	Men	Women
1890	26.1	22.0
1900	25.9	21.9
1910	25.1	21.6
1920	24.6	21.2
1930	24.3	21.3
1940	24.3	21.5
1950	22.8	20.3
1960	22.8	20.3
1961	22.8	20.3
1962	22.7	20.3
1963	22.8	20.5
1964	23.1	20.5
1965	22.8	20.6
1966	22.8	20.5
1967	23.1	20.6

SOURCE: U.S. Department of Commerce, "Marital Status and Family Status: March, 1967," *Population Characteristics,* February 23, 1968.

and the form of the service is usually one prescribed by the denomination in question, sometimes with modifications requested by the couple being married. The majority of American couples choose to be married under the aegis of the church and to have marriage characterized as a "holy state ordained by God" with commitments to be faithful, "so long as ye both shall live." The extent to which the service is regarded as ritual and passively accepted or the extent to which the views of the church on marriage are actively supported by the participants is a question for empirical verification.

Chambliss found that 74 percent of a sample of college-educated respondents listed the church as the place of marriage and an additional 10 percent indicated that they were married in a parsonage. Only 6 percent were married in a civil office and only 5 percent in the home of the bride.[5]

[5] Rollin Chambliss, "Married Students at a State University," *The Journal of Educational Sociology,* XXXIV (May, 1961), 409–416.

There is evidence of an increase in the proportion of church weddings over the generations. In a sample of Protestant middle-class people, Miles and Johnson found that fifty years ago eighty-three percent of the weddings were small private ceremonies, while only seventeen percent were public with large groups in attendance. On the other hand, in marriages performed between 1954 and 1961, thirty-nine percent were private weddings and sixty-one percent were public. In the grandparent generation only twelve percent of the weddings were held in churches; seventy percent were held in homes. In the present generation, seventy-two percent of the weddings were held in churches, while only seventeen percent were held in homes. Weddings had changed from an informal to a formal ceremony, from small private to large public gatherings, and from the home to the church.[6]

MARRIAGE AND FAMILY AS SEPARATE SOCIAL SYSTEMS

The emergence of marriage as a social system separate from the family reflects a key aspect of the American value system, namely, the freedom and the rights of the person over against ascribed institutional ties that would compromise his freedom of choice. It also reflects the American emphasis on the importance of affection in adult heterosexual relations.

Companionship and the giving and receiving of affection are primary functions of the marital system. Procreation is a secondary function in many marriages, as witnessed by the fact that couples are willing to divorce if the companionship and affectional functions have deteriorated, even if children have been born to the union. If they maintain the marriage for the sake of the children—in spite of the fact that it has lost its major functions—they maintain it primarily as family not as a marriage.

The genius of technology in providing ways of separating the conceiving function of coitus from the lovemaking function of coitus by providing chemical, mechanical, and surgical means of conception control is not least among the conditions that have made marriage as a social system a *de facto* reality apart and distinct from the family as a social system. When Ogburn and Nimkoff asked eighteen prominent students of the family to list the ten outstanding changes in the family in recent times, the second most commonly mentioned change was the wider diffusion of birth control and/or the decline in family size.[7] Before marriage could emerge as a separate system and remain a separate system, it was necessary that reliable methods of conception control be developed.

[6] Herbert J. Miles and Brooke R. Johnson, "Marriage Ceremony Trends," *Family Life*, XXIII (April, 1963), 1–4.
[7] W. F. Ogburn and M. F. Nimkoff, *Technology and the Changing Family* (New York: Houghton Mifflin, 1955), p. 12.

But do couples choose to remain a marriage and choose not to become a family? For a small minority of couples this is the case. But most see marriage as a relationship defined as including the presumption of offspring; the roles of husband and wife in marriage (during the child-rearing phase as well as before the birth of the first child and after the departure of the last child) are almost inextricably joined to their father and mother roles in the family.

Schneider and Homans[8] observe from their study of American kinship terminology that there is no clearly delineated kinship terminology that would suggest a responsibility on the part of couples to rear children for the sake of perpetuating the extended kinship group. This suggests that even those American couples who accept procreation as a function of their marriage are marriage (or at most nuclear family) oriented.

The development of reliable conception control techniques is so recent that it is too early to test the effects of reliable conception control techniques on choice. Most married couples become families, even those couples who have adequate knowledge of conception control and who embrace permissive values regarding the use of contraceptive methods. They apparently feel that the full expression of their roles calls for the production of offspring. With the emancipation of women and the acceptance of career roles outside of marriage as an alternative to motherhood, it is possible that there will be an increase in marriages as marriages rather than marriages as a prelude to or conjoint with family. The concern regarding overpopulation throughout the world may help to alter the climate of opinion. Pressures on couples to bear children may change; not bearing children may come to be positively sanctioned with even the possibility of rewards for infertility.

There are evidences of the desire of married couples to retain the marriage as a functioning entity even if they choose to raise children and even after the birth of the first child constitutes the base for performing family functions. By voluntarily limiting family size, couples find it possible to enact family roles and marriage roles without necessarily sacrificing the one for the other. In earlier times when family members had to spend most of their working hours in adaptive (economic) pursuits, and when families were large, the possibility of elaborating marriage roles was out of the question except for most insistent and resourceful persons.

The transfer of many functions previously performed in the home to other systems in society has played no small part in releasing time for marital functions. Much of the adaptive function, the religious function, the protective function, the educational function have been taken over by other social systems; sexual and companionship functions have remained largely

---

[8] David M. Schneider and George C. Homans, "Kinship Terminology and the American Kinship System," *American Anthropologist*, LVII (December, 1955), 1194–1208.

within the privacy of the home. One way in which married couples retain marriage as a system conjoint with the family of procreation is through the production of a limited number of children with the early departure of the last child from the home. This gives the married couple an opportunity for a period of uninterrupted concentration on personal and marriage roles following the departure of the last child.

The accompanying table emphasizes another aspect of the marriage *sans* family complex. As shown in the table the couple as a social entity usually develops one or more years prior to marriage. It is also common to have a period of life together as a married couple prior to the birth of the first child.

TABLE 15.2. STAGES IN THE COUPLE CYCLE AND THE FAMILY CYCLE

The Couple Cycle		The Family Cycle	
Random and serious			
dating couple	1.0 yr.[a]		
Engaged couple	1.0 yr.[b]		
Newly married couple	2.0 yrs.		
Married couple with		Child-bearing family	2.5 yrs.[a]
Children in the home	26.5 yrs.	Child-rearing family	17.5 yrs.[b]
Older married couple	13.5 yrs.	Child-launching family	6.5 yrs.[b]
Total years	44.0 yrs.[c]		26.5 yrs.

[a] Burgess and Wallin report that the average engaged couple had gone together for six months to one year before engagement.
[b] Source of data, U.S. Census, 1950.
[c] Conditions prevailing in 1950 point to 41 years of married life before the death of one spouse or the other, more commonly the husband. Paul C. Glick, *American Families* (New York: John Wiley & Sons, Inc., 1957).

SOURCE: Floyd M. Martinson, *Marriage and the American Ideal* (New York: Dodd, Mead & Co., 1960), p. 345.

Adding the period of time after the departure of the last child from the home, it is possible that two as a couple may have a life span of approximately forty-four years, while the family life span (the family as a functioning face-to-face social unit) is less than thirty years.

GOALS OF MARRIAGE

Societal Goals

Marriage as a social system receives full and unequivocal support from the American value system. The reasons that society maintains and supports such a system are in harmony with the goals of married couples themselves. Society maintains and supports marriage as a way of life that is regarded to be more compatible with human needs than is the single life.

Society is interested in marriage as a major source of a socialized adult population. Society recognizes the need for a system that will provide regular sexual outlet for adults and will serve as a major agency for controlling promiscuous sexual activity. Society desires that persons find the outcome for personal expression within rather than over against the structures of society. In a highly differentiated society, the marital system serves to articulate personalities with the larger social system. It socializes adults and provides mechanisms which meet many of their essential physiological, psychological, and social needs, thereby providing conditions of continuity and stability in the society.[9]

Society makes very few specific demands upon marriage when compared with the demands that it makes upon family. Historically, societies have been eager that marriage result in the production of offspring, but, today, there is little insistence in the societal value system that all marriages produce offspring.

Since society makes few demands on marriage, the spouses can, within rather broad limits, develop their own patterns of interaction. Research on marriage has centered on these satisfactions within marriage rather than on the adaptation of marriage to systems external to it. This is not to suggest that marriage is not affected by dependence upon the environment; major conditions affecting the functioning of marriage include the presence of and the behavior of children born to the union, and of relatives and in-laws, the influence of neighbors, the occupations of the spouses, the school system attended by the children, the church, and other conditions. In other words, marriage is not a closed system, but, compared with the family, it is relatively independent of outside pressures.

The differentiation process that has led to the recognition of marriage as a social system apart from family as a social system has accompanied and complements the emphasis on personal freedom and personal happiness as prime goals in life. Personal desire for each other—being in love—is made the basis of marriage, and a marriage is judged successful if it contributes to the happiness of both partners. At the heart of marriage is a reliance upon successful accommodation of the emotive elements in the lives of two adults living an intimate relationship.

Affective Attachment

Few societies have relied on the emotive aspect of personality as the basis for either establishing or maintaining marriage, and in America students of family have been uneasy and sometimes doleful in contemplating the outcome of marriages based and maintained on anything so fluctuating and volatile as the emotions. Americans have relegated to comparative unim-

[9] Talcott Parsons and Robert F. Bales, *Family, Socialization and Interaction Process* (Glencoe, Ill.: The Free Press, 1955), pp. 16 ff.

portance the social, cultural, and familial goals of marriage. By defining marriage as "a close, intimate interpersonal relationship between husband and wife in which the concept of personal fulfillment and the expression of need through close intimacy is the goal deliberately sought,"[10] Americans have put the elements that were so strictly and studiously avoided in older societies at the very center of marriage. "This means, of course, that our young people in getting married today are being encouraged to walk right into the burning, fiery furnace, right into the maelstrom, right into the things that are known to be capable of producing all sorts of conflict and cross currents of feeling and emotion."[11] Perhaps many societies have placed marriage on a level of expectancy that is unreasonably low; Americans have placed marriage on a level of expectancy that may be unreasonably high.

Despite the apparent American emphasis on the emotive side of personality as a basis for marriage, Blood and Wolfe[12] found that wives in the Detroit area ranked their husbands' expressions of love and affection as next to least valuable of five aspects of marriage. The other four aspects were companionship, understanding, standard of living, and children. Only 10 percent of the city and farm wives listed love first of all and nearly half omitted it completely from their first three choices. Despite an apparent lack of affection, wives in the study seldom indicated disappointment in their husbands. Blood and Wolfe suggest that love may be more of a prerequisite to marriage than a goal of marriage and that after marriage people stress doing things together as values desirable in the marriage rather than loving each other as the goal of marriage.

Companionship

Companionship is regarded by the participants as a major, if not the major, goal of modern marriage—a companionship based on an affective attachment that places a premium on mutuality and a companionship which does not recognize either spouse as having a superior status. In the Detroit study, 48 percent of the wives chose "companionship in doing things together with the husband" as the most valuable aspect of marriage. The chance to have children ran a poor second with only 27 percent first choices. In addition to being overwhelmingly popular as a first-choice item, companionship was chosen second by an additional 21 percent and third by 16 percent, leaving only 14 percent who did not choose it as one of the three most valuable aspects of marriage. This compares with 30 percent not choosing children and still more neglecting to choose other aspects of

---

[10] David Mace, "The Formative Years of Marriage," *The Bulletin on Family Development,* III (Spring, 1962), 2.

[11] *Ibid.,* p. 2.

[12] Robert O. Blood and Donald M. Wolfe, *Husbands and Wives: The Dynamics of Married Living* (Glencoe, Ill.: The Free Press, 1960), p. 223.

marriage. Blood and Wolfe found a close relationship between marital satisfaction and companionship, reflecting the high value which most wives placed on companionship as an aspect of marriage.

Couples see marriage as providing one of the enduring relationships in a highly mobile society. Fairchild and Wynn also found companionship to be very much on the minds of their respondents; they wanted to keep the marriage strong. Respondents tended to look upon marriage as a relationship between friends and often held marriage in higher esteem than parenthood. Suburban couples in particular saw a dilemma in attempting to balance the functions of companionship and parenthood; they saw themselves as personalities needing a life of their own as well as parents serving the needs of their children.[13] The family functions primarily on behalf of emergent youthful personalities; but marriage functions on behalf of adult personalities as well. Within the nuclear family there are only the two adults; they turn to each other. Neither party has any other adult kin on whom he can regularly lean for support in any sense comparable to the position of the spouse. Thus, the marriage relation is placed in a far more strategic position in meeting the needs of adult personalities than is true in kinship systems wherein solidarity with extended kin groups is pervasive.

Isolation also enhances the significance of parenthood for the emotional balance of parents. The two generations are, by virtue of the isolation of the nuclear family, drawn more closely to each other than in other kinship systems.

Confidentiality

Blood and Wolfe sought to find out to what extent the husband-wife relationship was functional in meeting the needs of wives by inquiring as to their use of the husband as a confidant in dealing with troubles. They found that women did not always take their troubles to their husbands. Many wives said that they thought the husband should not be bothered with their troubles. Wives who held this philosophy were seldom absolute in their resolve not to approach the husband with their problems, however; only eighteen percent of them never bothered their husbands with their troubles. Blood and Wolfe observe that wives who never utilized the husband in this way were apt to have found through actual experience that it did not work, either because the husband reacted negatively or because he was ineffective as a counselor. After trying to get help early in marriage, they gradually learned that it did not pay to try. They kept silent not from a conviction that the husband deserved respect, but from the bitter knowledge that it would be futile to try.

[13] Roy W. Fairchild and John Charles Wynn, *Families in the Church: A Protestant Survey* (New York: Association, 1961), p. 148.

Only a few wives reasoned that a mental-hygiene function properly belonged in marriage. Most gave pragmatic arguments for turning to their husbands—it paid off just by being able to tell someone or the husband actively relieved their depressing moods. Despite the rewarding reinforcement of their behavior, such wives modally exercised it "usually" rather than "always."

Wives who reported that they turned to their husbands because it was convenient or out of habit showed little discrimination between occasions. More than half of them always told their troubles no matter what the husband's circumstances were. Blood and Wolfe question how sensitive such wives are to their husband's own mental hygiene. Most satisfied was the wife whose husband was attentive to and directly helped to solve the problems she faced.

There appears to be a greater degree of segregation in the role relationships of husbands and wives among the working and lower-income classes than in the middle class; men and women do not have many relationships together. There is a sharp separation of man's work and woman's work and man's play and woman's play. Couple members do not appear to be dependent on each other emotionally, though each performs certain services for the other.[14] Working-class husbands and wives do not share the companionship of going out evenings or weekends together without the children, nor are working-class fathers inclined to relieve their wives of the burden of constant care of the children.[15]

Sexual Intimacy

A strong case can be made for viewing marriage and family as separate systems by referring to the sexual function. Generally speaking, couples keep the sexual function of marriage apart from and secretive from junior members of the family. In other words, two systems, a marriage and a family, operate within the same household, but one, marriage, keeps one of its major functions a secret. The family, on the other hand, has no secrets; all of its functions are known to, and most are supervised by the couple since the married pair serves as leadership coalition of the family.

Coitus as a core function of marriage receives statutory support. A woman in consenting to marry gives her consent to accept coition with her husband. A husband cannot be convicted of raping his wife no matter if coitus is against her wishes and the husband uses force. In most states, however, the husband can be prosecuted for assault and battery if he uses undue

---

[14] Lee Rainwater, "Marital Sexuality in Four Cultures of Poverty," *Journal of Marriage and the Family*, XXVI (November, 1964), 457–466.

[15] Melvin L. Kohn, "Social Class and Parent-Child Relationships: An Interpretation," *American Journal of Sociology*, LXVIII (January, 1963), 479.

force; such behavior may also be accepted as grounds for divorce proceedings brought against him by his wife.[16]

The frequency of coitus in marriages has been a subject for judicial review. Even in recent times in America, judges have been called upon to pass on the reasonableness of the coital demands of husbands. Husbands have been prosecuted on evidence indicating demand of intercourse at a frequency of three or four times per week.[17] Frequencies of approximately daily coitus have been cited as unreasonable and cruel in divorce proceedings.[18]

The rationale for marital coitus in the new sexual morality that is emerging differs somewhat from the rationale for coitus in marriage as interpreted from Hebrew, Christian,[19] and legal sources.[20] Not duty but desire, companionship, and the search for expression and happiness have become dominant motives for sexual conduct in marriage. Both husbands and wives have come to expect that coitus will be frequent, pleasurable, and a major contribution to marital happiness. Some students of marriage have felt that the decline of segregation of the sexes as it has been occurring in America would reduce the erotic and romantic behavior of couples. The opposite appears to be closer to reality. Interest in sex has increased, the repertoire of masculine and feminine sexual roles has widened, and many now enjoy experiences that once were the possessions or prerogative of a few.[21]

The changing attitudes toward coitus in marriage are reflected in the data on sexual conduct over several generations as reported by Kinsey. In the Kinsey sample of American women, the incidence and frequency of marital coitus reached a maximum in the first year or two of marriage. The average (active median) frequency of marital coitus in the sample was nearly 2.8 per week for females who had married in their late teens.[22] The rate dropped to 2.2 per week by the time they were thirty years of age. As many as fourteen percent had had marital coitus frequencies as high as seven or more times per week during their late teens, and there were those who had had coitus in marriage as frequently as four times a day as a regular pattern.

[16] For a discussion of laws covering marital coitus see Alfred Kinsey, Wardell B. Pomeroy, Clyde Martin, and Paul H. Gebhard, *Sexual Behavior in the Human Female* (Philadelphia: Saunders, 1953); Morris Ploscoe, "Sex Offenses: The American Legal Context," *Law and Contemporary Problems*, XXV (Spring, 1960), 217–224; Stanton Wheeler, "Sex Offenses: A Sociological Critique," *Law and Contemporary Problems*, XXV (Spring, 1960), 258–278.

[17] *Dittrick* v. *Brown County* (Minnesota), 1943:9, N.W. (2d) 510.

[18] For a review of the law see Kinsey, Pomeroy, Martin, and Gebhard, *op. cit.*, pp. 368–371.

[19] For a brief review of historical data see Kinsey, Pomeroy, Martin, and Gebhard, *op. cit.*, pp. 354–366.

[20] Nelson Foote, "Sex as Play," *Social Problems*, I (April, 1954), 159–163.

[21] Nelson N. Foote, "New Roles for Men and Women," *Marriage and Family Living*, XXIII (November, 1961), 325–329.

[22] Kinsey, Pomeroy, Martin and Gebhard, *op. cit.*, p. 392.

Kinsey found that most couples engaged in forms of sex play before intromission. The pre-coital techniques in marriage were not unlike those practiced in premarital petting. Extended sex play was more common among the better educated respondents. There were cases in which husband and wife spent two or three hours per day "in incidental or even intense erotic play."

Many females, particularly of the older generation, contributed little or nothing in sex play with their spouses preceding intromission. In the younger generation, an increasing proportion took an active part in the petting experience. Kinsey suggests that the earlier reticence of the female may have been due to a trained modesty, the belief that the male is normally so aroused that he does not need additional stimulation, and the belief that the gallant and romantic male is to provide his beloved with pleasure. The younger generation of females appeared to be aware that active participation in love play may contribute to their husbands' and their own pleasure.

Greater and more varied sex play was associated with more married females receiving satisfaction as evidenced on the greater incidence of those achieving orgasm.[23] Something between thirty-six and forty-four percent of the females in the sample had responded with orgasm in at least part of their coitus in marriage. Not even this latter group had experienced orgasm all of the time. About fourteen percent of the females in the sample regularly experienced multiple orgasm in coitus, but even those with multiple orgasm did not experience orgasm every time coital activity was engaged in. Some women had reached orgasm for the first time only late in marriage. Ten percent of the women had never reached orgasm at any time in marriage.

The number of females reaching orgasm was distinctly higher for the better educated females. This might reflect a factor of health, vitality, and freedom from fatigue; it might reflect the greater companionate activity of the educated classes; it might reflect the avante garde in adopting emergent permissive attitudes toward sexual behavior.

A distinct and steadily increasing number of females reach orgasm in their marital coitus. Complete frigidity for as much as five years was reduced from twenty-eight percent to 11 percent in one age group and from twenty to seven percent in another age group. Kinsey concludes that to have frigidity reduced so markedly in the course of only four decades cannot be attributed to biological factors alone; it may be credited in part at least to the more frank attitudes and freer discussion of sex that has prevailed in the United States, and to the scientific and clinical understanding of the biology and psychology of sex. The reduction of frigidity in marriage may also be a result of increased premarital socio-sexual experiences of young people.

[23] For an analysis of empirical data dealing with the anatomy and physiology of human sexual response see William H. Masters and Virginia E. Johnson, *Human Sexual Response* (Boston: Little, Brown, 1966).

Changes in marital roles. Behavioral scientists have noted a change in sex roles complementing the marked sexual emphasis in the husband-wife relationship. Marriage has been seen in the past as more functional for the personality of women than of men; particularly with the birth of children, the woman could give full expression to her maternal and domestic drives. It was felt that marriage stood in the way of man's desire or need for variety, and specifically for variety in sexual experience. On the other hand, American romanticism applied to marriage contends that love and companionship (including sexual companionship) with one spouse has the potential for providing all the satisfaction that any man can desire. The goal of making sex in marriage satisfying to married persons, including the variety-loving male, is reflected in the new roles of husband and wife in marriage. Much has been made of the declining importance of the woman's domestic role and of the pros and cons of a career role outside the home for the wife, while little responsible public discussion has surrounded a third rapidly emerging female role, namely, the glamour role or the role of seductress and sexual playmate matching the sexual desires and needs of the husband. The puritanical elements in American culture and the low esteem for the seductress in any culture and particularly in one informed by a Puritan ethic explains the reluctance to openly advocate or even to discuss this marital role. The glamour pattern[24] has been associated with the hussy, the woman of the world; it was therefore hestitantly at first that married women began to carry out their preening display with emphasis on diets, foundation garments (to assist in maintaining the attractive figure), cosmetics, and lounging and nightwear blatantly designed for seduction. The glamour role in marriage is a part of the emancipation of the American women, an emancipation that brought a new balance between domestic and marital roles. She has been freed from traditional and conventional restrictions on the free expression of her sexual attractiveness and her sexual impulses. She has become emancipated into a more complete femininity. The glamour role of married women does not lessen the difference between male and female roles in marriage; if anything, it enhances the difference.

There has been a concomitant change in the role of the married man. The male has always been recognized as a sexual creature quite given to acting out his sexual desires, but there has been a change in the conditions to his sexual activity. The male, like the female, has become self-conscious about his sexual image. Increasingly, men have become conscious of the desirability of the lean, athletic, well-groomed, flat-abdomened, virile appearance. Men dress with care and choose clothing with an eye toward fashion; they bathe, they use deodorants and sweet-smelling ointments; some dye

---

[24] Talcott Parsons, "Age and Sex in the Social Structure of the United States," *American Sociological Review,* VII (October, 1942), 224–225; Max Lerner, *America as a Civilization* (New York: Simon and Schuster, 1957), p. 590 ff.

their hair and manicure their nails. Men show some desire to be dashing and romantic and not necessarily as an alternative to marriage; they can be both sexually masculine and monogamous.

Kinsey found that improvement in the quality of coitus in marriage had occurred along with some reduction in the frequency of coitus. There are various interpretations of the relationship between increased satisfaction and reduced frequency. Kinsey contends that the data confirm the impression that males in the younger generation are more considerate of the wife's sexual needs and satisfaction and limit their sexual activity to frequencies more desirable to the wife.

The Kinsey data strongly support the contention that it is the male rather than the female who is chiefly responsible for the regularity of marital coitus. The regularity of coitus is more than a matter of physical urge; Kinsey found that the more religiously devout males carried their moral attitudes over into marriage and kept the coital rates lower in marriage than did the less devout husbands. That the rates for religiously-devout and less-devout females were essentially the same supports the contention that it was not the wife so much as the husband who controlled regularity.

Age and sexual intimacy. Kinsey found a steady decline with age in the frequency of coitus in marriage. From the high of 2.8 times per week for those married in their late teens, the frequency dropped to about once in twelve days (0.6 times per week) for those age sixty. Kinsey attributes the steady decline to the aging process in the male,[25] for there is little evidence of any aging in the sexual capacities of the female. According to Masters and Johnson there is no reason why menopause should blunt the human female's sexual capacity, performance, or drive: "The healthy aging woman normally has sex drives that need to be resolved."[26] As we previously pointed out though, it is the male who is largely responsible for controlling the coital rate.

Coitus as a satisfying marital function is not restricted to the early years of marriage, however. In a sample of men sixty-five years of age and over (predominantly educators, business leaders, attorneys, engineers, physicians, clergymen, and writers), seventy percent of the married men responding engaged in coitus, and the majority reported a satisfying sexual life with satisfactory potency.[27] Masters and Johnson report that the male over sixty years of age usually will be satisfied with one or, at the most, two ejaculations a week regardless of the number of coital opportunities or the depth of his female partner's sexual demand.[28]

[25] Alfred C. Kinsey, Wardell B. Pomeroy, and Clyde E. Martin, *Sexual Behavior in the Human Male* (Philadelphia: Saunders, 1948), pp. 252–257.

[26] Masters and Johnson, *op. cit.*, pp. 246–247.

[27] Mark Tarail, "Sex Over 65," *Sexology*, XXVIII (February, 1962), 440–445.

[28] Masters and Johnson, *op. cit.*, p. 249.

Sexual intimacy and marital success.   Empirical evidence supports the contention that satisfying sexual involvement with spouse is important to success in marriage. Kirkpatrick, in an exhaustive review of the literature on post-marital factors related to success in marriage, concluded that early and adequate orgasm capacity ranked first.[29] The failure of the woman to reach orgasm is a potential source of disappointment to the husband, especially among the better educated, younger group of males who feel under some obligation to see that the spouse secures gratification in coitus comparable to their own gratification.

Kinsey makes it clear that orgasm must not be taken as the sole criterion for determining the degree of satisfaction in sexual activity. The woman may experience considerable pleasure in sexual arousal which does not proceed to the point of orgasm, as well as in the social aspects of a sexual relationship. Whether or not she reaches orgasm herself, she may find satisfaction in knowing that her husband has enjoyed the contact and in realizing that she has contributed to his pleasure. Kinsey also reports histories of marriages of long duration in which the wife has never responded to the point of orgasm, but where the marriage has been maintained because of the high quality of the other adjustments in the marriage.

Social class and sexual intimacy.   Limited evidence of patterns of marital sexuality among the lower classes suggests a generally negative attitude toward wives' enjoyment of sexual relations. Rainwater hypothesizes that where there is a high degree of segregation in the role relationships of lower-status husbands and wives, the couple does not develop a close sexual relationship and the wife does not look upon sexual relations with her husband as gratifying. Sexual relations appear to exist for the pleasure of the man, and the enjoyment of the woman is either optional or disapproved. The lower value place on mutual sexual satisfaction can be seen as a part of the generalized pattern of separateness in the marital relationship in the lower classes.[30]

Children

Conception Control.   Enjoyment of coitus in marriage involves control of the procreative capacity of the couple. For the sterile couple wanting children, it involves finding the procedures—technical, medical, or surgical —that will render them fertile. Their childlessness may be the result of either the male's failure to impregnate or the female's failure to conceive. Down through the ages the female has been commonly regarded as the barren one, for the reason that a man who is functionally able to have coitus

[29] Clifford Kirkpatrick, *The Family as Process and Institution* (New York: Ronald Press, 1955), p. 394.
[30] Rainwater, *op. cit.* (see above, fn. 14).

may feel confident of his fertility. Actually, he may be sexually potent yet sterile; sterility involves only the presence or lack of spermatozoa in the semen. The male is solely or partially responsible for the involuntary childlessness of the couple in about half of those cases where some abnormality is found. If both partners are low in fertility, the marriage may be childless even though both spouses are capable of having children with a more fertile partner. Treatment of infertility is not impossible, though complicated; it is a relatively new field of research and practice.[31]

If the wife is fertile and the husband irremediably sterile or if both are fertile but conception does not occur, conception may be brought about by artificial (or therapeutic) insemination. Artificial insemination is of two kinds, homologous (wherein the husband's seminal fluid is used) and heterologous (where the semen is obtained from an outside donor). The medical aspects of artificial insemination are relatively simple, but the physiological, legal, psychological, and moral implications of heterologous insemination call forth the counsel of caution from both medical authorities and those religious authorities representing denominations that do not unequivocally brand heterologous insemination as wrong.

But sterile couples are in the minority; most couples are fertile though the degree of fertility may vary greatly from couple to couple and over time for a specific couple. For most couples, therefore, the problem of conception is in the nature of how to prevent too frequent conception rather than how to initiate conception. To be fully acceptable, a conception control method must not be injurious to the health of the user, must be reliable, inexpensive, free from interference with the spontaneity of the sex act, and psychologically, morally, and aesthetically acceptable to the couple. There are about a dozen methods currently in use that are regarded as not injurious. Of the newer methods, pills made of a steroid chemical which are taken orally and stop ovulation temporarily have been effective in preventing pregnancy; newer-type intrauterine devices also show promise.[32]

Sterilization procedures have enjoyed a growing popularity as a conception control method, primarily for use after the couple have had as many (or more) children than desired. Reactions of sterilized persons (especially males) to the operation is being studied. Of twenty-nine mainly skilled and semi-skilled workers who filled out a questionnaire, most reported increased enjoyment of coitus both for themselves and for their wives after the operation.[33] Rodgers found in data obtained from forty-eight subjects that most had tried alternative forms of contraceptives and found them to be a nuisance and

[31] Alan F. Guttmacher and the editors of Consumer Reports, *The Consumers Union Report on Family Planning* (Mount Vernon, N.Y.: Consumers Union of U.S., 1962).
[32] Alan F. Guttmacher, Winfield Best, and Frederick S. Jaffe, *Planning Your Family* (New York: Macmillan, 1964), pp. 67–69.
[33] Thomas and Shirley B. Poffenberger, "Vasectomy as a Preferred Method of Birth Control: A Preliminary Investigation," *Marriage and Family Living*, XXV (August, 1963), 326–333.

somewhat ineffective.[34] The findings support seemingly contradictory conclusions. There is expressed satisfaction with the operation and self-reports of either no change or favorable change in subjects' sexual, personal, and family lives with concurrent evidence of increased dysphoria and maladjustment, associated in some subjects with sexual decline. The operation may have adverse psychological effects for some persons who nevertheless profess satisfaction with it; they may be reluctant to admit that they have made a mistake. Sterilization may be disruptive for men whose psychosexual identification is vulnerable.[35]

The desire for children. Detroit-area wives counted children second only to companionship with the husband as a goal of marriage. Twenty-six percent listed the chance to have children as the most valuable part of marriage and twenty-eight percent more listed it second; fewer farm wives (22 percent) mentioned children first.

The desire for children was nearly universal. Marriages childless by choice were practically nonexistent. Good things about having children are listed in Table 15.3.

TABLE 15.3. GOOD THINGS ABOUT HAVING CHILDREN IN DETROIT-AREA CITY AND FARM FAMILIES

	Place of Residence	
	City	Farm
1. Pleasure, emotional satisfaction	48%	35%
2. Companionship for parents	18	24
3. Gives life purpose, meaning	16	17
4. Strengthens family, makes a real home	12	15
5. Strengthens marriage, brings husband and wife closer together	4	3
6. Children help parents, provide security	2	6
7. Nothing good	*	—
Total	100%	100%
Number of Families	599	155

* One case

SOURCE: Robert O. Blood and Donald M. Wolfe, *Husbands and Wives: The Dynamics of Married Living* (Glencoe, Ill.: The Free Press, 1960), p. 138.

[34] David A. Rogers, Frederick J. Ziegler, Patricia Rohr, and Robert J. Prentiss, "Sociopsychological Characteristics of Patients Obtaining Vasectomies from Urologists," *Marriage and Family Living*, XXV (August, 1963), 331–335.

[35] David A. Rodgers, Frederick J. Ziegler, John Altrocchi, and Nissim Levy, "A Longitudinal Study of the Psycho-Social Effects of Vasectomy," *Journal of Marriage and the Family*, XXVII (February, 1965), 59–64.

When asked what had been some of the good things about not having children, 36 percent of the childless wives could think of nothing good at all. The most common benefit (mentioned by 27 percent) was freedom from responsibility. Financial advantages in having fewer dependents was mentioned by 18 percent, and 9 percent appreciated not having to care for children and being able to enjoy the husband's companionship unencumbered by children.

Companionship was primarily what the wives reported that they missed in not having children. Forty-five percent reported that it was lonely being childless. An additional 27 percent felt that life without children lacked purpose; home was not complete or the role as woman was not fulfilled. Not having children reflected disappointed expectations; 9 percent of the childless couples reported that they felt especially frustrated when they looked at other families and saw what experiences they were missing.

TABLE 15.4. PREFERRED NUMBER OF CHILDREN IN DETROIT-AREA CITY AND FARM FAMILIES

Preferred Number of Children*	Place of Residence	
	City	Farm
None	3%	1%
One	2	3
Two	23	18
Three	24	25
Four	36	37
Five	5	6
Six	4	7
More than Six	3	3
Total	100%	100%
Mean	3.42	3.57
Number of families	724	174

* "If you could choose, or if you could start over again, how many children would you want to have?"

SOURCE: Robert O. Blood and Donald M. Wolfe, *Husbands and Wives: The Dynamics of Married Living* (Glencoe, Ill.: The Free Press, 1960), p. 118.

Blood and Wolfe labeled as deviant cases the 3 percent of all wives who wouldn't have wanted children if they had their lives to live over again. Most of these women had succeeded in avoiding childbirth. They could see nothing bad in not having children and usually gave economic reasons for not having them.

The one wife who complained that nothing was good about having children and who would go through life childless if she had it to do over again was grade-school educated, was very dissatisfied with her marriage, and her oldest child was past eighteen years of age and still living at home.

Preferred number of children.   As has been shown in other studies, the majority (eighty percent or more in the Detroit study) preferred either two, three, or four children. Not only did they choose this size family for themselves, but ninety-three percent of the Detroit wives and almost as many farm wives in the Detroit area gave between two and four as the "ideal number of children for the average American family."

Most wives did not expect to have their desired number of children. Nearly all who expected to miss their ideal felt that they would fall short of the mark rather than exceed it; nearly nine-tenths of those who expected to miss the mark expected a deficiency of children. Few complained that they expected more children than they would like.

Disadvantages of having children.   When asked what problems children present, the sentiment that "nothing is bad about having children" may be a nostalgic reaction because the statement was most often made by wives who no longer had any children living at home.[36] Others making the point were most commonly women too old to have any more children. Wives who had been unable to have any children or wives who had severe deficiencies due to physical difficulties also expressed this attitude. Factors reported as creating problems in the home due to the presence of children are listed in Table 15.5.

TABLE 15.5.   PROBLEMS CHILDREN PRESENT, BY STAGE IN FAMILY LIFE CYCLE, AS REPORTED IN DETROIT-AREA STUDY

| | | *Stage in Family-Life Cycle* | | | | |
| | | *Age of Oldest Child* | | | | |
Problems Children Present		*Under 6*	*6–12*	*13–18*	*19–*	*Postparental*
1. None		21%	22%	36%	39%	54%
2. Financial		14	19	10	17	10
3. Illness		15	19	12	9	10
4. Burdens		21	13	16	20	9
5. Worries		10	11	17	8	12
6. Restrictions		19	15	9	5	5
7. Conflict		—	1	—	2	—
Total		100	100	100	100	100
Number of Families		127	137	101	64	79

SOURCE: Robert O. Blood and Donald M. Wolfe, *Husbands and Wives: The Dynamics of Married Living* (Glencoe, Ill.: The Free Press, 1960), p. 118.

[36] Blood and Wolfe, *op. cit.,* p. 143.

Women who preferred fewer children than they had complained of the burden of caring for so many children and of the financial cost. Saddled with these tangible responsibilities, they seldom mentioned the loss of social life or merely worrying about children. The three top-ranking problems for college-educated wives and for families of high social status, on the other hand, were the burdensomeness of caring for children, worry, and restrictions. Being homebound and unable to participate in activities outside the home were seen as restrictions. It was financial problems and illness that plagued low-status wives, especially nonwhite wives. Thirty-nine percent of all nonwhite wives referred to economic hardships involved in raising children.[37] Couples in the Fairchild and Wynn study also saw children as contributing to one of their chief complaints, lack of time with spouse.[38]

Blood and Wolfe observe that children appear to have contrasting effects on different aspects of marriage. Young children may be treated as an expression of love and affection between husband and wife but not as associated with unfettered leisure-time companionship or a nice home and a high material standard of living. They found that wives who stressed the companionship they received from their children lacked companionship with their husbands. Children were apparently serving as a substitute source of love and companionship for emotionally estranged wives.

Wives were primarily concerned about the hardships experienced by their children, secondarily concerned by the extra burdens they had incurred personally, and hardly at all by the repercussions on their relationship to their husbands. No data were collected on the reaction of husbands to the dedication to children and to the maternal role.

Optimum number of children. Children can be a source of strength in marriage provided there are not too many of them, according to evidence from the Detroit study. Blood and Wolfe found that marital love tended to be strongest in homes with a moderate number (three) of children. The impact of more children than this moderate number on the husband-wife relationship seemed to be deleterious. Blood and Wolfe saw this as related to the fact that mothers of more than three or four children often wish they didn't have so many. However, some women want more children because they are dissatisfied with their husbands; and some women—such as those of low status, poorly educated, and immigrant groups, for instance—perhaps wouldn't have much more satisfactory marriages if they had fewer children, according to Blood and Wolfe.[39]

[37] *Ibid.,* p. 144.
[38] Fairchild and Wynn, *op. cit.* (see above, fn. 13), p. 149.
[39] Blood and Wolfe, *op. cit.,* pp. 262–263.

SUMMARY

Marriage as a social system has a different structure and different functions than the family as a social system. It does some injustice to the facts to treat marriage as a subsystem of the family system in American society.

The goals of marriage include affective attachment, companionship, sexual intimacy, confidence, and the procreation of children in moderation. The marked emphasis on effective attachment is seen as both a goal and a weakness of marriage.

The nature of the marital relationship is in part related to social class status.

Though children are a condition to rather than an integral part of a marriage, the majority of American couples choose to bear and rear children. Children are viewed as a pleasure and a source of emotional satisfaction, as companions, as giving life purpose or meaning. Two to four children is regarded as the ideal family size.

BIBLIOGRAPHY

Jessie Bernard. "The Adjustments of Married Mates," *Handbook of Marriage and the Family,* ed. Harold T. Christensen. Chicago: Rand McNally, 1964. Pp. 675–739.

Robert O. Blood and Donald M. Wolfe. *Husbands and Wives: The Dynamics of Married Living.* Glencoe, Ill.: The Free Press, 1960.

Lee G. Burchinal and Loren E. Chancellor. "Ages at Marriage, Occupation of Grooms, and Interreligious Marriage Rates," *Social Forces,* XL (May, 1962), 348–354.

Ernest W. Burgess and Paul Wallin. *Engagement and Marriage.* Chicago: Lippincott, 1953.

John H. Burma. "Interethnic Marriages in Los Angeles, 1948–1959," *Social Forces,* XLII (December, 1963), 156–165.

Nelson Foote. "New Roles for Men and Women," *Marriage and Family Living,* XXIII (November, 1961), 325–329.

Nelson Foote. "Sex as Play," *Social Problems,* I (April, 1954), 159–163.

Hannah Gavron. *The Captive Wife: Conflicts of Housebound Mothers.* London: Routledge & Kegan Paul, 1966.

Alan F. Guttmacher, Winfield Best, and Frederick S. Jaffe. *Planning Your Family.* New York: Macmillan, 1964.

Jerold S. Heiss. "Degree of Intimacy and Male-Female Interaction," *Sociometry,* XXV (June, 1962), 197–208.

Georg Karlsson. *Adaptability and Communication in Marriage* (2nd rev. ed.). Totowa, N.J.: Bedminister, 1963.

Alfred C. Kinsey, Wardell B. Pomeroy, Clyde Martin and Paul H. Gebhard. *Sexual Behavior in the Human Female.* Philadelphia: Saunders, 1953.

Alfred C. Kinsey, Wardell B. Pomeroy, and Clyde E. Martin. *Sexual Behavior in the Human Male.* Philadelphia: Saunders, 1948.

Mirra Komarovsky. *Blue-Collar Marriage.* New York: Random House, 1964.

Judson T. Landis and Mary G. Landis. *Building a Successful Marriage.* Englewood Cliffs, N.J.: Prentice-Hall, 1958.

Eleanore B. Luckey. "Number of Years Married as Related to Personality Perception and Marital Satisfaction," *Journal of Marriage and the Family,* XXVIII (February, 1966), 44–48.

Floyd M. Martinson. *Marriage and the American Ideal.* New York: Dodd, Mead, 1960.

William H. Masters and Virginia E. Johnson. *Human Sexual Response.* Boston: Little, Brown, 1966.

John E. Mayer. *Jewish-Gentile Courtships.* Glencoe, Ill.: The Free Press, 1961.

Herbert J. Miles and Brooke R. Johnson. "Marriage Ceremony Trends," *Family Life,* XXIII (April, 1963), 1–4.

Herbert J. Miles and Ray F. Koonce. "The Attitudes of Unmarried People Toward Marriage," *The Midwest Sociologist,* XXI (December, 1958), 39–43.

Harriet F. Pilpel and Theodora Zavin. *Your Marriage and the Law.* New York: Rinehart, 1952.

Lee Rainwater. "Marital Sexuality in Four Cultures of Poverty," *Journal of Marriage and the Family,* XXVI (November, 1964), 457–466.

David A. Rodgers, Frederick J. Ziegler, John Altrocchi, and Nissim Levy. "A Longitudinal Study of the Psycho-Social Effects of Vasectomy," *Journal of Marriage and the Family,* XXVII (February, 1965), 59–64.

Erich Rosenthal. "Studies of Jewish Intermarriage in the United States," Reprint from *American Jewish Year Book,* LXIV (1963), 3–53.

William Silverman and Reuben Hill. "Task Allocation in Marriage in the United States and Belgium," *Journal of Marriage and the Family,* XXIX (May, 1967), 353–359.

Marvin B. Sussman. "Parental Participation in Mate Selection," *Social Forces,* XXXII (1954), 76–81.

Jean A. Wells. "15 Years after College: A Study of Alumnae of the Class of 1945," U.S. Department of Labor, *Women's Bureau Bulletin,* CCLXXXIII (1962), 1–26.

Robert F. Winch. *Mate Selection: A Study of Complementary Needs.* New York: Harper, 1958.

PART VI

Crises and Their Resolution

CHAPTER 16

Marriage Crises

A MONOGAMOUS MARRIAGE is a unique social system in that its membership is restricted to two and only two adults. Hence a marriage in no case lasts beyond the life span of the initiating parties. If the marriage is dissolved and either of the partners remarries, the marriage is not a continuation of the first marriage; it constitutes a new marriage. Compared with other social systems, marriage and family are relatively short-lived. It is not unusual for other social units to continue to function beyond centenary; relatively few marriages continue beyond the "golden anniversary" —the fiftieth year, being limited by the life span of the partners.

Marriage is a system of process. Since it deals with life in process, a marriage system benefits less from experience than do most social systems. Its opportunities to deal effectively with a particular phase in the lives of its two participants are limited because each phase is a passing phase. Groups that continue to exist beyond the life span of their charter members accumulate a knowledge and wisdom from repeated experiences that is not shared in a marriage. A marriage goes through nonrepeatable cyclical phases.

Following early marriage there is a period of marriage plus parenthood with its various stages of preschool child, school child, and launching, and finally a period of post-parental marriage when the last child has departed from the home. Affective attachment through all the vicissitudes of changing conditions is a demanding goal of marriage. One would expect the proportion of failures to be high. The adjustments made necessary by changing conditions are complex and far-reaching; and the participants are relatively inexperienced, if not naïve, in advance of the onset of each new condition.

Despite all of this, Blood and Wolfe found in their Detroit-area sample that wives were relatively well satisfied with their marriages. Although few wives felt that their marriages could not be improved upon, the average wife was not far from enthusiastic.[1] Wives were satisfied with the way the marriage functioned; with the extent to which their husbands met their needs for companionship, children, understanding, love, and a comfortable standard of living.

[1] Robert O. Blood, Jr., and Donald M. Wolfe, *Husbands and Wives: The Dynamics of Married Living* (Glencoe, Ill.: The Free Press, 1960), p. 252.

322

An important source of marital satisfaction for the wife is the husband's prestige or standing in the community. Wives of men who were struggling to achieve status could take comfort in the thought that their children would experience a more satisfying way of life than they had known. Lowest status families, especially nonwhite families, found married life to be dissatisfying, as was life in general. These were the most unstable families in the community, most liable to divorce and desertion. A satisfactory family life under adverse conditions was found to be a rare achievement.

TENSION MANAGEMENT IN MARRIAGE

Both husbands and wives are subject to emotional disturbances and distractions which must be dealt with if a marriage is to be maintained and its goals are to be met. A successful marriage functions to keep its participants happy and free from the loneliness experienced by persons without friends or companions. Spouses realize that there must be interchange between the partners; they must give as well as receive satisfaction if the marriage is to be maintained.

Tension develops in marriage even before the first glow of romance has worn off. Adjustment and the need for tension management are apparent from the start.[2] There may be nothing that so effectively promotes the unity of conflicting parties as their ability to be objective and their ability to rely on deliberation and discussion: in other words, to enhance the intellectual while reducing the volitional form of the antagonism.[3] But to reduce the personal involvement in conflict is exceedingly difficult in a relationship built on the very element that needs to be subordinated in order to solve the conflict. To remove the emotive, feeling element from a relationship that is built on feeling leaves little for objective analysis. It is possible to deal rationally with conditions to the love relationship but difficult for the participants to translate into reason the emotional elements themselves.[4]

A problem of singular difficulty to the newly married couple is the impossibility of shifting duties or responsibilities onto the group. Once one

[2] Thomas P. Monahan, "When Married Couples Part: Statistical Trends and Relationships in Divorce," *American Sociological Review,* XXVII (October, 1962), 625–633.

[3] Georg Simmel, "The Number of Members as Determining the Sociological Form of the Group," *The American Journal of Sociology,* VIII (July, 1902), 1–46.

[4] Kenkel found that married college students show no great ability to judge aspects of the roles they play in decision-making sessions. Couples appear to be "unpracticed at even the relatively superficial degree of analysis necessary to recognize the part they play in a simple and structured interaction." A traditional conception of spousal roles appeared to characterize their interaction. Spouses expected influence to be differential, with the husband having the greater influence in decision-making. Husbands actually did have more influence but not nearly as much more as expected by the spouses. William F. Kenkel, "Observational Studies of Husband-Wife Interaction in Family Decision-Making," in Marvin B. Sussman, *Sourcebook in Marriage and The Family,* 2nd ed. (Boston: Houghton Mifflin, 1963).

member withdraws there is no group; there is only the other spouse. One can shift responsibility to his spouse, but the spouse is free to decline the responsibility. The decisive factor in a marriage is that each must perform, for when either refuses to do so only the other remains; there is no super-individual entity such as a group of three or more possesses. In a group of three persons, one can withdraw and a group remains. The very fact that each spouse knows that he can depend only on the other and not upon the group gives to marriage a tenuousness and an urgency that adds to the strain of adjustment and calls for personal responsibility and integrity or quickly reveals the immaturity or lack of concern for the other[5] on the part of the faltering member of the marriage.

A "marriage crisis" is defined as the breakdown of patterns of conduct and values which have been developed to guide the activities of husband and wife in relation to each other and in relation to external social systems.[6] A crisis may be either limited or general in scope, mild or severe in its effect on the marriage.

PARENTHOOD AS CRISES

Having a child, particularly the first child, disrupts marital routines and calls for the modification of conduct and values of both husband and wife. The crisis of birth normally affects conduct and values of the spouses differently. It may be a major crisis for the wife in that her occupational and social roles are markedly altered; it may be a minor crisis for the husband in that there is little interruption of his occupational role.

The parent-child relationship is another source of crisis. Fairchild and Wynn found couples responding with high involvement and interest to difficulties in parent-child relationships. The couples regarded parenthood, not marriage, as requiring the greater maturity.[7] Couples appeared to be romantic and more ill-prepared to face the realities of parenthood than they are the realities of marriage. Of forty-six couples interviewed, LeMasters found that thirty-eight, or 83 percent, reported extensive or severe crisis in adjust-

[5] Feldman and Rand found that if a married person is predominantly egocentric (self-concern with no concern for the other), he or she is most likely to win in conflict situations with the spouse; if cocentric (concern for self and other), a married person is most likely to be in a both-win situation; and if predominantly altercentric (denial of self in concern for needs of the other), the person is most likely to lose in conflict situations with the spouse. Harold Feldman and Martin E. Rand, "Egocentrism—Altercentrism in the Husband-Wife Relationship," *Journal of Marriage and the Family*, XXVII (August, 1965), 386–391.

[6] Bernard Farber, "Family Organization and Crisis: Maintenance of Integration in Families with a Severely Mentally Retarded Child," *Monographs of the Society for Research in Child Development*, XXV (1960), 1–95.

[7] Roy W. Fairchild and John Charles Wynn, *Families in the Church: A Protestant Survey* (New York: Association, 1961), p. 140.

ing to the first child.[8] Even though in thirty-five of the thirty-eight cases pregnancy was either planned, or unplanned but desired, the prospective parents appeared to be almost completely unprepared by training or experience to receive a baby into their homes. The crisis did not prove to be so severe or pervasive, however, but that all but a few eventually made what appeared to be a successful adjustment to parenthood.

Since marriage and the family are separate social systems, the crisis of parenthood must not be underestimated. It is precisely the birth of a child to a married couple that signals the beginning of a family. A marriage is a social unit structured around the similarities in age and sophistication of its members; a family is a social unit whose major interactions involve persons of marked age differences and differences in sophistication. A marriage is unique in that it does not add any members after its initial formation; hence it is distinct from most social systems—processing new recruits is no part of its function. The family, on the other hand, has the processing of new recruits as a central function and its recruits are the "rawest" recruits imaginable—newborn babies without the benefit of prior socialization.

There is a sociological enrichment in a three-person system (family) that is lacking in a two-person system (marriage). It is possible, however, that the relationship of a husband and wife might be so close that any third party as a condition to the marriage—even their own offspring—is treated as an interloper. A child as a condition to marriage, even though he could be indirectly an element of cohesion, might equally well operate as an impediment to marital interaction. Every mediator inserts itself between the elements to be combined and thus separates in the very act of uniting. There is no system of three in which interaction in pairs—leaving out one member—does not occur. This interaction in pairs—husband and wife to the neglect of the child, mother and baby to the neglect of the husband— may be harmless or acute, momentary or permanent. Sometimes, however, marital crisis develops only after the last child has departed from the home and the couple realizes that the marriage has died from neglect during the time that child rearing was a condition to the marriage.[9]

Blood and Wolfe delineate three trends that help to fill any void that may exist for the wife on the departure of the last child from the home, when her major family-system functions have been fulfilled.[10] First, wives continue mothering in the grandmother role; secondly, the housewife may resume work outside the home; and, thirdly, the husband-wife relationship may be enhanced when the wife has finished with the child-rearing phase of her life.

[8] E. E. LeMasters, "Parenthood as Crisis," *Marriage and Family Living,* XIX (November, 1957), 352–355.

[9] Margaret Mead, "The Contemporary American Family as an Anthropologist Sees It," *American Journal of Sociology,* LIII (May, 1948), 453–459.

[10] Blood and Wolfe, *op. cit.* (see above, fn. 1), p. 72.

If parenthood causes a marriage to disintegrate, then parenthood would have to be regarded as a tragic condition of marriage. On the other hand, if the marriage has remained strong and vital throughout the parenthood period the post-parental marriage period may be viewed with optimism and eagerness as the married pair again turn to some of the concerns they had prior to the parenthood period or that they have subsequently developed.

DISENCHANTMENT

A progressive loss of satisfaction in marriage appears to be a consequence of the passage of time in the marriage. This decrease in satisfaction or wearing away at the strength of marriage is referred to as disenchantment,[11] corrosion,[12] or the devitalized mode.[13]

The first months of marriage are characterized by a high degree of euphoria. Society, under the romantic influence, tells young couples that the honeymoon will be the height of ecstatic experience. The couple members are carried along by their fondness for each other, their enthusiasm about their romance, and the excitement of new experiences.[14] This early euphoria must subside, however, for people cannot continue to live at a high emotional pitch indefinitely. Conflicts arise in the process of adjustment. The conflicts will likely be resolved, but the very thought of conflicts in the love relationship has a sobering effect.

Kirkpatrick and Hobart[15] present empirical evidence of disenchantment early in marriage. They found a phase movement during early marriage that demonstrated more apparent disagreement than existed in the premarital phases of the relationship. For men, at least, a slight association appears to exist between increases in such disagreement and the tendency to romanticize during the premarital phase.

Pineo[16] found that men suffer more disenchantment in the earlier years of marriage than do women. The adjustment scores were approximately equal at engagement; by the time of early marriage, though, the men had adjustment scores that were typically lower than those for women. Dis-

[11] Peter C. Pineo, "Disenchantment in the Later Years of Marriage," *Marriage and Family Living*, XXIII (February, 1961), 3–11.

[12] Blood and Wolfe, *op. cit.* (see above, fn. 1), 263–264.

[13] John F. Cuber and Peggy B. Harrof, *The Significant Americans: A Study of Sexual Behavior among the Affluent* (New York: Appleton-Century, 1965), pp. 46–50.

[14] Willard H. Waller and Reuben Hill, *The Family: A Dynamic Interpretation* (New York: Dryden, 1951), p. 253.

[15] Clifford Kirkpatrick and Charles Hobart, "Disagreement, Disagreement Estimates and Non-Empathetic Imputations for Intimacy Groups Varying from Favorite Date to Married," *American Sociological Review*, XIX (February, 1954), 10–19; Charles W. Hobart, "Disillusionment in Marriage and Romanticism," *Marriage and Family Living*, XX (May, 1958), 156–192.

[16] Pineo, *op. cit.*, p. 10.

enchantment of the male was even more apparent when late-divorcing couples in the sample were compared with couples who were still married in the middle-years period. ("Middle years" is used to indicate couples married for up to twenty years.) The still-married men had had a mean engagement adjustment score of 148.2 and a mean early marriage adjustment score of 156.1. (This amount of "gain" represents a loss in adjustment because the engagement and early marriage adjustment scores are not exactly comparable.) The late-divorcing men, on the other hand, had a higher mean engagement adjustment score, 151.5 (3.3 points higher) and a mean early marriage adjustment score of 147.1 (9.0 points lower). It was the magnitude and the speed of disenchantment that characterized these husbands. Late-divorcing women, on the other hand, had scores of 144.1 and 144.7 and still-married women had scores of 149.0 and 150.2. The late-divorcing women began with a below-average mean adjustment score and although their losses were greater than the still-married women, their initially low mean adjustment was a factor in divorce. The women who divorced late in marriage tended to have doubts during the engagement period, but they did not act on them until late in the marriage. Men were more inclined to break the engagement if they had doubts.

Blood and Wolfe found that the arrival of children offset disenchantment; marital satisfaction tended to be heightened by the fulfillment of the desire for children. Even though the children's coming impaired the standard of living and the husband-wife companionship, the increased sense of understanding and love which young mothers experienced offset this. Conversely, by the time childless couples had been married as many as four to seven years, the disappointment of childlessness affected the wife's satisfaction to the extent that tangible compensations, like a high standard of living and continued husband-wife companionship, hardly compensated for the sense of tragedy.

In the middle years, Pineo found a general drop in marital satisfaction and adjustment. Men's early and sharp decrease in enchantment is contrasted with the larger increase in disenchantment for wives from early marriage to the middle years. As a result of gradual decrease in enchantment for women, the adjustment scores of husbands and wives are again equal (147.6 for husbands and 147.5 for wives) in the middle years. This finding is supported by the Blood and Wolfe data; whereas 52 percent of Detroit-area women married no more than two years expressed themselves as very satisfied with their marriage, only six percent among those married twenty years were very satisfied. Twenty-one percent were conspicuously dissatisfied.[17] Once the preschool stage of dependency (dependency of the child on the mother and of the mother on the husband) was passed, de-

17 Blood and Wolfe, *op. cit.* (see above, fn. 1), p. 264.

clining satisfaction characterized each succeeding stage in the family-life cycle, but the lessened enthusiasm was offset by deepened habituation in the later years.

A loss of certain types of intimacy in the later years of marriage has been noted. Confiding, kissing, and reciprocal settlement of disagreements become less frequent, and more persons report themselves as being lonely. Though Pineo did not find a major link between disenchantment and lessened sharing of activities or the reduction in frequency of coitus, Blood and Wolfe found a decline in satisfaction reflected in observable decreases in the number of things husbands and wives did with each other.

Personal adjustment and personality characteristics appear relatively unaffected by the process of disenchantment or loss of intimacy.[18] Perhaps middle-aged husbands and wives find satisfaction outside of marriage—in friends, employment, children—because they seldom find as much in each other as do younger couples.[19]

It may be reasonable to attribute the early decline in enchantment to exaggerated idealization of the mate or to intense romanticizing, but since the changes producing later disenchantment cannot be foretold, it is misleading to attribute the causes of later disenchantment to a lack of realism. Disenchantment after five years of marriage may be attributable to unforeseen changes in situation, personality, or behavior.

Is it not possible that unforeseen changes might result in increases as well as decreases in marital satisfaction? Pineo reasons that it is not. Marriage by personal confrontation implies that a couple has a self-contrived high degree of fit between the persons at the time they marry. For example, couples who marry in part because of identical social attitudes could only retain or lose this characteristic; they could not improve upon it. To the extent that fit and satisfaction are maximized at the time of entry into marriage they cannot be improved upon; the only direction of movement is a reduction in satisfaction on these indices. It is possible that a couple might find new goals and new reasons for marital satisfaction later in life. Neither the Blood and Wolfe nor the Pineo data suggest this as a common occurrence, however. The grounds upon which the couple decided to marry deteriorate or are no longer relevant. The grounds may have been sufficient for a high degree of satisfaction early in marriage but may be less relevant to the circumstances of middle age.

According to Pineo, the largest decrease in satisfaction appeared to be associated with generalized feelings of disenchantment with the spouse and the marriage, and with the reduction of intimate interaction.[20] The practice of kissing, confiding, and reciprocity in the settlement of disagreements was lost by couples who lost marital adjustment between early marriage and

---

[18] Pineo, *op. cit.* (see above, fn. 11), p. 3.

[19] *Ibid.*, p. 264.

[20] Pineo, *op. cit.*, p. 9.

the middle years; and it was among these persons that loneliness grew. Finally, it was the loss of agreement on affection which made the highest contribution to disenchantment. Pineo concludes that the "patterns of behavior which would seem most appropriate to the newly married couple are not readily given up. Their loss . . . is accompanied by the growth of real regrets and dissatisfaction in the marriage and is a core part of the process of disenchantment."

DISORGANIZATION

The majority of married persons go through life with their original spouses. Among women married thirty years, four out of every five have married only once and of those married at age twenty-one or older fully nine out of every ten have not remarried.[21] Permanence is a goal of marriage in America. Not all marriages that are characterized by disorganization— the breakdown of interaction patterns of the spouses—disintegrate. Many maintain their marriages through disenchantment and disorganization despite the emphasis on personal freedom in this country. These include the marriages that Cuber and Harrof label as "conflict-habituated."[22] Marital disintegration by desertion, separation, or divorce is only a crude index of marital disorganization. To be included in LeMasters' sample of unsuccessful marriages[23] both husband and wife had to regard their marriage as unsuccessful; this condition must have persisted at least ten years, and the marriage had to be intact. Although it was beyond the scope of the study to attempt to ascertain why these partners had chosen each other, two observations are in order: (1) lengthy courtships in themselves do not necessarily prevent unsuccessful marriages—39 percent of the couples had gone together for over three years before marrying; (2) the theory of the unconscious nature of psychodynamic attraction between future marital partners merits further attention. Some of the most incompatible couples in the sample appeared to have been drawn toward each other by forces of which they had no real understanding.

Of the seventy-two husbands and wives in the sample, 56 percent had lost their faith in romance and were cynical if not bitter. LeMasters raised the question as to whether or not couples with a long history of conflict ever solve their marital problems. A follow-up of the couples revealed that of the twenty-nine still living together, not one couple had been able to work out what seemed to them to be a satisfactory marriage adjustment.

A commonly stated reason for staying together was the desire to give the children a normal home life (66 percent). There was also the hope, at least in the early years of discord, that matters would improve.

21 Paul C. Glick, *American Families* (New York: Wiley, 1957), pp. 110–112.
22 Cuber and Harrof, *op. cit.* (see above, fn. 13), pp. 44–46.
23 E. E. LeMasters, "Holy Deadlock: A Study of Unsuccessful Marriages," *The Midwest Sociologist*, XXI (July, 1959), 86–90.

Do disorganized but intact marriages result in personal disorganization of the partners? LeMasters found that they did. Twenty-seven of the thirty-six cases (75 percent) showed personal disorganization. The most frequent types were alcoholism, chronic psychosomatic illness, neurotic or psychotic behavior, occupational disorganization, extramarital affairs, and disenchantment. As a substitute for lack of marital satisfaction, the husbands turned to their jobs, liquor, or other women. Extramarital affairs tended to follow rather than to precede marital failure. Wives turned to their children, jobs, religion, or community service. Of the two sets of substitute satisfactions, it appeared that those of the husbands were potentially more destructive. Husbands appeared to be more severely damaged by chronic marital failure than were wives.

Kinsey found that a total of 26 percent of the female population in his study had had sex relations with men other than their husbands by the time they were forty years of age. After that age only a few females began to have extramarital coitus. He estimated that about half of all married males have intercourse with women other than their wives at some time during their married lives. However, there are few types of sexual activity that are carried on with less regularity than extramarital coitus. The opportunities occur only sporadically; secrecy is required; and many men limit their extramarital activities in order to avoid emotional attachments which might break up their marriage.

Not infrequently extramarital activities lead to the development of emotional attachments that interfere with the relations with the lawfully wedded spouse. Kinsey found some females who had been able to carry on extramarital affairs—even to experience emotional satisfaction in the extramarital relationships—while maintaining reasonably good relations with their husbands; but few of either sex had been able to carry on satisfactory emotional relationships with two or more partners simultaneously.

In a society that considers marital fidelity to be a symbol and proof of social conformity, lawfulness, and love, guilt reactions and consequent social difficulties often attend extramarital involvement. It was those females who had been able to accept their extramarital activity as a form of shared pleasure who did not so often get into difficulty over their extramarital relationships.

Generally speaking, Kinsey found that extramarital relations to be successful had to be kept secret from the spouse. Though males might feel that extramarital activity is desirable and not entirely wrong, many feared that their extramarital histories would become known.

Of wives who had had extramarital coitus, 51 percent thought that the husbands did not know; 9 percent thought husbands suspected; and in 40 percent of the cases the husband knew. Wives reporting on the difficulties that ensued when the husband learned of or suspected the infidelity included

42 percent in which there was serious difficulty and 16 percent with minor difficulty; in 42 percent of the cases no difficulty was reported.

Kinsey collected some histories of long-continued extramarital relationships which seemed to have interfered in no way with marriage unless or until the other partner found out about the infidelity. It appeared to be the knowledge of extramarital coitus rather than the behavior itself that caused damage to the marital relationship. In some cases, divorce proceedings ensue immediately upon discovery of the infidelity.

In those cases where no difficulty was reported, even where knowledge of the relationship existed, difficulty sometimes developed later on. There were instances of what appeared to be acceptance of the spouse's extramarital activity which developed into conflict situations later. Sometimes circumstances unrelated to the infidelity—such as a new economic situation, the development of some insecurity on the part of the other spouse, or the appearance of a new extramarital partner—developed into conflict over extramarital relationships some five or ten years after they had begun. In some cases the difficulty was caused by an extramarital pregnancy. In most cases these pregnancies were terminated by abortion; in some cases the child was reared by the mother either with or without her husband's knowledge of the child's parentage. In some instances the pregnancies resulting from extramarital coitus led to divorce. Kinsey concludes that the reconciliation of the married individual's desire for coitus with a variety of sex partners and the maintenance of a stable marriage presents a problem which has not been satisfactorily resolved.

DISINTEGRATION

Divorce

The divorce rate (including annulment), based on total population and on married female population aged fifteen and over for the years 1920–1964, is given in Table 16.1.

Divorces have generally declined in times of economic depression and risen during times of prosperity. The divorce rate per 1,000 females aged fifteen years and over—the more sensitive rate—reached a peak of 8.0 per 1,000 in 1929. In the fall of that year the stock-market crash signaled the beginning of an economic depression. The divorce rate dropped to its lowest point in the forty-year period 1920–60 during the depression years of 1932–33. Following the depression, the rate of divorce moved upward almost steadily until the first postwar year, 1946, when the rate reached the all-time high of 17.9 per 1,000 married females fifteen years of age and over. After 1946 the rate dropped steadily; the nation had returned to more normal living conditions for the majority of its people. The divorce rate showed considerable stability during the fifteen years 1950–64 with slight declines during

TABLE 16.1.   DIVORCE RATE FOR TOTAL U.S. POPULATION AND FOR MARRIED FEMALES, 1920–1964

		Rate per 1,000	
Year	Number (000's)	Popu-lation	Married female aged 15+
1920	171	1.6	8.0
1921	160	1.5	7.2
1922	149	1.4	6.6
1923	165	1.5	7.1
1924	171	1.5	7.2
1925	175	1.5	7.2
1926	185	1.6	7.5
1927	196	1.6	7.8
1928	200	1.7	7.8
1929	206	1.7	8.0
1930	196	1.6	7.5
1931	188	1.5	7.1
1932	164	1.3	6.1
1933	165	1.3	6.1
1934	204	1.6	7.5
1935	218	1.7	7.8
1936	236	1.8	8.3
1937	249	1.9	8.7
1938	244	1.9	8.4
1939	251	1.9	8.5
1940	264	2.0	8.8
1941	293	2.2	9.4
1942	321	2.4	10.1
1943	359	2.6	11.0
1944	400	2.9	12.0

the economic recession years of 1954 and 1958. The rate of divorce for the decade 1950–60 was less than one for every one hundred married couples. Of males fourteen years of age and over in the United States in 1960, 1.9 percent were divorced; the comparable figure in March, 1967 was 2.1 percent. For women 2.6 percent of those fourteen years of age and over in 1960 were divorced and 3.2 percent in March, 1967.[24]

Divorce rates reflect regional, residential, racial, and nationality differences, as well as economic differences. In 1955 the overall rate of divorces ranged from 40.7 per 1,000 population in Nevada to 0.8 per 1,000 population in North Dakota. When the variables of race and place of residence are held constant, a significantly larger proportion of the population divorced in

[24] U.S. Department of Commerce, "Marital Status and Family Status: March, 1967," *Population Characteristics*, February 23, 1968.

TABLE 16.1   DIVORCE RATE FOR TOTAL U.S. POPULATION AND FOR
MARRIED FEMALES, 1920–1964 (Continued)

Year	Number (000's)	Rate per 1,000 Population	Married female aged 15+
1945	485	3.5	14.4
1946	610	4.3	17.9
1947	483	3.4	13.6
1948	408	2.8	11.2
1949	397	2.7	10.6
1950	385	2.6	10.3
1951	381	2.5	9.9
1952	392	2.5	10.1
1953	390	2.5	9.9
1954	379	2.4	9.5
1955	377	2.3	9.3
1956	382	2.3	9.4
1957	381	2.2	9.2
1958	368	2.1	8.9
1959	395	2.2	9.3
1960	393	2.2	9.2
1961	414	2.3	9.6
1962	413	2.2	9.4
1963	428	2.3	9.6
1964	450	2.4	10.0

SOURCE: U.S. Department of Health, Education and Welfare, Public Health Service, National Center for Health Statistics, *Vital Statistics of the United States, 1964*, Vol. III: *Marriage and Divorce* (Washington, D.C., 1968), Section 2–5.

1950 was in the West. Of fifteen states with the highest divorce rates in 1950, only Florida was located east of the Mississippi River. Ten of the fifteen states with the lowest rates were located either in New England or along the Atlantic Coast. In 1960 the lowest rate was also in the Northeast; the West had the highest divorce rate.

Regarding place of residence, urban communities include a higher percentage of divorced persons than do rural communities. In urban areas, the reported percentages of women who are divorced and separated are substantially higher than those of men; women exceeded men in these statuses in 1960 by about one-third. Not all couples seeking divorces do so in their own community or even in their own state of residence. The states with more lenient grounds for divorce—states recognizing emotional or psychic grounds—receive temporary citizens seeking divorces and seeking relief from the legal restrictions of the conservative states—states emphasizing physical infidelity or physical abuse as the bases for dissolving marriage.

Marriage instability is most common in the nonwhite population in the United States. The social circumstances arising from being a member of a particular race plus factors of residence and sex help to account for the fact that urban nonwhite females have the highest proportion of divorced persons in the population.[25]

Duration of marriage prior to divorce. There has been a significant decrease in the duration of marriage prior to divorce in the past fifty years. At the turn of the century, the peak in divorces came in the fifth year of marriage; in the period 1922–32 it fluctuated between the third and the fourth year; and in 1950 divorces were at their highest in the first and second years of marriage. In 1960 more than 30 percent of all divorces occurred within less than four years, and over one-half occurred within less than eight years after marriage.[26]

In most marriages that terminate in divorce, there is a period of separation of varied length preceding the divorce. Hence there is a difference between the legal and the actual duration of marriage if we define duration of marriage as the length of time that the marriage partners lived together. Kephart found, in Philadelphia, that the peak year for separations was in the first year of marriage; the peak for divorces fell between the second and the fourth years of marriage.[27] Monahan, using data with reference to Wisconsin in particular, found that the overall length of marriage to divorce had not changed greatly for several generations but that there had been a slight lengthening of the time from marriage to separation and a shortening of the period from separation to divorce.[28] The decrease in divorce frequency in times of economic recession and the increase in times of prosperity may be explained in part through a redefinition of duration of marriage. It is possible that some couples who would separate in less prosperous times obtain their divorces in the ensuing period of prosperity.

Grounds for divorce. Marriage partners may separate for reasons known only to themselves, but divorce calls for legal procedures and the grounds for divorce become a public affair.[28a] The legal grounds for granting

[25] Benjamin E. Haddox, *A Review of the Research on Divorce in the United States 1900–1957* (Gainesville, Florida: University of Florida, June, 1960, unpublished Ph.D. thesis); E. Franklin Frazier, *The Negro Family in the United States* (Chicago: University of Chicago Press, 1939), p. 79.

[26] Hugh Carter and Alexander Plateris, "Trends in Divorce and Family Disruption," *Health, Education and Welfare Indicators,* September, 1963; reprint, pp. v–xiv.

[27] William M. Kephart, "The Duration of Marriage," *American Sociological Review,* XIX (June, 1954), 287–295.

[28] Monahan, *op. cit.* (see above, fn. 2).

[28a] California's new divorce law is something of an exception. A couple can merely state that "irreconcilable differences" exist, and if the judge accepts this a divorce can be granted without corroborating evidence from witnesses. Also, the idea of fault has been eliminated; the assumption is that both parties likely share blame for an unsuccessful marriage.

divorces are the patterns into which actual reasons for divorce must be fitted before the state recognizes the cause as valid and grants a couple the right to terminate their marital relationship. The law stipulates that a divorce suit must involve a legal contest—that is, the marriage partners seeking a divorce are not permitted to do anything that could be interpreted as subverting the element of contest. For instance, the parties to the divorce litigation cannot agree in advance to submit false evidence to support fictitious grounds for divorce. One of the partners cannot commit an offense for the sole purpose of creating grounds for an agreed-upon divorce nor agree with his spouse to withhold evidence that might support a defense against the charges. To cooperate illegally to subvert a *bona fide* legal contest is defined as collusion. The temptation to cooperate illegally to make the actual grounds for divorce fit the statutory limitations is a very real one particularly in states with very restricted bases for divorce.

Lawyers recognize the discrepancy between the statutory grounds for divorce and the actual causes of marital conflict. According to Haumsworth and Minnis lawyers regard the real causes to be financial problems, infidelity, drunkenness, and basic incompatibility.[29] The lawyers were also aware that marital discord was often the result of a multiplicity of causes rather than one single cause.

Thomas, in a study of cases appearing before a chancery separation court (Roman Catholic), lists the factors in order of frequency of occurrence in the breakdown of marriage as follows: drink, adultery, irresponsibility, temperament, in-laws, sex, mental factors, religion, and money.[30]

Determining the grounds for divorce is a right reserved to the individual states; hence there is lack of uniformity in divorce statutes from state to state. The grounds most commonly appearing in statutes are, in order of their universality, adultery, desertion, imprisonment or conviction of crime, cruelty, alcoholism, impotence, nonsupport, and insanity.[31]

The most commonly used grounds in actual divorce proceedings as reported in 1958, in order of frequency used, were—after cruelty, which was the grounds used in 51.8 percent of the cases—desertion (15.8 percent), drunkenness (1.8 percent), nonsupport (1.5 percent), and adultery (1.3 percent). No other grounds were used in more than one percent of the cases.[32]

[29] Harry C. Haumsworth and Mhyra S. Minnis, "Non-Statutory Causes of Divorce: The Lawyers's Point of View," *Marriage and Family Living*, XVII (November, 1955), 316–321.

[30] John L. Thomas, *The American Catholic Family* (Englewood Cliffs, N.J.: Prentice-Hall, 1956), p. 220 ff.

[31] Ray E. Baber, *Marriage and the Family* (New York: McGraw-Hill, 1953), p. 450.

[32] U.S. Department of Health, Education and Welfare, National Office of Vital Statistics, *Divorces and Annulments: Detailed Statistics for Reporting Areas*, Vital Statistics—Special Reports, National Summaries, XLVIII, No. 2 (Mar. 25, 1958), 34.

Strict divorce laws within a state may serve as a deterrent to divorce; migratory divorce with the requirement of establishing residence in a liberal state is not a live option for most married couples. Actually, strict divorce laws may result in a higher proportion of illegal marriage units, as marriage partners separate and form new marital unions without the benefit of divorce.[33]

Length of acquaintance of the marriage pair prior to marriage is related to success in marriage. Locke found that a very short engagement was much more characteristic of divorced than of happily married couples, with the differences more significant for women than for men. An engagement of twelve months or more was favorably related to marital success.[34] Goode also found a positive association between divorce, brief acquaintance, and short engagement. More than seventy percent of the divorced females in his sample had had engagements of six months or less.[35]

There appears to be a relationship between divorce and age at time of marriage, although the relationship is not altogether clear. The very young, those under twenty years of age, are overrepresented in the divorce statistics. Sixteen percent of the divorced males and 45 percent of the divorced females in Goode's sample had been married in 1960 before reaching their twentieth birthday, while only 13 percent of all males marrying in 1960 were under twenty years of age and about 37 percent of all females married in that year were under twenty years of age.

In an attempt to determine the relationship between age at marriage and divorce, Monahan analyzed 8,040 divorces in Iowa for the period 1945–47.[36] Divorced couples had married about one year earlier than other couples, and youthful marriages were of shorter duration; but age in and of itself did not appear to be a major factor in marital accord.

A number of studies have included data on age differentials. The results are not consistent, but other things being equal similarity in age appears to be positively associated with marital accord.

Sexual problems and divorce. Three sexual problems have been empirically demonstrated to be related to divorce: premarital pregnancy; sexual incompatibility; and extramarital sexual intercourse, or adultery. It is generally supposed that marriages solemnized under the urgency of premarital pregnancy may be hasty and ill-conceived marriages subject to more than their share of marital difficulty. Christensen found a relationship be-

[33] Raymond B. Stevens, "Illegal Families among the Units of Family Agencies," *Social Forces,* XIX (October, 1940), 84–87.

[34] Harvey J. Locke, *Predicting Adjustment in Marriage: A Comparison of a Divorced and a Happily Married Group* (New York: Holt, 1951), pp. 93–94.

[35] William J. Goode, *After Divorce* (Glencoe, Ill.: The Free Press, 1956), pp. 77–78.

[36] Thomas P. Monahan, "Does Age at Marriage Matter in Divorce?" *Social Forces,* XXXII (October, 1953), 81–87.

tween premarital pregnancy and divorce, with premarital pregnancy apparently a part of a divorce-producing complex. Conflicts which may already exist between the marriage pair are intensified by the pregnancy; this results in the increased likelihood of a divorce.[37]

The nature of the relationship between sexual incompatibility and divorce is less clear than that between premarital pregnancy and divorce, for it has not been clearly determined whether sexual maladjustment is primarily a cause of marital tension, a result of marital tension, or both. It is reasonable to expect that the intimate and sensitive sexual relationship might be disturbed by tensions in other aspects of the relationship, and, since couples expect happiness from sexual activity, it is reasonable to assume that disappointment in this area might lead to disenchantment.

Sexual maladjustment was alleged to be a causal factor in 15 percent of the cases in a study of divorce suits in Philadelphia. Kephart characterized the complaints as follows: in those cases in which the husband was plaintiff, the chief sexual cause of complaint centered around the failure of the wife to show sufficient interest in sexual relations. In cases where the wife was the plaintiff, the usual complaint was either that the husband wanted sexual relations too often or that he wanted to engage in sexual practices which the wife disapproved of, such as oral-genital contacts.[38]

Kephart made comparisons between couples with a sexual complaint and couples without a sexual complaint. He found that marriages involving a sexual complaint were of significantly shorter duration. The peak year for divorce in the sexual-complaint group was the first year of marriage, while for the group not listing a sexual complaint the peak was not reached until the fourth and fifth years. Kephart's study does not tell us whether the sexual-adjustment factor is cause or effect of marital tension. It suggests that of marriages which ultimately end in divorce the ones reporting sexual maladjustment are subject to earlier termination. Thomas concludes with Kephart that in marriages terminating after short duration, sexual maladjustment appears frequently as a complaint. However, Thomas found that for marriages ending in the middle or later years, adultery appeared to be a major disorganizing element. Of marriages ending in less than five years, adultery was a factor in nineteen percent of the cases. It was a factor in 34.4 percent of the marriages ending in the eleventh through the fifteenth year. It decreased as a complaint to 23.5 percent of the marriages that broke after twenty-one years or more of marriage. A majority of Locke's divorced couples also checked adultery as one cause of conflict.

[37] Harold Christensen, "Child Spacing Analysis Via Record Linkage: New Data Plus a Summing Up from Earlier Reports," *Marriage and Family Living*, XXV (August, 1963), 272–280.

[38] William M. Kephart, "Some Variables in Cases of Reported Sexual Maladjustment," *Marriage and Family Living*, XVI (August, 1954), 241–243.

Divorce and social status. Three indices of social status (economic, educational, and occupational) show an inverse relationship to divorce. The indices used are crude and the relationships not altogether clear. Goode has made a convincing presentation of the inverse relationship existing between divorce incidence and economic status. He bases his conclusions on previous studies, census data, and his own findings.[39]

Goode,[40] Kephart,[41] Monahan,[42] and Kirkpatrick,[43] show an inverse relationship between occupational status and divorce incidence. Monahan found that the professional class contributed somewhat less than its proportion of divorces; the official-management-owner group accounted for half of its expected share of divorces; and the clerical sales group contributed almost exactly its expected proportion. Descending the occupational scale, the differential increases. The laboring class had about four times as many divorces as might be expected and the labor service group about three times its expectancy. The upper classes, particularly the professional men, may not appear in the divorced categories in their true proportion because they have a greater likelihood of remarriage.

The relationship of educational level to divorce is not clear. There appears to be an inverse relationship in the case of men, but for women, especially college graduates, the relationship is not clear. College graduates have a fairly low incidence of divorce when compared with groups at lower educational levels. Women graduates, however, are more likely to appear in the divorced category than are men graduates. The differential in availability of marriage partners for divorced males and divorced females may reduce the number of males showing up in the divorced category since women outlive men.

Drinking and divorce. The results of a number of studies indicate a direct relationship between excessive drinking and the incidence of divorce. In Locke's study about one-half of the divorced women cited drunkenness as a contributing factor in their divorces (about the same proportion as designated adultery as a contributing factor). About a fourth of the divorced men indicated that drunkenness of their wives was a factor in their marital difficulties. Kephart found drinking to be a factor in about a fourth of all divorces.[44]

[39] William J. Goode, "Economic Factors and Marital Stability," *American Sociological Review,* XVI (1951), 802–812.

[40] *Ibid.*

[41] William M. Kephart, "Occupational Level and Marital Disruption," *American Sociological Review,* XX (August, 1955), 456–465.

[42] Thomas P. Monahan, "Divorce by Occupational Level," *Marriage and Family Living,* XVII (November, 1955), 322–324.

[43] Clifford Kirkpatrick, *The Family: As Process and Institution,* 2nd ed. (New York: Ronald, 1963), pp. 587–589.

[44] William M. Kephart, "Drinking and Marital Disruption," *Quarterly Journal of the Studies of Alcohol,* XV (March, 1954), 63–73.

The importance of drinking as a factor in the breakdown of marriages varied with the length of duration of marriage prior to the breakdown.[45] Drink (the term "drink" was used to cover those cases in which drinking appeared as the major factor in the maladjustment) accounted for 30 percent of the cases, and drinking plus adultery accounted for over one-half (approximately 55 percent) of all cases. Thomas concluded that drinking was a major cause of discord and not a factor that arose as a consequence of marital discord.

In marriages that lasted less than one year, drink was the sixth most common factor mentioned, being a factor in 9 percent of the cases. The importance of drink as a factor increased steadily for each five-year period. For marriages lasting less than five years, drink was the second most common factor listed (18 percent of the cases). In marriages that lasted from six to ten years, drink was the most commonly mentioned factor; and it continued to increase in importance until in marriages that lasted twenty-one years or more drink was a factor in 43 percent of the cases.

Whether drink is causal or symptomatic of marital discord is a moot question. Locke sees drunkenness as one of the factors symptomatic of underlying maladjustment in marriage or as an expression of basic personality needs that are not being met. Whatever its cause, such behavior is predictive of marital disruption. On the other hand, Thomas sees drunkenness *per se* as a significant disintegrating factor in marriage. The drinking habit appeared to have been acquired gradually and to have started disrupting smooth-running family relationships "before its full seriousness" was recognized. Whatever the reasons for men drinking, serious frustration did not appear to have played a major role in maladjustment in the marriages. By the time the seriousness of the drinking factor was realized, the drinking partner was enmeshed in such a web of relationships at home, on the job, and socially that it became impossible for him to break the habit. What happened to the marriage depended in part on the patience of the spouse. Frequently, she deteriorated as a person, and the marriage relationship deteriorated with the result that the husband's propensity to drink was increased. By the time the case reached the chancery court, the principals and the relationship had deteriorated to the extent that there appeared to be little hope of reconciliation short of an extended period of rehabilitation for both partners.

Divorce and religion. Marital adjustment has been shown to be associated with conventionality, and conventionality is made up in part of conformity to certain characteristic religious behavior patterns—attendance at Sunday School during childhood, a religious wedding ceremony, and church affiliation and attendance.[46] Marriages in which both partners claim a reli-

[45] Thomas, *op. cit.* (see above, fn. 30), p. 220 ff.
[46] Locke, *op. cit.* (see above, fn. 34), p. 237.

gious identity, and the same religious identity, have a low rate of divorce; marriages involving couples with no religious preference have been found to have the highest incidence of divorce.[47]

Marriages in which both spouses are Protestant have a higher rate of divorce than have marriages in which both are either Roman Catholic or Jewish.[48] Though the Catholic divorce rate is lower than the Protestant rate, Catholics (in Philadelphia) accounted for much more than their proportionate share of desertion cases. Jews appeared least often in the marital disruption statistics.

Mixed religious, or interfaith, marriages are common in America even within groups with a strong endogamous tradition, such as the Christian Reformed Church[49] and the Roman Catholic Church.[50] Both the Christian Reformed Church and the Roman Catholic Church take strong stands against marrying outside the group. Nevertheless, Bouma found 41 percent of Christian Reformed Church members marrying outsiders, and Monahan and Chancellor found 42 percent of all marriages involving a Catholic were mixed-religious marriages.

Divorces are more common to religiously mixed than to nonmixed marriages. Landis found this to be true even when the marriage pair had agreed in advance that they would work things out. Couples were not able to find acceptable solutions, and the differences generally did not decrease with the passage of time.[51] Chancellor and Monahan found that marriages in which both partners were Catholics were less than half as likely to end in divorce as were mixed marriages.

However, when controls for certain variables other than interreligion are applied, much of the alleged greater divorce propensity among mixed marriages disappears. Burchinal found for first-married couples that when the survival rates of Catholic-Catholic marriages and the survival rates of marriages of Catholics with members of specific Protestant denominations were compared, the size of the differences in survival rates between the two was not very great. The differences hardly justified generalizations of consider-

[47] Thomas P. Monahan and Loren E. Chancellor, "Statistical Aspects of Marriage and Divorce by Religious Denomination in Iowa," *Eugenics Quarterly*, II (September, 1953), 162–173.

[48] Thomas P. Monahan and William M. Kephart, "Divorce and Desertion by Religious and Mixed Religious Groups," *American Journal of Sociology*, LIX (March, 1954), 454–465.

[49] Donald H. Bouma, "Religiously Mixed Marriages: Denominational Consequences in the Christian Reformed Church," *Marriage and Family Living*, XXV (November, 1963), 428–432.

[50] Loren E. Chancellor and Thomas P. Monahan, "Religious Preference and Interreligious Mixtures in Marriages and Divorces in Iowa," *American Journal of Sociology*, LXI (November, 1955), 233–239.

[51] Judson T. Landis, "Marriages of Mixed and Non-Mixed Religious Faith," *American Sociological Review*, XIV (June, 1949), 401–407.

ably greater marital difficulties facing Catholics who married outside of their faith as compared with Catholics who married Catholics, providing the person they married was identified or affiliated with a Protestant denomination. The lower survival rates of interreligious marriages were derived mainly from the marriages of Catholics with persons who apparently were not affiliated with any specific Protestant denomination.[52]

Burchinal found that differences in marital survival rates were more a function of social status and age at marriage than they were a function of religious identity. Smaller differences between survival rates for intrafaith and interfaith marriages were observed when brides were twenty years of age or older at time of marriage and when husbands were employed in high-status occupations.[53]

Desertion

The United States Census Bureau includes a category of broken marriages referred to as marital separations. According to the Census Bureau definition, persons reported as separated include those with legal separations, those living apart with intentions of obtaining a divorce, and other persons permanently or temporarily estranged from their spouse because of marital discord.[54] The 1956 Census Survey reported 1,242,000 married women separated from their husbands while the number of divorced women in 1956 was a reported 1,492,000. Women who had been divorced and were remarried are not included in the figures.

Persons who are not legally separated by divorce, annulment, or separate maintenance proceedings are commonly referred to as desertion cases. Desertion has been referred to in the sociological literature as "the poor man's divorce." Since desertions have been relatively high among the black population with its lower socio-economic status, it is at least in part correct to speak of desertion as "poor man's divorce." But for the white population, close to half of the deserters are in the skilled worker, clerical, proprietor, and professional classes. Of desertions involving whites, 44 percent derive from the upper half of the occupational ladder. Both in the proprietor and skilled worker groups desertions are higher than divorces. Kephart reports that for selected years from 1920 through 1955 in Philadelphia there have been more desertions per year than divorces, and in some years the number of desertions is more than double the number of divorces. In 1955 there were 2,812 divorces and 4,224 desertions.

[52] Lee Burchinal and Loren E. Chancellor, "Survival Rates Among Religiously Homogamous and Interreligious Marriages," *Social Forces,* XLI (May, 1963), 353–362.

[53] *Ibid.*

[54] See U.S. Bureau of Census, "Current Population Reports," Series P-20, No. 72, December 22, 1956.

The percentage separated and divorced in the population of the United States in 1960 is shown in Table 16.2. Separation rates are particularly high for the urban nonwhite population.

TABLE 16.2. PERCENT SEPARATED AND DIVORCED IN THE POPULA-TION BY RESIDENCE AND COLOR, 1960

Residence and Color	Males			Females		
	Total, marriage disrupted	Sepa-rated	Di-vorced	Total, marriage disrupted	Sepa-rated	Di-vorced
Total	3.6	1.5	2.1	4.8	2.0	2.8
White	3.1	1.0	2.1	4.0	1.3	2.7
Nonwhite	8.0	5.6	2.4	11.9	8.3	3.6
Urban	3.9	1.6	2.3	5.6	2.3	3.3
White	3.4	1.1	2.3	4.6	1.4	3.2
Nonwhite	9.0	6.2	2.8	13.7	9.4	4.3
Rural	2.8	1.1	1.7	2.7	1.2	1.5
White	2.7	0.9	1.8	2.3	0.8	1.5
Nonwhite	5.5	4.0	1.5	6.4	5.0	1.4

SOURCE: Hugh Carter and Alexander Plateris, "Trends in Divorce and Family Dis-ruption," *Health, Education and Welfare Indicators*, September, 1963; reprint, pp. v–xiv.

Both desertion and divorce constitute breaks in marriage relationships, but the consequences of the two are not the same. In the case of divorce, the marriage is legally terminated and the couple members are free to enter new relationships. Divorced persons do marry again and marry quite soon after having been divorced. But in a desertion case, the issue is not clear-cut. The whereabouts of the deserter (more often the husband) may not be known. Commonly, no arrangements have been made by the deserter for the sup-port of spouse and children. A larger proportion of desertions than divorces involve children who are minors. It may be difficult for the nondeserting partner to know what action he should take, even though desertion is a rec-ognized ground for divorce action. In that majority of cases in which the deserter was the major breadwinner, the care and support of the dependent family members commonly becomes a matter of public responsibility; they become "welfare families."

Death

For marriages that run the full natural course, the last and greatest crisis comes with the demise of the partner first to die; this ends the marriage. Women have a longer life expectancy than do men. This coupled with the fact that the groom is characteristically somewhat older than the bride at time of marriage means that many more marriages terminate by death of the male spouse. Women have an average expectation of living from five to seven years longer than males born on the same day. If the groom is two or three years older than the bride at marriage, the bride can expect to outlive her husband by seven to ten years.

PERSONAL ADJUSTMENT AND DIVORCE

Marriage functions on behalf of the personalities of its members. Divorce completely destroys the marriage system, the system sanctioned by society to meet adult personality needs. But divorce does not destroy personal needs. Since marriage rests directly on the one partner and the other, the departure of either destroys the whole.

There are no third parties in monogamous marriages; there is no possibility of the system continuing after one has withdrawn. In some societies (mostly primitive societies) the divorced person is taken back into his family of orientation or into the extended family of which his family of orientation is a part. American society provides no such system affiliation for the divorced person. The social status of the divorced person is less clear than is that of the person whose marriage has been terminated by the death of his spouse. In the case of death, kinsmen move in with offers of sympathy and support. Divorce, on the other hand, is apt to immobilize the kinfolk. There are no clearly defined norms for relating to the divorced person as there are to the bereaved person; kinsmen may not know how to relate to a divorced relative.

The roles of husbands and wives are well-defined when compared with the roles of divorced persons. The marriage system receives high esteem and status in the hierachy of American social system; on the other hand, divorce is regarded as a threat to social order and divorce status is thus not so highly esteemed. The divorced person is doubly burdened; he must learn to play new and ill-defined roles. On entering the new role of a divorced person he is not permitted the luxury of mourning the passing of his marital status or the departure of his spouse. The divorced woman is expected to appear composed, relieved, and even gay (the "gay divorcee" is one of the few divorce roles stereotyped by American society). In reality, her (or his) life may be marked by regret, guilt, and confusion.[55]

In a very practical way, divorce may affect the economic and other adaptive roles worked out in the broken marriage system. Divorce often leaves the wife without training or experience to step into an occupational role; she may not be prepared to step into a job that will provide the level of living

---

[55] Willard Waller, *The Family: A Dynamic Interpretation* (New York: Dryden, 1938), pp. 556, 582–584.

formerly enjoyed.[56] For the divorced man, a career in his chosen occupation (especially certain occupations) may be adversely affected because of public reaction to his divorce. Marriage is commonly viewed as a social system responsible for motivating proper and socially acceptable behavior, thus marriage partners interact in the assurance that their behavior is approved. But according to the traditional public morality, divorce was considered as a mark of failure. For one who subscribes to the traditional morality, the termination of marriage through divorce may have a disillusioning and disorganizing effect.[57] In marriage, thoughts of the beloved may motivate the spouse to actions that will please his mate; in divorce thoughts of the mate may depress and immobilize. Some divorced persons experience affection for the beloved after the relationship is broken; others identify with and accept the very things that in marriage resulted in conflict.

According to Goode, more divorced spouses desire to punish the ex-spouse than the data appear to indicate. His study revealed a significant amount of antagonism toward the former spouse even among women who had remarried subsequent to the divorce. The dissolving of the marriage as a social system does not automatically end the emotional relationship even though much of the guilt and hostility may be dissipated in the process of marital conflict. The divorced person cannot be said to have adjusted to his new status unless and until he has reorganized his affectional life, including its sexual expression, free of undue concern with the departed spouse. Finding sex partners that are personally and socially acceptable is not the least of the concerns of the divorced person.

The marriage system serves the function of integrating activities and sentiments for its participants and of mediating influences from the outside. The divorced person is left without such an entity. Goode found that something over one-half of the women in his study claimed to have kept their same friends throughout the separation and divorce period, but that generally the associates and friends of the divorced woman were not interested in her divorce problems. However, among those who changed their circle of friends, many did so not out of choice or because of rejection by their friends but rather out of a necessary change in residence.

Marriage at its best contributes to the internal stability of the person. There are many special mental health agencies and professionals in society, but marriage and the family are primary agencies of mental health. It is in marriage that care, sustenance, personal attention, warmth, and affection are given and received. The divorced person does not have such a unit. It

[56] Willard Waller, *The Old Love and the New: Divorce and Readjustment* (New York: H. Liveright, 1930), pp. 226–249; Kirkpatrick, *op. cit.* (see above fn. 43), pp. 610–614.

[57] Baber, *op. cit.* (see above, fn. 31), pp. 443–444.

must be recognized, of course, that one reason for the divorce may be that the marriage is no longer or never was such a unit.

A person's pride and self-esteem can be dealt a severe blow by the divorce experience; the divorced person may have feelings of shame and humility as a result of the experience. The fact that he regards his former mate as having been at fault does not assuage his negative feelings. He had a part with his spouse in the choice of each other as marriage mates, and he sees himself as having chosen poorly. The romantic attachment has ended in a traumatic way; there is wounded self-esteem.[58]

Regarding stability of the personality, the divorced person may have to settle a rebellion within himself and without the help of a family system. He has to learn to live with and by himself, to accept his wounds, and to try to move on toward a process of rebuilding self-esteem and self-confidence. One index of recovery from a divorce experience is the ability of the divorced person to objectify the experience and to see it in perspective without bitterness and undue longing for the past.

REMARRIAGE

If remarriage is a mark of adjustment to divorce, then many adjust to divorce. Of the three-quarters of a million persons divorced annually, many remarry; of 1,523,000 marriages in the United States in 1960, over one-fifth (22 percent) were remarriages. About three out of four remarriages involved a divorced person; one out of four involved a widow or widower. Using United States Census data, Glick found that for those who remarried subsequent to divorce the median length of time that elapsed between previous marriage dissolution and remarriage was 2.7 years. For those who remarried after having been widowed, the median years before remarriage was 3.5 years.[59]

Success of Remarriage

From society's point of view, remarriages are successful to the extent that they contribute to marital and familial stability. The high divorce rate does not in itself indicate an unstable society if large numbers of the divorced remarry successfully.

Regarding the effect of marriage on personality, Terman found that generally persons who remarried were as happy in their new marriages as were those who had not been divorced.[60] Locke and Klausner on the other

---

[58] Waller, *The Old Love and the New, op. cit.,* p. 8.

[59] Glick, *op. cit.* (see above, fn. 21), p. 138.

[60] Lewis M. Terman, *Psychological Factors in Marital Happiness* (New York: McGraw-Hill, 1938), p. 174.

hand, found a sex differential in adjustment to divorce. Divorced-remarried women appeared to be as well adjusted in their remarriages as were women married only once; divorced-remarried men were less well adjusted in their remarriages than were men living in their original marriages.[61] Remarriages are more likely to end in divorce than are first marriages, and the likelihood of divorce increases with each divorce experience.[62]

In a sample of divorced women who had remarried, Goode reports that 87 percent claimed their second marriage to be "much better" than the first marriage and that 8 percent claimed it to be a "little better." Eighty-four percent attributed their success in the subsequent marriage to be due in part to experience gained in the first marriage. Bernard, using a sample of remarried subjects including a disproportionate number of higher-class professional persons, found that a woman's remarriage was more likely to be successful if she had married a man whose first marriage had been successful (a widower), if she had married a well-educated professional man, and if she had retained custody of the children of her first marriage.[63]

DIVORCE TRENDS

The peak years in divorces in America was in 1946, when there were 610,000 divorces. From 1950 to 1960 the annual number of divorces remained under 400,000 per year. One change over the years has been a much heavier concentration of divorce in the early years of marriage than was previously true. Children born during the post-World War II years are now entering the marriageable age, and, if there is a continuance of marriage at an early age, other things being equal, there may be a higher proportion of marriages ending in divorce in the future.

SUMMARY

Marriage is a system of process beginning with the wedding and in no case lasting beyond the life span of either of the initiating parties. A marriage goes through nonrepeatable cyclical changes beginning with marital adjustment, continuing through the experiences of child bearing, rearing, and launching, and the eventual disruption of the marital relationship. The adjustments made necessary by the changing phases in the cycle are de-

---

[61] Harvey J. Locke and William J. Klausner, "Marital Adjustment of Divorced Persons in Subsequent Marriages," *Sociology and Social Research,* XXXIII (November, 1948), 97–101.

[62] Thomas P. Monahan, "How Stable Are Remarriages?" *American Journal of Sociology,* LVIII (November, 1952), 280–288.

[63] Jessie Bernard, *Remarriage: A Study of Marriage* (New York: Dryden, 1956), pp. 287–288.

manding on the personalities involved and on the relationship. Tensions that develop must be resolved if the marriage is to continue.

Progressive loss of satisfaction or disenchantment appears to characterize marriage. Men appear to suffer more disenchantment in the earlier years of marriage than do women. This early, marked decrease in enchantment for men is contrasted with a slower decline in enchantment for women from early marriage to the middle years. Despite disenchantment, the great majority of married persons go through life with their original spouse.

Some marriages that remain intact are beset by greater problems than disenchantment. These more seriously demoralized and disorganized marriages sometimes remain intact—in many cases for the sake of the children. Marriage partners in intact, disorganized marriages show signs of personal disorganization.

All marriages are eventually disrupted; most by the death of one of the partners, many by reason of divorce or desertion. America experienced a steady increase in divorce rates reaching a peak in the post World War II years. There has been some reduction in divorce rates since that time. The divorce rates reflect social conditions, regional, residential, racial, nationality, socio-economic differences, and a variety of personal and relational problems. Marriage disintegration calls for subsequent personality adjustment.

BIBLIOGRAPHY

John C. Belcher. "The One-Person Household: A Consequence of the Isolated Nuclear Family?" *Journal of Marriage and the Family*, XXIX (August, 1967), 534–540.

Jessie Bernard. *Remarriage: A Study of Marriage*. New York: Dryden, 1956.

Robert O. Blood, Jr. and Donald M. Wolfe. *Husbands and Wives: The Dynamics of Married Living*. Glencoe, Ill.: Free Press, 1960.

Donald H. Bouma. "Religiously Mixed Marriages: Denominational Consequences in the Christian Reformed Church," *Marriage and Family Living*, XXV (November, 1963), 428–432.

Lee Burchinal and Loren E. Chancellor. "Survival Rates Among Religiously Homagamous and Interreligious Marriages," *Social Forces*, XLI (May, 1963), 353–362.

Hugh Carter and Alexander Plateris. "Trends in Divorce and Family Disruption," *Health, Education, and Welfare Indicators*, September, 1963; reprint, pp. v–xiv.

Loren E. Chancellor and Thomas P. Monahan. "Religious Preference and Interreligious Mixtures in Marriages and Divorces in Iowa," *American Journal of Sociology*, LXI (November, 1955), 233–239.

Catherine S. Chilman. "Families in Development at Mid-Stage of the Family Life Cycle," *The Family Coordinator*, XVII (October, 1968), 297–312.

John F. Cuber and Peggy B. Harrof. *The Significant Americans: A Study of Sexual Behavior Among the Affluent*. New York: Appleton-Century, 1965.

Harold Feldman and Martin E. Rand. "Egocentrism—Altercentrism in the Husband-Wife Relationship," *Journal of Marriage and the Family*, XXVII (August, 1965), 386–391.

Paul C. Glick. *American Families*. New York: Wiley, 1957.

William J. Goode. *After Divorce*. Glencoe, Ill.: Free Press, 1956.

Harry C. Harmsworth and Mhyra S. Minnis. "Non-Statutory Causes of Divorce: The Lawyer's Point of View," *Marriage and Family Living*, XVII (November, 1955), 316–321.

Charles W. Hobart. "Disillusionment in Marriage and Romanticism," *Marriage and Family Living*, XX (May, 1958), 156–192.

Paul H. Jacobson. *American Marriage and Divorce*. New York: Rinehart, 1959.

William F. Kenkel. "Observational Studies of Husband-Wife Interaction in Family Decision-Making," *Sourcebook in Marriage and The Family* (2nd ed.), ed. Marvin B. Sussman. Boston: Houghton Mifflin, 1963. Pp. 144–156.

William M. Kephart. "Drinking and Marital Disruption," *Quarterly Journal of the Studies of Alcohol*, XV (March, 1954), 63–73.

William M. Kephart. "The Duration of Marriage," *American Sociological Review*, XIX (June, 1954), 287–295.

William M. Kephart. "Occupational Level and Marital Disruption," *American Sociological Review* XX (August, 1955), 456–465.

William M. Kephart. "Some Variables in Cases of Reported Sexual Maladjustment," *Marriage and Family Living*, XXVI (August, 1954), 241–243.

Clifford Kirkpatrick and Charles Hobart. "Disagreement, Disagreement Estimates and Non-Empathetic Imputations for Intimacy Groups Varying from Favorite Date to Married," *American Sociological Review*, XIX (February, 1954), 10–19.

Judson T. Landis. "Marriages of Mixed and Non-Mixed Religious Faith," *American Sociological Review*, XIV (June, 1949), 401–407.

E. E. LeMasters. "Holy Deadlock: A Study of Unsuccessful Marriages," *The Midwest Sociologist*, XXI (July, 1959), 86–90.

Gerald R. Leslie. "The Field of Marriage Counseling," *Handbook of Marriage and the Family*, ed. Harold T. Christensen. Chicago: Rand McNally, 1964. Pp. 912–943.

Harvey J. Locke. *Predicting Adjustment in Marriage: A Comparison of a Divorced and a Happily Married Group*. New York: Holt, 1951.

Harvey J. Locke and William J. Klausner. "Marital Adjustment of Divorced Persons in Subsequent Marriages," *Sociology and Social Research*, XXXIII (November, 1948), 97–101.

John E. Mayer. *The Disclosure of Marital Problems: Exploratory Study of Lower and Middle Class Wives*. New York: The Community Service Society of New York, 1966.

Thomas P. Monahan. "Divorce by Occupational Level," *Marriage and Family Living*, XVII (November, 1955), 322–324.

Thomas P. Monahan. "Does Age at Marriage Matter in Divorce?" *Social Forces*, XXXII (October, 1953), 81–87.

Thomas P. Monahan. "How Stable are Remarriages?" *American Journal of Sociology*, LVIII (November, 1952), 280–288.

Thomas P. Monahan. "Is Childlessness Related to Family Stability?" *American Sociological Review*, XX (August, 1955), 446–456.

Thomas P. Monahan. "When Married Couples Part: Statistical Trends and Relationships in Divorce," *American Sociological Review,* XXVII (October, 1962), 625–633.

Thomas P. Monahan and Loren E. Chancellor. "Statistical Aspects of Marriage and Divorce by Religious Denomination in Iowa," *Eugenics Quarterly,* II (September, 1953), 162–173.

Thomas P. Monahan and William M. Kephart. "Divorce and Desertion by Religious and Mixed Religious Groups," *American Journal of Sociology,* LIX (March, 1954), 454–465.

Ivan F. Nye. "Child Adjustment in Broken and in Unhappy Unbroken Homes," *Marriage and Family Living,* XIX (November, 1957), 356–361.

Maurice Pinard. "Marriage and Divorce Decisions and the Larger Social System: A Case Study in Social Change," *Social Forces,* XLIV (March, 1966), 341–355.

Philip M. Smith. "Broken Homes and Juvenile Delinquency," *Sociology and Social Research,* XXXIX (May, 1955), 307–311.

John L. Thomas. *The American Catholic Family.* Englewood Cliffs, N.J.: Prentice-Hall, 1956.

Willard H. Waller and Reuben Hill. *The Family: A Dynamic Interpretation.* New York: Dryden, 1951.

CHAPTER 17

Family Crises

THE FAMILY has been labeled as the great burden carrier of society. No family is completely free of tension and crisis. "Because the family is the bottleneck through which all troubles pass, no other association so reflects the strains and stresses of life."[1] Problem families are often characterized by more than one area of tension. Fairchild and Wynn found high-problem families to be characterized by more than one of the following tensions: (1) problems involving the family's present housing and furniture; (2) drinking by family members; (3) general tenseness and low morale in the family; (4) dissatisfaction with the amount of the family's income; (5) the wife's working outside the home; and (6) inadequate sexual relations.[2] Women were more likely than men to check (1) and (2); men tended to check (5) and (6).

Some stresses that cause crises in the family originate within, others originate outside of the family. Some arise from the caprice of nature, some from situations within the community, and some from the actions of family members themselves.[3] The various crisis situations to which the modern family is susceptible have been classified by Hill[4] under the following headings: dismemberment only, accession only, demoralization only, demoralization plus dismemberment or accession, and stresses involving status shifts.

The division into dismemberment only, accession only, etc., is for the purpose of clarification; most crisis situations of any severity usually involve demoralization sooner or later if for no other reason than that patterns of family roles are disturbed by the change in membership. In the case of dismemberment, the departed one's vital family roles must be reallocated to other members of the family or to nonfamily persons. There is a period of confusion and delay as participants in the family learn new roles.

---

[1] Reuben Hill, "Social Stresses on the Family: Generic Features of Families under Stress," *Social Casework,* XXXIX (February–March, 1958), 139–150.

[2] Roy W. Fairchild and John C. Wynn, *Families in the Church: A Protestant Survey* (New York: Association, 1961), pp. 152–153.

[3] Donald A. Hansen and Reuben Hill, "Families Under Stress," *Handbook of Marriage and the Family,* ed. Harold T. Christensen (Chicago: Rand McNally, 1964), pp. 782–819.

[4] Hill, *op. cit.*

Dismemberment Only

* Death of child, spouse, or parent
* Hospitalization of spouse
* War separation

Accession Only

Unwanted pregnancy
Deserter returns
Stepfather, stepmother addition
* Some war reunions
* Some adoptions, aged grandparents, orphan kin

Demoralization Only

* Nonsupport
Infidelity
* Alcoholism
Drug addiction
Delinquency and events bringing disgrace

Demoralization Plus Dismemberment or Accession

* Illegitimacy
Runaways
* Desertion
* Divorce
Imprisonment
Suicide or homicide
* Institutionalization for mental illness

* Starred items designate crisis situations in which study has been reported. Non-starred items represent areas of needed research.

As indicated by Figure 17.1, there has been an increase in the proportion of manless households since the turn of the century. Women's longevity is a principal reason. The population over sixty-five years of age in the United States grows at a rate of about 1,000 per day, and a majority of the aged are married women who have outlived their husbands. The number of divorces involving children has increased, as has the number of children in the families of divorcées. The number of children born out of wedlock has also increased. These trends indicate that a higher proportion of American children are growing up without continuing adult male influence in their families of orientation.

A family crisis may result from something that happens to one or more individuals in the family (voluntarily or involuntarily) or something that happens to the family as a whole. The severity of the crisis is related to the importance of the member affected in the activities of the family. Families are most vulnerable if something happens to one or both of the adult members, the leadership coalition. The reaction to a crisis in the life of a minor in the family may be severe, but other things being equal, its effect on the functioning of the family will not be pervasive. For example, if the father is incarcerated for a crime, a major breadwinner, a major decision-maker,

FIGURE 17.1.   HOUSEHOLDS HEADED BY A WOMAN

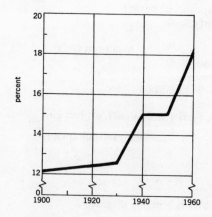

SOURCE: U.S. Bureau of the Census, *Historical Statistics: Colonial Times to 1957.* Series A-255–263. *Selected Characteristics of Households: 1790–1957.* U.S. Bureau of the Census, *Current Population Reports Series* P-20, No. 106.

FIGURE 17.2.   DIVORCES INVOLVING CHILDREN

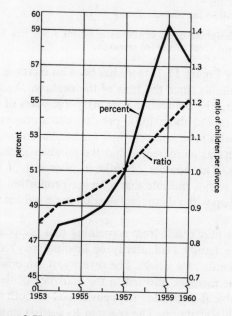

SOURCE: Department of Health, Education and Welfare, National Office of Vital Statistics, *Vital Statistics of the U.S., 1959, Health, Education and Welfare Indicators,* September, 1963.

a major disciplinarian may be lost to the family. On the other hand, if an adolescent son is incarcerated the effect on the family may be to cause embarrassment, but family support, decision-making, and discipline are not likely to be markedly affected.

A downward trend in the fortunes of a family or social disgrace will result in crisis; a dramatic upturn in economic and social status may also constitute a crisis—a crisis quite as disruptive as that caused by economic loss or social disgrace. The price of either upward or downward mobility for a family may be family disorganization. In the accompanying listing of stresses involving status shifts, the crisis situations that have received systematic study are again starred. The crisis potential of downward shifts have received relatively complete coverage; the same cannot be said of the crisis of sudden wealth and fame.[5]

Types of Stresses Involving Status Shifts

* Sudden impoverishment
* Prolonged unemployment
Sudden wealth and fame
* Refugee migrations, political and religious
* Disasters, tornadoes, floods, explosions
* War, bombings, deprivations
* Political declassing, denazification

* Starred items designate crisis situations in which study has been reported. Non-starred items represent areas of needed research.

Families differ in their capacity to adjust to crisis situations. Difficulties that would disrupt the functioning of one family will be taken in stride by another family. Utilizing data on the ability of families to solve a laboratory problem, Straus found working-class families to be less successful than middle-class families. This was true of sample populations in India, the United States and Puerto Rico.[6]

Some families appear by their very nature to be crisis-prone, while others are not. Crisis-prone families have limited crisis-meeting resources and fail to learn from past crisis experiences. Factors demonstrated to be conducive to adjustment to crisis include family adaptability, family integration, affectional relations among family members, good marital adjustment of husband and wife, companionable parent-child relationships, democratic control in decision-making, participation of the mother in activities other than home life, and previous successful experience with crisis.

[5] *Ibid.*
[6] Murray A. Straus, "Communication, Creativity, and Problem-solving Ability of Middle- and Working-Class Families in Three Societies," *American Journal of Sociology,* LXXIII (January, 1968), 417–430.

Research on family crisis within the context of war separation and re-union[7] corroborates these generalizations: demoralization that follows a war-related crisis usually stems from incipient demoralization that was present before the crisis; the length of time a family continues to be disorganized as a result of a war-related crisis is inversely related to the family's adequacy or organization; predicting the reaction to war-related crises for families that lack integration and adaptation is particularly difficult; knowing about a critical event and preparing for it in advance mitigates the hardship and improves chances of recovery; the effect of crisis on families may be punitive or strengthening depending on the margin of health, wealth, and adequacy possessed by the family.

Society and the community not only create problems for the family; they also assist in preparing for and alleviating the effects of stressful situations. Beach and Lucas in reporting on individual and family behavior in a coal-mining town indicate how the local culture keeps people alerted and prepared for the ever-present danger of a mine cave-in.[8] Within the local culture are ideas and expectations that can help a family adjust if the danger becomes a reality. In other words, the community can prepare the family and its members for crisis by providing crisis roles and norms that persons can assume should a dreaded crisis become a reality.

Studies of wartime stress have shown that the community can be supportive of the family in time of crisis. Rather than undermining family unity, the effects of war have been shown to strengthen family unity if neighbors are stimulated to cooperate with one another and even to assume some of the supportive functions that are ordinarily provided by other agencies in the community.

FAMILY WELFARE SERVICES

In Chapter 10 it was pointed out that kinsmen often play a significant part in time of family crisis. Organized formal systems of support take their places alongside informal neighborhood and kinship support patterns. What emerged in America was an acceptance of a principle of social responsibility for the welfare of individuals and families in crises but with the least challenge to private enterprise, the least burden on the taxpayer, and the greatest reliance on the voluntary principle.[9]

[7] Reuben Hill, *Families Under Stress* (New York: Harper, 1949), pp. 196–211.

[8] H. D. Beach and R. A. Lucas, ed., *Individual and Group Behavior in a Coal Mine Disaster* (Washington, D.C.: National Academy of Sciences-National Research Council, Disaster Research Group, 1962), as reported in Hansen and Hill, *op. cit.*

[9] Max Lerner, *America as a Civilization* (New York: Simon and Schuster, 1957), p. 129 ff.; David M. Potter, *People of Plenty: Economic Abundance and the American Character* (Chicago: University of Chicago, 1954), p. 92 ff.

Child-Welfare Services

It is strongly held in America that it is from parents that children receive the protection, care, and guidance which enables them to become healthy, well-balanced, happy adults. The rationale supporting child-welfare services is a belief in the importance to children of their parents and of family life *per se*. Child-welfare programs place major emphasis upon efforts to support and strengthen the family.[10] As one example of the extent of the implication of this rationale, public welfare systems provide casework services to 150,000 children living in their own homes or in the homes of relatives, per year. Many other children are cared for by substitute families, referred to as foster families. A lesser number are cared for in child-care institutions.

Since the nuclear family rather than the kinship system is the major organized, responsible family system in American society, family members, both adults and children, are without absolute assurance of kin protection or support if the nuclear family fails to function properly. For instance, it cannot be assumed that an infant or small child born out of wedlock or orphaned will be taken into one of the kin families. As a result, the state takes responsibility for supervising the permanent placement of homeless children into nuclear families. Adoption is the method provided by law for assuring children the security of a home under the same material rights and obligations as those existing between children and natural parents. Adoption establishes the legal relationship of parents and child between persons who are not so related.

Adoption in the United States as a method of caring for children without parents or without parents capable of providing for them is increasing every year.[11] For the past six years the average yearly increase in adoptions has been approximately 6 percent. There are nearly two million adopted children in the United States under eighteen years of age.

Of 142,000 children adopted in 1965, about 54 percent were adopted by persons not related to the child. Eighty-four percent of the children placed with nonrelatives were born to unmarried parents.

An adoption agency helps the natural parents in making plans for the child, makes studies of prospective adoptive homes, selects an adoptive home, places the child, and helps the adoptive couple in preparing for and receiving the child. Increased public acceptance of placement by an adoption agency is evidenced by a steady increase in the percentage of agency placements over direct placements by the natural parents or in other ways.

[10] Maurice O. Hunt, "Child Welfare," *Social Work Yearbook* (1960), pp. 141–156.
[11] The following discussion is based on Ursula M. Gallagher, "Adoption: Current Trends," *Welfare in Review*, V (February, 1967), 12–20.

In 1965, 69 percent of nonrelative adoptions were social agency placements, while in 1951 agency and independent adoptions were nearly equal in number.

The majority of children placed for adoption by agencies, until recently, were nonhandicapped children. One reason for confining adoptive placements to such children was the fact that many couples who wished to adopt a child requested one which was normal in every respect, feeling that agencies should "certify" the child. However, in recent years children in need of medical or surgical therapy, older children, and slow learners have been placed for adoption, as adoptive couples willing to provide a home for a handicapped child have been located.

Matching of physical characteristics is also considered less important than it formerly was. For example, children of nonwhite parentage are now being placed with white families. This has been true in the case of children of Oriental ancestry for some years. More recently, American Indian, black, and foreign-born Asian children have been increasingly placed.

Much research on adoption is in process, but there are very few findings to date. One study sponsored by the Children's Bureau[12] deals with a group of ninety-one children adopted after infancy. All of the children had experienced deprivations during infancy or childhood prior to adoption and the rights of their parents had been terminated through court action. The majority made a good adjustment to adoption, and the score of overall parental satisfaction in the adoptive experience was high. The degree of resiliency (the return to emotional stability) after adoption was marked. In the light of the encouraging results, the researcher suggested that agencies take greater risks in increasing the number of adoptive placements of older children. Research into the adoptive experience of American Indian children is also under way at present.

Annually, a total of about 115,000 different children are cared for in institutions, with the greater proportion in the nine- to twelve-year age group. Most children in institutions have one or both parents living. Most of them spend from one to three years in the institution; a few remain from infancy until they are ready for self-employment or college. Many child-caring institutions concentrate only on shelter, custody, and the child's adjustment to the institution's patterns and routines. During the last decade, however, more institutions have added casework services in an effort to work with parents before, during, and after the child's stay in residence.[13] It is no longer regarded as enough for the community to assume responsibility for

---

[12] Alfred Kadushin, *Adopted When Older: Final Report* (*Follow-up Study of Older Children Placed for Adoption*) (Madison, Wis.: University of Wisconsin, 1966).

[13] Clare Golden and Martin Gula, "Care of the Child Outside the Home," *Reference Papers on Children and Youth,* 1960 White House Conference on Children and Youth.

the care of the child who must be removed from his own family; the community must exhaust every effort to reconstruct the family so that the child can be returned as quickly as possible.

The circumstances necessitating services for children and their families vary widely. Sometimes parents come to the child-care agency when they are having difficulties with their children and when they feel the need for information or guidance on how to proceed. Some children themselves request assistance from the agency. Frequently children who present problems are referred to the agency by the court; complaints from the school or other community agencies also bring them to the agency's attention. A common situation bringing social services to bear upon families occurs in cases in which parents in the judgment of society are neglecting, abusing, or subjecting their children to demoralizing influences.

Child-welfare workers make extensive use of community services designed to supplement and assist families in carrying out their responsibilities. Among these are a wide variety of health services including psychiatric diagnostic and treatment facilities, group-work services, recreational facilities, services of the church, and educational programs.

Sometimes both parents (or the lone parent having responsibility for the children) find it necessary to be out of the home. The Children's Bureau reports that, as of January, 1959, nearly four million children under twelve years of age had to care for themselves while their mothers worked and that 138,000 of these children were less than ten years of age. Over one million children were looked after by nonrelatives who either came into the children's homes or cared for them in their own homes. About 24,000 children under three years of age and 67,000 children between three and five were in group care of some kind.

Services provided by public agencies are usually of two kinds: foster-family day care and care in group facilities known as day nurseries or nursery schools. The child-welfare agency makes studies of prospective foster homes and approved foster day-care homes are supervised by the agency as to program and standards of care. Traditionally, day nurseries have emphasized protective or custodial day care while nursery schools have stressed the education of the young child. The use of day-care centers has been recognized as a way of relieving overwhelmed and overburdened mothers of the care of their preschool children during the day and also as a way of giving attention to the youngsters. Day-care centers and camps have also been used experimentally as a means of partial separation when placement of the children seems to be indicated but when the mother is not able to face this possibility.[14]

14 Helen W. Hallinan, "Co-ordinating Agency Efforts in Behalf of the Hard-to-Reach Family," *Social Casework*, XXX (January, 1959), 9–17.

Another type of child-care program involves homemaker services. The larger part of these services have been supported by private rather than public funds. Under the homemaker plan, agencies employ and train capable women who can be placed in homes to carry the responsibility of looking after children or other persons needing care and for carrying on household functions, the idea being that in time of emergency in the home it might be better to use homemakers instead of removing children and placing them in foster care. Homemaker services are used to enable mothers to assume gradual responsibility for their families during periods of convalescence from mental illness or when a mother is chronically ill and cannot take full responsibility. In cases of parental neglect homemakers are also used in an attempt to help stabilize the home and to demonstrate satisfactory care of children. The homemaker services available are adequate to meet but a small portion of the need for such services, however.[15]

The Children's Bureau was created in 1912 with a mandate from the Congress to investigate and report upon all matters pertaining to the welfare of children and child life among all classes of people. Over the years as it has collected facts it has also worked with public and voluntary agencies dealing with the health and welfare of children in preparing standards for practice based on the best knowledge available. In 1936, under the Social Security Act, the Children's Bureau was delegated the responsibility for administering grants-in-aid to the states for maternal and child-welfare services. In the maternal and child health program well-child conferences are used to help parents in an attempt to understand how they can support and protect the child's emotional growth.

The states, partially through the impetus of federal funds, have also set up programs aimed at protecting the lives of prematurely born infants. In an affluent society that values persons, the categories of services available to children know few bounds.

The effect of broken homes on the healthy growth of children, the growing recognition that social services in their own homes can do much to strengthen relationships between parents and their own children, and the affirmation of the right of every child to his own home are factors spurring efforts of state child-welfare programs to meet the needs of an ever increasing number of children.

In recent years the Congress has earmarked maternal and child health funds for the development of state projects for mentally-retarded children and their families with the aim of keeping these children in their own families and home communities. The importance of school health services, with partnership between health, education, and parents is being emphasized and

---

[15] *Focus on Children and Youth,* Report of the Council of National Organization of Children and Youth for the 1960 White House Conference on Children and Youth, 1960.

there is a continuing and long-term interest in seeing that the services of a professionally trained child-welfare worker are made available in each community.

In all these areas of service to children, the Children's Bureau plays a double role. Not only does it supplement state funds through grants but its staff members also provide consultation to the states in planning new programs for children. The Bureau is also concerned with helping communities strengthen and improve services for the prevention and control of juvenile delinquency. A continuing service of the Bureau over the years has been its publications for parents.[16]

One last service to children (and we have not catalogued all of them) is the school social-work program, another program aimed at keeping children in their own homes. Schools began to employ special social-work staff in the early part of this century and this has become a nationally recognized field of service, though a minority of schools provide the service. School social workers operate as a part of the school system and within the aims and purposes of the schools. The school social worker gives assistance to children who are having problems in adjustment, working not only with them but also with their teachers and families.

Social Security Legislation

The year 1935 was especially significant in the development of social services, for it was the year of the passage of the Social Security Act. The act provided for employment insurance to protect persons of working age against the risks of short-term unemployment, a contributory system of social insurance, federal grants-in-aid to states for public assistance to needy aged and blind persons and dependent children, and various child welfare services. Subsequent legislation extended coverage within several of these categories; social insurance coverage was extended to include the disabled as were federal grants to states for public assistance.[17]

Social-insurance programs established by the Social Security Act provide protection against wage loss resulting from old age, prolonged disability, death, or unemployment. Under old-age, survivors, and disability insurance, protection against wage loss due to old age, disability, or death is available to the gainfully employed.[18] Programs providing health and welfare services are aided through federal grants to states for maternal and child-health services, services for crippled children, child-welfare services, vocational rehabilitation, and public-health services. Examples of maternal and child-

16 Katherine Brownell Oettinger, "Children in a Changing World," *Marriage and Family Living,* XX (August, 1958), 233–238.

17 Helen E. Martz, "The Contributions of Public Assistance to Family Life in the United States," *Marriage and Family Living,* XX (August, 1958), 213–220.

18 *Statistical Abstract of the United States, 1961* (Washington, D.C.: U.S. Department of Commerce, Bureau of the Census, 1961).

health services administered through Social Security are maternal medical clinic services; maternity nursing care services; well-child health service; nursing service for children; dental service; school health examination.

Public assistance is provided through a number of programs administered by the states and localities. Federal grants-in-aid help finance payments to the aged, the blind, the permanently and totally disabled, and children whose needs arise from certain given causes. The states may also receive grants for medical assistance to the aged who are recipients of old-age assistance and who cannot take care of these costs themselves. The federal aspects of these programs are the responsibility of the Bureau of Family Services of the Welfare Administration.

Many otherwise adequate families, plagued by unemployment, illness, or death of the breadwinner, may need no professional casework services but only the resource of public assistance to enable them to manage their lives in a way that provides for satisfying personal and family relationships. Family assistance programs as well as the other services available to needy persons and families under public assistance programs attempt, in a relatively uncomplicated and direct way, to provide a substantial contribution to the stability of the American family. All of the states now administer federally-aided programs of public assistance for the needy aged, the blind, and children who are dependent because of the death, disability, or absence of a parent; and most states administer the federally-aided program of aid to the permanently and totally disabled under provisions of the Social Security Act.

In families receiving aid to dependent children, nearly one-fourth of the fathers are incapacitated; in over one-half of the cases the father is absent because of divorce, separation, desertion, unmarried parenthood, or other reasons; and in about 13 percent of the cases the father is deceased. Many economically needy parents and their children have been sustained as family systems through public assistance.

Many public assistance workers, though limited in capacity and in the availability of community resources, in addition to providing financial aid, help needy persons and families find and use their own strengths and other resources to achieve more satisfying and independent lives. They help secure medical care and other rehabilitation services available either within the public welfare agency or elsewhere; they provide, or help to secure, services that enable the needy person to remain in his own home and with his family and friends as long as possible; they plan institutional care when necessary, and arrange for specialized services and home-helps that enable persons no longer in need of custodial care to return to normal community living. Some workers attempt to help with deep-seated emotional and interpersonal problems as well.

In the years since the passage of the Social Security Act, public assistance to persons and to families has been raised to national prominence. Amendments to the Social Security Act allowing for an additional wide range of services beyond financial assistance have been passed by the Congress (1) authorizing greater appropriations for maternal and child-health services; (2) extending aid to families with dependent children, including children who have passed their eighteenth birthday but who are still in high school or pursuing other training to equip them for employment; (3) helping unemployed fathers and other needy persons to secure and retain employment or to attain and retain capability for self-support and personal independence; (4) providing medical care for the aged.[19]

SERVICES TO THE FAMILY AS A SYSTEM

The focus of casework in a family agency is on the family as a system, while taking into account the needs of individual family members. Its intention is to contribute to harmonious family relationships and to promote healthy personality development and satisfactory social functioning of family members. The goals of a family casework program are based on family premises. One of the first of these premises is that family malfunctioning stems from negative relationships among the members of the family that result from cultural, economic, somatic, emotional, or any combination of causes. A second premise is that these negative relationships among family members are susceptible of improvement through casework techniques, except in cases where neurosis or psychosis is a causal factor.[20] The federal government, in adopting the social security program, refused to channelize financial aid through private family-service agencies. As a result these agencies were forced to emphasize functions other than the granting of relief; voluntary agencies in turn developed a technical interest in the psychology of the person.[21]

Private social agency services can be divided into two kinds: supportive, in which the effort is made to continue the family as a working system, and substitutional, in which the agency provides functions or services which the family cannot provide. It is in the supportive services to the family that social work focuses on family relationships, attempting to help a family member or members with problems which affect the stability of the family. The lack

[19] Charles E. Hawkins, "Legislation in the 88th Congress Concerning Welfare Administration Programs," *Welfare In Review*, III (January, 1965), 6–8.

[20] Earl L. Koos, "Private Social Agencies and Family Stability," *The Annals of the American Academy of Political and Social Science*, CCLXXII (November, 1950), 110–116.

[21] Harold L. Wilensky and Charles N. Lebeaus, *Industrial Society and Social Welfare* (New York: Russell Sage Foundation, 1958), pp. 149–167.

of adequate numbers of professionally trained caseworkers has been a serious deterrent to the program; a more fundamental problem is that many communities have shown themselves to be far from ready to accept the broadened services of a family casework agency. The development of family casework services by religious groups has resulted in great variation in the type and quality of services given. The availability of family casework services is closely related to the affluence of the community. In general, private family casework agencies exist only in the larger cities.

An association one of whose primary purposes was to promote the development of family social work was organized as early as 1911—the Family Service Association of America. The purposes and activities of the Association include the promotion of the development of family social work and of wholesome family life through field work with family service agencies, assistance in the development of qualified personnel in family casework, information and research on agency organization and programs, interpretation of the family-service movement to the public, and publications for professional social caseworkers and for laymen.[22]

The St. Paul Family-Centered Project, as well as other projects dealing with multi-problem families, confirmed the suspicion that a small percentage (6 percent in St. Paul) of families take a disproportionately large share (50 percent) of social welfare services and that there is a high concentration of problems such as dependency, ill health, and maladjustment in a relatively few families. Many agencies had worked concurrently with these families often over an extended period of time, but the treatment had been fragmentary, episodic, individually-oriented, and on an agency-by-agency basis according to the particular symptom that was causing trouble at the time.[23]

Discussions with medicine, casework, psychiatry, public welfare, and community organization services centered on classifying the families from the group who were still in the active case load of the county welfare board as potentially treatable, needing only a specialized service or supportive help. The discussions also worked on establishing detection centers for uncovering hard-core families in the making; development of a coordinated and directed plan of diagnosis and treatment for potentially treatable cases; and the working out of agreements with public and voluntary casework agencies whereby each would work with a block of these families under supervision and on a coordinated basis developed through family-centered treatment concepts. Directors of the project were convinced that the ap-

[22] Social Work Yearbook (1957), p. 670.

[23] Charles J. Birt, "Family-Centered Project of St. Paul," Social Work, I (October, 1956), 41–47; Ludwig L. Geismar and Michael A. LaSorte, Understanding the Multi-Problem Family: A Conceptual Analysis and Exploration in Early Identification (New York: Association, 1964), pp. 16–17.

proach had to be family-oriented, with work centered on the whole family in its total situation.

A study of the results of casework with a sample of fifty of the one hundred forty families in the project was completed in 1956. Fifty-eight percent of the sample families had made moderate or marked improvement in seven areas of social functioning, an additional 30 percent showed slight improvement, 8 percent showed no improvement, and 4 percent showed negative change. Sixty-four percent of the families showed positive change in attitudes toward and use of community resources—families who, based on past experience, were hostile toward and distrustful of all authority. Other projects aimed at dealing with the multi-problem or hard-to-reach family have been carried on elsewhere.

SETTLEMENTS AND NEIGHBORHOOD CENTERS

The National Federation of Settlements was organized in 1911, and today there are close to three hundred centers operating throughout the United States.[24] These settlements and neighborhood centers are multi-functional agencies existing to serve the needs of persons in a given geographical neighborhood; the neighborhood is their client. Improvement in living conditions is still a main objective of settlements. Other objectives are the strengthening of family life; helping persons and groups within the neighborhood to relate to one another; developing indigenous leadership; and integrating the local neighborhod within the larger social milieu. The services program of any settlement are as varied as the area served. They may include day care, nursery school, a program for the aged, an urban renewal program, clubs, classes, a clinic. The work falls into three general categories: work with individuals; work with groups; and work with, or on behalf of, the neighborhood as a whole.

A related new project is that of social work in a public housing project. The Philadelphia Housing Authority, for example, has established a Social Services Division as an administrative part of the organization—an informational and referral service staffed with graduate social workers. Eligible, interested tenants with complex health or social problems are helped in getting to the community agency that best can meet their needs or in continuing in contact with agencies through which they are already receiving help. Referral, not continued service, is the Division's primary function. There is only a small core of families who need specialized helping services. These families are not only the so-called hard core of difficult-to-reach families but are also those for whom community services are not readily available. These families sometimes have come from slum areas or have a

[24] Margaret Berry, "Settlement and Neighborhood Centers," *Social Work Year Book* (1960), 523–528.

long history of deprivation, dependency, and poor health, and find it difficult to adjust to living standards that seem alien to them, almost as if they represent a different culture.[25] Owing to long periods of economic and social dependency, they are apt to be apathetic, destructively aggressive, immature, and socially and economically maladjusted. They also include poor housekeepers, those who are chronically delinquent in paying rent, the maritally maladjusted whose disruptive behavior frequently requires police action, and the chronically ill and elderly, or families who are too ill to care for themselves yet not ill enough to require institutional care. Child behavior problems, vandalism, property destruction, adult and juvenile tensions are also frequent problems.[26] Since the project social worker is constantly present in the project, he can become aware of the intrafamilial, as well as the external factors that contribute to family problems. If no appropriate services are available in the community or if they are insufficient to meet the tenant's needs, the social worker participates in community planning for their establishment or extension.

Another program of services to families is that carried on by the Cooperative Extension Service, the field educational arm of the United States Department of Agriculture and the state land-grant colleges and universities. The Extension Service disseminates research findings and attempts to motivate their application in the fields of nutrition, clothing, home management and furnishings, family financial planning, child development and family relationships, housing, and in areas such as health, safety and citizenship. In several states the method known as farm and home development—an attempt to work with the family as a system—is carried on in a group setting. Groups of couples meet regularly, with specialists and extension agents as consultants, to consider ways and means of solving problems they face in the creation and management of the family's resources. Reportedly, one of the results of this method is increased understanding by husband and wife of each other's concerns and values. In some states work is carried on with individual families who are visited for consultation by the agents and by other specialists.

Volunteer leaders also assist in extension family-life work. Annual reports from 2,429 counties throughout the country showed that in 1956 a total of 88,941 volunteer leaders assisted in extension family-life work, and a total of 1,699,359 different families were assisted directly or indirectly by the program. In addition, 40,387 4-H Club members were reported as having completed project work in child care.[27]

[25] Walter B. Miller, "Implications of Urban Lower-Class Culture of Social Work," *Social Service Review*, XXXIII (September, 1959), 219–236.

[26] Osborne McLain, "Social Work in a Public Housing Project," *Social Casework*, XLI (October, 1960), 408–412.

[27] Edward Pope, "Extension Service Programs Affecting American Families," *Marriage and Family Living*, XX (August, 1958), 270–276.

Three other of the major organizations concerned with helping families are the National Council on Family Relations, the American Institute of Family Relations, and the American Social Health Association. The Institute is a private agency which, under the direction of Paul Popenoe, pioneered in marriage counseling and in developing family-life education for out-of-school groups in the Los Angeles area. The Institute now offers to a wider audience summer workshops in counseling, seminars and lectures, and publishes a monthly bulletin, *Family Life*.

The purposes of the National Council of Family Relations, begun in 1938, are mainly to provide opportunities for organized groups, agencies, members of allied professions (family sociology, home economics, social work, medicine, etc.), and individuals interested in family life—to meet, plan, and act together voluntarily for the advancement of marriage and family life. The Council probably joins together more of the professionals engaged in teaching, teacher-training, and research than any other national organization. The Council helps formulate proposals for the family through discussion by interested persons and groups, though it is not an organization designed or staffed to implement such proposals. The Council also publishes two journals, *The Journal of Marriage and the Family*, which publishes about one-fifth of all the research on sex, marriage, and the family, and *The Family Coordinator*.

The American Social Health Association, formerly the American Social Hygiene Association, began as an association for social protection and for the prevention of venereal disease. It now consists of some two hundred and fifty separate organizations. It has as its purpose the enrichment and strengthening of the family as a basic social system by promoting sound education for personal and family living, including training for marriage and parenthood, as well as improving conditions that might otherwise lead to delinquency and sexual promiscuity, especially among young people.

ANTI-POVERTY PROGRAMS

Recent measures to aid families and family members are an integral part of the so-called war on poverty. In his economic message to Congress in January, 1964, President Johnson emphasized the need to bring together the many existing federal, state, and local government programs and to mount a "frontal assault on the sources of poverty." The Economic Opportunities Act passed later in the same year was one form of response to the concern over poverty. Poverty programs are built on the conviction that families must have an adequate income for basic subsistence and that they must be provided a wide range of opportunities and services if they are to escape from insular poverty, case poverty, and poverty that persists from one generation to another within families. One title of the Economic Op-

FIGURE 17.3. PROPORTION OF POPULATION RECEIVING PUBLIC AS-
SISTANCE (RECIPIENT RATES) BY PROGRAM, JUNE OF EACH YEAR,
1940–1966[1] (ALL DATA EXCEPT GENERAL ASSISTANCE INCLUDES RE-
CIPIENTS RECEIVING ONLY VENDOR PAYMENTS FOR MEDICAL CARE)

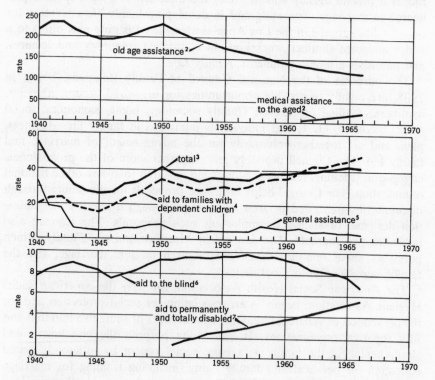

[1] Population for all jurisdictions used in computing rate even though some jurisdictions did not have specified programs in operation. Rate for GA slightly understated
for some years because data on number of recipients incomplete.
[2] Per 1,000 population age 65 and over.
[3] Per 1,000 population all ages.
[4] Per 1,000 population under age 18.
[5] Per 1,000 population under age 65.
[6] Per 1,000 population age 18 and over.
[7] Per 1,000 population age 18–64.

SOURCE: U.S. Department of Health, Education and Welfare, *Welfare in Review: Statistical Supplement*, 1966 Edition.

portunities Act attacks the problem of poverty by helping needy fathers and
mothers develop or improve their ability to earn a living for their families.[28]
The work experience program is administered through the federal-state-

[28] Andrew R. N. Truelson, "Helping Needy People Get Jobs and Hold Them: A
Report on the Work Experience Program," *Welfare in Review*, III (November, 1965),
14–19.

local public assistance system under the direction of the Welfare Administration's Bureau of Family Services. Work experience projects are established and supervised by local public-welfare systems, giving the program a social-services orientation. Members of the welfare agency's social services staff give each work experience trainee and members of his family continuing counsel and support throughout the trainee's participation in the project. The aim is the strengthening of family life and improvement of morale while the head of the family improves work skills and gains motivation.

The war on poverty is a war not only on economic privation but also on deprivation in health, education, creativity, training, family life, social relations. Concerted effort is under way to discover the peculiar needs of the poor in the varied community settings across the nation and to design programs especially tailored to meet these needs.

FAMILY CRISIS AND MARRIAGE CRISIS

Little is known about the relatedness of marriage problems and problems in the family of which the marriage pair serve as the leadership coalition. The empirical results to date are conflicting. Landis,[29] Nye,[30] and Baruch[31] find marital tension to be positively related to personal maladjustment of the child of that marriage. When either the values or roles in marriage are in conflict or in a state of tension, the development of patterns of consistent child raising are inhibited.[32]

There is a relationship, also, between wanting children but not having them and marital disintegration. Wilcox reported as early as 1897 that childless marriages were three to four times as likely to end in divorce as were marriages with children.[33] But Monahan, after a review of research findings, comes to the conclusion that childlessness is not as significant a characteristic of divorces as had been suggested—that the differences be-

---

[29] Judson T. Landis, "A Comparison of Children of Divorced Parents and Children of Happy or Unhappy Non-divorced Parents on Parent-Child Relationships, Dating, Maturation and Sex and Marriage Attitudes," paper read before the National Council on Family Relations, Minneapolis, Minnesota, August, 1955; Judson T. Landis, "Marriages of Mixed and Non-Mixed Religious Faiths," *American Sociological Review,* XIV (June, 1949), 401–407.

[30] F. Ivan Nye, "Child Adjustment in Broken and in Unhappy Unbroken Homes," *Marriage and Family Living,* XIX (November, 1957), 356–361.

[31] Dorothy Baruch, "A Study of Reported Tension in Interparental Relationships as Co-existent with Behavior Adjustment in Young Children," *Journal of Experimental Education,* VI (December, 1937), 187–204; Dorothy Baruch and Annie J. Wilcox, "A Study of Sex Differences in Pre-School Children's Adjustment Co-existent with Interparental Tensions," *Journal of Genetic Psychology,* LXIV (1944), 281–303.

[32] Bernard Farber and Julia L. McHale, "Marital Integration and Parent's Agreement on Satisfaction with their Child's Behavior," *Marriage and Family Living,* XXI (February, 1959), 65–69.

[33] Walter F. Wilcox, *The Divorce Problem* (New York: Columbia University, 1897), p. 34.

tween stable and divorced marriages with regard to the presence of children should be minimized.[34]

Locke finds no relationship between marital adjustment and the presence or absence of children, or between it and the size of family. He does, however, find a relationship between marital success and personality characteristics reflected in the desire for children. Stroup[35] and Burchinal, Hawkes, and Gardner[36] find little common variation between the personal and marital adjustment of parents and the adjustment of the child. Brim, Fairchild, and Borgatta concur, adding that there is no common variance among five factors: problems in child rearing, husband and wife relationship, style of life, community involvement, and religion.[37] They find family problems to be role-specific and isolated, and not to be the expression of general personality traits that pervade all family and marriage interaction. Nor are family problems necessarily the result of economic factors. The findings call in question the assumption that the economic problems of families are related to interpersonal ones, as well as the assumption that interpersonal problems in the marital and parental roles are closely related.

That marital problems and family problems are closely interrelated is also challenged by the findings of LeMasters' study of unhappy marriages. One would assume a high incidence of personal disorganization among the children of LeMasters' chronically unhappy couples. The data, however, do not support such an assumption. Of the seventy-six children in these marriages, only seven had ever been referred to a child guidance clinic or school psychologist for diagnosis or therapy for emotional or behavioral problems. Only three in the sample had ever been booked for a juvenile offense. LeMasters suggests that perhaps children are tougher emotionally than has been generally thought; that they may not be as aware of marital conflict as child psychiatrists have supposed; that modern society permits enough contacts with other persons to compensate for the difficulties at home; that the genetic factors are crucial in personality disorganization; and that these may operate independently of parental conflict.

Disorganized marriages do not necessarily result in disorganized families. This does not mean that we would expect to find in a majority of situations that a disorganized marriage would be coupled with an integrated family.

More and more couples who become divorced have children, hence many children are affected (for good or ill) by divorce. Children are affected

[34] Thomas P. Monahan, "Is Childlessness Related to Family Stability?" *American Sociological Review,* XX (August, 1955), 446–456.

[35] Atlee L. Stroup, "Marital Adjustment of the Mother and Personality of the Child," *Marriage and Family Living,* XVIII (May, 1956), 109–113.

[36] Lee Burchinal, G. R. Hawkes, and B. Gardner, "Marriage Adjustment, Personality of Parents and Personality Adjustment of Child," *Marriage and Family Living,* XIX (November, 1957), 366–372.

[37] Orville G. Brim, Roy W. Fairchild, and Edgar F. Borgatta, "Relation between Family Problems," *Marriage and Family Living,* XXIII (August, 1961), 219–226.

when marriage is broken. In 1960 there were almost three million children with separated or divorced parents.[38] Kinship help in dealing with the children of divorce cannot be taken for granted any more than it can be taken for granted that kinship help will be offered to the divorced parents.[39] Although we cannot assume that the same lines of disorganization will form in the family that formed in the related marriage, if the marriage disintegrates through desertion or divorce (rather than being disorganized but intact), the family system must of necessity experience the loss of at least one member. One of the parents leaves the home; the children are normally awarded to the custody of one of the parents with visiting privileges for the other parent. From the point of view of the good of the children there might be cases in which the marriage could be perpetuated as LeMaster's findings would suggest. On the other hand, Nye observes that unhappy unbroken homes seem to correlate with unfavorable behavior on the part of children, and Burchinal concludes that differences in the characteristics of adolescents from unbroken, broken, and reconstituted families require revision of beliefs about the detrimental effects of divorce upon children.[40] It has been generally accepted that broken homes relate to delinquent behavior in children. Actually, adolescents in broken homes may have less psychosomatic difficulties, less delinquent behavior, and better adjustment to parents than do children in disorganized unbroken homes. Children in homes broken by divorce do not exhibit poorer adjustment than do those in homes broken in other ways. High rates of broken homes and high rates of delinquency are both characteristics of depressed and disorganized urban areas; but when groups of delinquents are matched with nondelinquents on factors such as age, ethnic origin, socio-economic status, and residence, the incidence of delinquency among youth of broken homes begins to approach that of comparable youth in intact families.[41] Obviously, the relationship is a complicated one and one requiring additional research.

SUMMARY

Family crises develop out of a variety of situations both within and outside of the family. Situations contributing to a crisis situation include dismemberment, accession, demoralization, demoralization plus dismemberment or accession, and upward or downward status shifts. Families differ in

[38] "Marriage and the American Woman," *Population Profile*, (Washington, D.C.: Population Reference Bureau, Inc., June 3, 1963), pp. 1–5.

[39] Kingsley Davis, "Children of Divorce," *Law and Contemporary Problems*, X (1944), 700–710.

[40] Lee G. Burchinal, "Characteristics of Adolescents from Unbroken, Broken, and Reconstituted Families," *Journal of Marriage and the Family*, XXVI (February, 1964), 44–51.

[41] Philip M. Smith, "Broken Homes and Juvenile Delinquency," *Sociology and Social Research*, XXXIX (May, 1955), 307–311.

their capacity to adjust to crisis. Factors demonstrated to be conducive to adjustment to crisis include adaptability, integration, good affective relations, good marital adjustment, companionable relations, democratic control, participation of the mother outside the home, and previous successful experience with crisis.

Programs designed to help families and persons in families adjust to crisis situations include a variety of child-welfare services, social security provisions, family casework services, settlement and neighborhood centers, research, family-life education, marriage and family counseling, and a variety of programs aimed at the alleviation and destruction of poverty.

Family crises and marriage crises are related but the nature of the relationship is complex and imperfectly understood to date. Additional research regarding the complexities of the relationship is needed.

BIBLIOGRAPHY

Margaret Berry. "Settlement and Neighborhood Centers," *Social Work Year Book* (1960), pp. 523–528.

Charles J. Birt. "Family-Centered Project of St. Paul," *Social Work,* I (October, 1956), 41–47.

J. Douglas Brown. "The American Philosophy of Social Insurance," *Social Service Review,* XXX (March, 1956), 1–8.

Muriel Brown. "Organizational Programs to Strengthen the Family," *Handbook of Marriage and the Family,* ed. Harold T. Christensen. Chicago: Rand McNally, 1964. Pp. 823–880.

Harold T. Christensen. "The Intrusion of Values," *Handbook of Marriage and the Family,* ed. Harold T. Christensen. Chicago: Rand McNally, 1964. Pp. 969–1006.

Vincent DeFrancis. *The Fundamentals of Child Protection.* Denver: American Humane Association, 1955.

Evelyn M. Duvall. "American Families and NCFR—Since 1938," *Journal of Marriage and the Family,* XXVI (February, 1964), 10–19.

Ursula M. Gallagher. "Adoption: Current Trends," *Welfare in Review,* V (February, 1967), 12–20.

Ludwig L. Geismar and Michael A. LaSorte. *Understanding the Multi-Problem Family: A Conceptual Analysis and Exploration in Early Identification.* New York: Association, 1964.

Clare Golden and Martin Gula. "Care of the Child Outside the Home," *Reference Papers on Children and Youth,* 1960 White House Conference on Children and Youth.

Helen W. Hallinan. "Co-ordinating Agency Efforts in Behalf of the Hard-to-Reach Family," *Social Casework,* XXX (January, 1959), 9–17.

Donald A. Hansen and Reuben Hill. "Families Under Stress," *Handbook of Marriage and the Family,* ed. Harold T. Christensen. Chicago: Rand McNally, 1964. Pp. 782–819.

Maurice O. Hunt. "Child Welfare," *Social Work Year Book* (New York: National Association of Social Workers, 1960), pp. 141–156.

Alfred Kadushin. *Adopted When Older: Final Report (Follow-up Study of Older Children Placed for Adoption)*. Madison, Wis.: University of Wisconsin, 1966.

Helen E. Martz. "The Contributions of Public Assistance to Family Life in the United States," *Marriage and Family Living*, XX (August, 1958), 213–220.

Osborne McLain. "Social Work in a Public Housing Project," *Social Casework*, XLI (October, 1960), 408–412.

Elizabeth G. Meier. "Foster Care for Children," *Social Work Year Book* (New York: National Association of Social Workers, 1960), pp. 277–285.

Daniel R. Miller and Guy E. Swanson. *The Changing American Parent*. New York: Wiley, 1958.

Walter B. Miller. "Implications of Urban Lower-Class Culture for Social Work," *Social Service Review*, XXXIII (September, 1959), 219–236.

Robert Morris. "Governmental Health Programs Affecting the American Family: Some New Dimensions for Governmental Action," *Journal of Marriage and the Family*, XXIX (February, 1967), 64–70.

Katherine Brownell Oettinger. "Children in a Changing World," *Marriage and Family Living*, XX (August, 1958), 233–238.

Edward Pope. "Extension Service Programs Affecting American Families," *Marriage and Family Living*, XX (August, 1958), 270–276.

David M. Potter. *People of Plenty: Economic Abundance and the American Character*. Chicago: University of Chicago, 1954.

Milton I. Roemer. "Governmental Health Programs Affecting the American Family," *Journal of Marriage and the Family*, XXIX (February, 1967), 40–63.

Frances H. Scherz. "Strengthening Family Life through Social Security," *Social Casework*, XXXVI (October, 1955), 352–359.

Benjamin Schlesinger. "The One-Parent Family: Recent Literature," *Journal of Marriage and the Family*, XXVIII (February, 1966), 103–109.

Alvin L. Schorr. "Family Policy in the United States," *International Social Science Journal*, XIV (1962), 452–467.

Charles I. Schottland. "Government Economic Programs and Family Life," *Journal of Marriage and the Family*, XXIX (February, 1967), 71–123.

Murray A. Straus. "Communication Creativity, and Problem-Solving Ability of Middle- and Working-Class Families in Three Societies," *American Journal of Sociology*, LXXIII (January, 1968), 417–430.

Marvin B. Sussman (ed.). "Special Issue: American Poverty in the Mid-Sixties," *Journal of Marriage and the Family*, XXVI (November, 1964), 389–498.

Andrew R. N. Truelson. "Helping Needy People Get Jobs and Hold Them: A Report on the Work Experience Program," *Welfare in Review*, III (November, 1965), 14–19.

PART VII

Conclusion

CHAPTER 18

Family in Society:
Retrospect and Prospect

IN THE FIRST CHAPTER we raised the question: what happens to the family—this small, adaptive, vulnerable part of the total social structure—in complex societies characterized by rapid social change? More specifically, what has happened to the American family during the rapid emergence of America as a complex society? It is time to return to this question.

Two general answers can be given to it. First of all, the family has survived and, secondly, as the society has experienced change in structure and function, so has the family experienced change. The reader will recall the gloomy predictions of Sorokin, Zimmerman, and Ogburn indicating that the family had lost functions and that it was disintegrating. Still marriage and family appear to be taken as the *summum bonum* of existence by the majority of Americans. The vast majority of Americans choose marriage rather than nonmarriage or a life of "single bliss." In 1967, of males forty-five to fifty-four years of age 6 percent were single, 89 percent were married, and 5 percent widowed or divorced. Among women of the same ages 5 percent were single, 82 percent married, and 13 percent widowed or divorced.[1]

Rapid and pervasive social changes associated with urbanization and industrialization called for a family system that, both structurally and functionally, was adaptive to the demands of other social systems and to the needs of family members engaged in interchanges with the other social systems. The family system was severely tested but it adapted; it was not destroyed in the process.

Much attention has been devoted to the family by the polity system, indicating the importance of the family in contemporary society. The law regards a wide range of functions for which the contemporary family bears sole responsibility or is *primus inter pares* with other social systems. The many areas of interest of the courts and the law in the family serve as a reminder of the family's continuing role with regard to economic functions; sexual functions; procreative functions; the raising of children; psychological

[1] U.S. Department of Commerce, "Marital Status and Family Status: March 1967," *Population Characteristics,* February 23, 1968, p. 9.

374

and emotional impact of the family on its members; the provision of individual security and social identity; protection of mental and physical health; the encouragement of intellectual, vocational, and cultural developments; the care of the elderly; and arrangements for the dead. To catalogue even the variety of ways in which the state has interceded for the welfare of the child in the family is an almost interminable task.

While it is true that the family in the United States is no longer a major economic producing unit, it is a significant economic consuming unit. It is useless to argue whether or not one economic function is more important than the other. In the same vein, while the family has lost some conspicuous educational and religious functions, the majority of children hold religious, political, and social-class beliefs similar to those of their parents, suggesting a formidable socialization function in the family. It is more appropriate to emphasize change in kind and degree of function rather than loss of functions.

The loss-of-function formulation also obscures changes in the fields of medicine, in technology, in the natural sciences, and in the standard of living that have made it possible for other social systems to intervene in a way that supplements rather than substitutes for activities performed by the family. Changes in living conditions have made specialized supplementation and provision or services new and desirable additions to the interchanges between family and other social systems. In the process of differentiation and specialization, though, one function has, in a sense, been "taken away" from the family by other social systems: that is, the autonomy of setting its own standards. This is true in regard to certain goods and services available in the areas of medical care, insurance, specialized education, and many others. Not that the autonomy of the family was ever limitless, but it is now exposed to the demands of new standards set by personnel in other social systems who are equipped with the expertise, resources, and sometimes the power to render services which the family wants but which, without compliance with these standards, it cannot have. Many of the services cannot be obtained except at the price of dealing with large and powerful bureaucratic systems. American society is geared to large corporate organizations; the family is not one of these.

The family is not a dominant social system in initiating social change; on the other hand, it is not alone among the social systems that play an adaptive role. All systems play adaptive roles to some extent, but the family, to a greater extent than other major social systems, facilitates social change by adapting. The family's strategic socializing function is an adaptive or mediating function. The family works at preparing all of its members for roles in society; the changing demands, requirements, and goals of the society and its other social systems are translated and incorporated into the on-going process of socializing all members of the family, both children and adults.

Another reason for the lack of dominance on the part of the American family is that families lack an organizational structure and representative voice through which they might initiate change or resist change initiated by others.

Family changes are essentially a matter of redistribution of roles and functions within the family. There may be differentiation or integration, concentration or dispersion, in the course of redistribution which may be continuous or alternating over time.

RECIPROCAL ADAPTATION

The family is aided in its functioning in that other social systems respond to the changing needs and demands of the family. The family can be selective in its adaptations as well. In other words, in the interchanges between the family and other social systems there is reciprocal adaptation. For example, schools have had to expand their facilities considerably as a result of the "baby boom" that occurred in the middle and late 1940's. On the other hand, schools depend on the family for their "raw material" (children); hence there is a very basic dependence of school on families. Most American families have regarded this supply power "leverage" that they have over the school as inconsequential. Keeping one's children out of school in protest against various school programs and activities can be and is utilized, none the less. Compulsory attendance laws have strengthened the school's position, adding an authority that individual families are not able to cope with directly. Families can and do resist covertly by not encouraging the child in his school work, by insisting that he do other things, by not encouraging him to do his homework, by encouraging him to (or at least not discouraging him from) dropping out of school. But the vast majority of American families are on the side of the school; they depend upon the school for some critical services nowhere else available in society.

In the business world, also, there is reciprocal interchange with family. The market reflected numbers and ages of the population, for instance, as the baby-boom babies of World II moved up into the category of young adults. Governments also recognize the influence of the family to be considerable, as revolutionary leaders have found in other countries. There has been strong resistance within the home to policies of force or fraud. Since parents have the first contact with children, they can influence children to support or to oppose political regimes. Those bent on political revolution have given considerable attention to ways in which the influence of the home on the younger generation can be reduced or rendered ineffective. As another example of government-family interchange, except perhaps for a minority of families with a military heritage of which they are proud, families tend to be opposed to war. War brings separation of family members, imprisonment, maiming, and death—all of which are major catastrophes to families. Families attempt to influence draft boards; desertions are sometimes encouraged; and extensions of the draft are opposed.

THE FAMILY'S ROOT FUNCTIONS

Although the structural forms of marriage and the family vary from society to society and within societies, the trends in form and functioning appear very similar in all the industrialized countries in the world. Functions assigned to the family—bearing children, socializing, motivating, and revitalizing children and adults—appear to be common to industrialized societies.

The nuclear family is everywhere a differentiated or partially-differentiated system of the society. The social systems with which it experiences interchanges all have two things in common: they articulate with the nuclear family mainly through the nonfamilial roles of the adult members of the family and they constitute more highly differentiated structures than the nuclear family.

One of the requirements of bureaucratic, corporate structures is that individuals as workers must conform, be replaceable, and mobile, being willing to be transferred from one location to another. While the family plays a significant role in socializing persons in such ways as to equip them to function within bureaucratic structures, nevertheless, from the person's point of view, the family may in a real sense function uniquely as a counterpoint to bureaucratic adaptation. It may be that this is the family's most important function—the family as a potential place of intimacy in a world of bureaucratic relationships that are often demanding, impersonal, and depersonalized. The family may fulfill a retroactive, relief function for the individual in a bureaucratic society. Ideally the family takes on great significance in terms of the so-called root functions. Individuals frequently find themselves valued as persons in families in a way that is less likely in other social systems. To the extent that the family is able to provide affection, respect, and companionship for its members, we may, more nearly than ever before, have a situation in which the goals of individual family members and family goals *per se* are fully consonant one with the other. This is a major adaptation of the family to a highly differentiated social order.

There is some feeling that American society may have gone too far in allocating to the family too exclusive a right to the basic root function of socializing children. It is possible that families cannot adequately prepare their children for life in society because life in the family is different from life in the community in a society such as ours. Parents may give their children not only security, but they may also give them rigidity, an exaggerated sense of their own importance, and a life-style that makes them inflexible in adjusting to collective living. Socialization of the child as a parental function can be overemphasized.

FAMILY FORWARDNESS

Families do initiate change in that individual families and, derivatively, the family system, "lean toward the future." Individual families are constantly changing, and not all of the change is reactive to changes in the activities of family members or reactive to changes in the local community or in the larger society. Families not only have a past and a present, they also anticipate and plan for the future. Behavior in the family is often less closely determined by present situations than by what the family members anticipate and desire in the near or distant future. Forwardness, or anticipating and planning for the future, may be as important in determining present action of the family as are past experiences and the present situation.

The "leaning toward the future" on the part of the family is a significant factor not only in isolated cases; its existence is a general characteristic of the patterns particularly of middle-class families, as they work, invest, and save in anticipation of the achievement of long-range goals.

DIRECTION OF FAMILY CHANGE—
A THREE GENERATION STUDY[2]

One method of assessing the direction of change of the family is through longitudinal study of several generations. Reuben Hill's study of 312 Minneapolis area families within the same family lines covers three generations of nuclear families and affords an opportunity to trace persistence and change over three generations—from the grandparent, through the parent, and into the married-child generation.

A number of changes over the three generations are noted. Each generation surpasses its predecessor by an impressive margin in average years of schooling completed, especially in the case of husbands. Superiority in the amount of education of wives over their husbands decreases with each generation. The wife is no longer as likely to be the more educated and literate member of the couple.

Difference in age at marriage declines, showing a smaller gap between spouses in the third generation—from five years in the grandparent generation (hereafter referred to as the first generation) to two years in the married-child generation (hereafter referred to as the third generation). In

[2] Reuben Hill, "The American Family of the Future," *Journal of Marriage and the Family*, XXVI (February, 1964), 20–28.

regard to number of children per family, the first generation had an average of 5.2 children per family, with over a fourth bearing eight or more children. The last child was born after fifteen years of marriage. The second generation had an average of 3.5 children per family, with over half in the two and three child category. The last child was born after ten years of marriage for second-generation families, shortening the childbearing span by more than four years over the preceding generation. The third generation still had over twenty years of possible childbearing ahead at the time of the study but has already produced more than two-thirds the number of children of the second generation, averaging 2.4 children at the time of the study.

Comparing the occupational careers of the three generations, the third generation started below the second generation, in less skilled jobs at the beginning of their careers, but within a few years after marriage their rate of advancement was faster than that of the second generation during corresponding career phases. The first generation experienced the lowest start and the slowest movement upward over their entire working lives. More of the wives had worked the first several years of marriage in each succeeding generation, and more had returned to work as their children grew up. In the third generation, 60 percent of wives are working in the first years of marriage as compared with 20 percent of wives at the beginning of marriage in the second generation; and although still in the childbearing period, 40 percent of the wives in the third generation married six to ten years are employed. The increasing impact of the working wife on level of income, home ownership, and acquisition of durable goods is one of the major changes over the generations.

In all economic matters, the third generation appears destined to outstrip the previous generations based on the achievements of each generation during the first ten years of marriage. Eighty percent of the third generation has exceeded the first generation by becoming home owners, an achievement reached by that proportion of the second generation only after twenty years of marriage. In the acquisition of durable goods, the third generation overtook the second generation and is at the point in its inventory where the second generation was after thirty-five years of marriage. This acquisition of goods is not accomplished at the expense of providing insurance or retirement provisions, for the third generation is well along in the acquisition of a portfolio of insurance and investments. Over 50 percent have retirement provisions over and beyond social security, and 95 percent have life insurance. This generation started marriage with 82 percent coverage, which is higher than their grandparents ever reached and as high as their parents achieved after thirty years of marriage.

The change over the generations appears to be accelerated rather than being a linear movement upward, since changes occur at an accelerated rate in regard to education, occupational change in the direction of professionalization, increased education, increased employment of wives, upgrading of housing and the durable goods inventory, and increased insurance coverage and investments. Each generation has also become more innovative, as indicated by receptiveness to new home products adopted earlier in marriage in each generation.

In value orientations, Mill found the two older generations to be predominantly fatalistic, prudential, optimistic, and present- or past-oriented; whereas the third generation is the least fatalistic and is prudential, moderately optimistic, and oriented to the future rather than to the present or the past. Using typologies of traditional and developmental categories in regard to parenthood and childhood, the first generation was clearly the most traditional of the three generations, averaging less than half developmental responses; the second generation was more developmental, with some parents clearly falling on the developmental side of the scale. The third generation is the most developmental of all. Hill suggests that the higher education of the third generation and its greater accessibility to parent-education materials may account for its greater espousal of developmental beliefs.

In family organization, marked differences appear in authority patterns, division of labor, and marital integration of families by generation. In authority patterns, the shift to equalitarian patterns was greatest from the first to the second generation, but it holds up in the third generation. In division of tasks, there is more sharing of tasks and less specialization in the third generation, as well as less attention to the conventions about what is men's work and what is women's work. Eighty-three percent of the couples do some role crossing in the third generation, compared to 60 percent in the first generation.

Consensus on family values increases, but role integration decreases by generation; marital communication was especially low in the first generation where role integration was highest. Hill's interviewers found a greater readiness to enter into conflict among couples in the third generation. The second generation was loath to enter into conflict and slow to express hostility toward one another but proved to be lower on achievement consensus on the issues raised by the interviewer. The pattern of the third generation is frequently one of identifying differences, engaging in conflict, and then locating a basis for agreement with one party undertaking to smooth over the differences and seeking to "save face." The interviewers found the third generation to be the most colorful and interesting. The couples of this generation were most likely to experience conflict and to express hostility, but they were also most likely to conclude with consensus and gestures of affection.

Finally, in regard to planning and problem-solving performance of the three generations, in each succeeding generation the number of plans expressed was greater, the number of actions taken was greater, and the proportion of pre-planned action was greater. The differences may only reflect the stage in family development of the representatives of each generation. The third generation makes many plans and carries out many actions because it is in an expanding phase of need. Yet the so-called "flighty" young generation is the most likely to pre-plan its purchases, its residential moves, and its other consumer actions, with 51 percent of its actions during the year pre-planned compared with 44 percent in the first generation. Moreover, the components of rational decision-making are more faithfully met in the third generation than in earlier generations. That is, the child generation is more likely than the older generations to search for information outside the immediate family, to weigh satisfaction among alternatives, and to take into account long-term as well as short-term consequences.

A picture of increasing effectiveness, professional competence, and economic well-being, of greater courage in risk-taking accompanied by greater planning, of greater flexibility in family organization with greater communication and greater conflict between spouses emerges from the study. Looking toward the future, the educational aspirations of the third generation for their children (the fourth generation) are the highest of the three generations. These findings should be taken as suggestive rather than conclusive.

THE INDIVIDUAL AND SOCIO-SEXUAL SYSTEMS

Marriage and the family both reflect changes in society designed to improve the status of women, children, the economically and culturally disadvantaged, and the elderly. Improved status of individuals is not necessarily reflected in greater stability of marriages or of families, however. A high regard for the integrity and freedom of the individual may be reflected in a high rather than a low divorce rate, for example. Marriage has come more and more to be regarded as a relationship based on affection and companionship between consulting adults and based less on the responsibility of bearing and rearing children. New levels of efficiency of birth control techniques for the future will further increase the possibility of parenthood by design rather than by chance.

For adults, the marital relationship presents the individual with important functions not provided by the family or other social systems. The primary function of marriage is the provision of an age-appropriate, sex-appropriate partner as a source of intimate personal association—association provided only in part in childhood and adolescence by parents, siblings, and peers. This is not to say that the vast majority of married couples do not regard parenthood as a central focus of their marriage, however, but even for couples wanting and having children, early marriage and small family size contribute to the possibility of concentrating on the affectional and companionship features of marriage.

As previously indicated, marriage is popular with Americans. Persons who have experienced a broken marriage—the widowed or divorced—do not necessarily lose out on the possibility of a continued existence as a married person. The divorced are quick to remarry. There is approximately one divorced person for every thirty married persons in the United States; remarriage is the main reason for the relatively small number of divorced persons. The Census Bureau reports indicate that there are over 14,000,000 persons who have been married more than once. The majority of these are persons who have been divorced.

Marriage and parenthood are no longer thought of as synonymous; sexual intimacy and marriage are no longer necessarily thought of as synonymous either. The whole question of whether nonmarital (especially premarital) sexual experience is permissible and desirable or not is being debated. The sanctioning of sexual intimacy seems less likely to be a dominating factor in the decision to marry in the future. There is a feeling that sex expression should not necessarily be constrained to fit traditional morality and existing law, but that morality and law should give greater place to the realities of man's nature and the validity of human relationships *per se*.

The family experiences change as do other social systems and as does society at large. Change of structure and change of function are not synonymous with loss of function or disintegration of structure. Change in the direction of increased effectiveness and efficiency of operation in the various socio-sexual systems—aided by research, education, and constructive programs of social action—appears to be plausible.

The relationship of the American family *per se* to other social systems and to the individual is due for more attention than it has previously received. There is support for the further humanizing of the socio-sexual systems. On the other hand, developments may be pressing American society in the direction of formulating a more explicit national family policy than is true at present. The need for such a policy has been urged in many quarters and in the professional literature. Not that there is complete agreement on family goals. All groups interested in the family hold the family to be of importance, but definitions of family and goals for the family continue to be diverse, reflecting the pluralistic nature of contemporary American society.

BIBLIOGRAPHY

Jessie Bernard. "Developmental Tasks of the NCFR—1963–1968," *Journal of Marriage and the Family,* XXVI (February, 1964), 29–38.

Muriel W. Brown. "Organizational Programs to Strengthen the Family," *Handbook of Marriage and the Family,* ed. Harold T. Christensen. Chicago: Rand McNally, 1964.

Harold T. Christensen. "The Intrusion of Values," *Handbook of Marriage and the Family,* ed. Harold T. Christensen. Chicago: Rand McNally, 1964.

Ronald Fletcher. *The Family and Marriage in Britain: An Analysis and Moral Assessment.* Baltimore: Penguin Books, 1966.

William J. Goode. *World Revolution and Family Patterns.* New York: New York Free Press, a division of the Macmillan Company, 1963.

Reuben Hill. "The American Family of the Future," *Journal of Marriage and the Family,* XXVI (February, 1964), 20–28.

William M. Kephart. *The Family, Society, and the Individual* (2nd ed.). Boston: Houghton Mifflin, 1966. Chapter XXIII.

Richard K. Kerckhoff. "Family Life Education in America," *Handbook of Marriage and the Family,* ed. Harold T. Christensen. Chicago: Rand McNally, 1964.

Clifford Kirkpatrick. *The Family as Process and Institution* (2nd ed.). New York: Ronald Press, 1963. Chapter XXIII.

Gerald R. Leslie. "The Field of Marriage Counseling," *Handbook of Marriage and the Family,* ed. Harold T. Christensen. Chicago: Rand McNally, 1964.

David R. Mace. "Some Reflections on the American Family," *Marriage and Family Living,* XXIV (May, 1962), 109–112.

Floyd M. Martinson. "Value Assumptions in Family Research with Reference to Population," *The Sociological Quarterly,* II (October, 1961), 281–292.

Samuel Mencher. "Social Authority and the Family," *Journal of Marriage and the Family,* XXIX (February, 1967), 164–192.

Talcott Parsons and Robert F. Bales. *Family Socialization and Interaction Process.* Glencoe, Ill.: The Free Press, 1955.

Otto Pollak. "The Outlook for the American Family," *Journal of Marriage and the Family,* XXIX (February, 1967), 193–205.

Alvin L. Schorr. "Family Policy in the United States," *International Social Science Journal,* XIV, 3 (1962), 452–467.

Arthur B. Shostak. "Education and the Family," *Journal of Marriage and the Family,* XXIX (February, 1967), 124–139.

Clark E. Vincent. "Mental Health and the Family," *Journal of Marriage and the Family,* XXIX (February, 1967), 18–39.

Carle C. Zimmerman and Lucius F. Cervantes. *Marriage and the Family.* Chicago: Henry Regnery Co., 1956.

Index

385